THE MAN WHO WAS OLD MOTHER RILEY

The Lives and Films of Arthur Lucan and Kitty McShane

Robert V. Kenny

Foreword by Anthony Slide

The Man Who Was Old Mother Riley
The Lives and Films of Arthur Lucan and Kitty McShane
By Robert V. Kenny

Published in the USA by:
BearManor Media
P O Box 71426
Albany, Georgia 31708
www.bearmanormedia.com

ISBN: 978-1-59393-771-3
Printed in the United States of America
Book design by Robbie Adkins, www.adkinsconsult.com

Table of Contents

THE MAN WHO WAS OLD MOTHER RILEY

Photo 1: Arthur Towle, Studio portrait c. 1904-5. Mrs. Joan Towle

In loving memory of my mother,
Margaret Tiquin Kenny (1923-2002), and my grandmother,
Mary Tiquin Coyle (1893-1977), who adored Old Mother Riley,
and introduced me to her at the Scala cinema,
Stony Stratford, in 1953.

Acknowledgments and Thanks

In the course of my research I have had the good fortune to get to know members of Arthur Lucan's family; Arthur's granddaughter Marylyn Webster (Towle); Joan Towle, widow of Arthur's son Donald; Arthur's nephew and great-niece, Arthur and Sally Ladds. They have kindly given me access to hitherto unknown documents or facts, and I thank them all for their support and encouragement. I was also privileged to get to know Slim Ingram, Arthur's trusted friend and last company-manager. Sadly, Slim passed away on 15 June 2013, before this study was completed, but for over two years, frequently on the telephone, and at his home in Blackpool in 2012, Slim helped me to correct many common errors, and gave me important new facts, some of which he had withheld from publication for over sixty years. It was a privilege to have known Slim, and I owe him and his daughter Emma a very special debt of gratitude. I also owe warm thanks to Steve King, co-author of the first full-length biography of Lucan and McShane. Many years ago, Steve was fortunate to able to gather first-hand material from many people who had worked with the Lucans, and he has generously given me access to his research. Anthony Slide read an early draft of several chapters, and his wise blend of kind words and stern advice gave me the courage to persevere.

Professional photographer Mike Brown restored and edited the photographs. I am also grateful to the following organizations; The British Library, Leicester University Library, BBC Written Archives Caversham, The Cinema Museum, The British Film Institute, Fremantle Media, The Imperial War Museum, Skerries Historical Society, *Evergreen Magazine, The Stage, The Guardian*, the *Hull Daily Mail, The Boston Standard* and *The Call Boy*. BBC copyright material reproduced courtesy of the British Broadcasting Corporation. All rights reserved.

Many other people have given me help, encouragement and advice, all equally valuable in its way. There is no pecking order in the following list because all deserve an equal share of thanks; in my old-fashioned way, I have put the ladies first:

Angela Allen, Maureen Lipman, Emma Ingram, Mary Todd, Mrs. Urvashi Chudasama, Miriam Kite, Maree Baker, Gillian Swift, Sandra Skuse; Joy Rust, Bernadette and the Kennys at St. Rita's.

Michael Pointon, Steve King, Mike Brown, Jeffrey Richards, Steven Fielding, Edward Thomas, Brad Ashton, Lance Pettitt, Richard Anthony Baker, Karl Williams, Chris D'Grey, Roy Stockdill, John Fisher, Vivyan Ellacott, Nigel Ellacott, Roy Hudd, Roger Lewis, Patrick Prior, Ronald Grant, Martin Humphries, Alex Gleason, Roy Rust, Bob Marriot, Michael Dynan, Geoff Bowden, David McGillivray, Tony Parkinson, David Simpson, Theo Morgan, Mike Covell, Will Ramsey, Stephen Stray, Des Kerins, Stephen Poppitt, Lynton Black, Matthew Lloyd, Philip and David Williams, John Larkin, David E. Wilt, and Matt Grindley.

My thanks are due to the authors and publishers who have assured me that my use of quotations complies with academic 'fair usage.' All quotations are fully and gratefully attributed, both in the text and in the notes. If your name *should* be here and it is not, I hope and pray that you will forgive my disorganization and help me to put matters right as soon as possible.

Foreword

"National Treasure" is a phrase that has become overly popular in modern Britain, very similar to that over-worked word, "iconic," used to describe everyone from an aging, overweight ex-politician with no discernible talent except to spout oft-times offensive right-wing comments to aging matriarchal actresses with the talent to survive, as with Judi Dench and Maggie Smith. The term does not appear to be used too much in retrospect and that is unfortunate because I can think of no individual in British entertainment, British popular culture or British folklore more deserving of the title than Old Mother Riley and her creator, Arthur Lucan.

Of course, in reality there are no female impersonators of whom I am aware with the soubriquet of "national treasure." Not even gay men, with the possible exception of Sir Ian McKellen, have won such acclaim. But is that even an issue, in that Arthur Lucan as Old Mother Riley is hardly a female impersonator in the modern sense, and, as his marriage to Kitty McShane, his nemesis and overseer, should prove, poor Arthur Lucan, whatever else he might have been, was not gay. Perhaps at the heart of any debate concerning this extraordinary character is how does one speak or write of Old Mother Riley. A very real and very unique characterization, but is it a man? Is it a woman? Perhaps it is unfair to creator Arthur Lucan, but *his* characterization will always be a female to me. Just as much, as in our modern age, we don't think of Patrick Fyffe or Barry Humphries when we discuss Dame Hylda Brackett or Dame Edna Everage. They are ladies and so is Old Mother Riley.

Indeed, one might ask, and of far more importance than the title of "National Treasure," why, if we have Dame Hylda and Dame Edna, do we not have Dame Daphne Snowdrop Bluebell Riley? Dame Hylda Brackett is pretty much forgotten today, and, somewhat sadly, was never really known outside the United Kingdom. Dame Edna has retired, although she is probably too forceful a character to sink completely into anonymity. But Daphne Snowdrop Bluebell Riley will continue on through her marvelous films and through our memories. She will remain forever in our hearts.

We will smile at her antics, but we also perhaps quietly will shudder as we realize the reality of what lies behind the character. We may know just the same instincts, but we keep them under control. We may relish a fight as much as does Old Mother Riley. Or we know others, perhaps close relatives, with the same sense of wrong and outrage that Old Mother Riley displays so fervently, and often without a due sense of the reality of the situation.

In the Introduction to this magnificent book, I seem to be mentioned quite a few times, and often with fulsome praise, not always deserved and, I am sure, not influenced by my writing this introduction. I must confess that I came to Old Mother Riley somewhat late in life. I first saw her on screen as an adult thanks to a Saturday children's matinee at a local cinema. When I saw one of her films was to be screened, I plucked up the courage to go in and ask the manager if I might be allowed to attend. Highly suspicious of my interest in a children's matinee, with the emphasis on children, he agreed, but only if I sat, alone and in solitary confinement, upstairs in the balcony which the cinema did not usually open on a Saturday morning. Obviously, I appreciated the film more than the kids downstairs. But at least they laughed and cheered at Old Mother Riley, while the main feature, from the much vaunted Children's Film Foundation, was greeted with boos, jeers and general contempt. Again, we have this discrimination by the British establishment and British society. Awards for the work of the Children's Film Foundation, but none for Old Mother Riley. Where is *her* BAFTA?

The closest I ever came in person to Old Mother Riley was around 1970, I do not recall the date or even the exact year, when the British Music Hall Society hosted a tribute to female impersonation, hosted by its founder Ray Mackender, to whom I was very close. On the bill was Rex Jameson as Mrs. Shufflewick ("broad-mined to the point of obscenity") and Old Mother Riley understudy Roy Rolland, who was (admittedly very amusingly) over-the-top and "camp" in an outrageous style that Arthur Lucan would probably not even have known how to adopt. I brought along a good friend, actor John Stuart, who had been Kitty McShane's boyfriend in two films, *Old Mother Riley in Society* (1940) and *Old Mother Riley's Ghosts* (1941). After the show, John and I sat in the bar and we were joined by ventriloquist Bobbie Kimber, who had always appeared on stage as a woman since the late and British National Films. If Lady Yule represents the Empire and the best in British filmmaking, then so does Old Mother Riley.

And, of course, I would be remiss if I did not note that Dame Hylda had her partner, Dr. Evadne Hinge. Dame Edna had her partner, Madge. And Old Mother Riley had her partner, Kitty McShane. But enough about her. . . . If Arthur Lucan had been knighted, one can just imagine Lady McShane, hob-nobbing with the likes of Joan Collins and Pippa Middleton. Okay, I admit it. In search of that cheap laugh, beloved of all second-rate comedians such as myself, I have chosen to denigrate Kitty by comparing her to Collins and Middleton. No sooner had I written this than I felt a momentary sense of compassion for that redoubtable lady. Kitty McShane was never really nice, except perhaps in the very early years of the marriage, and yet she was crucial to the character of Old Mother Riley. In all sincerity, I doubt there was any other female performer capable of playing daughter Kitty to Old Mother Riley. She is a part of the act, a part of the film scenario at which we cringe but to which we secretly look forward. What inappropriate song will she sing? What inappropriate, girlish attire will she don? What half-baked British leading man will be forced into serving as her love interest? (If they had to kiss Kitty, one hopes that at least they were decently paid.)

I do not need, in fact, to write on Kitty McShane, as here Robert Kenny presents Kitty in all her terrifying reality, remorseless, relentless and ever-present, if not always physically, in Arthur Lucan's life. Kitty McShane is perhaps the supporting player—something which she never saw herself as in real life—in this book which provides a definitive and, I may add, refreshingly accurate and realistic examination of the man who was Old Mother Riley.

How lucky we are, and how lucky is Arthur Lucan, that Dr. Robert Kenny has chosen to devote a substantial number of years to researching, documenting, and writing this fantastic study. I find it somewhat amusing that in his professional life, Dr. Kenny was a university lecturer in French Language and French Literature. It seems so inappropriate for someone so learned and academic to take on a task such as this (as my mother might have described it, "so common"), and yet, it is absolutely delightful that he has. Arthur Lucan and Old Mother Riley are richly deserving of attention from an academic outside of the dreary field of cinema studies, someone

1930s. I can still recall my juvenile embarrassment at sitting next to a man in full female attire and yet talking with us in a male voice. And may I make a plea here for a serious study of Bobbie Kimber, a unique and unusual female impersonator. Like Arthur Lucan, one would never describe his performance as a "drag" act, and like Old Mother Riley, one always regarded him as being a "her."

In the United States, where I have lived for more than half of my life, I regret that Old Mother Riley is generally unknown, and so there is little likelihood of a posthumous Oscar, desirable as it might be. One American familiar with her work compared her to Francis the Talking Mule and Abbott and Costello. Well, the latter perhaps. Certainly, her last film, *Mother Riley Meets the Vampire*, is in the tradition of the Abbott and Costello films of the 1940s in which those comedians shared billing with Frankenstein and the Invisible Man.

Many critics and historians write with contempt of British films of the 1930s and 1940s, well actually of most decades, describing them as resolutely middle-class. The best of British cinema is represented by Anthony Asquith, Noël Coward or Terence Rattigan, or by well-spoken leading men such as Clive Brook, Ronald Colman or Eton-educated John Loder. One does not reference Arthur Askey, Frank Randle or George Formby. Well, obviously, these self-same elitist critics and historians have not seen Old Mother Riley. There is nothing middle-class about Daphne Snowdrop Bluebell Riley. She represents the very foundation upon which England is built: violence, drunkenness, questionable manners, and general contempt for everyone else, particularly those in authority. But also, and equally important, Old Mother Riley displays that strong yet controlled pathos which all great comedians have used to effect, beginning on screen with Charlie Chaplin.

Old Mother Riley appeared at a Royal Command Performance, and, it is reported, she "made the King laugh." As producer and British International Pictures Production Chief Walter Mycroft wrote in his autobiography, *The Time of My Life*, "Mr. Lucan was never debagged being always beskirted, but by comparison with Old Mother Riley, Leslie Fuller was practically high comedy, Arthur Askey almost Lubitsch." But as Walter Mycroft also points out, Old Mother Riley appeared under the cinematic banner of the idealistic Lady Yule, one of the richest women in the Empire, the woman who symbolized Elstree who understands the need to write sensibly and jargon-free. To read this book is to be present at the birth, the formative years, the starring years, and the sad decline of Old Mother Riley. In a way, the star here is quite definitely Old Mother Riley, and, in a strange fashion, both Arthur Lucan and Kitty McShane are supporting players.

During the golden age of Rock 'n' Roll, the Kinks performed a song titled "The Village Green Preservation Society." The second verse begins with the words, "God save Mrs. Mopp and good Old Mother Riley." And that is why we are here today, to save good Old Mother Riley. All of us should honor the words of the Kinks,

"Preserving the old ways from being abused

"Protecting the new ways for me and for you."

May we all praise, save and protect Old Mother Riley. And may we all join in praise for Dr. Robert Kenny, Old Mother Riley's friend, fan, biographer, and, indeed, savior.

Anthony Slide

PART ONE:
THE LIFE AND TIMES OF ARTHUR LUCAN AND KITTY McSHANE

Introduction

A Fruitful Misalliance?

"A Fruitful Misalliance" (without the question mark) was the title of Irving Wardle's review in *The Times* of the play *On Your Way Riley*, Alan Plater's 1981 tribute to "the comic genius of Old Mother Riley," which starred Brian Murphy as Arthur Lucan and Maureen Lipman as Kitty McShane.

In October 2013 a one-day celebration of the lives and films of Arthur Lucan (stage name of Arthur Towle, 1885-1954) and Kitty McShane (1897-1964) was held at the London Cinema Museum, the former Kennington workhouse that once sheltered the young Charlie Chaplin. For the very first time, before a large and appreciative audience, film, theater and political specialists and academics gave papers devoted to the exceptional talents of the comic actor Arthur Lucan. It was a timely moment for looking back and taking stock; 25 November 2013, was the hundredth anniversary of the marriage in Dublin in 1913 of Arthur Lucan and Kitty McShane. In May 2014 the sixtieth anniversary of Arthur's death was commemorated at his graveside in Hull's Eastern Cemetery; no such ceremony was held in March 2014 to mark the fiftieth anniversary of Kitty's death, for reasons which will become apparent later in this study. In October 2015, the families of Arthur and Kitty's only son, Donald Towle, will mark the centenary of his birth in Dublin. As "Lucan and McShane" Arthur and Kitty were one of the most successful double acts in the history of music hall and variety, eventually becoming "Old Mother Riley and her Daughter Kitty," the stars one of the longest-running comedy series in British film history. And yet to this day there exists only one attempt at a full-length biography of this unusual couple.[1] Steve King and Terry Cavender's book, published in 1999, before online search engines made life easier for the researcher, was sadly marred by a number of errors and inconsistencies, and suffered from patchy editing after the untimely death of Cavender. The book made no attempt to analyze the films but it did contain solid biographical information from reliable first-hand sources, and the present author gratefully acknowledges his debt to this valuable source. To mark the centenary of what Irving Wardle described as a "fruitful misalliance," it seems to me that a new and more comprehensive study of the lives and the films of Lucan and McShane is long overdue.

It is overdue because, in the opinion of many serious critics, led by the doyenne of British film historians, Rachael Low, Arthur Lucan was "a comedian of genius." Something of that genius was preserved, late in his career, in a popular series of cheaply made films, "which acquired a large and delighted following," with Arthur in the travesty role of Old Mother Riley. Leslie Halliwell agreed with Low that "Lucan at his best is a superb comedian" and he felt that "the brilliance of Arthur Lucan was never recognized in his own lifetime but now it shines through his ramshackle films."[2] In 1954, *The Times*, whose theater critics had never been particularly kind to Lucan and McShane, did in fact make amends in Arthur's obituary, speaking perceptively of "the endearing, bemused old woman, who seemed to those who laughed at her antics to enjoy a life of her own." As early as 1969, looking back at the "supposedly less sophisticated" comics of the late 1930s, David Robinson declared that "best of all was Arthur Lucan whose Old Mother Riley was at once vulgar, comic, touching and true to working-class life."[3] When Renown re-issued six of the Riley films in 2005, an internet critic, J. Black, wrote,

> Good, clean, 'silly' fun . . . The character was simple and the plots were basic but Arthur Lucan gave some magical performances on film. Old Mother Riley is a washerwoman who lives in a slum dwelling in a society that seems light years away from our world today; nevertheless I'm sure Lucan's penchant for parody and his talent to recreate traditional theater farce on film, which caused uproar amongst cinema-going children and adults when these films were released, will continue to appeal today.

Roger Wilmut summed up the view of most serious theater and film critics when he declared "Old Mother Riley is a magnificent creation, aggressive, leaping about and arguing, wheedling, coaxing . . . ready to confront anyone at any time."[4]

John Fisher in *Funny Way to Be a Hero* was among the first to capture the essence of Arthur Lucan's unique performing skills. He concluded his ground-breaking essay with one of the earliest and finest evaluations of the "magnificent creation" that was Old Mother Riley.

> By his complete absorption in the role of his chosen character, Lucan set himself head and shoulders above all others in a tradition which went back to the mediaeval mystery plays and had recently included the great Dan Leno." Fisher rightly sets Lucan alongside the great Dan Leno because there are striking similarities between the creations of these two utterly idiosyncratic performers. As Fisher goes on to stress, "However absurd [Old Mother Riley's] eccentricities, it was easy to peer beyond these and see that she possessed an intense awareness of life's tragedies. It was a subtle, humane, as well as outrageous characterization. It became legendary."[5]

Rachael Low, in her *History of British Film* echoed Fisher's assessment.

> With his wide acrobatic movements, tremendous but controlled waving of the arms, gesticulating with large, delicate and expressive hands, [Arthur Lucan] created a character of extreme subtlety. Servile yet aggressive, a little genteel but earthy when necessary, and occasionally exploding into unbridled fury, Old Mother Riley was an eager, helpful and independent type of woman, ready to stand up for herself.[6]

My only quibble with Low is that she also described Arthur as "a slight, pale ugly man approaching fifty, with sparse hair and a large bulbous nose." Arthur was indeed of slight build, and was in fact fifty-two in 1937, but the rest is Old Mother Riley, not Arthur Lucan. Arthur was far from ugly, and many women found his large dark eyes and expressive features very attractive. The bulbous nose was made of cosmetic putty, and his own hair was not sparse but thick, dark and wavy almost to the end of his life. But I have no quibble with the end of Low's description; "a comedian of genius."

Fisher and Low were followed by Jeffrey Richards and Anthony Slide, discerning critics who appreciated the ground-breaking nature of Lucan's unique Old Mother Riley characterization and the contemporary significance of what Halliwell called these "ramshackle films."[7] Elkan Allan, in his *Guide to World Cinema* went so far as to assert that we should "thank God for the cinema that this endearing, bemused old lady can never die."[8] One should however add that people who know only of the Lucan-Riley films are often unaware of the fact that before crossing to the cinema Arthur Lucan had spent almost forty years in the entertainment business, first in seaside Pierrot troupes, then in musical comedy, pantomime, music hall, and variety. It is therefore not surprising that in his films Lucan's extreme facial and gestural expressiveness harks back to those earlier genres, to circus clowning and to silent films including, most notably, Chaplin's *A Busy Day* (1914), a film from which Lucan seems to have derived several aspects of his belligerent dame. It is also just possible that Arthur Lucan saw Dan Leno perform live, as he was already nineteen years old when Leno died in October 1904. The fact that Lucan was born in 1885 also should be borne in mind when critics liken him to Gracie Fields and George Formby; these artists were many years (over fifteen) his junior, and his performance style provides a link to an earlier age. Stephen Shafer stresses the immense contribution of music hall stars to early films, both silent and talking, and concludes his list with the case of Arthur Lucan.

> One of the most prominent of these music hall performers was Arthur Lucan, whose 'Old Mother Riley' washer-woman character not only made a successful shift to the screen, but also became the central figure in one of the longest lasting movie series in British film history. Though admittedly a farce caricature, 'Old Mother Riley' is a good case study of this type of portrayal and helps to show the appeal of such music hall performers' work. Lucan's make-up and costume evoked a realistic impression of the harshness of life for the working classes; regardless of whether the situations being portrayed were farcical in nature, his rubbery, bony features when garbed in a long dress, shabby shawl, and tattered bonnet provided a remarkably authentic vision of real life existence to which working-class audiences responded.[9]

Throughout his entire career both on and off stage and film set, Arthur Lucan, "a nice little man, shy and self-effacing" according to Dora Bryan, was partnered by, or some say dogged by, his wife, "the appallingly untalented Kitty McShane, all saccharine and ham,"[10] a woman for whom not a single critic has had a kind word. By the time the Lucans began to appear in films, Kitty was seen by critics as "an unattractive, dowdy, slightly plump actress with no acting or singing ability."[11] In spite of this, "Kitty McShane served as stooge, songbird, and romantic interest, though the onset of middle-age severely restricted her effectiveness." Matters were made worse by the fact that "Plots for the films often revolved around Kitty's amours, especially if they involved social climbing."[12] David Quinlan adds, "Already rather mature for the role of the daughter, Kitty insisted on playing it to the point of ridicule for another 15 years. She did have a certain Irish prettiness, somewhat spoilt by a strong chin and thin penciled eyebrows. But she also insisted on wearing unsuitable clothes and singing sentimental and embarrassing Irish melodies in most of the films."[13] But offstage, things were far less benign, and unsuitable clothes were judged to be among the least of Kitty's faults. "From who knows what frustration or megalomania or just naturally ingrown bitchery, she became the dominant partner and, in her own view, the star. The more successful they got, the worse things went between them. "[14] Betty Driver witnessed Kitty's growing *folie de grandeur* at close quarters and insisted that Kitty "was a hard woman who browbeat the sweet old man [Arthur] until she ruined him. She had the biggest head and thought of herself as the star."[15]

Kitty McShane has fared badly at the hands of critics, and not without justification. By the time success came in the cinema she was already over forty, and no longer the attractive young woman she had clearly been in her earlier years onstage. Arthur's character on the other hand was by its very nature ageless, and so Kitty was in some ways a victim of his success, trapped in a role that could only become more unconvincing as she grew older and heavier. Worse still, while she must have once had a certain ability to appeal to large audiences in the vast spaces of a theater, she proved to be incapable of adapting comfortably to the very different conditions of the film studio; in close-ups she frequently appeared wooden, stilted, and ill-at-ease, whereas Arthur, at the advanced age of fifty-two, took to the cameras like a duck to water, and one can only grieve that his big break did not come many years earlier, in the era of Chaplin, Keaton and silent films. Whenever Riley is onscreen but silent, she always remains fully involved in the plot; her facial expressions, her amazingly expressive eye movements, the compulsively repetitive hand gestures, all dignify with utter verisimilitude even the most banal moments of plot or dialogue. The quality of Arthur's acting was underlined by Kitty's embarrassingly frequent inability to stay in role; her jerky, meaningless gestures, even when singing, and, above all, her panicked eyes which often seem to be looking for help from a passing stranger, formed a sad contrast with her consistently weird and wonderful mother. Nevertheless there are those who see Kitty as not only an essential component of the double act but also as the driving force behind Lucan's career. While acknowledging her many shortcomings, Anthony Slide maintains that "It is easy, indeed tempting, to ridicule Kitty McShane, whose lack of acting talent is matched only by her lack of personality and clothing sense . . . It is difficult to appreciate how crucial she was in helping Old Mother Riley become a star . . . She is the perfect foil for Old Mother Riley—and no one could have taken her place."

A more complex and, to my mind, in some ways misguided view was taken by playwright Alan Plater in an article in *The Observer* on 18 April 1982. Plater credits Kitty with a degree of lucid self-awareness and sophistication that she never once displayed in her dealings with anyone who knew her. However, his views need to be recorded if only in order to contest some of them later. "Her stage and screen personality was a simple extension of the private Kitty McShane: an urban peasant from Dublin with enormous gusto and energy, limitless ambition, and a streetfighter's knowledge that rich is better than poor." So far, so good, but I find it harder to agree with Plater when he says,

> My instinct is that Kitty's taste for over-dressing indicated an ironic self-awareness of the bizarre pretense she was obliged to take part in . . . She discerned and directed the near-genius within Lucan in a manner almost certainly beyond the capabilities of the man himself. Without her, he might well have spent his days as a journeyman stand-up comic with a good line in playing the dame; and without her—as she was very quick to point out— he died.

My profound disagreement, shared by others, with the second part of this analysis is based not on any animosity towards Kitty but on the facts I shall record in the following chapters.

In 1998 Ray Carradine provided a concise and more accurate restatement of the Lucan-McShane relationship.

> In real life Arthur Lucan was shy and sensitive, nothing like the garrulous, argumentative character that he portrayed on stage and screen, but he did have a fiery temper when roused. He was, without doubt, a comic genius who would have been a show business success even without Kitty, his partner in the act. In fact, cynics said that he became a star in spite of her. Kitty McShane, on the other hand, could never have made the big-time without Arthur; her talent in comparison was wafer-thin. As a team, though, they complemented each other well, even when Kitty stretched the audience's imagination to the limit by dressing like a young girl and playing the devoted daughter until well into middle age. It didn't matter, of course, because the real star of the show was Old Mother Riley herself.[16]

But for all Kitty's faults, there clearly was a chemistry between Lucan and McShane to which the public responded with enormous enthusiasm. Perhaps because Arthur was so obviously and genuinely fond of his "darlin' daughter" the public almost felt obliged to like Kitty for the sake of her weird and wonderful mother. One indicator of Kitty's popularity is to be found in the surviving recording of the first episode of *Old Mother Riley and Her Daughter Kitty*, recorded before a live audience in Bangor, North Wales, and broadcast on the BBC Home Service in 1942. Mother arrives onstage first and sets the scene for Kitty's entrance. "Where's my daughter? Ah, here she is!" As Kitty enters she is greeted with what feels like a spontaneous and enthusiastic round of applause and a few wolf whistles.

But as early as the mid-1920s it is clear that, offstage, Kitty could be difficult, demanding and at times offensive, as my account of her dealings with fellow artists Frank and Jen Latona will show. The actor Verne Morgan's reminiscences suggest that at this time the Lucans still had moments of relatively cordial married life, but both were touchy and volatile, and the theater orchestra violinist Fred Midgley, who was playing in Dublin in 1913 when the Lucans were married, told of their raucous arguments even in the 1920s.

Growing fame and success through the 1930s, and the belated acquisition of wealth beyond Kitty's wildest dreams, combined to exacerbate the difficulties in a personal relationship that was already becoming strained and acrimonious. When William Breach, a singer in their company, became Kitty's lover in 1943, the Lucans' marriage was over in all but name, and the hapless threesome became trapped in public roles which at times became a grotesque parody of their private lives. There were ever more frequent and violent verbal and physical disagreements both in public and in private until, by Arthur's own admission, Kitty's self-centered and demanding ways left him with nothing but "unhappiness and strife." In the first part of this study I intend to retrace the Lucans' troubled and ultimately destructive relationship from its idyllic beginning in 1910, through fame and fortune, to its sad and rather shabby end over forty years on.

After the biographical narrative, key aspects of the Old Mother Riley films, and critics' responses to them, will be examined. Considerations of space preclude a systematic film-by-film analysis but a number of major themes will be presented and discussed in some detail in order to offer a new and long overdue evaluation of Arthur Lucan's exceptional acting skills, to highlight his extraordinary physical dexterity and verbal fluency, and his uncanny ability to move from uproarious slapstick comedy to moments of genuine pathos. In 1982 *Movie Maker* said of the Lucans, "At the top of their profession, they performed before royalty and the British cinema clamored for them ... Arthur Lucan packed the music halls and cinemas with his rich portrayal of this arm-waving old hag with a heart of gold."[17] Jean-Louis Ginibre added that Lucan "departed from British music hall tradition in that his screechy voiced virago evoked humor clouded with a touch of darkness."[18] John Fisher noted that "For all her absurdity, Old Mother Riley did possess a definite credibility, a strict, even if zany fidelity to working class life ... whatever her vulgarity, her brashness, here was a touching portrayal of someone who was only too true a figure ... of the British social structure."[19] Fisher also asserted, "Many have been the actors and clowns who have helped to keep dame and aunt alive on the boards. But there was only one man who could ever play the hearty, and yet sad, Irish harridan."[20] The comedian Charlie Chester was in no doubt that pathos and sadness were crucial elements of Lucan's art. In his discussion of male and female impersonators and dames, he deliberately left Lucan until last, as if to place him in a special category all of his own.

> I have purposely left until the last the name of Arthur Lucan. Arthur was the perfect 'old hag,' small, fussy, garrulous Old Mother Riley. Yet with his acting ability he was able to move an audience to tears as well as make them laugh until they ached . . . Surely, Arthur was the greatest of them all.[21]

Film directors of the caliber of John Baxter (*Love on the Dole, The Common Touch, Say It with Flowers*), Lance Comfort (*When We Are Married*) "the most unjustly neglected director in British film history," and the seasoned screenwriter Con West, used several of the Riley films to convey wartime propaganda, but the films also managed to include a surprisingly wide range of incisive comment on society, politics, class, wealth, and even feminist issues, cleverly disguised as harmless comedy to escape the constant vigilance, especially in wartime, of the Board of Censors. John Baxter was in no doubt that Old Mother Riley was "a great character for propaganda purposes." He maintained that "overt war stories were inefficacious and that entertainment films left audiences with propaganda seeds planted in their mind to gain fruition later."[22] As he put it on another occasion, "If you can make them laugh, you can make them think." Arthur Lucan at his best certainly provoked thought as well as laughter, and to the intense annoyance of the establishment, working-class audiences adored this "screechy-voiced virago . . . always the underdog, shaking her scrawny fist at the world in defence of the downtrodden."[23] The screenwriters were aware of, and managed to exploit, Riley's relative freedom from interference by the censors. In spite of the strict control and manipulation of the media exercised by the government throughout the war years, I do not believe that a single commentator at the time or since has ever alluded to the social or political subtext of the Riley war films, which was staring them in the face and was fully understood by largely working-class audiences, and surely also by all those in favour of post-war social change. In the relevant films, Arthur can clearly be observed enjoying and exploiting to the full this added dimension to his earlier, comic stage personality. Evading the censor in order to address serious issues under the guise of comedy is also highly reminiscent of many aspects of the American Screwball film comedies of the 1930s, another facet of the Riley films that deserves further analysis.

> Screwball pictures also offered a kind of cultural escape valve: a safe battleground on which to explore serious issues like class under a comedic (and non-threatening) framework. Class issues are a strong component of screwball comedies: the upper class tends to be shown as idle and pampered, and have difficulty getting around in the real world.[24]

But whereas screwball comedies were noted for "blending the wacky with the sophisticated," Riley was usually content to blend the wacky with the wacky! Lucan was no sinister subversive, and in my discussion of the war years I will show that he actively co-operated with the Ministry of Information to add subtle government propaganda to his radio comedy series.

Many critics have wrongly labeled Lucan as a "northern comic," and claimed that his following was also largely confined to the industrial north, but theater programs and film distribution statistics prove that the Lucans were as popular in Brighton and Bournemouth as in Liverpool and Glasgow, and though they came late to the West End stage and screen, they were from the outset immensely popular in the London suburban theaters. Three of the most notable music hall comics of the day who made the transition to film, Gracie Fields, George Formby and Frank Randle, were indeed all firmly and correctly identified as "northern working class;" in fact, all three were from Lancashire. The film producer Richard Gordon, who worked with Lucan and Bela Lugosi on the last Riley film, was to the end of his days under the impression that the first Riley films were made in Manchester by Mancunian films. "Manchester is 'home territory' for Mother Riley because the early Mother Riley films were made in Manchester—Mancunian Films, which produced those pictures in the early days, was a Manchester film studio."[25] Dorothy Anger even goes so far as to reproduce without question the following quotation from a certain Philip Crookes. He claims that only romantic costume dramas were made in London studios, whereas, "Up in Manchester, at the Dickinson Road films, they made a series of funnies about

Old Mother Riley, a music-hall character played by a man in drag called Arthur Lucan . . . That was the social divide . . . working-class Britain lives in the north, speaks northern."[26] In reality all the Riley films were made in London studios for Butcher's Films and later for British National. Nor is the insistence of some critics on northern England borne out by closer examination of the plots and casts of the majority of the films. One example will suffice for the moment; in the first Riley film, Mother Riley's former neighbors who invade the Briggs' family mansion in Mayfair and hold an impromptu "knees-up" in the drawing room are, with one notable (Yorkshire, not Lancashire!) exception, clearly identifiable as cockneys. Peter Stead has erroneously claimed that "Formby and Old Mother Riley were loved in Bolton and hated in Surrey."[27] In spite of the snootiness of London-based critics, the Lancastrians George Formby and Gracie Fields were the two great *national* comedy icons of the 1930s, and as for Arthur Lucan, he too was immensely popular not solely in the North of England as many authors have previously claimed but throughout the entire country.

Philip Gillett, writing in 2003, was quite categorical in setting the record straight:

> Unlike the Mancunian comedies, the appeal of Old Mother Riley was considered to be national. In 1944, Len England observed that 'Old Mother Riley is the biggest money maker of all the British films. In some parts of England cinemas that nothing else can fill are packed to the doors by Old Mother Riley.' At the Granada Tooting an Old Mother Riley film in a double bill with *A Yank at Oxford* achieved a war-time box office record . . . *Old Mother Riley's New Venture* (1949) achieved excellent business on its London release on the Gaumont circuit, particularly in northeast London, while the management at Colchester, Essex, claimed it gave them their best business for twelve months. The film also proved successful in Chester, Dover and Cardiff.[28]

Clearly, "Ration Row near the gasworks" could have been found in any working-class area of any British town, north or south.

If Old Mother Riley was not especially at home in Liverpool or Manchester, it is equally debatable whether she was at home in Dublin.

Lance Pettitt, in his study of Irish films, *Screening Ireland*, touches briefly on another aspect of the Lucan-McShane phenomenon that has never been adequately examined, namely its links with the uneasy blend of mockery and anxiety which characterized Anglo-American portrayals of Irishness in general, and early twentieth-century British screen and stage images of the Irish in particular. "The darker side of Anglo-Irish history," writes Pettitt, "was avoided by the almost complete emphasis on light-hearted slapstick and whimsical (often musical) comedy." But paradoxically, Pettitt concedes that what he calls the "mayhem, mystery and madness that is 'Irishness' in these comedy films" does, in the case of Old Mother Riley have a rather sharper edge because "working-class concerns, regional characters and the Irish in Britain all represented forms of difference that posed non-conformity and potential disruption." Pettitt notes that "Both Lucan's eponymous Irish washerwoman mother and her daughter (played by Kitty McShane, his real-life Irish wife) are working-class Irish emigrants in northern England who stand up to authority figures in their films, puncture class snobbery, create anarchy and temporarily challenge existing power structures."[29] Jeffrey Richards, in the perceptive opening pages of his chapter on "Ireland, the Empire and Film," insists that "Violence has been integral to the Irish myth. Even comic films stress its centrality to the Irish psyche." And Richards clearly sees that Riley, the "combative Irish washerwoman as comic anti-heroine," takes her place in a long list of fighting Irish, real and imagined, tragic and grotesque[30].

In actual fact, all of the potentially disruptive characteristics evoked by Richards and Pettitt are aspects of Mother Riley alone; in no way are these attributes shared by Mother Riley's daughter, the "real-life" Irishwoman Kitty McShane. In the films, Kitty represented a completely different brand of Irishness, one which attempted to minimize the cultural and temperamental differences between the Irish and the British, and strove to escape from the twin evils of poverty and violence that had blighted so much of Irish history. Kitty's most ardent desire is not to rebel but to belong, to be assimilated into the host culture by the classic route of a good marriage. The serious significance of Kitty's role as an upwardly-mobile Irish girl working in Britain, and its enthusiastic reception as a role model for fellow Irish immigrants in England (and would-be emigrants back in

Ireland) has, to the best of my knowledge, been entirely overlooked or ignored by critics, and we shall return to it later.

Equally lacking is any attempt by critics to evaluate the cultural implications of the linguistic registers used by mother and daughter in the context of the differences between standard British forms of English speech and the specific vocabulary and idioms of what modern linguists call "Irish English," not "Stage-Irish" but the English spoken in Ireland which the "Irish" couple might have been expected to use quite differently from the English of regional comedians such as Fields, Formby or Randle.[31] As we shall see, there is hardly a single linguistic marker of genuine Irish-English (or for that matter even Stage-Irish) in Mother Riley's grammar, idiom or accent. Kitty on the other hand, in spite of several unintentionally comic attempts, was ultimately unable to modify her strong native Irish accent or her authentically idiomatic Irish-English usage, even when she became, for the umpteenth time, the bride of her handsome Englishman. We shall return later to the question of types of Irishness, not least because in one Riley film in particular it is referenced in one of its more graphically tasteless forms.

The most insightful critics have stressed the bizarre way in which Arthur Lucan as Old Mother Riley seemed somehow to escape or defy classification. He came neither from Ireland nor the north of England, nor did he sound identifiably Irish, northern, or for that matter anything else. He made not the slightest attempt to impersonate a woman, and long before academic gender theorists, his character deliberately drew attention to the constructed nature of gender via clothes, often performing a conscious parody of a striptease in order to reveal the flat-chested body of a man. "Bridget's Night Out," the first Lucan sketch to be filmed, contained the first such parody striptease, in which Mother removes layer after layer of deliberately drab underwear (definitely not "lingerie") and heightens the ridicule by stowing items in the oven and the bread bin. When it comes to her unresponsive corset, she cries in mock despair, "If only I had a spanner!" Sue Harper writes of this scene:

> Cross-dressing encourages a kind of sexual hide-and-seek. But what you think might be there is not; and what *is* there is not what you expect. This game is played with vigor in the

Old Mother Riley films . . . Mother disrobes for bed, and in a grotesque parody of the dance of the seven veils, seven petticoats are removed, four vests and a corset. Finally, the awful truth is revealed: the flat chest, the scrawny arms, the desexualizing effects of age. It is suggested to the audience that what gives Mother her insane energy is that time has made her like a man.[32]

In *Old Mother Riley's New Venture*, Mother refers specifically to her flat chest, in what may even be a sideswipe at female impersonators such as Norman Evans with their hefty artificial bosoms; "What God has forgotten, they'll fill out with cotton!" Arthur Lucan's Old Mother Riley is probably unique in the annals of dame comedy, and of comedy in general before Ben Elton, insofar as the "big boobs" of "saucy" seaside postcards are never once used as a grotesque prop to get a cheap laugh.[33]

"Lucan engaged in wild slapstick, wore his washerwoman's weeds without the slightest attempt at gender conviction, did violence to the language and invariably thwarted the pompous and the nefarious. The links with Music Hall are obvious and account for the bizarre charm of the films."[34] True enough, but the "the bizarre charm" of Arthur Lucan is far more complex, and cannot simply be ascribed to a nostalgic evocation of Music Hall or Variety. In Old Mother Riley, Arthur Lucan managed to create not so much a stereotype as an archetype, a character who took on a reality—or surreality—of her own, far transcending the sum of her disparate parts. For Roger Lewis, writing as recently as 2013, "It's the realism that's remarkable, the grace and dignity, despite the derangement and capering."[35] In 1941, just as their first radio series brought the Lucans to an even wider audience (judged at one point by the BBC to run into many millions), the *News Review* hailed Mother Riley, not as a clever dame or female impersonation, but as an actual person who was "The champion of the underdog, a hater of shams, a Valkyrie of the backstreets." In an article in *The Stage* in 2006, Patrick Newley described her as "perhaps unique in the annals of female impersonation. The act appealed to all generations. Children adored the knockabout qualities and some of the sketches had a touching sentimental air about them." Thus at one and the same time she incarnated "the inextinguishable life force of the slums, a veritable *Brünnhilde* of the backstreets," and yet she was also a pantomime dame character (another neglected aspect of Lucan's long career) as instantly recognizable and lovable as her storybook children, Dick Whittington, Jack Horner and Little Boy Blue. In fact, Lucan's creation became so deeply embedded in popular culture that she was the subject of a children's game-chant, "Old Mother Riley fell down the sink."[36] She even featured in camp-fire singsongs and playground chants. To this day one can hear cubs, scouts, guides and brownies lustily singing of a dame who died in 1954. "One man went to mow,/Went to mow a meadow./One man and his dog, Spot, bottle of pop, old Mother Riley and her cow,/Went to mow a meadow." Nostalgia websites on the internet indicate that the following smutty playground ditty was known in Liverpool in the 1930s, which suggests that it too was probably inspired by Lucan's antics with a pantomime cow at the Pavilion theater in the late 1930s and early 1940s. "Old Mother Riley She had a fat cow. /She wanted to milk it but she didn't know how./ She pulled its tail instead of its tit,/ And old Mother Riley got covered in sh**!" A doctor wrote on an internet blog website in 2006 that this song was "sung to me today by a 91 year old patient." The inimitable and quasi-iconic status of Lucan-Riley was also noted by Magill.

> Old Mother Riley is a peculiarly British phenomenon. She is the grand old lady of the British cinema, in the form of a female impersonator who is so much the character he created that not once watching any of the Old Mother Riley films does one ever stop to consider the incongruity of this character, an Irish washerwoman played by a music-hall comedian named Arthur Lucan.[37]

The American film historian and lecturer David Wilt adds a different but important comment on Lucan and the notions of "incongruity" and "gender conviction," a comment all the more telling given the fact that most Americans simply do not "get" this aspect of British comedy. "One of the truly unique characters in British cinema . . . There is never any overt hint of 'camp' in the Riley films with regards to the character's sex—indeed, I've always been convinced that an uninformed spectator would never suspect Old Mother Riley was being played by a male actor, the illusion was simply *that* good."[38]

Wilt's understanding of the British dame tradition is rare among Americans, who have even referred to Lucan as a "drag queen," imagining that he must have been gay because in *Mother Riley Meets the Vampire* the rent collector calls Riley an "old faggot." *Michael Grade's History of the Pantomime Dame*, a film made for BBC Television in 2012, made it clear that the pantomime dame and the drag queen are, and should be, two very different creatures. Peter Ackroyd made the same point with force in his study of the varieties of "dressing up." "The dame is never effeminate; she is never merely a drag artist, since she always retains her male identity. The performer is clearly a man dressed as an absurd and ugly woman, and much of the comedy is derived from the fact that he is burlesquing himself as a male actor."[39] In one of his essays on Lucan, Anthony Slide addressed his American readers' misplaced anxiety about male homosexual drag, explaining that in Britain a faggot is a meatball and a fag is a cigarette! But like many other critics he has also insisted on a paradox which seems peculiar to Lucan-Riley alone.

> To my way of thinking, the most important thing about Lucan is that you never look on him as a man ... He is not a cross-dressing entertainer. He is the character ... Old Mother Riley is to all intents and purposes real; watching her, we are not witnessing an impersonation but rather participating in the life of a foolish, garrulous old lady. She is 'she' and will remain so.[40]

And after Arthur's death she did remain so in her own right; Michael Dynan told me the following true story:

> When I was working at *The Stage* newspaper, a young researcher phoned me from Anglia Television, regarding the forthcoming series on comedians, including Lucan, and asked me what I knew about some of the stars they wished to present shows about. I was talking at some speed about Old Mother Riley, when she butted in. 'Excuse me,' she said, 'I'm a bit confused. You keep saying HE.' She had not been aware that Old Mother Riley was played by Arthur Lucan.

In September 2012 Arthur's last company manager, Slim Ingram, repeated to me his view that one never thought of Riley as a drag act. "Arthur created a character just as any other trained professional actor creates a character." Slim also said to me that Arthur was never "camp" whereas his last understudy, Roy Rolland, who was an excellent stand-in for a couple of performances, became too "camp" and affected in a longer run. In Rolland's obituary in *The Stage*, Dennis Gifford also noted that "Rolland was completely unable to manage the proper Riley gabble-talk."[41] Although (for brevity) Roger Lewis uses the term "drag act," his feelings perfectly reflect Lucan's uncanny, almost shamanistic, powers of persuasion. "Was Arthur Lucan the best drag act that ever lived? No one else affects me with such wonder and strangeness . . . ."[42] The way in which many critics have suggested that Mother Riley was somehow "beyond" considerations of gender was curiously reflected in her own day in Lucan's most loyal audiences; pre-pubescent children and post-menopausal older women.

Given critics' narrow focus on the image of the scruffy washerwoman, perhaps the most consistently neglected aspect of the Lucan-Riley films, is the fact that in most of them Mother Riley rarely spends more than a few early scenes in her drab widow's weeds. In a very different way from her daughter, Riley conspires to break the mold of the rigid conventions imposed on her by class, politics and gender. Never content with the status quo, Riley continually seeks to become *other*. In film after film, Riley's determination to break the career restrictions imposed on women, and her repeated casting off of her "base" identity of "scrubber" can be seen as an utterly serious and coherent statement of women's rights, several years before the persistent gender stereotyping of work began to be eroded by the wartime need for women to tackle absent "men's jobs." In a very real sense, Riley's speech on the hustings in *Old Mother Riley MP* is in fact her manifesto on behalf of all women. Why shouldn't she—a poor old woman— and the baby girl she takes in her arms, play any role or aspire to do any job they please, just because the powerful Mr. Wickers of this world, pompous old baskets, seek to disempower them, and "thousands like us?" Rarely content with mere comedy, Riley has here ventured into dangerous territory because, as Peter Ackroyd has suggested, "The mockery of sexual stereotypes involves the mockery of social stereotypes at the same time; when one social code is breached they are all at risk."[43]

In the light of Ackroyd's contention it is worth noting that a particular class of roles which Mother Riley plays with great relish has received no critical attention whatever, namely her frequent and delightfully amusing "send-up" impersonations of would-be upper class women; the wealthy Mrs. Briggs, concert pianist Madame Juanita, The Countess Wax-Vesta, Mrs. Montgomery-Jones, and Headmistress Riley, to name but a few of the Lucan ladies who aspire to be "lah-di-dah," but often with comical results. John Fisher, reflecting on the popularity of Danny La Rue in the 1970s felt that "It is hard to imagine that Arthur Lucan in his day could have met with the popular acclaim Old Mother Riley brought him, if he had ever veered away from the idea of the old Irish washerwoman in favor of a more sophisticated characterization."[44] Arthur did in fact veer away from the washerwoman in virtually every film, completely away in fact in *Old Mother Riley in Business*, where a well-dressed Riley has joined the ranks of middle-class shopkeepers. But in a sense Fisher was quite right, because always uppermost with Lucan was the potential for parody rather than glamour. Indeed, the way that the incorrigible old Riley (like the Franco-Italian Arlequin) often slipped out from beneath the posh disguise was a rich source of the comedy of incongruity. As a *Stage* reviewer put it, "Mr. Lucan as the Old Lady of the title is a host in himself." A complete list of the remarkable variety of roles and jobs (well over thirty) undertaken by Mother Riley would fill several pages.[45] As proof of how well the old scrubber could "scrub up" when the occasion demanded, see the magnificent portrait of Riley as Mrs. Briggs, one of the publicity photographs published by Butcher-Hope-Bell studios before the release of the first film in 1937. Daphne Snowdrop Bluebell is shown in an unusually elegant pose, wearing a full-length evening dress, with printed clusters of large peony-like flowers on a pale background, long evening gloves, a fur tippet on her shoulders, with an elegant tiara crowning her neatly brushed hair. But not for long!

Unlike her adventurous mother, Kitty aspires only to the predictable jobs of nice girls, stereotypes such as secretary, hotel receptionist or singing teacher. Disappointingly, her role as a doctor in *Old Mother Riley Joins Up* can be explained not by Women's Lib but by her bizarre need to upstage her own son, who had just graduated in medicine from Trinity College, Dublin.[46] All Kitty's efforts, unlike those of her insubordinate and combative mother, are geared towards the conventional and submissive role of adored fiancée and blushing bride. And yet, paradoxically, from the very first film, Kitty is staunchly aided and abetted in her stereotypical quest by her widowed mother, simply because "She's my daughter, and she's all I've got in the world." Kitty is the one chink in the armour of the otherwise impregnable "Valkyrie of the backstreets." She is the "Persian kitten" born of an "old tabby cat," the beloved "peacock chick" for whom Mother is content to be just an "old brown hen."[47] This powerful, albeit largely parodic, evocation of the theme of the "maternal melodrama" is present in almost all the films and is responsible for much genuine pathos, suggestive, as Roger Lewis has noted, of a darker subtext in the real world.

"Sitting on a hard chair before a weak fire, Old Mother Riley exists in the shadow of the workhouse. She is somehow desolate and oppressed—and terrified that Kitty too will fall. I look at the character shouting insults and I always wonder what injustices, wrongs, torments she has endured—or Lucan endured."[48]

For all its conventionality, Kitty's role had a contemporary resonance to which we shall return.

The fact that "one of the truly unique characters in British cinema" has received so little critical attention may be partly due to the immediate post-war Establishment's keen awareness of the political implications of these "ramshackle" films. The British Board of Film Censors was no friend to the Labor government, and as Sue Harper put it, "Throughout the post-war period strong hostility was expressed by the Board to popular forms, and towards any political system likely to celebrate these forms. Particular scorn was reserved for figures like Old Mother Riley and Frank Randle who appealed to a working-class audience."[49] Once the early Riley films had been ridiculed and vilified, their genuine and not inconsiderable contribution to wartime morale became obscured, and it was easy to consign them, and the post-war films, to children's matinees and late-night TV channels where their possible social and political implications could be ignored or forgotten by "serious" critics who, as Brian McFarlane put it, "no doubt lamented the vulgar taste that kept the escapades of the Irish washerwoman popular for fifteen years."[50]

More recently however, academic writers on cinema have come increasingly to agree with the view, long expressed by ordinary wartime cinemagoers, that the cheap British comedy movies of the 1940s probably did more for wartime morale than many of the more highminded British dramas or lavishly produced Hollywood blockbusters. Old Mother Riley, George Formby, Gert and Daisy, Arthur Askey, Tommy Trinder, and the team from John E. Blakeley's Mancunian Films, including Norman Evans and the irrepressible Frank Randle, raised flagging spirits and kept audiences laughing through Britain's darkest days. In 1994 the influential critic Wheeler W. Dixon wrote

> We can see now that 'A' films have for a long time been given an artificial precedence over 'B' films of equal or greater thematic interest. Often these more modest films question the dominant social order in ways that mainstream films would not dare to do, if only for fear of not recouping the substantial investment involved in their production. . . Even in the humblest British 'programmer,' the seeming predictability of the narrative often disguises implicit critiques of the British social, sexual, political, and class order.[51]

Things have come a long way since Norman Longmate who, after praising the "highbrow" film dramas of the war years, could write in deadly earnest, "Most wartime comedies are also best forgotten, like the appalling *Mother Riley* series, featuring a female impersonator, and some unfunny Crazy Gang performances."[52] In 1997 Stephen Shafer was among the first to reject categorically the views of Longmate and his ilk, and to examine the complex social and cultural implications of British film comedy.

> Clearly the glib, oft-repeated, unverified assumptions about British popular films during the 1930s must be discarded or at least re-evaluated. The highly influential London West-End critics, from whom so many of the perceptions about the British cinema at this time are derived, were unimpressed by the substantial contribution of the music hall tradition to British movies; they disdained the likes of Gracie Fields, George Formby, and 'Old Mother Riley,' whom they considered to be crude, vulgar, and cliché-ridden, in spite of the

enormous popularity with the working classes of these performers and of their feature films.[53]

In 2000, in *A Chorus of Raspberries: British Film Comedy 1929-
1939*, David Sutton undertook a timely and penetrating analysis
of a still relatively neglected genre, and in his review of the book
Tony Williams wrote, "Sutton argues that the low status and critical
invisibility of 1930s British comedies allowed them to deviate from
mainstream aesthetic and ideological parameters to explore issues of
class, gender, and sexuality absent in more prestigious texts." Williams
further noted that "Sutton's comments on *Old Mother Riley MP*
(1939) may even bring about a re-evaluation of this Arthur Lucan
series ... Sutton sees the figure as 'an embodied critique of both the
self-satisfied middle-class world view and of a middle-class art with
its emphasis on restraint and realism.'"[54]

But for Arthur Lucan, the full reevaluation for which Shafer,
Dixon, Sutton, and Williams all hoped has still not taken place. In
2003, Philip Gillett, in his perceptive study of *The British Working
Class in Postwar Film*, inevitably confined his analysis to the small
number of post-war Riley films. While minimizing the issue of Riley
and gender, wrongly in my opinion, Gillett does make a number of
perceptive observations on Riley and social class. Andy Medhurst
could have gone further in 2007 in his *National Joke: Popular Comedy
and English Cultural Identities*, with its avowed intention of "relating
comic traditions to questions of class, gender, sexuality and geogra-
phy," and its posing of the question, "why class influences what we
laugh at and why comedy has been so neglected in most theoretical
writing about cultural identity." Instead, while finding time for the
Carry On films, Medhurst simply admits in his introduction that his
omission of stars including "Arthur Lucan and Robb Wilton from
detailed consideration is deeply regrettable." Given Medhurst's central thesis, one might be forgiven for thinking that the omission of
Lucan's fifteen Riley films in particular was not only regrettable but
incomprehensible.[55] As recently as 2012, in *British Comedy Cinema*,
another volume of essays in celebration of the now fashionable genre,
the editors Ian Hunter and Laraine Porter note Lawrence Napper's
assertion that "The likes of Fields and Formby, the Crazy Gang and
Arthur Lucan are still subject to cultural snobbery. Many critics fail to

analyze these films in context or simply fail to appreciate the humor." That is the extent of this volume's discussion of fifteen of the most phenomenally successful British comedy films of the years 1937-1952. Lawrence Napper does at least go on to contend that "We need to adopt a much more sophisticated framework for understanding the popularity of 1930s comedy, whose appeal to its working class audiences may require a considerable effort of historical imagination."[56]

There are two notable recent exceptions to the strange degree of academic reluctance which surrounds Arthur Lucan in particular, and they may point the way forward for younger, more adventurous scholars. Paul Matthew St. Pierre, Associate Professor of English at Simon Fraser University, Vancouver, has discussed the Riley films in considerable depth and detail in his penetrating and scholarly analysis of music hall mimesis in British cinema, and Steven Fielding, Professor of Political History in the University of Nottingham, has made an interesting comparison between *Old Mother Riley MP* and Frank Capra's *Mr. Smith Goes to Washington* in an article (and forthcoming book) on screen representations of politics.[57] In terms of academic critical theory, Sam Friedman's recent essay, harnessing Pierre Bourdieu's theory of "The Field of Cultural Production" in his examination of British comedy, seems to me to offer a most promising framework within which to examine and properly evaluate issues of class, culture(s), and power in the rich corpus of Lucan-Riley stage and screen material. Unfortunately, Friedman's otherwise excellent essay is marred by its single passing reference to Arthur Lucan; "*The most famous drag queen of the music hall era* was Arthur Lucan's Old Mother Riley . . . [my italics]."[58] This is seriously inaccurate on two counts; the enthusiastically heterosexual Arthur Lucan was no "queen," and when he created Old Mother Riley the "music hall era" was already over.

The often surprising results of my research have obliged me to re-write most aspects of the Lucans' early years, and to correct many widely reproduced factual errors, inaccuracies and legends. The earliest documentary on Lucan and McShane, written and produced for Thames Television in 1969 by Margery Baker, was a sensitive and perceptive study to which Arthur's son Donald contributed many insights, though he asked not to be mentioned in the credits. The program also benefited enormously from the historical research of Raymond Mander and Joe Mitchenson. In 1980, to mark the twenty-fifth anniversary of Arthur's death, two timely and interesting documentaries were screened; one produced by John Graham for BBC North, the other produced by David Kenten for Anglia Television.[59] These programs actually contributed in some ways, thanks to people who should have known better, to perpetuating certain misconceptions. Perhaps the most glaring and unjust of these was the claim that towards the end Arthur was an erratic alcoholic, often incapable of playing the second house. Long-standing understudy Roy Rolland had indeed replaced Arthur in the earlier Mother Riley road show (as he repeatedly told television interviewers around 1980) but this was almost always during Arthur's periods of serious illness and hospitalization, a fact which Rolland neglected to mention. Nor was Rolland a regular understudy for Lucan in the films, as has been suggested. When Rolland was engaged for the Lucan-McShane road show, only three films remained to be made, and he may at most have been used as a body double for a few long shots. Throughout the 75 weeks of the show *Going Gay* (1952-1953) at a time when a chorus girl earned £6 per week, Rolland received the princely wage of £17. 10s., but, as company manager Slim Ingram assured me, he stood in for Arthur no more than half a dozen times, and he did not even appear in the company's 1952-1953 pantomime at Bristol. For this reason, at the end of the run of *Going Gay*, company boss James Gaston ordered Slim Ingram to dispense with Rolland's services, and he never again stood in for Arthur until the night after Arthur's death in Hull. Dennis Gifford, in his obituary for Rolland, wrongly asserted that Rolland had "gone on stage for his Guv'nor when Lucan's liquor consumption rose to an excess, an occurrence ever more frequent in Lucan's later life."[60]

After the Christmas 1953-1954 pantomime at Folkestone, when Slim protested that Arthur had to have an understudy for the new show, *Old Mother Riley in Paris*, James Gaston was so unconcerned that he told Slim to simply pick out any junior (and cheaper) member of the cast. Slim chose a newcomer, the repertory actor Frank Seton. Seton himself recounted in an interview filmed in 2002 that he was given no training and did not even try on Lucan's costumes. Contrary to endless rumors, which Seton himself flatly contradicted in the filmed interview, he was *never* called upon to perform as Riley until the night of 17 May 1954, and then only because Arthur was dead. As the years went by, these facts were forgotten, or brushed aside in favor of malevolent hearsay and juicy gossip, the black Lucan legend of a hopeless and jaded old drunk, a legend which, as we shall see, Kitty McShane actually encouraged and fostered for ten years after Arthur's death in order to present her own behavior, and her treatment of her husband, in a more favorable light. For years it was widely reported and believed that Frank Seton often did the second house when Arthur was too "tired" to go on. These claims were entirely without foundation, and yet to this day they have remained an uncontested part of the black Lucan legend. As recently as November 2013, in the new and augmented edition of his classic study *Funny Way to Be a Hero*, John Fisher sadly felt the need to add some "Afterthoughts" to his essay on Lucan and McShane.

> Just as he never appeared for his last performance, an understudy taking his place as the undertakers were called, so it has since come to light that understudies saved the day on many more occasions when alcohol prevented him going onstage. Audiences were unaware of the change. Full marks then, not only to Frank Seton, but also to Roy Rolland and George Beck, his most frequent double, for making their efforts so convincing, not least because of the extreme physicality that accounted for so much of Arthur's appeal.[61]

I do not for one moment wish to deny or minimize the fact that alcohol played an increasingly important part in Arthur's later life. As John Fisher went on to admit, Arthur probably needed Dutch courage to cope with "the megalomaniac monster that McShane had become," or, as George Melly called her, the "drunken termagant who made Lucan's life a hell." But it is a long way from that to the utterly fallacious tales of Arthur's being regularly made incapable of performing through drink. There are indeed well-documented examples of Arthur's understudies replacing him at moments of serious illness; there is no single properly verifiable instance of drink-related incapacity, and we have Frank Seton's testimony that in his own case there is no evidence whatsoever! We shall return this important topic later; but for the moment, on a lighter note, as Mother Riley said to Count Von Housen (Bela Lugosi), "Tipsy? Me, tipsy? Why, that's an insult to us Rileys! Do you know, there isn't enough of this stuff in the world to make me dizzy, never mind tipsy!"

Arthur Lucan was almost universally considered by his peers in show business and beyond to be both an exceptionally funny and intelligent actor, and a kind and generous man, a rare achievement in a profession famous for "bitching" and "acid drop" anecdotes. The sad and unpalatable truth, which cannot be avoided or exaggerated is the fact that, thanks largely to the unspeakably selfish and ungrateful behavior of Kitty McShane, the man who had brought laughter to millions on stage and screen was, on the night he died in the Tivoli Theater in Hull, as homeless and penniless as he had been when he first set out from Lincolnshire at the turn of the twentieth century. I have a copy of a hitherto unknown and unpublished letter from Arthur to his son Donald, written in February 1952, and another written to Donald by a trusted friend of Arthur in March 1955, both of which serve to make it undeniably and abundantly plain that Arthur was only too aware that the wife to whom he had given everything had repaid him with bankruptcy, "unhappiness and strife." The reluctant one-night understudy Frank Seton, just a few years before his own death, still recalled with great sadness an incident on Doncaster station early in 1954. While the company was in the refreshment room it began to rain heavily. Arthur had left his overcoat outside with the luggage on the platform, and when Frank pointed this out Arthur did not budge but said simply, "It doesn't matter chuck, I've already lost everything else!"

This long-overdue study aims to set many records straight and will, I hope, throw new light on the genius of Arthur Lucan, and the sadness of Kitty McShane.

Chapter One: Arthur Towle; Early Days and The Musical Cliftons 1885-1910

"*Sic parvis magna*—greatness from small beginnings" was the motto on the arms granted by Elizabeth I to Francis Drake after his circumnavigation of the globe. In his own more humble way, firstly on a "world tour" in 1924, and later thanks to the silver screen, Arthur Towle as Old Mother Riley went around the world (the films were dubbed into many languages) and achieved a degree of fame and fortune beyond the wildest dreams of his Lincolnshire childhood. Long before the theorizing of psychologists and psychoanalysts, it was widely understood that, in Wordsworth's words, "The Child is father of the Man," and to the end of his days Arthur Towle remained a Lincolnshire lad who never forgot or denied his humble roots as a "yellowbelly," the rather odd nickname given to Lincolnshire folk. In later years, his flamboyant wife Kitty McShane, while regularly visiting her family in Dublin, had little time for Arthur's provincial ways, or his provincial siblings, and rarely agreed to visit them in Boston, Lincolnshire. But while appearing (without Kitty) at Peterborough barely two months before he died, Arthur made one last visit to Boston, to see the brothers, sisters, nieces and nephews he had never completely forgotten. Several times during Arthur's last two years, on the Sundays when they changed theaters, company manager Slim Ingram drove Arthur to Boston in his Hillman Minx, and Slim remembered how, if they had time, Arthur would love to go to the vast parish church of St. Botolph to hear the choir sing the Morning Service. His older sister Annie, now Mrs. Butler, had been given the task in 1943 of placing a stone on their mother's grave in Horncastle road cemetery, and Arthur may well have visited it. Slim particularly remembered meeting Arthur's youngest sister Kate, the diminutive Mrs. Ladds, with her burly fisherman husband and their seven children, one of whom she had named after her famous brother.

Just a few months later, the Boston Towles were present in Hull's Eastern Cemetery, along with crowds of mourners, when their brother was laid to rest. Tom Towle may well have stood near Kitty at the graveside and heard her ungrateful parting words to the man who had literally given her his last penny; we shall return in due course to those words. Years later Tom told Margery Baker of Thames Television, "She broke his heart, and if she were here now I'd tell her to her face." On a happier note, Tom Towle had been the privileged witness of his brother's very first steps on the road to a career which began in Shodfriars Hall Boston in the reign of Queen Victoria, and ended in the wings of Hull's Tivoli Theater one year after the coronation of Elizabeth II. It may well be that the childhood of the boy Arthur Towle among what the poet Thomas Gray in his famous "Elegy" called "the rude forefathers of the hamlet," will help us towards a better understanding of the man who years later became Old Mother Riley. Thomas Gray also forewarned his readers against dismissing the stories of simple folk.

> Let not Ambition mock their useful toil,
> Their homely joys, and destiny obscure;
> Nor Grandeur hear with a disdainful smile,
> The short and simple annals of the poor.

Here are those annals.

Arthur Towle's father, Tom Towle, was born in 1855 in the isolated village of Waddingham, seventeen miles due north of Lincoln. As a young man Tom became a groom, working with the horses that were Britain's only means of general road haulage and agricultural traction until well into the twentieth century. Arthur's mother, Lucy Ann Mawer, was born in the town of Sleaford, seventeen miles due south of Lincoln, in the year 1858. The couple were married in St. Mary's church in South Kelsey in the autumn of 1881. South Kelsey was a hamlet of just six hundred souls, not far from Tom's native Waddingham, and set in the midst of the flat and fertile plain of north Lincolnshire, through which runs the straight line of the Ermine Street, the major Roman road connecting London with York via Lincoln. In the sleepy hamlet of South Kelsey, "far from the madding crowd's ignoble strife," Tom and Lucy Ann's first two children were born, Annie in 1883 and George in 1884.

Early in 1885 Tom found employment as groom to the local doctor in the village of Sibsey, forty-three miles to the south, just outside Boston. This village was not much bigger than South Kelsey but it had a railway station and also boasted one of England's tallest working windmills. The Trader Windmill, built in 1877, is one of six sail windmills which survive in England today, and it still operates on occasional "milling Sundays."

Arthur Towle was born in Sibsey on 15 September 1885, in a two-roomed cottage, lit only by candles and oil lamps, and with water drawn from a communal pump in the yard. Years later, the semi-derelict cottage was used by a farmer to store potatoes. When the farmer died the cottage was threatened with demolition, but in 2003 it was saved and renovated by Roy and Joy Rust, and today it proudly bears the name "Old Mother Riley's Cottage" and a commemorative blue plaque. In his first week of life Arthur contracted scarlet fever, a common cause of infant mortality in the days before antibiotics. But he survived, and on 14 November 1885 he was christened by the vicar Frank Besant (estranged husband of Annie Besant) at the ancient font in St. Margaret's church, just across the road from the cottage in the Workhouse yard. Arthur's sister Kate was also born in Sibsey in 1889. Then, in a major move for these country folk, the Towles left the peace and quiet of village life behind and moved into Boston, a bustling, thriving port and market-town, dominated by the "Boston Stump," the soaring 272 ft. tower of the magnificent mediaeval parish church of St. Botolph. The tower is visible for miles around above the flat fenland countryside and far out into the Wash, and the church itself has been described by Nicholas Pevsner as "a giant among English parish churches." But there was also a much earthier side to Boston which would have been a familiar part of the Towles' everyday life and Arthur's growing up. The vast Market Place was constantly crowded with the horse-drawn wooden stalls of local traders, and customers flocked here from all over the south-east of the county, especially at the time of the great May Fair, held annually since at least 1125. Wide Bar Gate, with its iron pens, was the setting for regular auctions of sheep and cattle. The new docks, opened in 1884, were filled with large commercial vessels, both steam and sail, coasters, tugs and fishing boats. Great catches of shellfish would be hauled through the streets as an old Bostonian, Bob Marriott, remembered years later.

> The railway horses were stabled on the Dock. They would pull the wagons along the line to where they were needed. It

was strenuous work for the horses, I've seen them fall on their knees, straining to get the fully loaded wagons to start to roll; once they started to roll, the handler would quickly unhook the chain. They also worked on the Mussel Stage. When the cockles and mussels were unloaded off the boats onto the mussel stage, they were then loaded into the railway wagons. The horses then would pull them along the Mussel Stage, to a turntable where they could turn the wagons to go across the road into the railway yard to be transported to various destinations. It was really hard work for the animals." Bob Marriott also remembered the huge herds of cattle which passed through the docks and competed with the horses to fill the streets with manure.

In our school holidays, I and one or two more used to go with cattle drovers. There were often a thousand Irish cattle arriving at the cattle dock on some Saturdays. The front of the herd would be at the Town Bridge as other cattle were still leaving the cattle dock. We would guard all the side streets and passageways. Cattle would be sold at the market, and then were taken to various fields outside of town. The roads and pavements were so splattered with cow muck, you didn't want a poop scoop, a JCB would have been handy."

Boston was also once an important railway junction, and the Lincolnshire headquarters of the Great Northern Railway. A branch line crossed the river and into the docks by means of a swing bridge which had to be opened to allow fishing boats to return to the quays. The swing bridge was operated for many years by a jovial man called Bill Box, who was a favorite with Boston children. But there was also an aspect of the bridge which may well have frightened the Towle children as it did many others.

For years and years, all those who lived along the river had to put up with the fishermen blowing their horns, to warn the chap who was on duty at the swing bridge that they wanted to pass through. We would be awakened in the early hours, often from a deep sleep, for the chap who was on duty to open the swing bridge, a most disturbing sound when awakened from deep sleep, an eerie sound when it was foggy. All the boats had a battered bugle on board.

At the heart of this busy town Tom Towle had found work as head groom at one of the finest inns in the county, The Peacock and Royal Hotel which overlooked the Market Place. The Peacock, which added "Royal" to its name when Queen Victoria's second son Alfred, Duke of Edinburgh stayed there in the 1890s, was a seventeenth-century building with a late eighteenth-century facade, to which bay windows and a balcony were added in the early 1800s. In 1904 an American tourist, Josephine Tozier, published her travel book, *Among English Inns*, a book which she noted in her introduction had already been "several years in the making." It contains a picturesque and sharply observed account of a visit to Boston and a description of the Peacock Hotel, offering a rare and interesting evocation of the town at the turn of the twentieth century, exactly as Arthur would have known it shortly before leaving home.

On the street leading from the station the low brick houses were all exactly alike, and out of them poured forth large families of dirty children. After two minutes' walk through this uninviting beginning of the town, the street suddenly stopped, and we stood above the parapet where the river ran swift beneath, and we looked across the water at the great tower of St. Botolph's Church shooting up into the red sky. This is the finest view in Boston, and, as we saw it in sharp contrast to the dull commonplace street by which we had come, our enthusiasm was correspondingly great. From this spectacle we understood plainly why Boston is said, by the English, to look like a Dutch town. Along the river gorgeously painted fishing-boats were making their way out at high tide to the Wash. Bridges spanned the river, and gardens grew along the side behind the high walls required to curb the River Wytham's ardor. As a tidal river, it has a way of climbing over barriers and even at intervals invading the great church. From the river-bank we went to the bridge, through a distracting maze of narrow lanes, before we reached our hotel on the marketplace. The Peacock and Royal is a commercial hotel of cheerful aspect. The front is decorated by bright flowers and long trailing vines growing from the window-boxes on the balconies, and above all is a most gorgeous sign of the most gorgeous of birds, from which it takes its name. We ate our comfortable little dinner in the coffee-room, our table placed in a bow-window.[62]

The Peacock Hotel was sold by Bateman's Brewery in 1965 and demolished to make way for Boots the Chemists, a dreary concrete box which now stands where once old Tom Towle was groom and Arthur's brother Tom had been a "Boots," a shoe-shine boy!

The Towles lived just behind Shodfriars Hall in a small terraced house at 10 Woodyard, an enclosed yard at the bottom of Jail Lane. The census of 1891 reveals that among their neighbors in Woodyard were a sail maker, a rag and bone collector, and, at No. 2 which was a lodging house, a motley assortment of characters to amuse and fascinate young Arthur; sailors, cattle drovers, agricultural and bricklayers' laborers, and a "female pedlar" from faraway Sheffield. Three more Towle children were born in Woodyard; Tom in 1890, Edwin in 1891 and Lucy in 1893. When they were of school age the children all went to the local National School in the corner of Pump Square, nicknamed "Nasty Cats" because of the very strict Headmaster's five-foot cane. A school photograph was unearthed around 1980 by a former headmaster, showing Arthur in a class photograph shortly before he left school. One pupil holds a slate on which is clearly chalked, "Boston National, 17 March 1899." This was a Friday two weeks before Easter, probably the last day of the Spring term, and Arthur was not yet fourteen years old.

In the 1890s Jail Lane was re-named Sibsey Lane and Arthur liked to claim that this was in honor of his birthplace. This of course was not true but today at the top of Sibsey Lane there is a blue plaque commemorating Arthur on the side of Shodfriars Hall. This is truly fitting because Shodfriars Hall was the most important building in Arthur's formative childhood years. It was a handsome 15th-century black-and-white timber-framed building, extensively remodeled and restored in 1874 by J. O. Scott, son of the more famous architect Sir George Gilbert Scott. A large brick hall in a sort of Flemish Gothic style that Scott added to the rear of the older building housed a first-floor theater which hosted regular visits from professional touring

Photo 2: Arthur (second left top) at the National School, Pump Square, Boston, March, 1899. *The Boston Standard*

companies, although the visits usually lasted only a few days. The building closed as a theater in 1929 but is still standing today. Arthur's brother Tom remembered the "bloodthirsty plays that everybody loved" and the pantomimes at Christmas. Arthur recalled that when he was ten, thanks to an outbreak of measles among the cast, the lessee of Shodfriars, Bartell Storr, gave Arthur a small part as a native in the pantomime *Robinson Crusoe*. It was from this humble beginning that Arthur went on to become probably the greatest pantomime dame of the twentieth century.

In *Jeremy*, a semi-autobiographical novel of childhood published to great critical acclaim in 1919, Hugh Walpole, who was just one year older than Arthur Lucan, evokes his young hero's sense of wonder on being taken to see a provincial pantomime, undoubtedly similar to the productions at Shodfriars Hall. In the opinion of the *Daily Telegraph* reviewer, Walpole's novel was "the real thing, wonderfully remembered, and most sympathetically and unaffectedly recorded." Walpole's account of a small-town performance of *Dick Whittington* perfectly captures what must have been the contemporary experience and feelings of the ten-year-old Arthur Towle, as he encountered his first pantomime dame.

In the middle of the scene was a funny old woman, her hat tumbling off her head, her shabby skirt dragging, large boots, and a red nose. It was from this strange creature that the deep ugly voice proceeded. She had, this old woman, a number of bales of cloth under her arms and she tried to carry them all, but one slipped, and then another, and then another; she bent to pick them up and her hat fell off; she turned for her hat and all the bales tumbled together. Jeremy began to laugh— everyone laughed; the strange voice came again and again, lamenting, bewailing, she had secured one bale, a smile of cautious triumph began to spread over her ugly face, then the bales all fell again and once more she was on her knees. It was then that her voice or some movement brought to Jeremy's eyes so vividly the figure of their old gardener, Jordan, that he turned round to Uncle Samuel, and suddenly grasping that gentleman's fat thigh, exclaimed convulsively: 'Why, she's a man!' What a strange topsy-turvy world this was in which women were men and shops turned (as with a sudden creaking and darkness and clattering did this one) into gardens by the sea. Jeremy drew his breath deeply and held on. His mouth was open and his hair on end . . . It cannot in reality have been a very wonderful pantomime, and it is unlikely that a touring company fitted into an old building like our assembly rooms would have provided anything very fine. But Jeremy will never again discover so complete a realization of his illusions.

As the finale to the first half of the entertainment, there was given Dick's dream at the Cross-Roads. He lay on the hard ground, his head upon his bundle, the cat as large as he watching sympathetically beside him. In the distance were the lights of London, and then, out of the half dusk, fairies glittering with stars and silver danced up and down the dusky road whilst all the London bells rang out 'Turn again, Whittington, Lord Mayor of London.' Had Jeremy been of the age and wisdom of Uncle Samuel he would have discovered that Dick was a stout lady and probably the mother of a growing family; that the fairies knew as much about dancing as the Glebeshire wives sitting on the bench behind; that the London bells were two hand instruments worked by a youth in shirt sleeves behind the scenes so energetically that the High Road and the painted London blew backwards and forwards in sympathy with his movements. Jeremy, happily, was not so worldly wise as his uncle. This scene created for him then a tradition of imperishable beauty that would never fade again. The world after that night would be a more magical place than it had ever been before.[63]

It must have been thanks to an experience such as the one Benson so lovingly evokes that Arthur was clearly "stage-struck" from his earliest years. His sister Kate remembered him dressing up as a clown and transforming his face with some sticks of greasepaint which the Shodfriars actors had given him. He then went busking in Boston Market Place and, in spite of his mother's disapproval, managed to earn a few pennies, his very first paid engagement! By a curious coincidence this sounds strangely similar to an amusing incident witnessed on the very same spot by the American tourist Josephine Tozier, and, as the dates correspond, it could well be an actual account of one of Arthur's earliest forays into the world of show business. (Margery Baker, in her 1968 TV documentary, claimed that Arthur left home "with his mandolin.") After dinner at the Peacock Hotel, Mrs. Tozier again takes up the story.

It was nine o'clock before we left the table. We were too tired to explore Boston's winding ways, and, as it was too early for bed, I had this time secured a large front room looking over the market-place, and my sleepy friends soon found entertainment there. The sound of a twanging banjo [mandolin?], which came from beneath our window, gathered the few stragglers in the market-place into a circle around the door of the Peacock. We could not see the musician from our window, but he broke forth as soon as the audience had gathered into the usual sentimental ballad dear to English ears. Some boys, with dogs at their heels, formed the outside of the meagre crowd, and then from a side street came belated mothers, pushing their babies home in perambulators. Three of these useful carriages joined the circle, the mothers, in true

Boston fashion, being unable to resist music. The audience grew larger and the circle wider; the songs were succeeded by dialogues, and coppers rained plentifully into the collector's hand, until a baby set up an opposition concert, and an enterprising dog was encouraged by the noise to fight his four-legged neighbor. During the rumpus which succeeded, the musicians vanished. The dog riot was finally quelled, the babies trundled home, and the market-place in a few minutes was absolutely deserted for the night.

Many years later Tom Towle recalled that long before he left school, "Arthur's interests always seemed to be in the theater and finally he took a job at the Shodfriars, cleaning in the mornings and selling programs in the evenings. He was eight years of age then." This gave young Arthur the chance to see some very serious theater. For example, when he was nine, in October 1894, *The Stage* records a visiting company giving *Hamlet*, *Romeo and Juliet* and Sheridan's *The School for Scandal*. The following year he may have seen Nicholas Rowe's 1715 "she-tragedy," *Jane Shore*. In April 1898 when Arthur was twelve, the actor-singer-composer George Grossmith, creator of some of Gilbert and Sullivan's greatest characters and co-writer of Mr. Pooter's *Diary of a Nobody*, gave his "entertainment" at Shodfriars. Grossmith was also famous in his day for performing his own comic sketches and songs at the piano, becoming the most popular British solo performer of the 1890s. Arthur may well have heard in person the creator of the magnificent patter-songs from, among others, *H.M.S. Pinafore*, *The Pirates of Penzance*, *The Mikado* and *The Yeomen of the Guard*, and his own highly idiosyncratic gabble-talk might thus be distantly related to W. S. Gilbert's "particularly rapid, unintelligible patter . . . ."

In 1967, Arthur's brother Tom told a reporter from the *Lincolnshire Standard* a revealing anecdote about Arthur's growing passion for the stage at about this time.

> One day Arthur was late home at dinner time and our mother sent us out to look for him. I looked in the theater [Shodfriars] and heard someone muttering on the stage behind the curtains—it was Arthur pretending to act all on his own. He was

about twelve then. There was a play running called *The Bells*, and he was trying to be the hero, Martin-Harvey.

This is especially interesting as it is the very first authentic account of Arthur onstage, and not in comedy or slapstick but trying to reproduce the tragic and melodramatic role of the murderer Mathias in the immensely popular play *The Bells*, which had been the vehicle for Henry Irving's spectacular rise to fame in the 1870s. The actor Sir John Martin-Harvey (1863-1944) whose biographer called him "one of last great romantic actors of the English theater," was a junior member of Irving's Lyceum Company, and after Irving's death in 1905 took on many of his roles, costumes, props... and mannerisms. From 1888 Martin-Harvey led provincial "Vacation Tours" of the company, "with the express permission of Mr. Henry Irving." In 1899 Martin-Harvey and his wife scored a huge personal triumph as Sydney Carton and Mimi in *The Only Way*, an adaptation of Dickens' *A Tale of Two Cities*, which they claimed they performed over three thousand times.[64] I can find no record of the Vacation Company having performed at Boston, although a brief visit en route to larger venues may simply not have been reported. Whatever the case, Arthur told Tom that he wanted to act like John Martin-Harvey, and just what Arthur was copying from Martin-Harvey's performing style may well be summed up in Edward Gordon Craig's description of Irving's own acting style as Mathias the Burgomaster in *The Bells*. "The thing Irving set out to do was to show us the sorrow which slowly and remorselessly beat him down. The sorrow, which he suffers, must appeal to our hearts. Irving set out to wring our hearts, not to give a clever exhibition of antics . . . .

What Tom Towle overheard that evening at Shodfriars, without really understanding it, was evidence that Arthur intended to be not just a clown but an actor capable of tragedy as well as comedy, *pathos* as well as *bathos*. Tom Towle was about seven when he heard his brother's performance. In 1905, another stage-struck schoolboy, the seven-year-old Eric Jones-Evans, remembered how Irving's own performance in *The Bells* in the theater at Boscombe (a favorite Lucan-McShane venue in later years) made him decide to become an actor. Like Tom and Arthur Towle, Eric remembered the moment years later. "It was at that moment that he heard, and so did we, the far-off jingling of sleigh-bells. 'Bells!' he whispered. 'Sleigh-bells on the road!' The sense of fear and horror conveyed by Irving in that whisper still has the power to make me shudder."[65] There are a number of sound-recordings of Martin-Harvey's performances, and the influence of his rather old-fashioned diction and manner on the tone and delivery of Old Mother Riley's pleading in the courtroom scene in the first Riley film (to give just one example among many) seems to me to be beyond question.

Incidentally, Arthur's mother Lucy Ann and Sir Henry Irving's wife may have had more in common than might be suspected. In the carriage on the way home after the triumphant first night of *The Bells*, Florence Irving asked her husband, "Are you going on making a fool of yourself like this all your life?" Irving instantly got out of the carriage and left his wife for good. Lucy Ann Towle's unrecorded chastisement of her histrionic son may well have produced a similar effect! In 1976, an elderly Bostonian, R. G. Wright, recalled another example of Arthur's youthful love of the theater. Long before he left home

> Arthur's interest in the theater had already been shown by the fact that he collected a group of boys together and under his own steam produced a play entitled *Maria Marten, or The Murder in the Red Barn*. This was performed in a loft above a slaughter house and bacon warehouse belonging to Mr. Thorpe, a butcher in Dolphin Lane. The admission was 6 pins. The play attracted about 50 children from the area including me. The only mishap on the first night was that the curtain became stuck and could not be lowered, much to the amusement of the audience.

But the birth of Arthur's love of the stage and the world of theatrical illusion seems to have coincided almost exactly with an event of a very different sort; the death from heart failure in March 1895 of his father Tom, at the relatively young age of thirty-nine. Early death among working people and a high rate of infant mortality were still an inescapable part of everyday life, but this surely did nothing to lessen the grief or hardship of the bereaved, however humble their station. Lucy Ann Towle was left with seven children, of whom the eldest was twelve years old, still (just) too young to work. Lucy Ann survived by becoming an efficient laundress, and Arthur was instructed to drum up business from the actors at Shodfriars Hall. However, Mrs. Towle was far from the almost saintly widow depicted by Steve King, who piously claimed that "the only luxury that she allowed herself was a ha'porth of stout, which she would get daily in a pint jug from the New Inn in Pen Street." In reality, there were many pubs far closer to Woodyard than the New Inn, and Lucy Ann did not bother with take-away jugs! In the 1980s, several elderly Bostonians had insisted in interviews with a local newspaper that there was something of the widow Lucy Ann Towle in Old Mother Riley. One old gentleman who claimed to have been a childhood friend of Arthur remembered Mrs. Towle as a "forthright figure who used to frequent the New Inn in Pen St, complete with rolling pin." Another elderly Boston resident said in 1979, "Anyone seeing Mrs. Towle's son as Old Mother Riley would see his mother in his dress, carriage and forceful ways." Back in the 1980s the euphemism "forceful ways" was a polite cover-up for something rather more earthy and shocking. But today, Lucy Ann's descendants are rather less "economical with the truth" and this helps us to understand how Mrs. Towle and Mother Riley really resembled one another. Arthur's nephew and namesake Arthur Ladds, son of Kate Towle, told me in 2012 that his grandmother Lucy Ann was remembered in the family as "a bit of a rum character. She enjoyed a drink, was often in the pub, and would frequently get so drunk that they would have to bring her home in a wheelbarrow." Given these facts the probable reason for Lucy Ann's choice of the New Inn was its unusual license. The present building, opened in 1874, was not only licensed from very early in the morning to accommodate the drovers bringing their cattle into the market on Wide Bargate, but it also had the right to open at high tide at any hour of day or night when the fishing boats returned to harbor. No doubt in honor of its double clientele, the inn was also known as the Haven and Bar. Lucy Ann Towle must have been one of very few women whose "forceful ways" were a match for the drovers and fishermen of the New Inn.

The image of a garrulous and argumentative widow tippling down at the pub, a rough and ready man's world rarely frequented by women, bears an uncanny resemblance to the character Arthur was to evolve in the years ahead, "a step washer with a propensity for sojourns at a nearby public house." In the final and most complete incarnation, as the widow-washerwoman Daphne Snowdrop Bluebell Riley, Arthur perhaps became a parody, albeit a poignant and affectionate parody, of the widow-washerwoman mother he had observed trying, not always successfully, to fend for her orphaned brood after 1895. Mother Riley was, as David Robinson put it, "a very affectionately observed caricature of the ignorance and strength of a back-street granny." But at a deeper level the caricature may also have been one of the coping mechanisms frequently observed in the children of alcoholics, laughter acting as a kind of exorcism for an abiding sense of sadness and shame. It is surely no coincidence that to the very end, Mother Riley's costume, with its full-length skirts, tattered shawls and bonnets, is frozen in time around the turn of the century, the time of Arthur's last powerful visual memories of Lucy Ann Towle. Sigmund Freud noted a very similar regression in Charlie Chaplin's heroes;

> Certainly he always portrays one and the same figure; only the weakly poor, helpless, clumsy . . . for whom, however, things turn out well in the end . . . He cannot get away from those impressions and humiliations of that past period of his life . . . The idea that the achievements of artists are intimately bound up with their childhood memories, impressions, repressions and disappointments, has already brought in much enlightenment and has, for that reason, become very precious to us.[66]

A further insight into Mother Riley's arm-waving and gabble talk was given to me in Boston in 2013 during conversation with Arthur Lucan's nephew and namesake, Arthur Ladds, and his daughter Sally Ladds. The Towles of Boston have always maintained that the arm-waving and gabble-talk "ran in the family," and that another of Arthur's nephews, Stanley Ladds, whenever he became animated, looked and sounded just like Arthur as Old Mother Riley. Slim Ingram also confirmed to me that even offstage Arthur "spoke with his hands." As several old Bostonians maintained that to see Arthur as Riley was to see his mother Lucy Ann, it seems that Arthur really did base his character's voice and movements on the "rum character" of his mother. Old Bostonian R. G. Wright was in no doubt; "Was it just an old Irish washerwoman that he was portraying, or his mother? The resemblance was rather uncanny."

At the time of the Census of April 1901 Arthur, now aged fifteen, is still living with the rest of the family at 10 Woodyard. The evidence of the Census flatly contradicts the often repeated legend, never denied by Arthur, that he had run away at the age of fourteen. The younger children, Tom, Edwin and Lucy are scholars, but Annie is working in a factory (she married in 1902); George is an errand boy; Kate, aged twelve, was absent for the Census but was still part of the family. Arthur is described in the return as employed as an "office boy," and this was the period when he was errand boy for printer Harold Dodds in the Market Place, and for Harry Fountain, who had re-opened the old Corn Exchange in 1899 as a music hall and theatre. Far from running away, it seems that before plucking up the courage to go further afield Arthur the office boy paid summer visits by train to the seaside at Skegness. There, on a covered wooden stage on the lawn at the edge of the sands, he would have seen Fred Clements's Pierrot troupe.

Clements came to Skegness in 1900 and was at the heart of its entertainment industry for almost forty years. Blackface minstrel troupes had been popular in music hall and then at the seaside throughout the second half of the nineteenth century. But in 1891, thanks to the success of Michel Carré's *L'Enfant Prodigue*, a "musical play without words" starring Jane May at the Prince of Wales Theater, they were replaced almost overnight by troupes of Pierrots or "whiteface coons," dressed all in white, with ruffles, black pompoms and conical hats. The image of the Pierrot was so new to British audiences that the Prince of Wales program actually contained a brief explanation of the origin and nature of the character. The very first troupe was formed by Clifford Essex, a singer and banjo player who had seen *L'Enfant Prodigue*. They played at Henley and Cowes during the Regatta and after performing for the Prince of Wales, who became Edward VII, Essex was given permission to call his troupe the Royal Pierrots. Essex was followed by Will Catlin, "the King of the Pierrots," who led one of the first alfresco seaside troupes, followed in turn by Will Pepper, one of whose "White Coon" parties was the first Pierrot troupe to appear on the promenade at Bray in Ireland. Catlin's Pierrots were to be found on rudimentary stages on beaches all around Britain, from Bournemouth to Scarborough. It should be stressed that the word "coon" was not meant to be offensive;

Sophie Nield notes that "by the turn of the century, the use of terms such as 'coon' had become disconnected from their earlier connotation of color, becoming shorthand for a particular style of popular program."[67] At Skegness, Will Catlin's players performed as the "Happy Valley Pierrots" or, in evening dress or blazers and boaters, as "The London Concert Party."

Arthur's love of theater had already set him apart from his down-to-earth family of manual workers. Now his position as "office boy" clearly suggests someone who was not content to be a manual worker but aspired to a role requiring a higher degree of literacy. In later years, his brother and sister, Tom and Kate, both remembered this sense of Arthur's being "different," and "his strange power of injecting humor into our lives at a time when there wasn't much to laugh about." He was more articulate, more verbal and vocal than his siblings, and clearly not destined for a life of heavy physical labor. Arthur was of slight build; Tom called him "the frailest one of us," and whatever Arthur's vocation might be, he would not fulfil it among the dockers and drovers of Boston. His first awakening had been on the stage at Shodfriars, but the revelation which was to prove decisive seems to have come on those visits to the seaside at nearby Skegness, and his discovery there of the world of the Pierrots, in the alfresco concert parties. At last Arthur knew exactly what he wanted to do, and this led directly to what Tom Towle called "Arthur's first disappearance." Before long, Arthur himself would be performing in the ruffles and pom-poms he first saw and admired on the beach at Skegness. Geoff Mellor claimed that Arthur's actual debut was with Catlin's Pierrots at Skegness in 1902, though there is scant evidence to confirm this.[68]

The Census of April 1901 may possibly suggest one further reason for Arthur's desire to leave home, namely the presence of a lodger. Along with the Towles at 10 Woodyard lived "boarder" John William Barton, a thirty-seven year old dock worker who, like Lucy Ann, was a widower. Local records reveal that John William Barton had married Caroline Pick in Boston in the summer of 1894. Caroline died barely a year later (possibly in childbirth) at about the same time as Tom Towle senior. At 8 Woodyard, two doors away from the Towles, there was a James Barton, a fisherman, living with his young family, possibly a relation of John Barton. If they were neighbors, Lucy Ann and John Barton may have been brought together as much by their mutual loss as by Lucy's need for money to feed her children; but it is also possible that in the crowded four-roomed house the bereaved couple, Lucy Ann and boarder John, grew close and shared (or appeared to share) more than mere board. Arthur, now a sensitive fifteen year-old youth, may have resented the intrusive presence of this older man soon after the death of his father, especially if, since Tom Towle and John Barton were about the same age, the lodger seemed to usurp the place of the dead father. Arthur, the aspiring actor, now perhaps shared something of the predicament of one of the most famous distressed adolescents in all literature, not a groom's son from Sibsey but the prince of Denmark whom Arthur may very well have seen on the stage at Shodfriars Hall in 1894. Hamlet's first reaction to the emotional turmoil provoked by his father's death and his mother's remarriage is his longing to disappear, to die or simply melt away. "O that this too, too solid flesh would melt / Thaw and resolve itself into a dew . . . ." Hamlet's first soliloquy may well reflect Arthur's predicament, albeit in language he still would barely have understood, except insofar as he too sensed that "It is not, nor it cannot come to good: But break, my heart; for I must hold my tongue."

The novelist Hugh Walpole once wrote, "It is the tragedy of childhood that its catastrophes are eternal." Biographical experiences such as those we have evoked from the formative years of Arthur's emotional and psychological personality, may well have contributed to the unusual vein of authentic pathos, of world weariness and genuine sadness even in the midst of slapstick which, as the most perceptive critics were to note, ran through all of Arthur's best work. Indeed it may well be that the "hearty, and yet, sad" Old Mother Riley, "that lovable old bundle of comedy,"[69] was in some strange way a memorial to the sad and funny ways of Lucy Ann Towle. And so, at some point after the Census of 1901, Arthur Towle "disappeared" as Tom Towle put it, melted away, spirited not quite into thin air, but to the bright lights of Blackpool and Llandudno, where he began his new life busking on the piers and beaches, and singing in the light and tuneful tenor voice which played such an important part in his early career and of which, sadly, so little has been preserved.

Another highly popular feature of a seaside holiday at the turn of the twentieth century was a day-trip on one of the sea-going paddle steamers which ferried excited landlubbers between various coastal resorts. In later life Arthur spoke of having sung on the steamers which plied between Liverpool, Fleetwood and North Wales, and also the steamers of the White Funnel fleet which sailed from the Bristol Channel resorts including Ilfracombe and Weston-super-Mare, to Newport, Cardiff and Swansea. One of the attractions for Welshmen when Wales was dry on Sundays was that the ships had bars, and the pubs in Weston and Ilfracombe were all open. Many of the magnificent boats later served in two wars before going out of fashion during the mass exodus to Benidorm of the swinging sixties. The world's last seagoing passenger-carrying paddle steamer, The *Waverley*, has recently been rebuilt and restored to almost new condition, with towering funnels, timber decks, brilliant varnish, and polished brass. In the summer of 2013 The *Waverley* returned to the Bristol Channel and to Llandudno, where for a few weeks the lost world of Arthur Lucan's earliest performing space was brought vividly back to life. Although about seventeen years old in 1903 and well able to fend for himself, it was while busking on a paddle steamer to Llandudno that Arthur allowed himself to be adopted for seven years into a substitute family, an adoption which involved the loss of his name, and the assumption of a new identity, the first of many.

Arthur and the Musical Cliftons
c. 1903-1910

The only firm information Arthur ever offered concerning his whereabouts in the years between about 1902-1903 and 1910 was that he sang on the promenades and the pleasure steamers, and was then apprenticed to a travelling troupe of seaside Pierrots called The Musical Cliftons. There are just a handful of contemporary press references to The Musical Cliftons, and the earliest three are all in Wales. In October 1895 *The Stage* reports that at Newtown Public Hall "Victor Gordon and Percy Clifton's Variety Co. opened here on Monday . . . The Cliftons (Percy and Lizzie) caused plenty of fun as musical eccentrics."[70] At the Swansea Empire in 1896, a program was presented which included "The Musical Cliftons, exceedingly good instrumentalists." In February 1897 at the Pavilion, Carnarvon, the list of acts ends with, "Other good artists engaged are The Cliftons, musical eccentrics." The title of "eccentric" at this time was shared by

Will Evans, "The Musical Eccentric," whose nephew Fred created the early British comic film character "Pimple." The BFI Screenonline describes Will as a well-known music hall performer "in the circus and pantomime tradition (eccentric in this case meaning acrobatic); he also sang, danced and played the mandolin." A brief film clip at the BFI of Evans's onstage acrobatics in 1899, and some sound recordings, may provide a link to the performance style of The Musical Cliftons during Arthur's formative years.

In June 1899 Percy Clifton advertised in *The Stage* for new recruits. "Wanted at once for seaside Minstrels, good Portable player and Violinist; also good Tenor and Baritone; double-handed men preferred. Apply, stating abilities to PERCY CLIFTON, VICTORIA STREET, BLACKPOOL."[71] As well as giving seaside seasons, the Cliftons also appeared in pantomime. From November 1899 to May 1900 the Cliftons toured widely in the pantomime *Beauty and the Beast*, in which Lizzie Clifton was highly praised for her acting and singing as the wicked fairy Henbane. At Radcliffe, among the specialty acts the Cliftons received special praise; "The Clifton Family gave a clever and refined musical performance;" at Long Eaton their act was encored, while at Bishop Auckland, "The Clifton Family handled their mandolins in a praiseworthy fashion." They also received favorable reviews at Bootle, Gateshead, Wednesbury, Wakefield, Seacombe and Whitehaven. At Gloucester in February 1901 they appeared in *Dick Whittington* as "The Clifton Family (musical experts)." In December 1902 at the Lecture Hall in Altrincham, the Musical Cliftons gave "an entertainment in aid of a local charity." The evening included "A selection on the mandolins. Master H. Clifton's rendering of 'Soldiers of the Empire' was worthy of the applause received. There were many songs and one or two sketches given during the evening, which met with untiring appreciation. The evening concluded with a sketch by the Cliftons, entitled *The Wilful Woman*." As there is no record of a young Clifton with the initial H, this might be a misprint for A (a common typo), making it Arthur Towle's Clifton debut at the age of seventeen, although I think this is highly unlikely. On 26 December 1902 at St. John's Hall, Penzance, and later on tour, the pantomime *Babes in the Wood*, included "specialties by The Musical Cliftons" and also "a shadow harlequinade." By an odd coincidence the pantomime which Hugh Walpole described in

Jeremy was almost certainly based on one he saw as a child in nearby Truro, performed by just such a troupe as the Cliftons, with farmers and sailors in the audience. In April 1903, *The Stage* reported that "At the Queen's Theater Fleetwood this week Mr. Solly is providing a variety entertainment, which includes clever vocal and instrumental turns by the Musical Cliftons, under the direction of Mr. Percy Clifton." In early December 1903 the Cliftons were at the Clay Cross Town Hall in Derbyshire.

These few sparse accounts do at least reveal that the Cliftons were seen as a versatile, accomplished and "eccentric" group of actors, singers and musicians who travelled widely around the country. The fact that Percy Clifton was the manager of the Musical Cliftons is further supported by several more advertisements for new artists which he placed in *The Stage* between 1904 and 1906. Indeed it seems very possible that Arthur's formal association with the Cliftons did not begin until the spring of 1904, with his reply to Percy Clifton's advertisements of 28 April and 5 May 1904. If Arthur had already been a member of The Musical Cliftons, Percy Clifton would hardly have needed to advertise for a boy who perfectly answers the following description of Arthur Towle. "Wanted, Boy or Girl, with a good Voice, for Alfresco Concerts. Good Amateurs may apply. One able to play mandolin or other instrument preferred. Long engagement.

Photo 3: Arthur (top right) with the Musical Cliftons as Pierrots, Llandudno, c. 1904-5. Steve King

State age and full particulars to P. CLIFTON, Deganwy, N. Wales."
Deganwy is barely a mile from Llandudno where Arthur was pho-
tographed with the Cliftons in Pierrot costumes at about this time.
Thanks to Arthur's presence among them, just three photographs of
The Musical Cliftons survive today, two of which Arthur sent to his
mother. The first photograph was taken in front of the Town Hall at
Llandudno, not far from the beach and pier, and shows the Cliftons
(including Arthur) in white Pierrot costumes. The group of eight
is made up of four adult men, presumably including Danny and
Percy, two younger men, Alan and Arthur, and two women, Lizzie
and Vera.[72] Some of the group's mandolins are visible, and one man
is seated at a small keyboard, probably a portable organ of the kind
much used by alfresco groups. The portable harmonium which Percy
offered for sale in *The Stage* in 1906 may be the instrument which
appears in this photograph. The fact that parts of Llandudno Town
Hall are visible in the background helps to date the photograph. The
Town Hall was not completed and opened until 1902 so the photograph cannot be earlier.

The second photograph, with the caption "The Musical Cliftons,"
shows two older men, two younger men and two women, all holding
banjos, mandolins or ukuleles. All are dressed in white but in naval
rather than Pierrot style, with flat peaked caps. This would seem to
be the summer concert party for which Percy Clifton had advertised
in *The Stage* and Arthur appears to me to be slightly older than in
the Llandudno photograph. The third photograph is a very formal
studio portrait of Danny and Vera Clifton with their son Alan, and
Arthur, posing rather solemnly in outdoor clothes. The three men are
all wearing hats and overcoats, and Vera has elaborate feathers and a
hat with a full-face veil. These photographs, and the brief references
in *The Stage* are all that is known for certain about the Cliftons, apart
from what Arthur told his mother when he wrote home, "These are
the kind people who are looking after me." Tom Towle recalled that
his mother told the children that Arthur had gone to Canada with
friends of the family, so they were surprised to hear from Llandudno
where Arthur claimed to be apprenticed to the Cliftons for seven
years so that, according to Tom Towle, "no-one could grab him."

This story of an apprenticeship has a rather odd ring to it.
Aspiring actors did not have a formal system of apprenticeship, and

itinerant entertainers such as the Cliftons could most certainly not give any guarantees of employment beyond the run of their current engagements. But from the little Arthur divulged of these years it would seem that he was more or less adopted by the highly musical and literate Clifton family, and remained with them until 1910, learning to speak, sing, dance and act, with an ever-growing sense of comic timing, and a rare degree of physical dexterity and mimetic expressiveness, all of which were to stand him in good stead to the very end of his career. Thanks to the benign influence and example of the Cliftons, he became far more culturally polished and articulate than the untutored lad who, when he left Boston, must still have spoken with the broad accent of a town that was the meeting place of fishermen and farmers, "Cow town and Fish town" as the locals say in Brixham, Devon.

Another clue to the Cliftons' contribution to Arthur's skills may lie in the repeated description of the group as "musical eccentrics." Perhaps as "eccentrics" themselves, they recognized and fostered this aspect of young Arthur's talent and, as regular pantomime performers themselves, perhaps they also saw that his eccentricity would one day make him the perfect pantomime dame. Curiously one of Arthur's very first pantomime reviews described him as "weird and comical," and Anthony Slide's excellent essay on Lucan appears in his appropriately entitled book, *Eccentrics of Comedy*. After these apprentice years, in 1910 Arthur went with the Cliftons to Ireland, and there his long association with his substitute family at last came to an end.

One further photograph of Arthur from this period exists, and has never been published before its appearance here. It was treasured by Arthur's son Donald to the very end of his life, and was lent to me by his widow Joan. It shows Arthur as a very young man dressed in a kind of bell-boy or cadet's uniform with a cap covering his dark, curly hair. He is holding what appears to be a long thin cigarette, but in the 1950s Arthur told an old friend, Jill Denman, that it was merely rolled paper. Jill also claimed that Arthur told her, "The photo of Arthur as a boy was taken when he was twelve, and in fancy dress in which he used to sing in a Concert Party on a boat which crossed the Bristol Channel." Arthur's estimate of his age (twelve in 1897) must be inaccurate as he was still in Boston long after his twelfth birthday. The photograph would seem to date from his time with the Cliftons and it strongly resembles his image in the studio group photograph with Danny, Vera and Alan Clifton. A date around 1903-1905 seems far more likely.

Ireland

The Dublin of 1910 bore little resemblance to the prosperous and welcoming city so successfully promoted today by the Irish Tourist Board. The text of an online exhibition mounted by the National Archives of Ireland, "Ireland in the Early Twentieth Century," paints a gloomy but honest picture of life in Dublin around the time of Arthur's arrival.

Dublin had the worst housing conditions of any city in the United Kingdom. Its extensive slums were not limited to the back-streets or to impoverished ghettos. By 1911 the city slums also incorporated great Georgian houses on previously fashionable streets and squares. As the wealthy moved to the suburbs over the course of the 19th century, their huge, red-brick buildings were abandoned to the rent-paying poor. Tenements in inner-city Dublin were filthy, overcrowded, disease-ridden, teeming with malnourished children and very much at odds with the elite world of colonial and middle-class Dublin.

The decay of Dublin was epitomized by Henrietta Street, which had once been home to generations of lawyers, but was, by 1911, overflowing with poverty; an astonishing 835 people lived in 15 houses. Life in the slums was raw and desperate. In 1911 nearly 26,000 families lived in inner-city tenements, and 20,000 of these families lived in just one room.

Death emphasized the precariousness of life for the poor: tenement dwellers died younger, died more often from tuberculosis, died more often in childhood. Overall, the death rate in Dublin per thousand was 22.3; in London it was just 15.6. The death rate in the city was not helped by the unsanitary conditions in inner-city tenements, where livestock were kept in dairy yards, cattle yards and down side-lanes. Drainage was little better than rudimentary, and the majority of meat eaten in the city came from beasts slaughtered in small private abattoirs and slaughter-houses. Offal and other substances lay on city streets despite being forbidden in a series of acts.[73]

In these daunting conditions, both middle-class and working-class Dubliners somehow struggled to make sense of their marginalized "colonial" status in what had become a stagnant backwater of the British Empire. Some found diversion in the music-halls, others in the innumerable pubs, but there were also many at all levels of society who were already planning a far more drastic solution to the "Irish Question." But for the moment, both literally and metaphorically Dublin was behind the times. In 1911, Cork was 11 minutes behind Dublin which was 25 minutes behind London, and it was not until 1916 that Greenwich Mean Time was extended to Ireland.

According to Arthur's obituary in the *Irish Independent*, he first found work

> in Samuel's Bazaar in Henry St, where the admission fee was 2d. Mr. Percy Clifton, then manager of the old Tivoli Theater on Burgh Quay, took an interest in him and obtained an engagement for him in [the seaside village] Skerries in the Martello Tower, then converted into an entertainment center in which Mr. Clifton had an interest. He also played at the sixpenny bazaar in Henry St, which ran a 2d sideshow as an additional attraction.

Although this information must have come from a local Dublin source, probably connected to the writer Seamus de Burca, whose family knew the McShanes and had a long involvement with the Queen's Theater, the chronology is gravely misleading. Percy Clifton's name appears as manager of the Tivoli only in the early 1920s, so it is far from certain that he would have been in a position to help Arthur earlier in his career. And there is only one earlier reference to Cliftons in the Irish Press, but "The Five Cliftons" who were at the Hippodrome in March 1912, were strongmen and quite unrelated to the musical family. Percy Clifton did indeed settle in Skerries, but not until 1922. Only then did he buy and convert the Tower Pavilion and the Arcadia ballroom in the main square. His wife Mrs. E. Clifton (Lizzie?) is described as the proprietor, and their son Walter was manager. Walter was also a violinist and there had been a violinist with the Musical Cliftons. The Musical Cliftons connection is further strengthened by the fact that Walter's wife, Minnie, played the trumpet and the French horn. Walter died unexpectedly in 1939, leaving two young children, but his father remained a pillar of local Skerries society until he retired and sold his businesses in 1947.[74] It is of course perfectly possible that the Lucans performed for their old friends at Skerries on one of their later visits to Dublin, but there is no firm evidence linking Lucan to Skerries other than the mention in Arthur's *Irish Times* obituary.

Chapter Two: Arthur Lucan and Catherine McShane 1910-1914

In 1910, in the bazaars and arcades of Henry Street, there were "singing booths" which employed singers to perform the latest popular melodies in order to encourage the public to buy the sheet-music to sing at home around the piano. It was apparently while singing in one such booth that Arthur Clifton first saw, and heard, Kitty McShane, who at the age of thirteen was also singing in the booths. It has also been claimed that Arthur lodged with the family, but this could not have been possible at this point as the McShanes were still living in two rooms in Cook Street. Kitty's mother Kathleen McShane became a theatrical landlady only after the family's move to Great Brunswick Street in 1911.

Catherine McShane (her name as it appears on her birth certificate) was born at the Coombe Lying-in Hospital in Dublin on 19 May 1897, the third of the eight surviving children of Daniel (Dan) McShane, a fireman who came originally from County Armagh in Ulster, and his wife, Kathleen Hudson, a midwife. The family had lived for many years in Cook Street, but shortly after the birth of Annie in March 1911 they moved to 208a Great Brunswick Street, next door to the Queen's Theater. The theater had closed in 1907 and after extensive refurbishment reopened in 1909 under the management of Charles F. Wright, "another remarkable Englishman" according to the theater's historian, Seamus de Burca. Wright was in charge until 1921. The McShane family forged a number of links with the theater world of the Queen's. Dan McShane had worked for the Dublin Fire Brigade, whose vast red-brick fire station (today a hotel) still stands on the corner of Tara Street, directly across the road from the theater. Many of the firemen drank and socialized in the bar at the Queen's, and there was even a call system to alert on-duty firemen that they were required back at the station! After leaving the brigade Dan found work as the theater's fire-officer, a post he held for so many years that he became a kind of fixture. Seamus de Burca, in his memories of the Queen's published many years later, gives us a fleeting glimpse of Kitty McShane's father.

The Queen's was a warren of staircases worthy of a king's palace; one can fancy conspirators sneaking through doorways, or watching from behind box curtains. Someone should have written about the Phantom of the Queen's but it had no ghosts I knew of . . . except Dan McShane the fireman making his final rounds at night.[75]

In later years members of Kitty's family recalled that the young Kitty had been by far the prettiest of the McShane girls. Early photographs reveal that her mane of dark wavy hair was elaborately curled into ringlets like a Victorian china doll. When still little more than a child, she began to develop a promising singing voice and seemed to enjoy performing. Her father Daniel would take her to sing, not in pubs as has been claimed, for this would have been forbidden, but outside pubs including the Station Inn in Winetavern Street, not far from Cook Street, where the locals would give her money. Kitty must have been prettily dressed up for these occasions, at which she would presumably have been the only child, and certainly the only girl present, and thus the center of much admiring attention. Dublin pubs were still an almost exclusively male preserve, often malodorous, insanitary and frequently the scene of noisy, drunken behavior. But such, it would appear, was the backdrop to some of Kitty's earliest performances. Several of the very earliest surviving photographs of a very young Kitty show her in the enormous frilly frocks which were to become her lifelong trademark. With her frilly frocks and her elaborate ringlets she must have been an extremely striking and unusual figure in the streets of Dublin at that time, a child-star in the making.

Seamus de Burca's essay also provides evidence that the McShanes actively pushed another of their daughters towards the stage at a very young age. Annie, who was born in 1911, was already treading the boards in the early 1920s. When listing the melodramas presented at the Queen's by William Macready and his company in 1924, de Burca wrote, "In *The Collier's Daughter*, Macready played the outraged father, denouncing his erring daughter... 'Go, go and take your bastard with you!' The little girl was always Annie McShane, as good a child actress as I ever saw." This little-known fact may help to explain why, years later, Kitty feared even her own sister as a rival.

Photo 4: Early photograph of young Kitty McShane. Mrs. Joan Towle

Every available written account of Arthur Towle's time in Dublin in 1910, repeats a version of the story of Arthur and Kitty's intended debut together in Arthur's version of *Little Red Riding Hood* at the Queen's Theater in Great Brunswick Street, written overnight according to some versions. Steve King gave an elaborate version complete with invented dialogue, and Michael Pointon's account in the *Dictionary of National Biography* follows King for the essentials.

On hearing that the manager of the Queen's Theater, Dublin, wished to book an English pantomime in 1910, Towle (by then using the surname Clifton professionally) wrote his own script for *Little Red Riding Hood*, which was accepted for the seasonal attraction; he was allowed to play the part of Granny and produce it himself. The title-role was given to a local thirteen-year-old girl singer . . . During rehearsals for *Little Red Riding Hood* Kitty was prevented from appearing [some versions mention the police] as she was under age, but the show was still a success, with Towle creating his first part as a dame.

A similar account, again relying on King, appears on the Britmovie website. "In 1910 [Lucan] managed to secure a pantomime, *Little Red Riding Hood*, at the Queen's Theater, Dublin, by literally writing the script overnight, with himself playing the role of Granny. The title role in the pantomime had been given to a beautiful thirteen-year-old raven-haired brown-eyed local girl, Catherine 'Kitty' McShane." Most recently, John Fisher has added these details to his earlier essay in the new 2013 edition of his classic *Funny Way to Be a Hero*.

During their lifetime neither Arthur nor Kitty ever contradicted these stories or gave an alternative account of their earliest days together. But the above version of events is quite simply apocryphal, wholly and completely untrue. My research has uncovered incontrovertible proof of this in reviews in the Dublin newspapers for December and January 1910-1911. For some reason in late 1910 and early 1911, the playbills for the Queen's Theater do not appear alongside the usual theater advertisements in the *Irish Independent* or *The Freeman's Journal*. Fortunately, reviews were published in *The Sunday Independent* at this time. In December 1910 a preview announced that the Queen's was indeed staging *Little Red Riding Hood* but the detailed account makes it clear that neither Arthur nor Kitty could possibly have been in any way involved in the production.

> We have had an opportunity of witnessing a full dress-rehearsal of the pantomime to be produced at 2 o'clock on Boxing Day at the pretty Brunswick Street house, and patrons of the theater will agree that never has a better show been provided for their Christmas fare. Nothing has been left undone by Messrs. Cullen and Carthy, and their able henchman, M. C. Baker, to ensure the complete success of 'Little Red Riding Hood.' Besides being as gorgeous and beautiful as any production can be, great stress has been laid, as it ought to be in every show of the kind, on the comic element, and in the hands of Miss Doris Vessey (Martha Miggs), Mr. Fred Dunstone (Baron Badlotte), Messrs. Cullen and Carthy, (Johnny Stout and Jimmy Green), and Mr. Will

Sullivan (Mother Hubbard), not forgetting Little Cluley as Dumpling, the fun will be fast and furious.

The principal boy, Nan Taylor, who was praised for her singing, and the principal girl, Miss G. Denza, provided the "love interest of the story," and there were eight "juvenile dancers, the Daffodil Troupe."

This article, written on the very eve of the first performance, makes it clear that Arthur could have had no hand in the script, nor played the part of the Dame, Old Mother Hubbard, which was taken by Will Sullivan. The comedians Cullen and Carthy who topped the bill were a famous music-hall act throughout the United Kingdom; "And what is one to say of the drolleries of these peerless jokers, Cullen and Carthy? Truly they are fellows of infinite jest." Worst of all, the charming story of the thirteen-year-old Kitty being denied the title role because of her age is flatly contradicted by what the preview has to say about the person who actually took the part of Red Riding Hood. "Wee Ellie Fields, who sustains the title role, is indeed an infant prodigy. Scarcely past her tenth year, she acts with a style and finish that may well excite the envy of many senior artistes."

Not only is the story of Kitty's being too young to play the part at thirteen apocryphal, but it is made nonsensical by the fact that the real Red Riding Hood was even younger! Perhaps the ten-year-old "infant prodigy" Ellie Fields was the first of the many people who excited the envy of Kitty McShane . . . .

On New Year's Day 1911, in "Flashes from the Footlights," the *Sunday Independent* returned to the success of the Queen's pantomime.

'Little Red Riding Hood' at the Queen's continues to draw crowded and appreciative houses, and there is every sign that this welcome condition of affairs will continue. The popular taste was struck by a four weeks' pantomime production at the Brunswick street house, and the management are to be congratulated on their enterprise. The piece abounds in diverting fun. It may well be said that there is not a dull moment from start to finish. This could hardly be otherwise with two such really clever comedians as Messrs. Cullen and Carthy to the forefront, assisted by Little Cluley. They are the life and soul of the piece, and their very names on the poster will ensure

crowded audiences. In addition to the comedy of the pantomime, and there is plenty of it, and rightly so, the production is
staged very prettily and attractively, and scenery, effects, songs
and specialties are excellent. Everything foreshows a successful
production during the weeks yet to come.

The pantomime closed at the end of January with further lavish
praise for Cullen and Carthy, but no word of Arthur or Kitty, who
were clearly not involved in any way whatsoever.

Steve King, in his version of the legend of 1910, even drama-
tizes the underage Kitty anecdote with imaginary "Oirish" comments
from "Charles Wright the owner of the Queen's Theater." The actor-
manager Charles F. Wright (who was *not* Irish) was not the owner
but the manager of the theater from 1910 to 1920. His obituary in
1940 confirmed a quite different version of events which will be more
fully discussed later; "A pantomime, *Little Red Riding Hood*, produced
by him in 1919, starring Arthur Lucan and Kitty McShane, ran for
13 weeks."

In the light of all the evidence I have collated, the version of
Christmas 1910, which appears in every biography of Lucan and
McShane must now be completely discounted and, sadly perhaps,
prosaic but solid fact must replace the pretty legend. No authentic
record exists for any kind of performance by either Arthur or Kitty in
1910; in fact no *corroborated* evidence exists of their even having met
in 1910 rather than in 1911. And yet there remains the very odd coincidence of an infant prodigy, even younger than Kitty, playing Red
Riding Hood at the Queen's in 1910-1911. Could it be that Kitty,
whose proud father clearly saw his favorite little girl as a budding
child star, was taken for an audition but was turned down? Kitty was
spoiled and precocious, and her sisters remembered her flying into
rages and threatening to run away in order to get what she wanted.
But this time she did not get her way, and in later life she may well
have re-arranged the legend to soothe the wounded and enraged
sensibilities of the damaged child she was to remain all her life.

Arthur Lucan

The commonly given reason for Arthur's name change around
1910 is that he felt he needed something "more Irish" in order to

get work. This seems rather odd on a number of grounds. By 1910 it would seem that Arthur had already been in Ireland for quite some time, barnstorming across the country with The Musical Cliftons, the family Arthur said "adopted him" for seven years. From the time (around 1902-1903) when he joined their troupe he was known as Arthur Clifton; Henry Desborough's memorial notice in *The Stage* in 1954 confirms this. So during his first season in Ireland, the English surname Clifton seems to have been no obstacle to work. Ireland was after all still an integral part of the United Kingdom, legislation for Home Rule was proceeding peacefully, and almost a million Irishmen of every religious persuasion enlisted in 1914. All that was utterly changed in the years after 1916, but in 1910 the Union flag flew over Sackville St, (later re-named for O'Connell), and in Dublin, English names, including Clifton, were ten a penny. Kitty's own mother was a Hudson, hardly a typical Irish name!

The next oddity is the very choice of the name Lucan, if indeed the intention was to sound more Irish, because Lucan is quite simply not an Irish surname. There is not a single Lucan household in the exhaustive *Griffiths All Ireland Primary Valuation Property Surveys* between 1847 and 1864. Worse still, the online ancestry website of the *Irish Times* contains no entry for Lucan in its *Dictionary of Irish Surnames*. Lucan is not a surname but the name of a place. In the Irish language, "Leamhcán" means "place of the elm trees." In 1910, Lucan was still a charming rustic village on the banks of the Liffey not many miles from Dublin, and was the seat of the Earls of Lucan, a title first created by James II for Patrick Sarsfield at the siege of Limerick in 1691. (The disappearing Lord Lucan was the most notorious recent title-holder.) Arthur himself told the story of spotting a passing milk-wagon with the words "Lucan Dairies" painted on its side. Arthur may have been aware of the aristocratic connection, or maybe just liked the sound of the word, perhaps because its two syllables were not so different in fact from the "Clifton" he had decided to discard because his formal association with that family was coming to an end. The end of the "Clifton years" is almost certainly one reason for the need for a new surname in Dublin in 1910. Another, perhaps the most decisive, is the fact that the archives of *The Stage* show that another actor, a "swell comedian" named Arthur Clifton was already working in England and Dublin, making the name quite simply unavailable.

But why, one might ask, did Arthur not simply revert to his own family name of Towle? Thereby hangs a curious tale, and one which Arthur himself may well have relished! Firstly, with its "w" the name does look very un-Irish, adding to the possibility of confused pronunciation; there is even today an internet blog on Facebook where young Towles from all over the world bewail people's inability to pronounce their name correctly! The two Arthur Lucan television documentaries of the 1980s used the pronunciation rhyming with "howl" but Arthur's granddaughter and daughter-in-law and their families now rhyme their name with "whole." In 2012 in Boston I asked Sally Ladds, Arthur's great-niece, how the name was pronounced there today; her answer was the version rhyming with "howl," so both pronunciations are in use to this day.

The Dublin of 1910 was in many ways a big village and Dubliners were, and still are, famous for gossip, the "craic," and a withering and sarcastic sense of humor. Arthur himself is reputed to have said that he developed his "gabble-talk," a quick-fire patter which his impersonators found so hard to copy, by listening to the blather of the street-sellers and fishwives of the Dublin backstreets. And it is, I believe, among those very fishwives that we find one more reason why Arthur would prefer Lucan to Towle because, although he admired the fishwives' loquacity, he did not wish to be associated with their coarseness or vulgarity

At the time of the Census of Ireland in April 1911, we find the McShanes still living in two rooms at 5 Cook Street, but there is no trace of Arthur in the census, under any of his three possible surnames. As we shall see shortly, "Arthur Lucan" was already back in England. However the April census does reveal the presence in Dublin of a family Arthur might have known, or at least known of, one of Ireland's very few Towl/Towel/Towell families (inconsistent spellings on the census return).

Living in just two rooms in Beresford St, just across the river from Cook St, was "Cathrin Towel" aged 49. Born in Co Wexford, she was a widow with seven children. Her three oldest children, Patrick, Catherine and Elizabeth, were all born in Scotland, suggesting the non-Irish origins of her late Towel husband; her four young boys, aged 13 to 4, were born in Dublin. Neither she nor her eldest son could read or write, and she signed the census with a cross. The four younger boys were still "scholars," leaving two girls to help support them. Catherine was a "Match factory girl," a dangerous and unhealthy occupation. But mother and daughter Elizabeth are both described as "Fish dealers." In plain language, away from the formalities of the census, they were Dublin fishwives! The very words instantly bring to mind disagreeable definitions; "foul-mouthed, squalid," "a coarse-mannered woman who is prone to shouting." And by all accounts, the Dublin fishwives of the day lived up to their stereotype! Those of Arthur's friends who knew his legal surname may have delighted in teasing him by cruelly suggesting that his closest relations in Dublin were a widowed fishwife and her brood of orphans, the Towells of Arran Quay! Offstage, Arthur was a gentle, well-mannered chap who clearly would not have relished the association; indeed, one of Arthur's earliest dame impersonations was the "Countess of Alagazam," a zany but rather *grande dame*!

Clifton was the name of the past, and in those early years it was by no means certain that Arthur would leave Ireland or find work in England, making the negative and potentially grotesque Dublin Towell connotation far more important than it may appear today. So a passing milk-cart, and possibly a well-known building, came to the rescue and suggested the more sonorous "Arthur Lucan." In 1910, the main Dublin depot for the Lucan Dairy was located at the junction of Parkgate Street and Conyngham Street, at the end of the quays, on the road leading up to Phoenix Park. One contemporary photograph of the depot still exists, but the building was long ago demolished. Arthur and Kitty must have passed the depot many times on their way to walk in Phoenix Park, and will have read the sign in large capital letters, "ENTRANCE—LUCAN DAIRY—DEPOT." Arthur, with his love of wordplay, may well have jokingly stressed the second syllable of the word "en-TRANCE" instead of the first, and then decided that he found the name Lucan "entrancing." This spot on Parkgate Street is probably the exact birthplace of the name Arthur Lucan, just a few yards from the little park which today contains the water-sculpture of James Joyce's mock-Latin personification of the river Liffey, Anna Livia Pluribelle. The sculpture is better known to Dubliners as "The Floozy in the Jacuzzi," a name which would surely have delighted both the Joyce of *Finnegan's Wake* and Arthur Lucan with his alliterative "gabble-talk."

While the Lucan dairy was the obvious source for the new surname, Arthur may also have had, perhaps unconsciously, a deeper emotional reason for being drawn to the name. If one removes just one letter from Lucy Ann, one is left with… Lucann, a salute to the memory of Lucy Ann Towle, the mother he had not seen for seven years.

Arthur Lucan's Debut

Arthur seems to have worked briefly in Ireland with an alfresco Pierrot troupe, Will Pepper's White Coons. Pepper, a banjoist, ran a number of "White Coon" concert parties around Britain, fourteen at one point, and he was famous for introducing the songs "Ma Curly Headed Babby" and "The Honeysuckle and the Bee." Pepper's troupes did not tour Ireland as some have claimed, but for several years one troupe gave a resident summer season at the fashionable seaside resort of Bray in County Wicklow, performing in the imposing bandstand which may still be seen today on the promenade.

The name Arthur Lucan appeared in print for the very first time in June 1911 in the pages of *The Stage*. Arthur (without Kitty) had joined an alfresco concert party, The Scottish White Coons, based at Carnoustie, a seaside resort near Dundee. The group, (in no way related to Will Pepper's company) had been founded in 1903 by the Yorkshire-born comedian Gilbert Payne (1877-1951) whose motto was "There is no pleasure without Payne!" Payne's company performed each summer at Carnoustie until 1914, and his advertisements in *The Stage* for new recruits give a sense of what Arthur must have been capable of by 1911.

> Payne's Original Scottish White Coons Eighth Season. Wanted to complete companies, Artists in all lines, including first-class Soubrette. Must be thoroughly used to refined alfresco and have good repertoire. Can arrange autumn tour to follow to really competent artist.—Photos, refs and full particulars to GILBERT PAYNE, 48 Union St, Dundee.

Payne evidently judged Arthur to be among the "really competent" because, as we shall see, he was given the promised autumn tour. In the local history section of its website, the Angus Council has an excellent account of Carnoustie's heyday and Gilbert Payne's contribution to it.

> Carnoustie, promoted as 'The Brighton of the North,' had been popular as a sea bathing resort in the early years of the nineteenth century when people would spend a month sampling the healthy sea water and air. Its heyday was from approximately 1900 to the outbreak of World War Two. The Season began in mid-June and finished at the end of August. Carnoustie's attractions included alfresco Pierrot shows, band concerts, sea bathing, fairs and sport. Visitors came from all over the country. The Pierrots' alfresco concerts were one of Carnoustie's biggest attractions. Gilbert Payne and his troupe entertained Carnoustie's holidaymakers for many years. Gilbert Payne was very well known in the world of the music hall. In his day he was rated as one of the six best comedians in the country, and in the same league as his contemporary Harry Lauder. His main character, Mr. Bingle, was known nationally and his trade mark was a big red wig. Payne played the comic but he also wrote and managed the shows, engaged the entertainers and staged the numbers. His troupe performed two shows daily after a morning rehearsal. It was a hard life, as he organized these shows in Broughty Ferry, Arbroath and St. Andrews too.[76]

Payne had begun his career as a musician in Leeds, and he played "fiddle, cornet, banjo and mandolin." He not only wrote the scripts of his sketches and musical comedies but also the original songs.

The very first documented performance in Arthur Lucan's long theatrical career took place on 22 June 1911, the day of King George V's coronation. On 6 July, The Stage reported that,

> Mr. Gilbert Payne opened his eight season at Carnoustie on Coronation Day. The company this season includes Miss Fanny Adamson, soubrette; Miss Dorothy Verton, pianist and entertainer; Mr. Alec Daimler, comedian; Mr. Bertram Edwards, tenor; Mr. Arthur Lucan, light comedian; Mr. Theodore Jones, baritone; and Mr. Gilbert Payne, comedian. Tonight (Thursday) Mr. Payne holds his first Japanese night

of the season, when he will produce a Japanese scena, "My Little Yo-San".

This "Japanese scena" was far from being a piece of merely decorative "japonaiserie" and was based on the seriously topical music hall song *Farewell, My Little Yo San*, published in 1904 by Francis, Day and Hunter, and recorded by two of the earliest recording artists, Hamilton Hill and Tom Costello. Hill sometimes accompanied his singing with appropriate lantern slide shows, and in 1905 Bamforth published *Farewell, My Little Yo San*, as a highly popular set of nine lantern slides, which were also issued as postcards. The lyrics and pictures tell how "Sweet little Yo San loved a sailor man," and how her Japanese sailor man comes to bid his sweetheart farewell as he goes off to fight in the Russo-Japanese war of 1904-1905. By the terms of the Anglo-Japanese Alliance of 1902, Britain and Japan were united against Russian expansionism, and the alliance suddenly and dramatically became front-page news when in 1904 the Russian Navy fired on a fleet of unarmed Hull trawlers on the Dogger Bank, mistaking them for Japanese torpedo boats. Six trawlers were hit and several fishermen were injured. The captain and third hand of the trawler *Crane* were killed and their boat sunk. This "Russian Outrage" almost led to war between Britain and Russia, and Royal Navy battleships were preparing to go into action when the matter was settled by the International Commission of Inquiry at The Hague.

Reflecting the intensity of local feeling, in 1905 Will Catlin's Pierrots at Withernsea performed a song entitled "The Russian Bear," during which an easel displayed a picture of the sinking of the *Crane*, and in 1906 an impressive memorial statue (still standing) was erected in Hull by public subscription to the memory of the dead fishermen. This major incident would still have been fresh in the minds of contemporary audiences, and the patriotic sentiments expressed in Gilbert Payne's Japanese scena "My Little Yo San," would have gone down especially well in the week of the coronation of George V, ruler of the vast British Empire.[77] Arthur seems to have been the youngest man in Payne's company and may have played the role of the sailor. If so he would have sung this verse in praise of Britain and her Navy:

There is a nation glorious and free,
Known to the world as 'Mistress of the Sea.'

She is our true friend, for her sturdy sons,
Built our ships, and taught us how to man our guns.
We shall fight and fight on,' said the sailor-man,
'With this stirring battle-cry,
For freedom we will do or die!'

At the very least, Arthur will have joined the company in the chorus, making these the first known words Arthur ever performed onstage.

Farewell my little Yo San,
Farewell my sweetheart true.
Over the mighty ocean
I've a duty there to do.
Sometimes, will you remember
To Ki your Sailor man,
Who is going out to fight,
For the cause of the right
And the freedom of dear Japan?

The theme of battle in the last verse is a chilling reminder that war and death had almost become a reality for British sailors, as well as the Japanese.

When guns are booming over land and sea,
Hope, little Yo San, hope for victory.
Should I in battle fall, my little maid,
Do not weep, 'tis but the toll of war that must be paid.
Wish your sailor good luck when he's far away,
If I'm spared when war is o'er,
To you my love I'll come once more.

Such was Arthur Lucan's very first documented role, a Japanese sailor boy and a far cry from Old Mother Riley.

There is an interview with Slim Ingram in the BBC documentary *The Lost World of Mitchell and Kenyon*. While viewing a film of one of Harry Flockton-Foster's concert parties entertaining crowds near Victoria Pier Blackpool in 1904, Slim (wrongly alas!) identified a member of the party as Arthur Lucan. In his hand Slim was holding a photograph for comparison. I have identified this posed group photograph of the Flockton-Foster company and it definitely does not include Arthur Lucan.[78]

Photo 5: Arthur (top right) with Gilbert Payne's "White Coons," Carnoustie, Summer, 1912. Steve King

In a letter to *The Stage* in 1938 Gilbert Payne reminisced about the many actors who had worked with him at Carnoustie, including "Arthur Lucan for a few seasons. He also toured in the winter with me in my musical comedy *The Honeymoon* as a light comedian." In all, Arthur did two seasons with Payne at Carnoustie, and one known photograph exists of Arthur with the company in the 1912 summer season. Up to this point there is no firm evidence of Arthur's attempting any Dame studies. He is evidently singing, dancing and acting male roles as a "light comedian." At the end of the Carnoustie season, in September 1911, Payne judged Arthur to be a "really competent artist," good enough to be taken on tour in the musical comedy *The Honeymoon*. Both the words and music (some twenty songs) of this "musical absurdity" were by Payne himself and he had taken the production on tour regularly since its premiere in 1906. On 28 September 1911 Arthur's name appears in *The Stage* for only the second time, in the cast list of *The Honeymoon*. "Exceptionally strong cast including . . . Mr. ARTHUR LUCAN as Archie." The plot of *The Honeymoon* was summed up in an early review.

> *The Honeymoon* is complicated and amusing, and deals chiefly with the efforts of Mr. and Mrs. Jack Armstrong and their friends to keep Jack's marriage hidden from Jack's uncle, Col.

Vandyke Brown, who has promised Jack half his fortune if he remains a bachelor. This, the charms of Madge prevent Jack's doing and the pair risk matrimony on the chance of the colonel's never returning from India to England. But he does, and quickly guesses how the land lies, although much dust is thrown in his eyes. Jack's friends pose as his servants, and many complications ensue, particularly over the discovery of a baby on the seashore. After much confusion, and many difficulties, Jack confesses, and all ends happily. The piece is brightly written, capitally dressed, and most effectively staged. Amongst the happiest musical numbers are the sextet 'Three sailor girls and three sailor men,' the quartet 'The Widow,' the duet 'Longing for you,' and the duet 'The policeman and the dude.'

The singing dude in this last duet is none other than Arthur Lucan. Payne starred as the country bumpkin, Nathaniel Noodle, and his second wife, Ethyl Errol, played Emeretta Noodle. Arthur played Archie Mashington, described in reviews as "a typical Johnny" and "dude." Brewer's dictionary defines dude as "a masher. One who renders himself conspicuous by affectation of dress, manners, and speech. The word was first familiarized in London in 1881, and is a revival of the old word dudes (clothes)." The now obsolete word "masher" also meant a flirtatious dandy or womanizer, probably a derivative of the slang word "*mash*, to attract sexually." Audiences would have immediately understood the implications of the surname Mashington, suggesting a swaggering, womanizing man-about-town, providing a comic contrast to Payne's portrayal of the bumpkin Nathaniel Noodle. So it would seem that far from wearing the skirts, Arthur as Archie Mashington was busy chasing them during *The Honeymoon's* extensive three-month tour of Britain. Reviews also reveal that the part of Archie included much comic patter, singing and dancing. "Stella le Brun (always in love) and Archie Mashington (always idiotic) engage in many saucy words duels and mincing mannerisms, besides exhibiting specialty dances." At Longton in Staffordshire, on 9 November, a reviewer reported that "The company is a remarkably good one, and every member of the cast is excellent. The merry songs, the tuneful choruses and the graceful dancing are delightful, and the whole performance goes with a splendid swing."

Arthur must have learned a great deal from Gilbert Payne. Since the turn of the century this gifted and versatile comic actor had also been a regular performer in pantomime, and for many years was the comic partner of Florrie Forde, one of the greatest music-hall performers. Payne wrote many pantomime scripts for Forde and often played a naive bumpkin figure, such as his Idle Jack in *Dick Whittington*. But the versatile Payne had also played Dame Trot in 1910 in his own production of *The House that Jack Built*, and played dame parts on many other occasions. A few samples of the many reviews of Payne's performance as Idle Jack strongly suggest some of the skills which Arthur may have adopted and adapted to his own needs:

> Among a host of clever comedians, Gilbert Payne as Idle Jack Was deservedly popular. He is an artist with a rare conception of his opportunities, and whether in song, patter, or dance, he was irresistibly amusing." *Glasgow News.*

> Gilbert Payne has a part which is very suitable as a medium for his quaint mannerisms and funny sayings. His appearance on the stage invariably coincided with a good deal of laughter in the auditorium." *The Scotsman.*

> Mr. Payne is irresistibly droll and genuinely funny. He dominates the pantomime. When he is off the stage one waits impatiently for him to return." *The Manchester Guardian.*

> Gilbert Payne fully merits the time-honored definition of 'screamingly funny,' and after his first appearance his re-entry is greeted with applause before he has the opportunity of doing anything else funny." *Nuneaton Record.*

Gilbert Payne's standing in the profession will certainly have been instrumental in helping Arthur to secure parts in concert parties and pantomimes over the next few years.

By the spring of 1912 at the latest, Arthur had returned to Dublin and the name Arthur Lucan appeared in the Irish press for the first time on Saturday 4 May when *The Connacht Tribune* announced the appearance on Monday of "MOOR'S MERRY MAKERS" for three nights only at the Galway Cinema Theater. The theater's name is a reminder of just how early in the century the cinema began to threaten the supremacy of music hall and variety, even in the most distant corners of what still was the United Kingdom. Kitty was only fourteen years old, and her name appears separately from Arthur's, a full eighteen months before their marriage. The company members were listed as follows:

> Mr. Arthur Lucan, Popular light comedian and chorus singer
> Miss Kitty McShane, Dainty Soubrette and Dancer
> Miss M. Morton, Soprano Vocalist
> Willie Harrison, The one to make you laugh
> Bertram Edwards, Tenor Vocalist
> Como, The great Japanese Equilibrist and Juggler
> THE MERRY MAKERS, in their repertoire of laughable sketches, including 'The Lights of London,' 'The Race for Wealth,' etc.[79]

Arthur acted and sang in this show, but there is still no evidence of his attempting any kind of "Dame Study." The description "chorus singer" did not mean he could only sing in a chorus line, but rather that he could lead an audience to join him in the choruses of his solo songs; Gilbert Payne's friend Florrie Forde was sometimes billed as "The World's greatest Chorus Singer."

After touring the "smalls" in Ireland in the spring of 1912, Arthur returned alone to Scotland for his second summer season with Gilbert Payne at Carnoustie. A photograph of Arthur in the company from this season shows that, like many other seaside concert parties around this time, they sometimes changed from ruffles and pom-poms into the fashionably smart naval-cadet style double-breasted blazers and peaked caps. For the women, now in skirts, this restored the gender differentiation which the Pierrot costume had blurred. At around this time Arthur made friends with an actor called Henry (Harry) Desborough, sometimes known as Fletcher-Desborough. Henry had worked in Ireland from 1903 and later with Gilbert Payne at Carnoustie as a comic actor and "smart illusionist." Henry and Arthur developed a sketch based around the character of "The Countess of Alagazam," played by Arthur. This seems to be the first known example of Arthur's writing his own material, and this is also the first documented example of Arthur attempting a "Dame Study." Fortunately, the dame in question is clearly identifiable, and not quite what one might have expected.

The word "Alagazam" was the title of a March, two-step and cake-walk, written in 1902 by the American composer Abe Holzmann, best known for his march "Blaze Away" (used in the television series *Monty Python's Flying Circus*.) In a note in the sheet music, Holzmann explained that during a trip to the South he met "a colored regiment, who, while marking time during drill, to the strains of 'Blaze-Away' March, were uttering a peculiar refrain which sounded like 'Alagazam! Alagazam! Alagazam! Zam! Zam!'" The front page of the sheet music also informed the public that Alagazam was "published also as a song with humorous darky text." Two years later in 1904, Cole and Johnson, the popular team of African-American singer-songwriters, simply borrowed the name and created the comic song "The Countess of Alagazam." The song, published as "the latest comic craze in Town," was taken up in New York by Lew Dockstader's Minstrels, non-Africans who performed in "blackface," and included, for a time, the great Al Jolson. A sketch on the front cover of the sheet music showed a very dotty dame with a funny hat on her head and an inane grin on her face. She has a rather glum-looking sheep on a lead, clipped like a poodle and wearing a top hat! The lyrics are a kind of nonsense rhyme, telling of the ridiculous exploits of a caricature countess who ends up being kicked into the blue yonder by a passing circus elephant. The following year, 1905, the singer Bob Roberts (another non-African-American) recorded the song with orchestra on a wax cylinder which has survived to this day and can be heard on YouTube.

The crazy antics of this surreal and eccentric countess must have appealed to Arthur's sense of the absurd, and the lyrics may well have been the starting point for the sketch he elaborated, with Henry Desborough as the straight man trying to instruct a foreign count-ess in the ways of polite society, and failing dismally. In the light of Arthur's known ability as a singer, it also seems very likely that he would have performed the whole song, perhaps with the verses punc-tuated by comic patter. The lyrics deserve to be resurrected here as the probable origin of one of Arthur's earliest dames, particularly as they contain many examples of the kind of zany alliterative word-play, rhythmic repetition and obsessive verbal patterning which became an abiding feature of Arthur's performance style.

They christen'd a girl somewhere in the world,
the Countess of Alagazam,
This dear little prize was wond'rously wise, the Countess of Alagazam,
She read all the time, her Nursery rhyme, of Mary and her lamb,
She said, "I'll have one, and I'll have lots of fun, the Countess of Alagazam."
The Countess of Alagazam, the lady from Rotterdam,
She went all the way to Birmingham,
Trying to find an innocent lamb;
The Countess of Alagazam, is now up in Amsterdam,
She got the lamb, but got in a jam,
The Countess of Alagazam.
The Countess of Alagazoop, the lady from Guadaloupe,
She sailed away on a full-rigged sloop,
As the gay soubrette in a burlesque troupe.
The manager flew the coop, the Sherriff he made a swoop,
So she looped the loop in a bowl of soup,
The Countess of Alagazoop.
The Countess of Alagazip, a lady decidedly flip,
She picked up a paper and found a tip,
So down to the races she took a trip;
She bet on a horse called Cyp, with a cow-puncher's mark on his hip,
But the tip, it slipped, now she's got the pip,
The Countess of Alagazip.
The Countess of Alagazee, the lady from Kankakee,
One day saw a cute little bumble bee,
A-buzzing around near a chestnut tree;
"I don't think he'll sting," said she,
But the bee drew his Stingaree,
And stung her between the gate and the tree,
This Countess of Alagazee.
The Countess of Alagazi, the maid with the dreamy eye,

One day when the circus was passing by,
She happened to get too dangerously nigh;
With the elephant she got fly, and he boosted her to the sky,
And the choir it sang 'In the sweet Bye and Bye,'
O'er the Countess of Alagazi.
The Countess of Alagazay, a lady decidedly gay,
One morning, upon a summer day,
Was leisurely strolling along Broadway;
She met with a country jay, with a roll like a bale of hay,
But he had to walk back to old Hackensack,
For a ticket, the jay couldn't pay.
The Countess of Alagazum, a lady addicted to gum,
Was chewing one day, when her piece of wax,
Slipped down and stuck in her little thorax;
On her back they began to drum, and they gave her a dose
of rum,
But the rum got stuck on the chewing gum
In the Countess of Alagazum.

It is truly remarkable just how many pre-echoes there are in these absurd lyrics of Arthur's style and character. For instance, "And stung her between the gate and the tree" perfectly anticipates the recurring gag which the Lucans used in their very first known mother-daughter sketch, "Come Over" (1919) and again in "Bridget's Night Out" (1934).

"Come over! (*Business*)
Where did he kiss you?"
"Between the Post Office and the Railway Station."

But the most striking pre-echo is the Countess and the circus. In *Old Mother Riley's Circus* (1941), for which Arthur is credited with the original story, Riley disguises herself as the Countess Wax-Vesta ("A match for any one of you!") in order to fob off the bailiff and save the circus from closure. This was one of Arthur's frequent and delightfully amusing send-ups of would-be upper class women who aspire to be "lah-di-dah" but often with comical results. The very fact that the Countess of Alagazam has a series of adventures in which she gains a new persona, only to get into another scrape, seems to predict the various film reincarnations of Old Mother Riley; the gay

Photo 6: Sheet music cover "The Countess of Alagazam," Arthur's first known dame. John Hopkins Library

soubrette in a burlesque troupe, the trip to the races, the circus, the dose of rum, all find their place almost forty years later in the films to which Arthur frequently contributed scripts and story-lines. As we shall see, the Riley films contain a number of re-workings of Arthur's past characters and situations, as well as many thinly veiled social and political reflections which are only now being properly acknowledged and evaluated.

After the summer of 1912 spent in Carnoustie, Arthur again toured with Gilbert Payne's company in the musical comedy *The Honeymoon*. At Leeds the company appeared at the city's largest theater, the Queen's in Holbeck (demolished in 1968), which could seat 3,500 people. A handsome color-printed playbill from October 1912, which still exists in the Leeds City Council archives, gives the full cast list, including "Archie Mashington, always idiotic, Arthur Lucan."[80] This is the first appearance of Arthur's name on a playbill in England. The last was to be over forty years later, in Hull in May 1954. These tours as Archie Mashington, along with the two summer seasons at Carnoustie, were the culmination of Arthur's "apprenticeship," Gilbert Payne's own description of Arthur's time with him.

In the autumn of 1912, almost certainly with the help of Gilbert Payne's Scottish connections, Arthur was engaged for his first recorded pantomime. As we have shown, this was not *Little Red Riding Hood* in Dublin, but a production of *Cinderella* by James Kiddie, a long-established impresario and producer of highly successful pantomimes. A brief review of the show at Paisley does not give the roles, only the names of the artists.

"Mr. James Kiddie's company presents *Cinderella* twice nightly. Leading parts are in the capable hands of Messrs. Bert Beswick, Tom H. Sally, Arthur Lucan and Sid Dean; the ladies, Misses Violet Thorne, Flo Edens, and Jean Kent, give an excellent account of themselves. The piece is cleverly staged." Arthur's name is listed next to Sid Dean who regularly played dame parts, which suggests that the two of them were the Ugly Sisters, a part which Arthur was to repeat for James Kiddie the following year, with Violet Thorne again as Cinderella. It may well be that something of the zany Countess of Alagazam found its way into the role of the more pretentious Ugly Sister.

Meanwhile, Kitty remained in Dublin and continued to pursue what she clearly still saw as her solo career. While Arthur was on tour with Gilbert Payne in England, she appeared twice nightly at the Tivoli Theater on Burgh Quay in October 1912, in a bill headed by "Duncan's Scotch Collies, the Educated Canines." The name Kitty McShane (again alone) made its very first appearance in the pages of *The Stage* on 16 January 1913 when she was called for rehearsal at the World's Fair Variety Theater in Dublin. This was a grandiose name for the music hall which was also known as Charley James's

Waxworks in Henry Street, (immortalized in Joyce's *Ulysses*) close to where she and Arthur had first met. The Englishman Charles James established a hardware and fancy business at 30 Henry Street in the early 1890s, which he named rather grandly after the forthcoming World's Fair in Chicago and advertised everything at 6½d. The establishment was on four floors, and upstairs he set up a waxworks "mostly illustrating Irish history or sentiment" according to the *Era* of 18 September 1897. There was also a small theater under the roof and it was here that James encouraged the population of Dublin to catch a glimpse of Marcella, the Midget Queen, not a waxworks but a very small girl with a sweet singing voice. This was also the venue for Kitty's official Dublin debut. In March 1913 Kitty again appeared without Arthur, this time back at the Cinema Theater in Galway. *The Connacht Tribune* lists her as part of a "Star Company" hired at "great expense" to appear on Easter Monday and Tuesday. She was still only fifteen years old (two months from her sixteenth birthday) and already must have achieved a considerable degree of independence from her parents who, tied down by work and younger children, could not have accompanied her. By now she may well have decided that if she was old enough to travel across Ireland as a singing star in a concert party, she was probably old enough to marry the little Englishman now known as Arthur Lucan, and to escape with him from dreary Dublin and the Irish provinces to the bright lights of London. Arthur too must already have been contemplating marriage to Kitty because at some point he took instruction and was received into the Catholic Church, although exactly when and where this took place is not known.

After touring England in *Cinderella*, Arthur went back up to Scotland in the summer of 1913, not to Carnoustie this time but to the seaside resort of West Kilbride on the west coast, where he joined an alfresco concert party called The Smart Cadets. The Cadets had been founded at the Beach Pavilion in Prestwick in 1903 by a friend and colleague of Gilbert Payne, the comedian Alvin Sawyer, and they continued to perform there, at Largs, and at the Seamill Pavilion, West Kilbride, for many years. Sawyer's advertisements for recruits give some idea of what he expected of his players:

"Wanted for season of 1914. A REALLY FIRST CLASS PRODUCER, for plays, comedies, burlesques, etc, to play about 35 minutes. Well up in Concerted Movements and with good ideas for Special Nights. FIRST CLASS PIANIST (Gent) to do turn. FIRST CLASS DANCER. PROBABLE OTHER VACANCIES."

In another advertisement Sawyer insists that the pianist must be an excellent sight-reader and violin accompanist. The Cadets season lasted sixteen weeks and Arthur's presence without Kitty is supported by a solo advertisement he placed in *The Stage* in July 1913: "Lucan, Arthur, comic. A success. Alvin Sawyer's Smart Cadets, WEST KILBRIDE. Vacant Autumn. Musical Comedy or Variety." Here again is evidence of the range of Arthur's material, including yet another reference to his singing, which was clearly an important element of his early repertoire. Up until now, most of the evidence points to the fact that Arthur Lucan was slowly but surely building up a successful career as a male singer, dancer and actor in musical comedy with, like many of his peers, only a Christmas season as a pantomime dame. But at the end of the summer season of 1913, Arthur returned to Dublin and there he took a step which, for good or ill, was to affect the entire course of both his career and his life: he married Kitty McShane.

Chapter Three: McShane and Lucan or Lucan and McShane? 1913-1924

The Dublin to which Arthur returned in the autumn of 1913 was going through one of the bleakest moments in its troubled history. The city was in the throes of a major industrial dispute concerning trade union rights between over 20,000 workers and 300 employers that came to be known as the Dublin Lock-out. The dispute lasted from August 1913 to January 1914. On 31 August (Bloody Sunday), the Dublin police force baton-charged demonstrators in Sackville Street, killing two men and injuring many more. The lock-out affected tens of thousands of impoverished Dublin workers and their families, and led to the formation of the Irish Citizens' Army. Worse still, at the very same moment, the passage of the Irish Home Rule Bill at Westminster was being resisted by the Ulster Protestants who had formed the armed Ulster Volunteers. This led to the creation in Dublin of the nationalist Irish Volunteers, publicly launched on Tuesday 25 November, explicitly to safeguard the granting of Home Rule. On the very same day, in a city dominated by hunger, anxiety and fear, "Arthur Towle, actor," and "Kitty McShane, spinster" were married at the elegant neo-classical church of St. Andrew on Westland Row, a five-minute walk from the McShane household next door to the Queen's Theater on Great Brunswick Street. The wedding certificate gives Arthur's address as 31, Lower Gardiner Street, and his late father's occupation as "Coachbuilder." Kitty's father's occupation is given as "Foreman." (This transcription of the certificate was copied out in 1980, and "Foreman" is surely a misreading of "Fireman.") Arthur was twenty-eight and Kitty's age was entered as nineteen, although she was in fact sixteen.

It has been claimed that Kitty married without the consent of her parents, who only learned of the wedding after the event. This, like many other details of the early Dublin years, seems highly improbable. Towards the end of his life Arthur told one of his chorus girl friends that he would meet Kitty after school and give her sweets and ribbons. This must have been early in 1910 as Kitty would have left school at the age of thirteen at the latest, and the census of April 1911 shows that she has left school but has "no business."[81] Kitty's parents must have been aware of this intense relationship, and must also have approved of the couple appearing onstage together in 1912, more than a year before their marriage. Marriage, like virtually every aspect of Irish daily life at that time, was closely regimented by the ever-vigilant clergy of the Catholic Church, to such an extent that the anti-Home Rule parties claimed that "Home Rule" would be "Rome Rule." The McShanes were practicing Catholics, and many years later Donald Towle remembered home visits from the parish priest. The banns of marriage would have had to be read in church, and the candidates' status would have had to be verified, especially with regard to Arthur's Catholic conversion, which could not have been effected without a period of instruction followed by confession, communion and confirmation, the last two of which are normally public acts. Although at sixteen Kitty was eligible to marry, as a women under twenty-one she needed the consent of her parents. It seems highly unlikely, in fact inconceivable, that the parish priest of nearby St. Andrew's, Father McNevin, would marry the "popular comedienne" daughter of one of his parishioners, a tough fireman from Northern Ireland, without the father's express permission; in fact "clandestinity" is one of the grounds in Catholic Canon Law which renders a marriage invalid. Giving Kitty's age as 19 would also have altered nothing in legal terms, but it may have been done to gloss over the considerable age difference between bride and groom. Romantic rumors of an almost "runaway" wedding have perhaps served to glamorize the rather more mundane facts of the matter; the McShanes must have hoped that Kitty's marriage to Arthur, a promising young British actor, would be her passport from the gloomy backwater of strife-torn Dublin to theatrical fame and fortune in what was still thought of as "mainland Britain."

The couple did not settle down together in Dublin because Arthur was obliged to return almost at once to England where he played an Ugly Sister in his second tour with James Kiddie's *Cinderella*. Once again, a review in *The Stage* shows that Kitty was not in the cast. This time the pantomime was seen at the elegant Shakespeare Theater in Lavender Hill, Wandsworth. Arthur Lucan had arrived on the London stage!

Mr. James Kiddie's pantomime, *Cinderella*, is doing good business at this theater. It is a very pleasing production, for its songs, which have been well selected, are numerous, and are well sung. The pantomime company are particularly strong in vocalists. The scenery is admirable; the Palace exterior, glistening with silver, calls forth great applause. Numerically, and in ability, the players are strong, and the ladies are winsomely graceful as well. Miss Violet Thorne is an ideal Cinderella, mignonne and lithe; she sings very sweetly. The Prince Perfect of Miss Lily Ennis has a courtly dignity; Miss Ada Tyrrell is a dashing Dandini, and both are pleasing in song. Abundance of fun is provided by the comedians, Mr. Ernie Percival, the Baron, Mr. George Bray, his page; Messrs. Arthur Lucan and Billy Wesley, the Sisters, and Mr. Fred Melt. The amount that is compressed into a two-hour's entertainment (for *Cinderella* is performed twice nightly) gains one's admiration; and all is excellent, the ballets, the specialty dancing, the acting, and the fun. The company give a wholesome and enjoyable show.

After the pantomime, *The Stage* contains no information concerning Arthur's whereabouts throughout the summer of 1914. When he returned to West Kilbride in the summer of 1915 he says it is his "second season." As his first was in 1913 it would seem that he did not secure a place with the Smart Cadets in 1914 and so returned to Dublin. In *The Stage* in November 1914 he gives his address as 208a Great Brunswick Street, Dublin, with the McShanes. The tone of this advertisement suggests that work had not been easy to find in the troubled months preceding and following the outbreak of the Great War in August 1914. This was also the married couple's first joint advertisement in *The Stage*. It is worded to suggest strongly that Kitty had also appeared in Kiddie's *Cinderella*, whereas, as we have seen, she did not. The "joint engagement preferred" is the first of many warnings that if you wanted Lucan you had to take McShane!

Wanted panto. KITTY MCSHANE, 2nd Boy or Girl. ARTHUR LUCAN, Ugly Sister or Dame, or anything that's going these hard times. Last two years James Kiddie's *Cinderella*. Joint engagement preferred. All comms. A. Lucan, 208a Great Brunswick Street, Dublin.

The advertisement was reinserted the following week with Kitty's name again above Arthur's. This time it reveals that these "two useful people" as it calls them, were once again on the road to Galway, and doing the provincial halls en route at Newbridge and Athlone.

Gilbert Payne had been at the Theater Royal in Dublin in June 1914, and Arthur may have introduced his young wife to his former mentor. Perhaps the well-connected Payne lent a helping hand because the "two useful people in these hard times" eventually managed to secure a much needed pantomime in England. This was to be Kitty's first crossing of the Irish Sea and her theatrical debut in England. She was only seventeen, and had the fresh good looks of a young colleen, a mane of wavy black hair, a pretty little singing voice and an appealing Irish brogue. On these basic facts, in the early years at least, the critics seemed to concur.

Lucan and McShane's very first pantomime together was to be Nelson Barrett's production of *Little Jack Horner*. However, when the show opened in December 1914, neither Lucan nor McShane figured in the cast list. First boy Jack Horner was Emmie Carr, Dame Horner, "the village schoolmistress," was Eugene McCabe, and Baron Graball was Jack Ennis. But by the time the tour reached Derby in January and Peterborough in February 1915, while other cast members remain the same, Arthur and Kitty had replaced Jack Ennis and Emmie Carr. According to her very first review in *The Stage*, "Miss Kitty McShane in the title role acted and sang with charming effect." But there was to be no opportunity for mother-daughter business because Kitty was principal boy and Arthur was not the Dame but the wicked Baron Graball. At Stafford in April 1915 *The Stage* reported that "Mr. Eugene McCabe as the Dame and Mr. Arthur Lucan as the Baron, splendidly sustained the comic element." Once again, documentary evidence reveals that the early careers of Lucan and McShane were rather different from the legend that over the years has come to be accepted as fact. This late substitution could perhaps be the original source of the story of Arthur's taking over a dame role at the last minute; but it was a baron not a dame, and the year was not 1910 but 1915. Now, at the moment when the Lucans at last launched themselves as a successful duo on the English comedy stage, their only child Donald was conceived, so Donald Towle's father was not Dame Horner but Baron Graball!

In the summer of 1915 Arthur returned to Alvin Sawyer's Cadets at East Kilbride, this time with Kitty, who by now was almost six months pregnant. Their advertisements in *The Stage* continue to highlight Kitty's name above Arthur's, and Arthur still offers to work "revue, panto, dude, dame." At the end of the season Kitty returned alone to Dublin, where Donald Daniel Towle was born on 2 October at 208a Great Brunswick Street, delivered by his midwife grandmother Kate McShane. Arthur remained in England, and his name appears in November in the cast of a musical comedy revue, *Money for Nothing*, at the Grand Theater in Manchester. This is supported by the fact that Donald's birth certificate gives his father's address as "33 Ormond Street, All Saints, Manchester," less than a mile from the Grand Theater. Arthur wrote proudly to Kitty, his handwriting an irregular back-sloping scrawl which he radically changed in later years. "To my little wife, for being a brick and sticking it. Arthur." (To correct his spidery scrawl, Arthur later took to using a ruler to force himself to write in straight lines. This explains the strangely flattened lower edge of all later examples of his handwriting.)[82]

From the very outset, according to her family, motherhood did not suit Kitty one little bit, and her actions made this perfectly clear. When Donald was just over two months old, she left him in the care of her mother in Dublin and joined Arthur in England. In December, at a time when most women would still be physically recovering from childbirth, Kitty was back in costume, singing and dancing as principal boy, again in Nelson Barrett's *Little Jack Horner*, which opened at Great Yarmouth on 27 December, with Arthur at last playing her mother, Dame Horner. This is the very first time that Arthur played a pantomime dame with Kitty as principal boy or girl. Now, as one amused commentator has observed, we have a husband playing a mother to a daughter playing a son but who is in fact his wife! The pantomime, advertised to "go on tour for twenty weeks or more," visited Hitchin, Coalville, Cinderford and Crewe, with "great success." The Lucans' card in *The Stage* again placed Kitty's name first and in much larger type than Arthur's, but an unfortunate misprint turned her into McTHANE, perhaps a theatrical ill omen of evil things to come! The tour lasted well into the spring of 1916, so the Lucans were far from Dublin at the time of the Easter Rising on 24 April. But from the family flat on Great Brunswick Street, Kate

McShane, nursing the six-month-old Donald, would have heard the gun battles which raged around the General Post Office in nearby Sackville Street. After the Easter Rising, daily life in Dublin appeared to return to normal fairly quickly, although in reality, as W. B. Yeats saw clearly, all was "changed, changed utterly" in the story of relations between Britain and Ireland.[83] But the theaters were soon open again and by September Gilbert Payne was back at the Theater Royal with another re-working of his musical comedy *The Honeymoon*, now entitled *Wedding Bell(e)s*. Dublin theatergoers could now admire the dude Archie Mashington, which had been Arthur's first major role on the English stage.

After their 1915-1916 pantomime, Arthur and Kitty's names do not reappear in *The Stage* for over three years. Most of this time seems to have been spent in Ireland, which gave Kitty the opportunity, if not the inclination, to help her mother in bringing up Donald. Cast lists and reviews in Dublin newspapers make it clear that Lucan and McShane were in no way involved in the 1916-1917 pantomime *Dick Whittington* at the Queen's Theater. Another source of work for the young couple in "these hard times" was mentioned by Philip Ryan in his book *The Lost Theaters of Dublin*.[84] Ryan quotes the reminiscences of Charlie Jones, a booking agent for theaters and halls throughout Ireland. Because of travel difficulties caused by the 1914-1918 war it was not uncommon for artists to fail to travel, and so Jones had a stable of artists based in Dublin who all assembled on Monday mornings for a sort of roll-call. At this meeting artists were dispatched to various theaters to fill-in for the missing people. As the Lucans recalled many years later, they spent a number of years "doing the smalls," the provincial halls and picture palaces up and down the country. Touring in fit-up was a very hard school, and did not die out in Ireland until the belated advent of television. Provincial audiences may have been unsophisticated but they were also very demanding. Galway writer M. J. Molloy said of them, "The rural Irish audience is an Elizabethan audience. They're very tough—they come out for a night's fun and if they don't get it from the stage they'll make it for themselves in the auditorium."[85]

It truly was a school of hard knocks, but the Lucans seem to have provided the required fun, and their next recorded presence was on Monday 12 November 1917 at the Victoria Cinema Theater in Galway. Kitty had not returned to Galway for several years, as the poster in the *Connacht Tribune* makes clear. "Return Visit after a long absence of a Galway favorite, KITTY MCSHANE, dainty Irish comedienne and dancer." Kitty is given pride of place, probably because she had appeared alone in Galway in 1913. Arthur is not mentioned directly by name, instead the poster continues, "And THE LUCANS, the Irish comedy couple." On Wednesday and Friday they are again billed rather oddly as "KITTY MCSHANE AND THE LUCANS, in a complete change of program." Their last night was Sunday 18 November, and throughout the week they shared the program with silent comedy films and newsreels.

Arthur and Kitty were now becoming well known as the "Irish comedy couple," and their colleagues in the Dublin theaters had heard of their success in pantomime, musical revue and summer alfresco in England. But up to this point, the couple had not appeared together in a Dublin theater, and Arthur had still never written a full-length show. When chatting to Charles Wright, manager of the Queen's Theater next door to the McShane household, he may well have exaggerated the amount of material he had written in England in order to get the commission to write a show for Christmas 1917. But get it he did and, building on his not inconsiderable years of experience in the business, he wrote his first pantomime. Now at last, on Monday 17 December 1917 (seven years later than hitherto believed) the true story of the Lucans' involvement in Dublin pantomime begins, not with *Red Riding Hood* but with the Queen's Theater production of Arthur's *Little Jack Horner*.

The pantomime featured a very strong cast of local talent. On the printed program Marion Scott and Clarice Chesney topped the bill in large capital letters, followed in much smaller print by "J. B. Strain, Frank Joy, Arthur Lucan, Doyle and Massey, Norman Carroll, Cathal MacGarvey, Kitty McShane, Moira Breffni [mother of Cyril Cusack], Greta Mack, the Sisters Colley, the Lennox troupe of Dancers and the Little Avoca Dancing Gems." Kitty had played Jack Horner in England but she was not given the role in Dublin. *The Freeman's Journal* reported that "The title role was sustained by Miss Marion Scott, who makes a charming and vivacious boy," and Clarice Chesney was principal girl. The same paper reported that "Most of the fun-making falls to Mr. Cathal MacGarvey who, needless to say, is equal to every emergency." MacGarvey was described elsewhere as "Ireland's premier original humorist in song, monologue and story." He also played the dame in pantomimes, appearing the following year as Widow Twankey in *Aladdin*. So at first it appears unlikely that Arthur was the dame, and Kitty definitely did not play principal boy or girl. Their names were not even listed as a couple, but Arthur's authorship of the script was acknowledged; "The pantomime is written and produced by Mr. Arthur Lucan, and large audiences yielded a full measure of well-deserved applause." Fortunately, one single advertisement in *The Stage* on 10 January 1918 provides solid evidence of the exact nature of Arthur and Kitty's major involvement in the production. "The Lucans, Comedy Duo, Dame and Frolic, Queen's Dublin. *Jack Horner*, written and produced by Arthur Lucan and acknowledged by the management to be the best Panto put on for years." At the bottom, in capitals and inverted commas, appears what must be some kind of reference to Kitty. "ISN'T SHE GORGEOUS."

"Popular," "dainty," and now "gorgeous." From her earliest childhood pub performances onwards, Kitty was being actively encouraged to think of herself as someone very special indeed, with lasting consequences for herself and all those who came into contact with her through the years.

The Dublin press described *Jack Horner* as a "Gigantic success. The Pantomime of Pantomimes. Everybody's opinion, the best ever staged at the Queen's. A riot of fun from start to finish. All-star Company … hundreds turned away last night." Another critic praised the "thoroughly Irish" nature of the program, thereby revealing the extent to which a sense of nationalism, inflamed by the events of 1916, had now permeated all areas of public life, especially at the Queen's which was already well known for the patriotic and Irish nationalist slant of its repertoire. By the end of the thirteen-week run of *Jack Horner* in early February, the management estimated that it had been seen by well over sixty thousand people. The legend of Arthur's last-minute involvement either as writer or as dame is contradicted by the facts; had it been true it would have merited and received admiring coverage in the press. And as we have seen, long before the Dublin *Jack Horner*, Arthur had already played Countess,

Ugly Sister and Dame in England, demolishing the legend of a reluctant or last minute Dublin damehood!

In the first week of March 1918 "The Lucans, The Irish Comedy
Couple," were back at the Tivoli in Dublin and at the end of the
month they returned to Galway for a week where, as before, Kitty
headed the bill over Arthur. "Kitty McShane, songs and dances. The
Lucans, Irish comedy couple in new acts. Ned Joyce, Galway's best
baritone, in a sketch entitled 'The Billposter,' written by Mr. A. Lucan,
who will take part in it."

Here is further evidence that Arthur was writing material for
others as well as for the Lucans, and acting in sketches without Kitty.
In Dublin in April 1918, Arthur and Kitty are billed together properly
by name for the first time, and for the first time as dame and girl. In
a variety show at the Queen's they are at last listed as "Arthur Lucan
and Kitty McShane, the Dame and the Dainty Maid." This simply
referred to the roles they had played in the recent highly successful
pantomime; the fact that Arthur continued to appear in male roles
is revealed by an account of another "all-Irish" show at the Queen's
in May with Power and Bendon heading the bill. "An excellent 'all-
Irish' variety program drew large audiences last night. Chief among
the entertainers were Arthur Lucan and Kitty McShane in a farce,
'The Railway Porter and the Girl' which was hugely enjoyed." *The
Freeman's Journal* added, "Miss Kitty McShane and Arthur Lucan of
pantomime fame, in an act entitled 'The Railway Porter and the Girl'
made a distinct hit before large audiences at the Queen's last night."
Arthur's porter may have been distantly related to Dan Leno's famous
depiction of "The Railway Guard." Throughout 1918 the Lucans
toured "the smalls" across Ireland, leaving very few records of their
passage. In the autumn they were in Ulster where *The Donegal News*
on 12 October 1918, reported that they appeared for one week at St.
Columb's Hall in Derry before "crowded and appreciative audiences.
The bill includes an amusing comedy scena by the Lucans, a duo of
Irish artistes, who display great cleverness in their mirth-making
entertainment."

Given the resounding success of Arthur's *Jack Horner*, it was hardly
surprising that the management of the Queen's Theater wanted to
secure his services again. In December 1918 he at last presented *Little
Red Riding Hood* in which he played an "Irish" Dame Hubbard, but

contrary to the accepted legend, Kitty was again neither principal boy nor girl, those roles being taken by Jean Robb and Clarice Chesney. Kitty played Dolly Dimple, written in by Arthur as a comic partner for Dame Hubbard. The pantomime was advertised as "show, lyrics and original songs written and produced by Arthur Lucan," but top billing went to the Scottish comedy duo Power and Bendon, followed by "Tom Warden, Harry O'Donovan, Arthur Lucan, Sisters Colley, Kitty McShane, Jean Robb, Clarice Chesney and full chorus and ballet." On 4 February *The Freemans Journal* reported,

> Crowded houses are still the rule at the Queen's Theater where the remarkably successful pantomime 'Little Red Riding Hood' still holds the boards. The four comedians, Power and Bendon, Tom Warden and Arthur Lucan—one and all deserve the phrase applied to Yorick; they are fellows of infinite jest . . . For robust fun, picturesque staging and tuneful song, 'Red Riding Hood' would be hard to beat.

The Irish Independent reported enthusiastically,

> Bumper audiences attended last night at both performances of the remarkably successful pantomime 'Little Red Riding Hood,' which has been given fresh life by new songs and new comedy business. Tonight will be the benefit of Miss Clarice Chesney (Principal Girl) and Miss Jean Robb (Principal Boy), when special attractions will be provided at both houses. On Thursday night the benefit of Arthur Lucan, and his partner Miss Kitty McShane, the popular Dublin comedienne, will take place with added attractions. To avoid disappointment, seats should be booked early.

Once again, the separate popularity of Kitty is stressed. Quite by chance, Arthur's old friend Gilbert Payne was at the Gaiety starring in the "Grand British Victory" pantomime *Boy Blue*. On Payne's benefit night, artists from the other theaters, including the Queen's, volunteered their services, so Arthur was able to show his gratitude to his former mentor. Also in Dublin, at the Theater Royal, was the singer and pianist Jen Latona, who some six years later would play a brief but important part in the story of Lucan and McShane.

The Lucans now describe themselves in *The Stage* as "The Great Comedy Couple" and "The Dainty Damsel and the Different Dame." In March 1919, billed as "The Lucans, the Irish comedy couple," they appeared at the Tivoli Theater on Burgh Quay. They had clearly scored a great success with *Red Riding Hood* as they are presented as "the well-known and popular duo . . . fresh from their triumphs in local pantomime." But the two pantomimes at the Queen's Theater were the only two in which the Lucans ever performed in Ireland. Dennis J. Clarke, the legendary talent-spotting manager of the Argyle, Birkenhead, was in Ireland in January 1919, where he was involved in theater management in both Dublin and Belfast.[86] Clarke, whose eye for talent gave early opportunities to Harry Lauder, George Formby, Charlie Chaplin, Stan Laurel and many more, became an instant admirer of the Lucans and seems to have set up their English tour of 1919. He also became a life-long friend, mourned by the grateful couple at his funeral in September 1934, where their wreath bore the inscription, "Goodbye, dear friend. The curtain has rung down but you put up a good show. Lucan and McShane."

In March 1919, the Lucans at last returned to England and embarked on their first real tour of the halls together. They began at the Portsmouth Hippodrome, and the sketch "Come Over," their prototype domestic quarrel routine as "Kathleen and Mother," was first mentioned in *The Stage* on 3 May 1919, when they performed it at the Palace Burnley. The following week at the Empire in Grantham they contributed "an immensely amusing sketch," and at the Queen's Varieties in Castleford they presented "a scena full of mirth." At Hanley Grand in June 1919 they are described as "Lucan and McShane, a clever comedy character couple." But the couple's first really significant and unusually perceptive review (as far as Arthur is concerned) appeared in *The Manchester Guardian* on 7 June 1919, when they were playing at the Ardwick Empire.

> Mr. Arthur Lucan and Kitty McShane surprised us into great liking for nearly everything they did in their Irish cabin. Mr. Lucan succeeded by a humorous manner which makes him independent of jokes which are necessarily comic or never used before. His treatment of several worn jests last night was

considerably better than the mere recital of good jokes which earlier in the program were delivered in a different manner.

The "scena full of mirth" is again identified as "Come Over" in July in a performance at the Rochdale Hippodrome, and in October at the Olympia in Dunfermline. The couple returned briefly to Dublin at the end of the year and the "well-known and popular duo" performed "Come Over" at the Tivoli Theater on Burgh Quay in the second week of December. *The Freeman's Journal* reported, "Arthur Lucan and Kitty McShane have an aptitude for rollicking comedy and their scena 'Come Over' kept the audience in good humor." But Ireland was now in the throes of an armed struggle for independence, and by Christmas the Lucans were again back in England where they were more or less obliged by the Irish situation to remain for several years. They did not return to Dublin until after the creation of the Irish Free State. Fortunately, in December 1919 their growing reputation on both sides of the Irish Sea led to their first pantomime engagement at the Pavilion Theater in Liverpool ("The Pav") where they were to become firm favorites and regular visitors over the years. *The Stage* reported that in *Aladdin*, "the principals are taking it through right merrily, Kitty McShane being the celestial hero, with a weird and comical mother (Widow Twankey) in Arthur Lucan."

"A weird and comical mother." At last Arthur Lucan's greatest creation was beginning to take shape! In February 1920, *Aladdin* moved to the Nottingham Hippodrome where Chinese dancing was provided by "Lotte Stone's Eight Pekin Belles."

Years later, the Mother Riley films contained scenes which were inserted at the suggestion of Arthur and Kitty, perhaps as poignant reminders of moments of earlier triumph, and maybe even unclouded happiness (or wishful thinking!) In *Old Mother Riley in Society* (1940) there is a wonderfully evocative sequence set in a theater during a performance of the pantomime *Aladdin*. Chorus girl Kitty is mocked by the other girls because her "weird and comical mother" is a mere theater washerwoman. When, with a flash and a bang, Mother Riley is accidentally hoisted onto the stage in place of the Genie of the Lamp the audience loves her wildly disruptive antics and decides "It's all part of the show!" But the principal boy Aladdin storms out and Kitty gets her big break. When filming this sequence in 1940, although they had played *Aladdin* in South Africa a year earlier, the Lucans may well have thought back to that first *Aladdin* in Liverpool. Sadly, the Aladdin in the film was played by a "difficult" woman of forty-three, not the twenty-two-year-old colleen of 1919. Nevertheless, the camera seems to capture the genuine and intense affection with which the long-suffering Arthur as Riley proudly watches from the darkness of the wings as his wife/her daughter sings onstage; in reality, the number "No Matter Where You Are" was dubbed by the genuinely affecting voice of the young Celia Lipton. No film footage, and very few photographs seem to have survived of Arthur and Kitty in any of over twenty pantomimes, so this *Aladdin* sequence, with its atmospheric back-stage business, and a fine entrance number for the chorus, lovingly and nostalgically spun out by director John Baxter, is the only visual reminder we have of what had been, before the Riley films, a hugely important part of the Lucans' working lives, and would, for Arthur at least, remain so to the end. A complete list of the Lucans' pantomimes, 1895-1954, can be found at the end of this study.

There is no record of the Lucans in pantomime at Christmas 1920, and the years 1921 and 1922 were spent, well down the bills, touring with "Come Over" described as their "Irish scena that abounds in fun ... and some capital singing and dancing ... an act which shows Mr. Lucan as a very funny and unexpectedly agile old Dame." At Christmas 1921-1922, they were in Fred Collins new production of *Aladdin* at the Glasgow Pavilion. Once again, as in Dublin, the cast included the Scottish comedy duo Power and Bendon playing the Chinese policemen. Arthur again played the Widow Twankey but Kitty was not first principal boy or girl; she played second boy Prince Pekoe, like the original Tuan Kay, another brand of tea, but one which has disappeared from modern pantomimes! The seven-week run was followed by a tour. In August 1922, the couple went back briefly to Dublin, now the capital of the new Irish Free State but already in the throes of a civil war. They took part in an "All-Irish" program at the Tivoli and *The Freeman's Journal* noted that "the quick-change character scena presented by Arthur Lucan and Kitty McShane was as interesting as it was entertaining." On 14 August they were booked to appear at the Hippodrome in Belfast. Belfast now lay beyond the border of the Free State, in the British six counties of Northern

Ireland, and within the south there were armed skirmishes in the countryside between the pro- and anti-Free State forces. Perhaps not quite by chance, Kitty became unwell and Arthur wrote from Great Brunswick Street to the Belfast management enclosing a doctor's certificate and an apology. This letter, preserved at the London Cinema Museum, reveals that the Lucans had an agent and permanent business address at "Will Lund's Agency, Adelphi Chambers, Lime Street, Liverpool" and the notepaper was headed "Lucan and McShane, Character Comedy Scena 'Come Over.'" Will Lund was for many years an important Liverpool-based variety agent who also represented Tom D. Newell, billed as "One of England's greatest Dames." In September *The Irish Independent* reported that "the clever Dublin comedy couple continue to do well with 'Come Over' and are fully booked for the next year." Kitty's long absence must also have been noted by her son Donald. He had been just a child when his mother left him (for the second time) early in 1919. Now a strapping eight-year-old lad, he regarded her as a complete stranger; she for her part sometimes passed him off as her little brother to make her feel younger.

It was around this time that young Donald, who in spite of his grandmother McShane's best efforts was never a pious Catholic child, committed a *faux pas* which he enjoyed retelling in later years. The McShane boys had taken him to the seaside where he gathered some bulbous seaweed. When he returned home the parish priest was visiting the house. The priest asked him what it was he had in his hand and before his uncles could stop him he repeated what they had wickedly told him; "Mermaids' bollocks, Father."

During the Christmas season of 1922-1923, the Lucans were back at the Glasgow Pavilion again, for a nine-week run in Fred Collins' *Babes in the Wood*, with Power and Bendon as the robbers. On this occasion there are very full reports in both *The Stage* and *The Glasgow Herald*. Arthur played Dame Priscilla and Kitty was principal girl Maid Marian opposite the male Robin Hood of Randolph Sutton. Arthur received praise for both acting and singing, and he scored a particular hit with a recent song by Irving Berlin, "Some Sunny Day with a smile on my face, I'll go back to that place far away." The sheet music was advertised in *The Stage* as "sung by Arthur Lucan." In the midst of high praise, the *Glasgow Herald* reviewer made an unusual point. "Arthur Lucan makes a first-rate Dame; he cracks his many jokes in a rich Irish brogue that is irresistible." All extant recordings of Arthur's voice date from almost twenty years later than this performance. The reviewer was presumably competent to detect a rich Irish brogue when he heard one, so it would seem that, contrary to his later practice, Arthur could and did adopt some kind of Irish accent, at least in the early part of his career. This would make more sense of the fact that Irish audiences readily accepted the Lucans as an "Irish comedy duo" and that they were often referred to as a "Dublin couple." Years later, this was reflected in the headline of Arthur's obituary in the *Irish Independent*, "Death of noted Irish Dame Comedian." Only when they appeared at the Royal Command Performance in 1934 did *The Times* describe them as "British comedy couple."

The *Glasgow Herald* review of *Babes in the Wood* had praise for Kitty and Randolph Sutton, as well as Arthur. "Randolph Sutton makes a most dashing Robin Hood, and his singing is one of the features of the show, winning rapturous applause. Maid Marian is sympathetically played by Kitty McShane whose work, in conjunction with Arthur Lucan as Dame Priscilla is most effective. Arthur Lucan scores with 'Some Sunny Day.'" The *Herald* adds, "Miss Kitty McShane makes a winsome Maid Marian, clever alike in song and dance." As Maid Marian Kitty must have worked hard to earn her praise from the critics because during the same season she faced competition from the Glasgow Alhambra which was presenting the pantomime *Queen of Hearts* with the immensely popular singing principal boy Mona Vivian. Mona, said *The Stage*, was "versatile, vivacious, and dances extremely well." Like young Kitty back in Dublin, Mona had begun performing as "Wee Mona" when barely ten years old. After *Babes in the Wood*, which ran for nine weeks, the Lucans returned to presenting the sketch "Come Over" on the variety circuit, and there seems to be a gap of ten years before they return to pantomime. The Lucans' long association with Bristol began at this time. They appeared at the Hippodrome in three consecutive summers from 1920 to 1922, in "Come Over," "brisk witticisms and stirring dancing being among their features," according to the *Western Daily Press*. In 1928 they were at the Bristol Empire, and when they returned to the Hippodrome in 1929 the press hailed Arthur as "one of the cleverest dames seen in Bristol for a long time."

In the spring of 1923 the Lucans were back in Ireland, still playing "Come Over." On 14 April *The Freeman's Journal* reported, "The success achieved in Dublin some time ago by Arthur Lucan and Kitty McShane will ensure for them a flattering reception at the Theater Royal when they are seen and heard in their character comedy scena 'Come Over.'" After the performance the critic noted that the Lucans were "responsible for much genuine fun, especially [Arthur's] impersonation of a Washerwoman." In August they were in Exeter, where the *Exeter and Plymouth Gazette* commented "While this alleged washerwoman and 'her' pretty daughter occupy the boards, clever patter keeps everyone in the best of spirits. Their comedy is clean and original."

In November 1923, back in Dublin, no doubt encouraged by the labels "popular, pretty, winsome, dainty and gorgeous," Kitty entered the Dublin *Saturday Herald* Beauty Contest. Although she was among the winners she was probably not really pleased to be awarded second prize. Her photograph was published in the *Sunday Independent* along with the information that "Miss Kitty McShane is well known in Dublin theatrical circles. She appeared recently in the sketch 'Come Over' and leaves soon for a tour in Australia." The article contained no mention of Arthur Lucan.

Indeed, in Ireland at least, the impression one gets from the press is that from around 1910, young Kitty McShane was, in her own right, an extremely popular, glamorous and talented artiste, and that Arthur was merely her comical sidekick. Even in 1934, when reporting the appearance of the Lucans at the Royal Command Performance, the *Irish Independent* (unlike the London *Times*) headlined two short news items as "Honor for Dublin Comedienne" and "Dublin artiste [singular] at Command Performance." In both articles Arthur was somewhat dismissively tacked on at the end. "Miss Kitty McShane, the popular Dublin comedienne, and Arthur Lucan, her whimsical partner, have been summoned to appear ... Among the artistes who contributed were Miss Kitty McShane, the popular Dublin comedienne, and Arthur Lucan, her whimsical partner." In view of all this, unless some kind of collective delusion had seized the entire press corps of Britain and Ireland, one is forced to concede, in spite of the evidence of the later Riley films, that the young Kitty must have had some measure of theatrical talent in acting, singing and dancing. But as we shall see later, by the time "Bridget's Night Out" was filmed late in 1935, Kitty, who was by then approaching forty, already seems not only to have lost the freshness of youth but also any natural grace of movement or sense of stagecraft she may once have had. And this is only made worse by the fact that Arthur's consummate skills remain undimmed and, unlike Kitty, his intuitive understanding of performance to camera at the age of fifty is astonishing.

The overseas tour which the Dublin press had announced was in fact a booking by the J. C. Williamson theater organization for Lucan and McShane to join a tour of the variety theater circuits of South Africa, Australia and New Zealand. In order to seize this opportunity, the Lucans turned down the offer of a pantomime at the Bradford Alhambra, and thereby hangs a sad tale. They were replaced by the "bashful'" music hall singer-comedian Jack Pleasants, two of whose hits from the 1910s, "I'm shy Mary Ellen" and "Twenty-one today," are still remembered. Early in the run, at the age of forty-nine, Pleasants collapsed and died onstage, a feat which Arthur was to emulate thirty years later.

The Lucans now set sail for a "world tour" which was to last a full year. Their Christmas card for 1923 consisted of a portrait of Kitty with the proud caption "Africa and Australia till August 1924." By Christmas they were in Capetown, where they opened at the Tivoli Theater and basked in the South African sunshine. But it was here that Kitty, the gorgeous, popular Dublin Beauty Queen was to receive her first unfavorable notice.

> I cannot say that I have been impressed by the dancing of Kitty McShane in the Lucan and McShane scena either last week or this. She is a trifle heavy and forced in getting about. I would rather hear her sing than see her dance. I think that some of these over versatile vaudeville artistes are bound to suffer from mediocrity, for it takes a bit more than talent to develop equally well in three lines at once, such as singing, dancing and patter. As dance turns they can't be taken seriously, though in their own way, they might be quite amusing.

Once again we are reminded of an important aspect of the Lucans' act which the Riley films did not depict or preserve; Arthur and Kitty *both* did a great deal of singing and dancing. In the Riley films Arthur only occasionally sang or danced, but when he did so the effect could be poignant or utterly hilarious. Kitty on the other hand, as one critic acutely observed, "had a habit of bursting into song whether the audience liked it or not," and increasingly in the later films, whether the plot required it or not! It is noticeable that in none of the Riley films does she show any evidence whatsoever of ever having been a competent dancer.

In the spring of 1924 the Lucans arrived in Australia, making their début at the Tivoli Theater Sydney on 8 March in a bill which also included the British comedian Robb Wilton. They then toured extensively, and succeeded in impressing both the public and the critics, who noted Arthur's remarkable identification with his role.

> Mr. Lucan plays a pantomime Dame so well, that for a moment one is deceived as to her sex, while Miss McShane is entirely charming as the daughter. Typically Irish, in both conception and interpretation, the sketch causes howls of laughter by reason of its wit and humorous portrayal. Quite the funniest act I have seen in Australia.[87]

Arthur Lucan took Australia by storm long before Priscilla, Queen of the Desert!

In Perth on 19 May 1924, Kitty celebrated her twenty-seventh birthday and received a good review when the couple opened at the Prince of Wales Theater. "Arthur Lucan and Kitty McShane present a humorous sketch entitled 'Come Over' which creates much laughter. Mr. Lucan gives a skilful characterization of an Irish Dame and Miss McShane appears as a colleen, whose confession of her love affair gives her partner opportunity for some clever comedy." On 25 May *The Perth Sunday Times* featured a large photograph of "Miss Kitty McShane of McShane and Lucan" on its "Movies and Mummers" page;

> A bright program: A large audience witnessed the initial pre-sentation of the new program last night. On the vaudeville side two newcomers, Arthur Lucan and Kitty McShane were

received with enthusiasm. They presented a novel act, while their clever offerings of songs and dances are made most effective by a broad Irish accent in their patter.

Once again Arthur is clearly included in the "broad Irish accent" as had been noted in Glasgow a couple of years earlier, and singing and dancing by both of them is again a feature. On 27 May *The Daily News* also mentions Arthur's brogue, and Kitty's frocks.

The principal item is a humorous sketch entitled 'Come Over' by Arthur Lucan and Kitty McShane, London comedy entertainers direct from Sydney. Mr. Lucan impersonates an Irish 'dame,' and his broad Irish brogue and witty patter are most amusing. Miss McShane's frocks are a very pleasing feature of the act, and her singing and dancing earn much applause.

A few days later another critic again mentions Kitty's frocks. "Well-merited applause followed a 20-minute sketch in which Arthur Lucan impersonated an Irish dame, and Kitty McShane took the part of a colleen. Their dialogue was original and bright; and Miss McShane was most strikingly frocked."

"Most strikingly frocked." Throughout Kitty's career, observers were to comment, often uncharitably, on Kitty's obsession with what Sybil Rowse in 1941 christened "Kitty's frilly frocks."

Still in Perth, on 1 June the couple gave the first performance of the sketch "The Old Match-seller" which was the second of their major sketch routines, but not as mother and daughter. Arthur played an elderly widow selling matches and balloons on the Thames Embankment. She meets a jilted bride in her wedding dress, and together they bewail their fate as victims of men and society in general. The bride's anguish is comically punctuated by the match seller's cynical responses, most famous of which was "Every man before wedlock should be padlocked!" At the end, the unlikely pair simply go their separate ways, in a riskily downbeat ending for a comic sketch.

The West Australian reported that "The comedy sketch presented by Arthur Lucan and Kitty McShane, 'The Old Match-seller,' causes much laughter and Mr. Lucan's impersonation of an Irish dame meets with cordial recognition." This last point must refer to the significant Irish-Australian element in the audience.

Arthur Lucan and Kitty McShane, who commenced the second week of their season, gave another humorous sketch entitled 'The Old Match-Seller.' In this skit Mr. Lucan was again successful in his impersonation of a dame, his high-pitched voice and mannerisms causing roars of laughter. Miss McShane wore some dainty costumes and was heartily applauded for her singing and dancing.

Once again Kitty's dainty costumes are as notable as her singing and dancing. Arthur continued to perform male roles in sketches, including a routine called "In the Dressing Room" which they gave on 7 June, the third week of their Perth season. "The popular comedy duo Arthur Lucan and Kitty McShane will commence the third week of their season with another original humorous sketch, entitled 'In the Dressing Room.' The male member will play the part of an old theatrical dresser, and Miss McShane will appear as a young actress." The press later reported, "Much laughter was caused by the humorous sketch, 'In the Dressing Room,' presented by the popular burlesque artists Arthur Lucan and Kitty McShane. Mr. Lucan gave an excellent characterization of an old theatrical dresser, and Miss McShane played the part of a young actress with a dainty charm." Kitty was, once again, surrounded by frilly frocks, and the critics loved Arthur as a man, just as much as they appreciated him as a Dame. "The funniest sketch I have ever seen. A peep behind the scenes in a theater where we see Arthur, the one and only, getting into difficulties with costume changes. Kitty, the winsome one, helps him. Can you imagine the dialogue? My sides still ache with laughter. Surely it must be the night of nights to witness such an event! A very excruciatingly funny act!"

The Lucans remained in Perth until early July, when they moved on to Fremantle and Adelaide, where the press described them as "the delightful . . . the brilliant . . . Irish performers . . . an exquisite comedy duo, Dame and Colleen." They performed "Come Over" and "The Old Match-seller," "which is considered by many to be even funnier and more artistic than 'Come Over.'" In Adelaide *The Mail* repeated a frequent press comment. "Arthur Lucan and Kitty McShane were irresistibly comic in the sketch 'Come Over,' and showed that, in addition to comedy, they were experts in dancing and singing." The *Bunbury Herald* was equally enthusiastic.

Photo 7: Arthur as the Match seller. John Fisher

A CLEVER DUO. What is voted by general opinion, and who is a better judge than the paying public, to be the best variety turn which has appeared in Bunbury for a long time is provided by the clever comedy duo now appearing at the Princess Theater. After a most successful season at the Prince of Wales Theater, Perth, and the Princess, Fremantle, Arthur Lucan and Kitty McShane have been engaged by Mr. Hands for the entertainment of Bunbury people along clean comedy

To Viani the "Shepherd" of the "Bush" with best wishes from two of the "flock" Lucan & McShane

Photo 8: Kitty as the jilted bride with the Match seller. Anthony Slide

lines. Described as the Irish Comedy Duo, they were seen and appreciated by a large audience last evening in 'The Match-seller,' a highly diverting item which met with a splendid reception. To-night the same sketch will be repeated with a complete change of program on Wednesday and Thursday. To those who appreciate a clever, sparkling entertainment, we commend Lucan and McShane as the best yet. A riot of comedy from start to finish.

The Lucans were even appreciated by the gold miners of Kalgoorlie. On 15 July the *Kalgoorlie Miner* reported "Arthur Lucan and Kitty McShane made their farewell to goldfields audiences at the Kalgoorlie Town Hall last night, when they appeared in two of their inimitable sketches respectively entitled 'Come Over' and 'Fun in the Dressing Room.' They were conspicuously successful."

After an equally successful three-month season in New Zealand, the couple sailed for England at the end of 1924. On the long sea voyage home they were befriended by Viscount Jellicoe and his wife. Jellicoe had had a distinguished naval career as Admiral of the Fleet and First Sea Lord, and had commanded the British Grand Fleet at the Battle of Jutland in 1917. He then served as Governor-General of New Zealand from September 1920 to November 1924. Quite what the noble viscount made of the subversive Irish dame, history does not record, but I have managed to find an anecdote from six years later which clearly concerns Arthur and Viscount Jellicoe. In March 1930 the *Hull Daily Mail* published an interview with the "unique dame" and "great mirth maker Arthur Lucan," which reveals that he and Kitty and the company must have given performances for the passengers during the long voyage home from New Zealand. The anecdote also appears to suggest that only at this point did Arthur start to use the "putty nose" which was to become such a distinguishing feature of the face of Old Mother Riley.

> Arthur Lucan is a dame whose style is as unique as it is successful. During a chat with him in his dressing-room the other night, I discovered the secret of his prominent nose. It is, of course, now constructed of cosmetic clay, but when it was just created, Mr. Lucan told me, it was composed of dough commandeered from a ship's bake house. It was during a voyage on one of the comedian's numerous tours when the company endeavored to entertain a famous English Admiral who was one of the passengers. The Admiral accused Arthur of suffering from indigestion after his nose had been on view. This, the comedian denied but admitted that the phenomenon was due to indigestible material. It is certainly a nose which speaks volumes for the artist's individuality. Mr. Lucan

is a disciple of broad slapstick comedy, and he is a past master in the art of comical gesture and facial expression.

At the end of the voyage, the Jellicoes gave the Lucans a memento, a mascot doll which accompanied them on their travels for many years. On his return to England in 1925, Viscount Jellicoe was made an earl . . . while Arthur remained a Dame!

Chapter Four: The Lucans and the Latonas 1925-1926

Between February and September 1925 the Lucans were again touring the British and Irish variety circuit with "Come Over" and "The Match-seller," not given top billing but often bringing up the rear; at the Alhambra in London, for instance, they were well down a bill headed by Harry Tate and Little Tich. But in the course of 1925, they had the immense good fortune to be befriended by the well-established and highly popular music hall couple Frank and Jen Latona. The partnership which ensued, though short-lived, was of tremendous importance, for both good and ill, to the career of Lucan and McShane. The full story of this doomed association has never been properly told and deserves to be added to the complex history of the genius of Arthur Lucan and the sadness of Kitty McShane. The variety artistes Frank and Jen Latona, although completely forgotten today, were by all accounts a remarkably interesting, talented, and likeable couple, renowned in the profession for their good nature and generous attitude towards their fellow performers.

Frank Latona's early life reads like an episode from a *Boys' Own Adventure Book*. He was born Benjamin Franklyn Titus in Frankfort, Michigan in 1857 and as a young man ran away to join a circus. He had a successful career in the American and British music halls as a "tramp comedian" and was also regarded as one of the finest trombonists of his day. He acquired or inherited considerable amounts of property in Jackson, Michigan, and a farm at Darien in Genesee County, New York. Frank had performed in England in the 1880s but by 1898 when he returned to perform in the London halls he was already divorced, with three grown children.[88] Frank appeared in Music Hall with all the greatest stars of the day including Dan Leno, George Robey, Eugene Stratton, Vesta Tilley, Marie Lloyd and Florrie Forde.

Jen Latona, who was twenty-four years younger than Frank, was born Emma Jane Letty Carter in Birmingham in 1881. Aged barely sixteen she took the stage-name Jennie Gabrielle and performed in theaters all around the country as "the marvelous child pianist and vocalist." She also played the concertina. Contemporary reviews speak of her exceptional skills at the piano, "her execution and finesse being something wonderful." She sometimes played blindfolded, "the keys of the instrument being covered by a flag." Critics frequently praised her extremely beautiful voice, one comparing her to Jenny Lind, the great nineteenth-century soprano known as "the Swedish Nightingale." Jen and Frank were married in Birmingham in March 1900. They had one daughter who worked with them briefly in the late 1920s under the names of Madeline Joy and Madeline Latona. The Latonas undertook several world tours and regularly won high praise for their comic patter as well as their singing and playing. Back in London in July 1910 after an extensive tour of Australia and New Zealand, the couple bought a large old house in Streatham. At about that time Frank retired from the stage but continued to manage Jen who was much in demand all over the country, both as a performer and a prolific song-writer. Jen continued to perform until Frank's death in 1930. She lived on in the house they had bought until her own death in 1955; as her only daughter Madeline had died two years before her mother, Jen's property, costumes and memorabilia were sold at auction. A retired actress, Jean Kennedy, bought a cupboard and in it she found two diaries written by Frank, including one from the year 1910, which clearly documented the Latonas' wealth and success, and their enormous prestige within their profession at that time. A few snippets from the diary were published in *The Stage* in May 1956.

The Latonas were in Ireland in 1910, and Arthur and Kitty must have known of them, especially as the young Kitty already aspired to be a performer and must have learned her craft by copying the popular artistes of the day. Around this time Jen became a prolific recording artist and during her extensive recording career made dozens of documented recordings, mostly for Zonophone; a few of her comic songs can still be heard today on CD compilations. Her name figured on the sheet music of many songs, and her portrait also appeared on the cover of an Australian edition of MacDonald and Tate's hit song from 1909, "If I should plant a tiny seed of love." When the Latonas bought their London house in 1910, Jen gave an interview to the magazine *Madame*. At that time the thirteen-year-old stage-struck Kitty McShane, living next-door to the Queen's

Theater in Dublin and singing in bars and song booths for a few pence, would have lapped up glamorous accounts of the fame and fortune of the pretty young-ish singer (Jen was already 29) who had been on tour in Ireland that same year. Kitty could well have seen Jen perform at the Empire in Dublin in April-May 1910, and very possibly dreamed of emulating her as she read these tantalizing lines from the fashionable magazine which would have been on sale in "British" Dublin.

"*Madame*, London, Saturday, 13 August 1910. 'The Artiste at Home'

> One usually thinks of the successful variety artiste as rushing from city to city at the end of each week, but this is not always the case. The extraordinary growth of music-halls in and around the Metropolis enables some of our entertainers to spend the greater part of the year in their own homes, and, thanks to the success of her amusing songs at the piano, this is the happy lot of Miss Jen Latona. After some years touring in every continent of the globe, Miss Latona returned to England to make an instant hit, and she had so many offers from managers that she was able to pick and choose. She selected engagements as far as possible in the London district and, being thus able to settle down, she has just purchased a fine old mansion and estate on Streatham Hill. All her spare time is being devoted to the collection of decorative furniture and to wandering in her newly-acquired orchard. 'Success is very sweet, but home is sweeter,' says Miss Latona, and one can well believe that a permanent abode is pleasant after a long course of hotels, steamers, and sleeping berths on trains."

So at the very moment of Arthur and Kitty's first meeting, the immensely popular and talented Latonas were much in the news in ways which the younger couple still only dreamed of emulating. It was to be fourteen years before Kitty, like Jen, would taste the delights of "touring in every continent of the globe" and taking luxury liners to foreign climes; but when at last she did, Jen Latona was still going strong as "the stage's happiest and most gifted Songs at the Piano Girl," an accomplished keyboard and concertina player, but also capable of singing Verdian Grand Opera.

A possible link between Jen and the young Lucans is to be found in the song "If I Should Plant a Tiny Seed of Love." This sweetly sentimental ballad was written in 1909 by James W. Tate (brother of the operatic soprano Maggie Teyte, creator of Debussy's Mélisande), with lyrics by Ballard MacDonald. The song, which tells of the bashful beginnings of a young couple's courtship, was a huge popular success in variety and pantomime and was recorded by several artists. The edition of the sheet music from 1909, which features Jen's photograph on the cover, also asserts that that the song was "the biggest ballad hit of the century, as sung with raging success in 200 pantomimes in England." In 1909 The Warwick Trading Company also produced a short Cinephone film, which was synchronized to a recording of the song. Contemporary Irish newspapers show that the song was equally appreciated in Ireland, having penetrated as far inland as concert parties in Ballinasloe, and it is perfectly possible, indeed highly likely, that Jen included it in her Dublin program in the spring of 1910. The 1910 Christmas season was, of course, Arthur and Kitty's first Christmas together, and they must have known of this "raging success" whose lyrics seem remarkably appropriate to the tentative courtship of the older man and the thirteen-year-old schoolgirl. The lyrics were also published in 1910 on a number of sentimental picture postcards that Kitty might well have known; indeed it may well have been the Lucans' courtship song.

Busy little honey bees were buzzing to and fro,
Humming in the summer air,
Gathering the honey and the little drops of dew
That lay within the blossoms fair.
A youth and a maid thro' the garden stray'd
And the youth seemed out of sorts,
So the maid with a smile just to tease him said,
'I'll give penny for your thoughts.'
'I was wondering,' said he,
'If I should plant a tiny seed of love,
In the garden of your heart,
Would it grow to be a great big love some day
Or would it die and fade away?
Would you care for it and tend it every day,

Till the time when all must part,
If I should plant a tiny seed of love,
In the garden of your heart.'

The Latonas returned to perform in Dublin in June 1913, with Jen topping the bill at the Empire. Arthur was in England at that time, preparing to return and marry Kitty in November. Jen again topped the Empire bill in October 1914. Up until then the two couples' paths may not have crossed in Dublin, but when Jen appeared at the Theater Royal in January 1919, the Lucans were in pantomime at the Queen's Theater, just round the corner in Great Brunswick Street (now Pearse Street) on the other side of Trinity College. By this time at the very latest the Lucans and Latonas must have been well aware of each other's existence, having followed each other round the theater circuits, and read each other's reviews in *The Stage* and the local press. When the Lucans embarked on their first tour to South Africa, Australia and New Zealand in 1923-1924, the Latonas, who had been on frequent "world tours" since the turn of the century were also "down under" at precisely the same time, and the two couples clearly must have been aware of each other's presence, although working for different tour management companies. Both couples were in Perth in July 1924, and the Lucans must have seen the highly laudatory press reviews of Jen's performances in Australia and known of her enormous popularity there as well as at home, at a time when they were still much lower down the bills.[89]

According to the comedian Wee Duggie Doyle, quoted by Steve King, the Lucans met the Latonas at the Cork Opera House in Ireland in the spring of 1925. However, I have recently discovered that Jen and the Lucans were on the same bill at the Glasgow Pavilion during the first week of March. Jen also headed the bill in Belfast and at the Theater Royal in Dublin in April 1925, and this may be when the two couples really got to know each other. It seems that Frank was particularly impressed by Arthur's attitude towards his work; something of that attitude may be gleaned from an autograph Arthur gave to an admirer at the Hippodrome in Belfast on 3 April 1925, offering sound advice to a budding thespian. "Work well! Speak well! And you'll do well. Best wishes from yours faithfully, Arthur Lucan and Kitty McShane 'Come Over.'"

Frank invited the Lucans to join him and Jen in a formal partnership in order to take a new variety show on the road, combining all
their talents. Not that Jen was in any way short of talent herself. In
July 1925 *The Stage* carried a music publisher's advertisement which
sang her praises. "Miss Latona possesses the great and invaluable gift
of personality which reveals itself to the best possible advantage in
one of the prettiest song hits of the year." But Frank may also have
turned to Arthur because a reviewer at the Holborn Empire in July
had dared to suggest that Jen was "rather in need of some fresher
patter." In accepting the Latonas' offer of partnership, the Lucans
must have been aware of the exceptional favor being shown to them
by two established professional artists who already enjoyed theatrical
fame and fortune.

In September 1925 *The Stage* carried advertisements for acts and
crew for the new Lucan-Latona joint venture, *Some Show*, which was
due to go on tour in October. Arthur was involved with Frank in the
production side of the show, and in a call for carpenters he gave his
address as 25 Christchurch Road. This was the address of one of the
two houses the Latonas owned in Streatham from 1910 until Jen's
death in 1955. When number 25 was sold in that year it contained
seven flats, so it would appear that the Lucans, who were still very
far from well-off, had been offered hospitality in one of the Latonas'
flats, as well as the very first chance to be their own bosses. In 1925
Frank was 68 and Jen was 44. Arthur was 41, and Kitty was 28. One
curious coincidence was the fact that both husbands were considerably older than their wives. Kitty, the "baby" of the team was now
the age of Jen when Jen had toured Ireland in 1910 and given her
interview to *Madame* magazine. But Kitty was still a long way from
enjoying the material possessions which the Latonas had prudently
gathered over the years. Now that the Lucans and Latonas were
better acquainted, Kitty will no doubt have heard stories of Frank's
properties in America, and his invention of the patented "Ednor Tank
Washer" at his factory at Streatham Hill. She will have wandered
in Jen's orchard, and, in Jen's drawing room, she will have seen the
contents of Jen's shelves and cabinets, her scrapbooks of cuttings and
mementos, including the souvenir program of the glittering Special
Performance organized by Sarah Bernhardt at the London Coliseum
on 11 October 1913 in aid of the Charing Cross Hospital and the

London French Hospital. The concert was given in the presence of King George V, Queen Mary, and the many members of European royal families who were in London for the wedding two days later of Prince Arthur of Connaught to the Duchess of Fife. Kitty's eyes must have opened wide in wonder as she studied this silk-bound memento, a copy of which is preserved in the Victoria and Albert museum. The evening featured some of the greatest stars of the day from all the theater and musical arts. As well as Bernhardt there was Ellen Terry, George Robey, Cicely Courtneidge, Lydia Kyasht, Sir Edward Elgar, Sir Henry J. Wood, W. C. Fields, Yvette Guilbert and Yvonne Arnaud, with society ladies acting as program-sellers for the night.[90] There is no mention of Jen by name among the performers but she must have been among the many music hall stars who took part in the concerted finale, a musical medley called *The House of Sticks*, "in which the principal ladies and gentlemen in musical comedy and opera will appear." Jen, who had recorded a song entitled "You Can't Blame the Suffragettes for That," may have enjoyed telling Kitty that as the royal party left the theater "despite the presence of a large body of police, women suffragists succeeded in creating some little disturbance." Shortly before her death in 1955, Jen donated her scrapbooks to the Mayor of Fulham, but the Royal Performance program was auctioned with her houses and their contents after her death. With characteristic generosity, Jen bequeathed the entire proceeds of the auction to the Variety Artists' Benevolent Fund.

As Kitty's subsequent behavior amply demonstrated, all this (and more) was clearly what she now aspired to. She had to wait another nine years before her own Royal Command Performance, but for a few months in late 1925 and early 1926, she seems to have used the wealth, influence and the obvious kindness of the Latonas to further her own quasi-imperial ambitions.

The new production *Some Show*, "presented by Jen Latona and Arthur Lucan" opened at the Metropole in Manchester on 19 October 1925, and was immediately booked by impresario Percy Broadhead for his circuit. The title was based on a turn of phrase much in vogue at the time to signify powerful approval, most famously used years later by Churchill in his riposte to the Canadian generals who said Britain's neck would be wrung like a chicken; "Some chicken! Some neck!"

The comic actor Verne Morgan (1900–1984) was a member of the cast who, like Arthur, also specialized in what were known as "Dame Studies." Many years later, with a long career in theater and television behind him, Verne recalled his memories of working with the Lucans and the Latonas. As a young actor in 1924 he had been touring in Ireland, and when in Dublin he found what he called "humble lodgings" next to the Queen's Theater with a certain Mrs. McShane and her numerous children. Mrs. McShane proudly informed him that her daughter Kitty was on the stage in London. What she did not tell him was that one of the children in the house, the nine-year-old Donald, was not her son but her daughter Kitty's. A year later, Verne answered an advertisement in *The Stage* that called for a young comedian to work with Lucan and McShane in a new touring revue. The name McShane may not have rung a bell at first but before long it most certainly did.

> I got the job and we started rehearsals for a revue called *Some Show* in Manchester, where we opened at the Metropole. The show was run jointly by Frank and Jen Latona and Lucan and McShane. Frank supplied all the finance because Arthur didn't have any money. Instead, Arthur wrote all of the material. The Latonas were nice people. Frank was elderly and a big-built man, who at one time had been a star in America as a trombone player. Jen was well known on the variety stage as an entertainer at the piano, and one of her big hits was 'The First Forty Years Are the Hardest'. She was quite a homely person, kind and charming in a self-effacing sort of way. They had a nice home in Christchurch road, Streatham, where some of us were invited from time to time for tea and a sing-song." Verne also remembered Arthur with affection; "Arthur was a really lovable man, kind and gentle. He was never known to swear. I don't think he knew how to be horrid to anybody.[91]

Sadly, Verne Morgan's memories of Kitty were rather different.

> Kitty was the exact opposite of Arthur, as hard as nails and the epitome of the word 'extrovert.' I well remember the first morning's rehearsals. We were all gathered together in the

usual slightly self-conscious way, when in walked the three stars, Arthur, Kitty and Jen. We had a troupe of girls, the Margo Girls, one of whom looked very much like Kitty, with similar long black curly hair. Before any of us had been introduced Kitty pointed to the girl and said in a commanding voice, 'She's out before she starts!' It so happened that the sacked girl was one half of a sister act, and this resulted in the dismissal of both girls.

This may account for the fact that the company needed to advertise in *The Stage* for new "chorus ladies" in November 1925, the advertisement promising a "long engagement." Verne went on,

> That was just the start. She continued to scare the living daylights out of everybody from then on. She was a terror if anybody fell foul of her. As she and Arthur progressed in their careers, so did her temper and her flair for showing who was boss to all who worked with them. Somehow she would relish the fact that people were frightened of her.

On a happier note, Verne Morgan also remembered that the Lucans seemed to have a soft spot for him and his friend, the show's musical director, Harry Carmichael. For a time "the boys" were taken under Arthur and Kitty's wing, as long as they showed due deference to "Miss McShane," as Kitty now insisted on being called. When on tour Kitty never allowed other members of the cast to stay in the same lodgings as her and Arthur, but she once made an allowance for "the boys." Verne remembered that "as the weeks wore on Arthur and Kitty would invite us into their room for cocoa and a chat. They showed us photos of their son Donald whom I had seen two years earlier at Mrs. McShane's in Dublin. They also told us stories of the days when they toured 'the smalls' in Ireland." Theater folk cannot resist a good anecdote, and by the time Verne committed these memories to paper, both Lucan and McShane were long dead, and lurid tales were doing the rounds. But far from contributing to them, Verne seems to imply that regardless of her other failings, Kitty was not at that time notorious for chasing other men; indeed the cocoa, the chat and the photos of Donald suggest that the Lucans were still a relatively contented couple.

In spite of Kitty's high-handed ways, *Some Show* had got off to a good start and was well reviewed when it opened in Manchester.

"Bright and tuneful music, smart dances, and a fund of enjoyable humor are the features of the fourteen-scene revue 'Some Show' in which Jen Latona, Kitty McShane and Arthur Lucan are the leading artists." This was one of the earliest times the Lucans had been described as the "leading artists" and it marked an important moment in their progress up the playbills. This warm reception was repeated all around the country, with Arthur receiving particularly high praise in some of the finest reviews he had received up to that point in his career. In November the show was at the Grand Pavilion Scarborough, in early December it was in Aberdeen, and the week before Christmas, on 21 December *Some Show* opened at the Empire Hippodrome, Ashton-Under-Lyne, where the critic on the *Ashton Herald* gave a very full account of what was clearly an impressive production, thanks to Arthur's skills as both writer and actor-director, and Jen's established popularity as a singer-songwriter. Kitty also received her share of praise for some, for her, unusual character acting.

Latona and Lucan are presenting their revue 'Some Show' at the Hippodrome, and truly it is 'some' show, with far more originality and variety than most shows now on the road. There are fourteen scenes, some of them little entertainments on their own. 'The Lady of the Garden' is artistic and musical; 'Come Over' is delightfully comic; 'The Apache Den' is semi-tragic; 'The Embankment' is a notable scene where Arthur Lucan is at his best as the old Match-seller. 'The Beauty Parlor' is at once spectacular and a screaming barber's burlesque, and embraces a pretty mannequin parade. Full details are impossible in our disposable space. Jen Latona, who, by the way, is also the creator of the music and lyrics, is a most accomplished artist. She has a sweet voice, a quaint and taking way, she is an accomplished concertinist and pianist, and her musical scene at the piano is a decided hit, both in melody and humor. No one should miss her 'The First Forty Years Are the Hardest' and her gags on married life are quite away from the time-honored chestnuts.

Kitty McShane is her equal on different lines, for while an excellent vocalist, she shines more in her admirable comedy acting and dancing. As an Irish colleen she scores, and by a sudden transformation she becomes an Italian and then a Spanish senora, dress and deportment following suit. She has a most winning style with her. These two principal ladies are brought together in scene twelve as schoolchildren in a humorous duet, and their partnership evokes loud applause. Encores were many but time only permitted of Miss Latona giving 'Mother Kelly's Doorstep,' which she rendered in fine style.

The writer and producer, Arthur Lucan, is a 'scream.' Of course, as the author, he should know what he wants, but few authors can do both jobs. He is a sort of blend of Formby [the elder] and half-a-dozen other comedy stars on first impression, but his versatility and ability stamp him as an artist on his own, and no mere imitator. He has more originality to the square inch than some have to the square mile. That this was fully appreciated was proved by the frequency of the laughter and the heartiness of the applause. Mr. Harry Carmichael is the company's musical director, and gets the best out of our local orchestra.

Arthur must have loved the complimentary "square inch square mile" image, and will surely have delighted in repeating it in his inimitable gabble-patter for the amusement of the whole company. Another local paper, The *Ashton Herald*, after reporting that the show closed on Christmas Day and re-opened on Boxing Day, added some further interesting details.

Those who intend visiting the Empire Hippodrome, Ashton, at the afternoon or evening performances on Boxing Day, will be well advised if they book early. There is certain to be a run on the tickets, as the production is one of the very best in the boards ... staged in fourteen scenes which for variety and sparkle would be hard to beat. It is indeed difficult to say which part of the show stands out most prominently, as there are so many attractive episodes. Perhaps 'The Apache

Den' will appeal strongly to the average person as there are plenty of thrills, especially where the vicar and the curate are molested by robbers. The former's escape is of a sensational character being well arranged and carried out. The Embankment scene, where Arthur Lucan appears as an old woman is a striking personal expression of the humor and pathos of the underworld. The jokes about the matches, the bitter experiences of poverty and the assumed deafness cause rounds of applause ... Of the artists, Arthur Lucan is a great comedian of an original character, with not a stale joke; they are all good and above average. Jen Latona is a sweet singer and makes her best effort in the garden scene ... while Kitty McShane does well as The Jilted One and Marie.

This review shows that the wistful, downbeat ending of the Match-seller sketch was not an oddity but reflected the mood of earlier parts of the sketch; "There's laughter and tears, smiles and regrets, sunshine and showers, but we must all carry on to the end." The Match-seller script is unavailable, and the usual quotations from it are a couple of gags ("Every man before wedlock should be padlocked" and "I'll swing for you!"). But in the light of this review it would seem that Mother Riley's speech from the dock at the end of the first film was partly based on the "striking personal expression of the humor and pathos of the underworld" and the Match-seller's "bitter experiences of poverty," further evidence of the degree to which the film scripts were based around Arthur's long experience of writing his own material for the stage. The fact that this material provoked "rounds of applause" from the audience, is also evidence of the element of socio-political awareness in Lucan's work, "always topical" as the critics put it, long before the films. In 2013, in his revised Lucan and McShane essay, John Fisher added this telling detail concerning the end of the Match-seller sketch; "Shrugging her shoulders with more than a touch of Chaplin about her, she shuffles offstage, repeating her opening cry, which fades away into the distance: 'Matches, penny a box, matches, penny a box ...' There couldn't have been a dry eye in the house."[92] The *Ashton Herald* review was repeated almost word for word in the *Bath Chronicle and Weekly Gazette*, on Saturday 9 January 1926, when the show was at the Palace Theater, Bath, and was illustrated with one of the earliest photographs of Arthur as a dame. Another full account of the program appeared in *The Stage* when the show was at the Queen's, Poplar, later in January 1926.

> Jen Latona and Arthur Lucan's new revue 'Some Show' realizes its title to a large extent and though no author's name is given, it is well put together, its chief aim being laughter. There is plenty of other palatable matter, however, in this review, including an attractive choice of popular songs, some smart dancing and agreeable vocalism, while the whole is staged effectively and at times with originality. Arthur Lucan and Kitty McShane's sketch 'Come Over' forms an acceptable part of the general scheme while Jen Latona finds time for some of her familiar concertina playing, as well as scoring a big success in other directions. Arthur Lucan has most of the comic lines to deliver, winning the heartiest laughter in one of his clever dame studies, and also doing well as a curate, a match-seller, and a barber, all invested with a fantastic humor which tells.

These last two reviews constitute an important reminder that well into the late 1920s Arthur was still playing male roles alongside his dame and girl sketches, which at Poplar received only a passing mention as an "acceptable part." The reviewers all go on to praise the other singers and actors by name, including Verne Morgan "who is another who gives full attention to his various characters." Verne recalled that for him one of the high spots of the show was an original sketch written by Arthur called "A Princess from a Sunny Clime" in which he (Verne) appeared with Jen Latona, and that Arthur also rewrote part of his Match-seller sketch to include Verne as an awkward customer, perhaps the prototype of the one who appears in the opening scene of first Riley film. Ice cream bicycles were introduced to London by Walls around 1924, and a year or so later Cecil Rodd of Walls came up with the slogan "Stop Me and Buy One" which was affixed to the front of the bicycles. Verne remembered that Arthur added the cry "Stop me and strike one!" to the Match-seller sketch. This duly got a laugh but it was horribly prophetic because a very different strike, the great strike of 1926, began in May!

For the first few months of the *Some Show* tour, harmony prevailed between Jen and Kitty to such an extent that, as we have seen, they actually appeared together in a humorous vocal duet as a pair of schoolgirls. All in all, the show seemed to be a huge success and heading for a long run. This is borne out by one of the advertisements in *The Stage*, which warned theater managers that *Some Show* had very few weekly slots available right up to Christmas 1926. So happy was young Verne Morgan that he had announced in *The Stage* that he would not be available as a dame for pantomime at Christmas 1926 because he was staying with *Some Show*. Arthur and Kitty would also normally have gone into pantomime but instead stayed with this highly promising new venture, which was clearly expected to carry on touring throughout 1926. Financially too, the Lucans seemed to be reaping the benefits of the confidence which the Latonas had placed in them. Verne Morgan remembered that "At the end of the first week it was common knowledge that the Latonas and Lucans had made £100 each. On the Sunday morning at the train call, Kitty turned up in a beautiful mink coat which she let it be known had cost her £100." This was an enormous sum of money for ordinary people in 1925, and Kitty's mink coat was one of the very first items in what was to become her notoriously lavish wardrobe when, more than ten years later, she finally made it to the film star status she already craved on that Sunday morning in 1925, in a steam train somewhere in the suburbs of Manchester. The mink coat may also have had a curiously symbolic significance, revealing an aspect of Kitty's attitude to Jen. In the 1955 advertisement in *The Stage* for the auction of the late Jen Latona's possessions there were offered for sale, "Clothing, Theatrical Costumes and FURS, including MINK COAT." Jen already possessed all of these things in abundance by 1925 and Kitty, either in lodgings in one of the Latona's flats, or as a guest at Frank and Jen's tea parties and sing-songs with the rest of the cast, will have seen the wealth of possessions, including the furs (in the plural!) which Jen had been accumulating since 1910. Instead of responding to "homely" Jen's unforced kindness, Kitty in her mink on the station platform seems to have been implying that "anything *she* can do I can do better!"

Such a scenario would help to explain the fact that after barely a couple of months of touring (again according to Verne Morgan) Jen and Kitty began to quarrel. Given all we know of the personalities of the two women it would probably be fairer to say that Kitty turned against Jen and started to pick quarrels with her. Kitty would refer to Jen behind her back in a loud stage whisper as "that old woman," rubbing Jen's nose in the fact that Jen was over forty while she, Kitty, was still in her twenties, and still believed the billing she got in the 1919 Dublin pantomime: "Isn't she Gorgeous." The company manager, Robert Winlow, sided with Jen, and Kitty would often complain about him to Verne Morgan, hoping that she might learn something Jen had said about her, in order to stir up more trouble. In such an unhealthy atmosphere the company soon found it difficult to know where its loyalties lay and this created division and mistrust in what had at first been a bright and friendly team. Matters deteriorated rapidly until, on 26 February 1926, *The Stage* carried the announcement which gossips in the business were surely by now expecting.

NOTICE TO PROPRIETORS, MANAGERS AND AGENTS. DISSOLUTION OF PARTNERSHIP. From 10 April 1926 the partnership agreement between Frank and Jen Latona, and Lucan and McShane will be dissolved by mutual agreement."

The show had seemed set to run until at least early 1927, heralding what might have been a long and lucrative partnership for the two couples, but it had come unstuck after barely five months, and the rest of the year's bookings had to be cancelled. The other members of the company announced in *The Stage* that they were staying with Frank and Jen; before long they were touring in a successful new show with the ironic title *Still Smiling*, in which Verne Morgan did dame studies reminiscent of Arthur's. This ran for a couple of years, later changing its name to *Vaudeville Follies*, perhaps as an ironic echo of the title of the show in which the Lucans were by then appearing. In March 1930, at the age of 73, Frank Latona died after failing to recover from major surgery. Jen retired from the stage but continued for many years to be active in good causes and theatrical charities. Years later, in 1955, it must have been a cruel experience for the aging and recently widowed Kitty, now growing old with boyfriend Billy in her increasingly threadbare Mayfair flat, to read in *The Stage* the impressive list of contents of the late Jen Latona's properties, which were to be sold at auction on 7 December, and to see listed the Sarah

Berhardt Royal program which she may well have perused with more envy than admiration at Christchurch Road back in 1925.

Chapter Five: Lew Lake to the Rescue
1926-1931

In green rooms and agents' offices in early 1926, rumors of the impending Lucan-Latona split must have been rife. This would help to explain the fact that in spite of advertised bookings to the end of the year, the producer Lew Lake came to see *Some Show* at the Queen's, Poplar, in January 1926, and afterwards had a long conversation with the Lucans in their dressing room. Lake may in fact have "poached" the Lucans from the Latonas as his visit was quickly followed by the notice of dissolution of their partnership.

When Lew Lake decided to turn to management he already had a long career as a performer behind him. Lew (1874–1939) and his colleague Bob Morris (1866–1945) had started on the music halls as stand-up comedians at the turn of the century. After teaming up, they toured the halls for seven years as "Nobbler and Jerry" in their two-act knockabout sketch "The Bloomsbury Burglars." During the First World War they coined the catch phrase "Stick it Jerry!" This, as Gordon Williams put it, "gave a humorous cast to that endless exhortation to the lower orders, both before and during the war, to endure their lot rather than seek to improve it."[93] We noted earlier that Arthur had borrowed the expression and used it in a note congratulating Kitty on the birth of Donald in 1915; "Thanks for being a brick and sticking it." This context explains the rather odd choice of imagery to celebrate the birth of a baby! Lake's reputation in his own day stood as high as that of his contemporary Fred Karno, who had launched Charlie Chaplin and Stan Laurel on their path to stardom in America. Along with Karno, Lake's name was immortalized in the ribald song sung by Lord Kitchener's hastily trained Tommies in 1914, to the tune of "The Church's One Foundation:" "We are Fred Karno's army, we're Lew Lake's cavalry. We cannot fight, we cannot shoot, what bleeding use are we?" After 1918 Lake turned to production and artists' agency. Until his death in 1939 he was the proprietor of Collin's Music Hall in Islington, where Jen Latona appeared many times. With Murray Mills, Alfred Lyon and producer Stephanie Anderson, Lake formed the company United

Variety Artists. In all, Lucan and McShane were to be represented by Murray Mills for five years from 1926 to 1931.

During Lake's meeting with the Lucans at Poplar, Verne Morgan was in the next-door dressing room and remembered hearing virtually the whole discussion through the flimsy partition walls. According to Verne, Lew Lake wanted Arthur to feature in a new show to be called *Irish Follies*. He was to be teamed up with a silent partner, a comedian named Bert Arnold, and Lake assured Arthur that Lucan and Arnold could become a new comedy sensation in America, as Laurel and Hardy were to prove a year later in *Duck Soup*. At this point Kitty, who had at first assumed she was to be included in the act, realized with growing annoyance that she was not in fact wanted, and that the show had been conceived with the new comic team of Lucan and Arnold in mind. Kitty's reputation in the business was by now fearsome, and her treatment of the lovable Jen Latona was common knowledge. It may well be that this move by Lew Lake was part of a concerted effort, a deliberate attempt by members of the profession to prize Arthur away from a partnership which, while it still worked on the stage, was becoming increasingly intolerable for all those who had to put up with it in real life. Kitty was shocked and angry but was not be fobbed off. She flew into one of the loud and colorful rages which were by now one of her trademarks. When it subsided Lew Lake had to accept the fact that if he wanted Lucan he would have to take McShane, and so he reluctantly agreed. Nevertheless the mother-daughter material in the next show was to be largely eclipsed by the new and successful comic relationship between Arthur and his silent partner Bert Arnold, while in the vocal department Kitty's "charming" work was overshadowed by the praise lavished on a very fine tenor, Eric Randolph.

In 1926, as we have seen, Frank and Jen Latona were well known and highly respected members of their profession, and in view of Frank's age, they were probably looking forward to a well-earned and comfortable retirement in the near future. In theaters all across the country Arthur Lucan was still probably best known as a pantomime Dame and Kitty McShane as principal boy or girl. This had been a regular feature of their career since 1913-1914, when Arthur (without Kitty) played an Ugly Sister in *Cinderella*. Their "old widow and girl" sketches, while attracting some positive comments, were just one item alongside Arthur's repertoire of male characters which had begun in 1911 with the "masher" Archie Mashington, and included a curate, a barber, an elderly theater dresser and a railway porter. After their first "world tour" Lucan and McShane were still just a moderately successful act among many others on the theater circuits, but certainly not top of the bill. The partnership with the Latonas lifted them overnight to the top of the bill and seemed to promise far greater artistic satisfaction and financial rewards. Instead, as a result of Kitty's outlandishly egocentric and spiteful behavior, the partnership was prematurely dissolved, almost certainly by Frank Latona, who held the purse-strings and who was no longer prepared to tolerate the insults to his wife. Thanks to the Latonas the Lucans had briefly been their own bosses but now returned to working for others for over ten years.

At this point, Kitty McShane's theatrical career may well have been saved from total collapse, but only because Lew Lake, another prestigious "old-timer," had a high regard for the talent of Arthur Lucan, and was prepared to pick up the pieces after the Lucan-Latona fiasco. Kitty's realization that people could happily envisage an Arthur Lucan without a Kitty McShane must have come as a profound shock to the woman who had long thought of herself as the indispensable and superior part of the act. From this point on however, she was determined never again to allow herself to be placed in such jeopardy, and as her later behavior showed, if she could not achieve her goals by fair means then she was prepared to resort to foul. Indeed, from Verne Morgan onwards, the general consensus seems to have been that she actually derived more pleasure from being nasty than being nice!

Irish Follies

When *Some Show* folded, and before Lew Lake's new show opened, the Lucans made several appearances as a one-off act on a mixed bill. On 20 May they did a split week (Thursday to Saturday) back at the Ashton Empire Hippodrome where they had been so warmly received just months earlier. But far from starring in a series of lavish numbers, this time they were simply billed to give their old "Irish Comedy Scena, 'Come Over.'"

The new show, *Irish Follies*, which Lew Lake devised principally as a showcase for Arthur Lucan and Bert Arnold, finally went on tour in July 1926 (not 25 August as Steve King asserts). At the Birmingham Hippodrome the reviewer noted, "Arthur Lucan, a comedian we have not preciously seen here, should go a long way; at all events Birmingham would be glad to welcome him again." At the end of July at the Palace Theater Hull, where Jen Latona had long been a firm favorite, Kitty was described as "a singer and dancer of international experience," while Arthur "makes a ludicrous dame and his quips and sallies never lack laughter-making qualities." The show's comedy scenes (which seem to have contained recycled material from *Some Show*) were written by Arthur, and the show was produced by Stephanie Anderson who also provided the dancing girls. *Irish Follies* was in Dublin in August 1926, where the *Irish Independent* reviewer noted that the show did not attempt to be "stage-Irish," and had unusual praise for Arthur; "Many of his topical jokes were clever." Reviewers pointed out that only a couple of scenes were strictly Hibernian, but that the show was none the worse for that. In March 1927, the *Derby Daily Telegraph* noted that "Lew Lake will not pretend that the majority of his principals have even a smattering of the brogue," and in July the *Hull Daily Mail* said that at the Palace Theater "The atmosphere of the Shamrock is not too vigorously introduced, but is one of a number of pleasantly varied ingredients of a fast-moving and attractive show." Indeed, such was the success of the team assembled by Lew Lake that *Irish Follies* ran, with minor changes, for over two years, until November 1928, touring extensively in the London suburban theaters, the south of England (including Eastbourne, Southampton, Brighton, Boscombe and Southend) and throughout the rest of England, Scotland, and Dublin and Belfast in Ireland. In August 1926 the *Hull Daily Mail* said Arthur was a "ludicrous dame," but that "with Bert Arnold his chief assistant, he is equally funny as a prospective film star, clergyman and a Match-seller," and when they returned to Hull in July 1927, the critic spoke of Arthur Lucan as "a comedian who scores as much with his facial expressions and his actions, as with his witticisms. He has a slow-motion assistant in Bert Arnold."

Irish Follies still featured some of the male roles which Arthur had played in *Some Show* in 1925-1926. A review of the show at

Aberdeen in May 1928 and at Eastbourne in August lists a plumber and a vicar. For the latter role he was teamed with Bert Arnold "in an underground den where two zealous parsons try to do some 'saving.'" Or, as the *Burnley Express* put it, "disguised as clerics, they visit the underworld and attempt to steal the booty of other members of their crooked fraternity." An account of a similar sketch in *Some Show* in 1925 says "there are plenty of thrills, especially where the vicar and curate are molested by robbers. The former's escape is of a sensational character, being well arranged and carried out." This tantalizing scrap suggests that the escape may have been one of Arthur's spectacular acrobatic turns, of which only the shadow was captured in the films eleven years later. The *Aberdeen Journal* of Tuesday 29 May 1928 carried one of many reviews which stressed both the range and the quality of Lew Lake's program.

> A show sent out by Lew Lake can be depended upon to satisfy a taste for the spectacular. His 'Irish Follies' at the Tivoli this week does more. It satisfies the artistic and, indeed, all kinds of taste. There is high-brow music and high-brow dancing for the high brows, and good, broad comedy stuff for everybody. The music must take pride of place. It first makes itself felt when Eric Randolph sings an introduction to an elaborate Aladdin's Cave scene, and Dulac and Debois dance with harp, 'cello, and violin accompaniment 'off.' The accompanists, The Venetian Trio, appear in the flesh in a delightful Irish scene as wandering players. Arthur Lucan, whether as a plumber, a slavey, or a dame is irresistibly funny, while his partner, Bert Arnold, is a quaint comedian of the Weary Willie type.

A detailed review of the performance at the Kilburn Empire on 25 April 1927 published in *The Performer*, gives a very good sense of how a variety show at the time was a fitting together of a number of disparate acts.

> The Emerald Isle is much to the fore this week. 'The Irish Follies' as presented by Mr. Lew Lake, consists of eleven scenes, some very beautiful ones, and a splendid company, including Arthur Lucan, a most amusing and versatile comedian, ably assisted by Bert Arnold, Kitty McShane

(a dainty soubrette), Eric Randolph (a tenor baritone with a fine range), Dimitri and Lorina (dancers). The Strolling Players (a band of really fine musicians and a capable and attractive chorus, each of whom is allowed to display his or her individuality during the show). The principal scenes in this production are as follows: Scene III. 'The Spirit of the Lamp.' A fantasy depicting the interior of Aladdin's cave, with a cleverly arranged lighting arrangement [*sic*]. Song by Eric Randolph and dances by Dimitri and Lorina. Scene V. 'My Irish Home Sweet Home,' a typical southern Irish Village, with national songs and dances by Eric Randolph and chorus respectively, and music by the Strolling Players. Scene VIII. 'The Cinema Studio,' a boisterous scene, getting much laughter, with Arthur Lucan as a flapper burlesquing an irate director's descriptive scenario.

Scene IX. 'Carnival Time in Venice,' a gorgeous setting of Venetian canals by night, allowing Eric Randolph full scope as a singing gondolier, to the accompaniment of violin, 'cello and harp.

This reviewer, along with many others, was impressed by the voice and performance of the fine tenor Eric Randolph, including an Irish scene in which, rather surprisingly, Randolph seems to have stolen the show from Kitty. Above all, throughout the long run of *Irish Follies* the reviews make it abundantly clear that, in spite of Kitty's earlier protestations, the pairing of Arthur with Bert Arnold was a very important and much appreciated part of the show.

The major part of the humor falls to the lot of Arthur Lucan, whose delineation of feminine characters, especially those of the elderly matron type, are excellent. He bubbles with vivacity, and his admirable foil, Bert Arnold, one of the slow motion types, causes many a smile with his innate drollness.

The Derby Daily Telegraph reviewer in March 1927 spoke of "Arthur Lucan, a comedian new to Derby, whose style is entirely different from that of any other comedian, but very effective," and he also noted the pairing of Lucan and Arnold.

Broad comedy is dispensed with a generous hand, and hardly a scene passes without the appearance of Arthur Lucan and the inevitable Bert Arnold at his heels. They make a queer pair. Both are obviously funny; and while Lucan gets more laughs because he works harder for them, Bert Arnold is a man who adopts the guise of half-witted yokel, who requires few words.

When the show returned to Derby in its second year, the reviewer's emphasis is still on Lucan and Arnold, with Kitty "a sweet and clever colleen" but relegated to an afterthought.

The comedy parts are in the hands of Arthur Lucan and Bert Arnold, who are capably portrayed. Judging by the laughter which Lucan drew from his audience, his funny ways are still as popular with Derby people as they were when he last visited the town with his 'follies,' his masquerade as an old woman being particularly appreciated. Of course he is never without Bert Arnold, the man who needs to say little or do little when on the stage to raise a laugh. His looks are absurd. Kitty McShane is a capable leading lady.

Time and again reviewers in *The Stage* return to the Lucan and Arnold team.

The humorous parts are well sustained by Arthur Lucan and Bert Arnold.

He [Arthur] has at times a funny partner in Bert Arnold.

Bert Arnold helps him well.

The contrasted comicalities of Arthur Lucan and Bert Arnold …

Bert Arnold as the silent confrere of Mr. Lucan does excellently.

Some clever comedy is introduced by Arthur Lucan and his 'sleepy' partner, Bert Arnold.

Arthur Lucan is a comedian brimful of humor, and he keeps things moving in happy vein.

Bert Arnold also provides excellent comedy.

Only one review actually couples the names of Arthur and Kitty, but then adds Bert Arnold. "Arthur Lucan is the leading comedian, and he is capably assisted by Kitty McShane and Bert Arnold." The reviews also list the range of parts played by Arthur. "Arthur Lucan, a well-liked comedian, causes no end of fun as an old Irish mother, a dilapidated match-seller on the Embankment, and a flapper with film ambitions in a Kinema scene, while Bert Arnold is also funny in his own particular quiet style." *The Derby Daily Telegraph* on 22 March 1927 gave further information on the flapper;

> On the comedy side an easy winner is 'The Cinema Studio' where Arthur Lucan, essentially a 'dame,' has the funniest pseudo-modern get-up that could be imagined, complete with jumper suit, jeweled garters, and spats. This is an episode of talk and no action, but a riotously funny affair for all that.

Many of the advertisements for *Irish Follies* which I have found in the regional press include a photograph of Arthur in suit, collar, and tie. Kitty "is applauded for her singing and acting in a number of parts," and most reviews include a fairly standard compliment such as "Kitty McShane is a delightful leading lady, whether as colleen or bride in search of a husband."

In September 1926, *The Stage* recorded that the songs in *Irish Follies* included "Keep Your Skirts down, Mary Ann" and "Momma Pin a Rose on Me." Both of these had been recorded by the Irish-American singer Billy Murray, but "Keep your skirts down Mary Ann" was a comic duet with words by Andrew Sterling and music by Robert King, recorded in August 1925 by Billy Murray and Aileen Stanley. This song is particularly important as it contains vital clues to a hitherto unnoticed source of the Lucan and McShane double act, and its later evolution. According to William Ruhlmann's online biography,

> Billy Murray was the most successful recording artist of the acoustic era of recording that stretched from before the turn

of the 20th century to the mid-20s. He possessed a penetrating tenor voice, a strong sense of phrasing and enunciation, and a comic style that overcame the sonic limitations of early recording. The first singer ever to make a living solely from recording, Murray won great popularity for his topical comedy songs, ethnic dialects including French, Italian and Irish, and 'coon' songs. His hits included 'The Yankee Doodle Boy,' 'The Grand Old Flag,' 'Casey Jones,' and 'Alexander's Ragtime Band.'

Aileen Stanley, one America's most popular female vocalists of the 1920s, sold some 25 million copies of her Victrola recordings, outselling those of the renowned tenor Enrico Caruso. Aileen was a comedienne and vaudevillian but she could also project a blues-influenced sensuality that was rare in white female vocalists at that time. Billy and Aileen were regular singing partners throughout the 1920s, recording over thirty duets, some serious but mostly comic. In four of these duets Billy Murray, whose parents were Irish immigrants, employed his convincing brogue in the role of an old Irish mother chastising her wayward and flighty daughter. The first example "Maggie," with words by Leslie Moore and music by Johnny Tucker, was recorded in 1923. It was followed by three duets by Sterling and King, "Keep Your Skirts Down, Mary Ann" in 1925, "Bridget O'Flynn, Where've Ya Been?" in 1926, and the couple's last duet together, "Katie, keep your feet on the ground," recorded in 1929. Coincidentally, in this last duet the daughter is actually called Katie McShane, in order to rhyme with "aery-o-plane."

In the performance of "Keep Your Skirts Down, Mary Ann" in *Irish Follies*, Arthur must have taken the role of the "old Irish mother," Kitty was Mary Ann, and the song was one of the items which helped to justify the show's title. The song's title (itself a distant parody of two wartime soldiers' songs) refers to the old Irish mother's disapproval of the shortening of skirts by the "flappers" as the Charleston dance craze swept across America. In the 1925 recording, the opening spoken exchange between Mrs. O'Flynn and a Mrs. Clancy is a clear foretaste of the tone and style of Arthur's washerwomen, and also of some of Mother Riley's exchanges with Mrs. Ginnochie. Both parts were spoken by Billy Murray.

How d'ye do Mrs. Clancy?

I'm well thank you Mrs. McCann, and how's yourself?

Ah sure I'm all in after the week's wash. Me daughter Mary Ann gives me enough to break the back of me!

Well, after the looks of her today your wash will be much lighter next week! I'm just after seeing most of her comin' down the street, and all I can say is, thank God all me girls are boys! Here she comes now!

Well, well, would you look at her! Wait till I lay me hands on her. . . . Mary Ann!!!

A couple of verses from the song will suffice to show a remarkable affinity in tone and style with the characters Arthur was developing for himself and Kitty. The closing reference to "your father" is a comic trope which Arthur re-used frequently.
(Billy Murray is mother, Aileen Stanley is daughter.)

BM–Mary Ann, Mary Ann,

AS–Yes?

BM–Girl, you'll never get a man.

AS–Oh, I'll grab one, never fear.

BM–Mary Ann, just listen here.

Men like the old-fashioned kind.

AS–Mama, dear, you're way behind.

BM–Sure, you'll make them lose their minds!

AS–Oh, what am I gonna do?

BM–Keep your skirts down!

AS–Ahhh!

BM–Keep them way down!

AS–Gee whiz!

BM–Keep your skirts down, Mary Ann!

AS–You make me tired!

I might catch a fellow with my stockings rolled.

BM–All that you will ever catch will be a cold!

BM–Keep your skirts down!

AS–Ah, what d'ya mean, down?

BM–Keep 'em down when you sit down, if you can.

AS–Nowadays you must dress like this to win a lad.

BM–Mmm, but I didn't do it, and I won your dad.

AS–Well, he was no bargain!

BM–Don't get fresh.

Keep your skirts down!

AS–They're going up!

BM–Well keep 'em down, Mary Ann!

The fact that Arthur was familiar with the recorded duets and the available sheet music of Murray and Stanley seems to me to make it clear beyond doubt that his 1934 script for "Bridget's Night Out" was inspired by, and in part copied from, Murray and Stanley's comic spoken patter duet "Bridget O'Flynn, Where've Ya Been?" Arthur's Irish mother waiting up for the return of her flighty daughter after a night on the town is an exact copy of the theme of the Murray-Stanley duet, and this will be more fully discussed later. It also seems highly likely that this song was the source of the name Mrs. Bridget O'Flynn, which Arthur adopted in the next Lew Lake show in 1929.

In August 1926 *Irish Follies* was in Belfast and at the Theater Royal in Dublin, where all the McShanes and young Donald Towle must have turned out proudly to see the grandest Lucan-McShane

Photo 9: Portrait given by Kitty to violinist Fred Midgley in Dublin, 1926.
Roy Stockdill

show so far. The Theater Royal had a fine orchestra, which included a young violinist from Yorkshire named Fred Midgley. Fred was a keen collector of autographed photos of the stars for whom he played, and his album, a veritable roll call of music hall and variety artists, eventually passed down to his grandson, the genealogist Roy Stockdill. In October 2013, Roy brought his album to the Lucan day at the London Cinema Museum and presented the photograph which Kitty gave to Fred in August 1926. This photograph, hitherto unknown, is one of the finest of the younger Kitty, and shows off her much admired mane of wavy black hair. It was probably not taken in 1926, as it closely resembles the photographs of Kitty that appeared at the time of the Dublin beauty contest in 1923. The photographer's stamp is from Liverpool, which means that the photograph might even date from late 1922; Kitty's pose is also very reminiscent of a famous photograph of Lilian Gish from 1921. The show at the Theater Royal in 1926 was one of the Lucans' many visits to Dublin since their marriage. Perhaps because Donald Towle was being brought up in the McShane household, Kitty lavished money and gifts on her family, and this perhaps made Arthur painfully aware that in thirteen years of marriage he had never managed to persuade Kitty to meet *his* mother, who was, after all, Donald's other granny. At last, in the spring of 1927, he finally took Kitty to visit Lucy Ann Towle in Boston. This was to be Kitty's first, and Arthur's last meeting with Lucy Ann. She died aged 71 on Friday, 4 November 1927 (not 1926 as Steve King states). *Irish Follies* had been playing at Kingston and Arthur travelled up to Boston on the Sunday. His mother was buried in Horncastle Road cemetery on Monday, 7 November. After the funeral he returned to open the show in Aldershot. Lucy Ann's grave remained unmarked until 1943; the grave of her husband Tom, just a few yards away, was never purchased by the family and so remains unmarked to this day.[94]

Back on the variety circuit, Arthur, Kitty and Bert Arnold shared the limelight in *Irish Follies* with one other leading artist, the tenor Eric Randolph. Randolph's career had begun in 1913 and he received high praise as a comic "vagabond" actor as well being an excellent tenor with a pure high C. He made many gramophone recordings during his long career, which continued until 1946. I have a couple of these records in my collection and they reveal that Randolph did indeed possess a very pure and pleasing voice. In *Irish Follies* he was hailed as "a vocalist of quality. Eric Randolph is an outstanding success." Randolph wrote some of the show's musical numbers and, no doubt with this in mind, another critic wrote, "The music is above the average. Some of it is reminiscent of light opera." Several of Randolph's scenes are described in appreciative detail, and in one Irish number, undoubtedly to Kitty's great chagrin, he almost stole the show.

Photo 10: Arthur in mid to late 1920s. Mrs. Joan Towle

The most Irish feature is a scene called 'My Irish Home Sweet Home' in which Eric Randolph, as an old tramp, sings several number admirably. Indeed his vocalism is a great feature of the review, and is most strikingly in evidence, perhaps, in the finely staged Venetian scene in which it reaches operatic qualities. His rendering before the tabs of 'My Tumbledown Cottage of Dreams' is also highly successful.

With very few alterations, *Irish Follies* ran for over two years, receiving excellent reviews to the end of the run. In October 1928 the *Western Daily Press* reviewed *Irish Follies* at the Bristol Empire and the perceptive critic singled out Arthur as "a character actor of no mean order."

It is many a long day since a comedian made his audience laugh to the extent that Arthur Lucan did at the first house last night. Lucan makes an excellent dame and he was singularly successful as a down and out woman who sells matches on the Thames Embankment. Further to being a distributor of quips and jokes, Arthur Lucan is a character actor of no mean order. His 'flapper' impersonation in the Cinema Studio scene was well portrayed. His 'mate,' a man of few words and fewer actions, Bert Arnold, was a good foil. Dainty Kitty McShane wore some gorgeous costumes, sang some pretty songs, and danced well.

Reviews repeatedly stressed the operatic qualities of Eric Randolph's music and, again and again, "the contrasted comicalities of Arthur Lucan and Bert Arnold." Kitty was perhaps momentarily chastened by the growing threat to her stage partnership posed by Bert Arnold, and she seems outwardly to have toed the line. Throughout the whole run, just one review at Derby in July 1928 linked Kitty positively with Arthur. "The bulk of the comedy is in the safe hands of Arthur Lucan and vivacious Kitty McShane, the adorable colleen. The fun these two talented artists get out of the most trivial situations is remarkable, but their personality simply oozes from them." Kitty seems to have sought consolation in "some gorgeous costumes," and Lew Lake indulged her growing extravagance. At the Eastbourne Hippodrome in August 1928, shortly before the end of the run, the review in the *Eastbourne Gazette* must have delighted the "fair lady of Erin's isle."

The features of the show are the dresses and the scenery, which are of quite unusual splendor, but their beauty is necessary to form an adequate background for Kitty McShane, the pretty colleen of *My Irish Home Sweet Home*, whose luxuriant fall of black tresses is indeed a crowning glory, and whose brogue is one of the most charming experiences possible to encounter. To offset this fair lady of Erin's isle is her 'mother,' a grotesque but human and lovable figure, Arthur Lucan, who, in turn, is also a romantic slavey, a plumber, a vicar, a flapper, and a match-seller, and at all times a boisterous and excruciating figure.

In spite of the cosmetic glamour, Kitty must have felt insecure, and jealous of Bert Arnold's increasingly important role, a role which she was determined to undermine in order to salvage her own. At last she saw her chance; when *Irish Follies* closed in November 1928 so too did the budding career of Lucan and Arnold. The *Derby Daily Telegraph* reported one rather ominous gag from *Irish Follies*.

"Kitty: 'He said he wanted to marry a girl with black eyes, but I haven't got black eyes, have I Mother?

Mother: 'Have patience, daughter, have patience!'"

Kitty's patience was rewarded, and it was poor Bert Arnold who got the "black eye."

Paris 1929

In January 1929 Murray Mills sent out a new show, *Paris 1929*, again "devised and produced" by Stephanie Anderson. The tenor Eric Randolph remained an important member of the team, but now, at Kitty's insistence, and to the extreme annoyance of Lew Lake, who had protested loudly but in vain, Bert Arnold was banished from the cast. Kitty was back with a vengeance, and her position would never again be challenged! As if to make the point more explicit, it was in this show that the resurgent mother-daughter team were first given names; Mrs. Bridget O'Flynn and her daughter Noreen. Arthur's choice (he wrote the "book" of the show) of the name Bridget O'Flynn was significant and revealing, and it could not possibly have been mere coincidence. The facts are presented here for the first time, and they throw new light on the evolution of Arthur's career.

We have already noted that from early February 1926 the Lucans were performing "Keep Your Skirts Down, Mary Ann," a comic duet made popular on both sides of the Atlantic in the recording by Murray and Stanley, and with sheet music published in London by Feldman. The fact that Lucan and McShane are on record as having performed two of Billy Murray's songs in *Irish Follies* suggests that they may well have followed his releases with interest. They would therefore certainly have been aware of the appearance in England early in 1927 of another comic duet with Aileen Stanley, a duet which again featured the characters of the old Irish mother and her daughter.

The comic duet "Bridget O'Flynn, Where've Ya Been?" with words by Andrew Sterling and music by Robert King was the third Murray and Stanley comic duet to feature Murray as the irate Irish mother and Stanley as her wayward daughter. They recorded it for HMV Victor Talking Machine Co. on 24 August 1926, (record No. 20240-A) with Frank Banta at the piano. The sheet music was published by Shapiro, Bernstein and Co. in New York in 1926, and also under license in Australia and New Zealand by J. Albert and Son of Sydney. I have not yet found a London edition of the sheet music but it would be most odd if it was published "down under" and not in the capital of the Empire. With or without the sheet music, the Murray and Stanley recording of "Bridget O'Flynn" was most certainly on sale in England and it even attracted a "rave review." *The Gramophone* magazine reviewer reported in February 1927, "Of duets and such-like I am glad to be able to recommend a really good effort by Aileen Stanley and Billy Murray in 'Bridget O'Flynn, Where've Ya Been?' with 'Who Could Be More Wonderful than You?' on the reverse." So impressed was the reviewer that the following month he complained, "There's nothing so good to report this month as the 'Bridget O'Flynn' record of Aileen Stanley and Billy Murray." In April 1927, in his Quarterly Review of recordings, the distinguished editor of *The Gramophone*, Sir Compton Mackenzie, lamenting the dearth of good quality popular music, singled out "Bridget O'Flynn" as an exception. The recording was also exceptional in that it was the very first recording of the new electrical microphone era to include a whispered opening scene, the first successful whispering record ever made, and something which had not been possible with the acoustic system. This may partly account for the fact that, according to another critic, the song "attracted more attention than any other of Murray and Stanley's records. That was especially true in England *where it was a sensation.*" (my italics).

Not only was the recording a sensation, but English audiences were also treated to the real thing. After a successful first London season in 1925, Aileen Stanley returned in 1927 to perform in London's West End and the provinces, and her stay lasted from August to the end of the year. She again appeared at the Alhambra, Leicester square, and on 15 September *The Stage* reported, "Aileen Stanley in her third week here, submits an almost entirely new selection of songs and character studies, and is heartily enjoyed. 'Side by Side' and 'Bridget O'Flynn' are among her best-liked numbers." The comedian Gillie Potter, a long-time friend of Arthur, was also on the bill at the Alhambra with Aileen. During the very same week just a couple of miles away, Arthur Lucan was appearing as Mrs. Bridget O'Flynn at the Metropolitan Theater, Edgware Road. One cannot help wondering if Aileen took time out to see the guy who was pretending to be her at the Met!

Given the interest the Lucans had already shown in the Murray-Stanley comic duets it would be extremely surprising if they were not aware of, and indeed familiar with, not only the recording of "Bridget O'Flynn," but also Aileen's live performances during her 1927 English season. It is also possible that they were aware of another version to which Anthony Slide has kindly drawn my attention. The highly popular American vaudeville performers Gus Van and Joe Schenck had also recorded several comic duets on "stage-Irish" themes, performed with a convincing Irish brogue; these had included "That's How You Can Tell They're Irish" (1917), and "In the Good Old Irish Way" (1918). They also performed "Bridget O'Flynn" in a Vitaphone short released in February 1927. It was obviously part of the act they performed on stage, and the Vitaphone shorts were widely distributed as supporting programs to the Warner Bros. shorts. It is therefore possible that Lucan and McShane may have seen and heard Van and Schenck sing the song at the cinema. In light of all this, it stretches the bounds of credibility to suppose that Arthur's adoption of the name Bridget O'Flynn at this time could be pure coincidence. The enthusiastic reviews in both *The Gramophone* and *The Stage* make it clear that British theater audiences would certainly have made the connection with the Murray-Stanley or Van and Schenck duet. Thus the seed was sown for what eventually grew into one of Arthur's classic routines. Quite by chance, when the Lucans created "Bridget's Night Out" in 1934, Aileen Stanley was again touring in Britain, and may have seen the sketch for which she and Billy Murray had provided the initial inspiration. Indeed, fear of infringement of copyright or an accusation of plagiarism were probably among the reasons which in 1937 made the screenwriter Con West feel obliged to change the name which Arthur had been using onstage since 1929. In their brief sketch in the 1937 film *Kathleen Mavourneen*, Arthur was still called Mrs. O'Flynn, and his daughter was emphatically named "Bridget Mary Josephine O'Flynn." Con West's creation of the name Old Mother Riley for their first starring vehicle broke the visible link with the songs of Sterling and King, but the first audiences for the Riley films will have remembered Arthur's earlier stage name and its links with the mother-daughter quarrel duets of Sterling and King performed by Stanley and Murray or Van and Schenck.

The title of the new show, *Paris 1929*, was explained by a review from the Cardiff Playhouse:

On Tuesday, 8 January 1929, was produced at the Playhouse, Cardiff, a revue, book by Arthur Lucas [misspelt for Lucan], music by Leon Jesse and Eric Randolph, entitled 'Paris 1929.' The revue, which is in fourteen scenes, was presented by Murray Mills. Two hours of unalloyed delight rewarded the full house which witnessed this production. Interest centers upon the experiences of a Mrs. O'Flynn, an old tourist on a trip round the world. . . The whole review bears witness to the direction by a fresh and inventive mind. There are four most excellent things in the show. First, the well-contrived scenas, for which Ireland forms a happy background for the droll dame studies of Arthur Lucan as O'Flynn. His gestures and mastery of mimetic art were the joy of the evening.

A later review adds further details of the plot:

Here is told a story beginning in the romantic city of the Arabian Nights and continually changing its venue, finally ending in the heart of 'Gay Paree' itself. Eric Randolph, the silver-voiced tenor, as an impetuous son of an old-fashioned

Photo 11: Mrs. O'Flynn and her daughter Bridget, late 1920s. Mrs. Joan Towle

sheik, leaves his home in the East with Paris as his goal. Mrs. O'Flynn and her daughter, as a pair of tourists travelling round the world, continually cross the path of the young sheik, and sufficient merriment results to satisfy even the most ardent and critical theatergoer.[95]

The romantic and sentimental tone-poems of the composer Albert Ketèlby are still well known and admired, and this allows us to form a very clear impression of one of Eric Randolph's scenes, described in the earlier Cardiff review.

Another effectively beautiful act was that depicting Albert Ketèlby's 'In a Monastery Garden' in which Eric Randolph as an erring monk of jovial mood is disciplined amid the tranquil pleasances outside the monastery. He was recalled for his rich and resonant tenor work. Anthony Gordon as the old Abbé, together with Hamilton Evans, Jack Sinclair, Leo Doherty and Jack Bruce, as the Brotherhood, gave support.

In this impressive scena, the "Brotherhood" must have sung the monks' "Kyrie Eleison" and Randolph sang the "big tune" which followed, decorated with mechanical bird-calls. This is indeed quasi-operatic music as described in reviews of *Irish Follies*, and provided a sharp contrast to the capering of Lucan and McShane. Another sharp contrast was provided by a tableau vivant, "A posing scene of three classic dancing maidens in a setting which might well recall bas-relief studies of Flaxman's designs, with sweet discourse of melody from 'cello and harp." We can visualize this still-life posing scene thanks to a remarkable example of the genre preserved in the film *Stars on Parade*; more recently, the "living statue" has been revived by buskers in holiday resorts around the world. The Cardiff review goes on to praise Lucan and McShane in a comic scena "Never Any Morning Anywhere" which included "the irresistible fun of Mr. Lucan's maidservant, Martha the Maid," another of his dame studies. After mentioning the supporting acts, the reviewer concludes, "They do not seek effect; they achieve it."

At the Brixton Empress in February, another favorable review reveals more of the show's contents:

> The reason for the show's title is far to seek, as most of the happenings occur in Bagdad, Ireland, Canada, and other places, and it is not until the final scene that Paris is reached . . . The Hibernian humor of Arthur Lucan has a welcome freshness, and Mr. Lucan's study of an eccentric dame is very funny. He is very well supported by Kitty McShane, whose talents and appearance are readily appreciated. The principal vocalist is Eric Randolph, who not only sings to the general joy but also acts intelligently in his different characters. He has the choral help of the Eight Canadian Lumberjacks in at least two scenes, and their admirable harmonizing greatly helps the effect.

So the monks also doubled as lumberjacks! The show toured the country throughout the year and returned to London over Christmas and the New Year. It then simply changed its name to *Paris 1930* and carried on until the summer. In February and March 1930, *The Derby Daily Telegraph* and the *Burnley Express* carried a photograph of Kitty alone, not a recent portrait but one taken seven years earlier in 1923, when she won second prize in a Dublin beauty contest. The Lucans had used the photograph for their 1923 Christmas card. Another photograph of Kitty, last seen in Australia in 1924, appeared in the *Hull Daily Mail* in March 1930.

Throughout November 1930 a revamped show with the title *Still Going Strong* included the "dancing violinist" Mareski as well as Lucan, McShane, and Eric Randolph. Randolph appeared in a very serious scene, providing the kind of extreme contrasts of mood and emotion which audiences clearly seemed to enjoy. "Eric Randolph pleases with his songs. The scena 'Call of the Menin Gate' is applicable just now [approaching Armistice Day, 11 November], and provides a pathos which contrasts with the irresistible humor." The Menin Gate at Ypres was built as memorial to the unidentified dead of the Great War; it was inaugurated in 1927 but it was only in 1928 that the nightly custom of sounding the Last Post began. Randolph's scena was undoubtedly inspired by the fact that in August 1930 a play was produced at the Palladium called *The Road of Poplars*, set in an inn near the Menin Gate. In the play, a deranged former soldier who survived the war and has come back on a sentimental pilgrimage believes that his dead comrades return to the Menin Gate each night at the sounding of the Last Post. In the macabre *dénouement* the old soldier is spirited away to "the other side" to join them. In his scena, Randolph played a dual role as "a jolly fusilier and an old soldier," very reminiscent of the play at the Palladium, and also gave an "impressive rendering" of a number entitled "The Trumpeter," probably including a few notes of the Last Post. That such a theme as the "Call of the Menin Gate," described by one review as "both reverent and touching," could be dealt with in all seriousness in the context of a variety show in which "Kitty McShane gave an Irish jig" and Arthur Lucan appeared as a "district nurse in a mental hospital" and "a step washer with a propensity for sojourns at a nearby public house," underlines the very different sensibilities of variety theater audiences at the time.

Pathos and sentimentality were quickly swept away at the end of the month when the show was re-named *The Jazz Parade* in honor of Al Jolson and "the talkies." The show went to the Hippodrome Belfast and to the Theater Royal Dublin, where Kitty's photo in the press was captioned "the Dublin leading lady of 'The Jazz Parade.'" The show then ran until June 1931, when Lucan and McShane announced in

The Stage that they were "concluding five happy years' service with Murray Mills Esq." Whether or not the five years were really happy is not so certain. Lew Lake had clearly intended to launch the new comic team of Lucan and Arnold, but had been thwarted by Kitty's determination to retain her position. Lake was extremely angry when Kitty successfully insisted on Arnold's exclusion from *Paris 1929*, and he felt that the show was weaker as a result. Thanks to the Latonas, Lew Lake and Murray Mills, the Lucans had had a long and successful run of regular work, from 1925 to 1931, something which was the envy of many in their precarious profession. But their growing fame was accompanied by an equally growing awareness in the variety world of Kitty's reputation for gratuitous and inexplicable unpleasantness, accompanied by an inflated sense of her own importance within the Lucan-McShane partnership. This may well account for the fact that after they left Murray Mills in June 1931 the Lucans found themselves "resting." The scant information contained in *The Stage* shows that for a while they were back down the bills again as one among many turns, sometimes giving "The Match-seller," sometimes merely listed as "Lucan and McShane, etc." Over the next few months their engagements seem to have become rather thin on the ground, and their names hardly ever appear in the pages of *The Stage*. Worse still, after topping the bills for six years, in August 1931 they appeared at the bottom of the bill in a variety show at the Aberdeen Tivoli, and in September they had just a "comedy cameo" spot in a variety road show called *Hike and Be Happy* at the Hull Tivoli.

For seven long years the Lucans had neglected the Christmas pantomimes which had been the scene of their earliest triumphs, preferring to stay with their lucrative road shows; now that Christmas was coming without a road show, they were eager to get back in harness. This led to an unusual partnership which to this day remains virtually unknown and unacknowledged; the Lucans were engaged for a touring production of *Dick Whittington* with George Formby junior. Although Formby had been in the business for some years, he was still laboring in the shadow of his brilliant father, and was far from being the star he would eventually become; in fact it would be no exaggeration to say his career was in the doldrums, and his wife Beryl and mother Eliza harangued him endlessly for his lack of originality and initiative. Formby expert Kevin Daly takes up the story, based on a filmed interview with the impresario Bert Loman.

> In 1931 Formby's mother Eliza, had a meeting with Bert Loman, a well-known and respected theatrical impresario who specialized in booking supporting acts. He'd been in the business since 1919 and knew everybody. Eliza confided that George couldn't get any theater work and spent all his time playing around with cars and motorbikes. She asked Loman to see him, and the two met at the Grand Theater, Bolton, where George was performing. George explained that he wanted Loman to get him into pantomime. Loman, typically blunt, told him to forget it, as George knew absolutely nothing about it. 'That's what I want to come to you for, to learn it.' George replied apologetically. Loman then met Beryl to propose his deal. He'd get George into pantomime and teach him the business, but he wanted paying for it; £300 (£15,000 in today's money) over the next three seasons to make it happen. Beryl agreed. Three contracts were drawn up for 1931, 1932 and 1933, and George's career finally got on track. It was money well spent; it not only gave George invaluable experience, it pushed him up the bill.'

What Kevin Daly does not reveal, nor, as far as I can ascertain, do any of Formby's biographies or television documentaries, is the fact that for his first foray into pantomime Formby was teamed up with, one might almost say apprenticed to, the seasoned Dame and Principal Boy/Girl, Arthur Lucan and Kitty McShane, who had first appeared in pantomime together in 1914. Loman's experiment clearly worked, and he recalled, 'It was a tremendous success, and first started George Formby in the money class.'"[96] *Dick Whittington* opened at the Liverpool Shakespeare in December 1931, and although details are hard to come by Formby must have played Idle Jack, a role he often returned to in later years. When the show reached the Leeds Hippodrome in January 1932, *The Yorkshire Post* revealed that Miss Lalla Dodd played Dick, Kitty played Alice Fitzwarren, and Arthur presumably played the dame role of Sara the Cook. Bert Loman must have been delighted to read in the *Yorkshire Post* that "The cast is one that would carry along a resident pantomime for weeks and weeks."

Above all, Loman's strategy of teaming Formby with Arthur Lucan paid off magnificently because, as the *Post* declared, "the combination of Arthur Lucan and George Formby in the comedy lead is tremendous." This tantalizing snippet is all I have been able to discover of what must have been a fascinating collaboration between the reluctant twenty-six-year-old and a comedian almost old enough to be his father; Lucan was now, in fact, a year older than Formby senior, who had died at the age of forty-six. A few years later, Formby remarked that his wife Beryl always played in pantomime with him, so the combination of Mrs. Lucan and Mrs. Formby must also have been, to say the least, rather interesting. *Dick Whittington* closed, rather appropriately, at the Hippodrome in Formby's home town of Wigan. This was the Lucans' one and only appearance in this pantomime, probably chosen because Bert Loman thought Idle Jack was a suitable role for George. In February, a re-energized George Formby appeared in variety at the Bristol Hippodrome, and Lucan and McShane were supporting Hetty King at the Islington Empire. By the end of the decade both the Formbys and the Lucans were rolling in films and money, and Beryl and Eliza Formby must have been secretly grateful to Arthur and Kitty for showing George how to "do it!"[97] Strangely, not a word of the Lucans' crucial role in the re-launching of George Formby's spectacular career can be found in any of the standard histories of British music hall or variety.

And yet, if fate had decreed differently, if Lew Lake had managed to get the better of Kitty in the late 1920s, Arthur's celebrity might have been on a far greater international scale. With Lew Lake's help, Arthur Lucan and Bert Arnold might have followed Chaplin and Stan Laurel to fame and fortune across the Atlantic. It was not to be, and years later Arthur may well have looked back with regret to this crucial turning point in his career, and recalled with sadness some chillingly apposite lines from Shakespeare's *Julius Caesar*.

There is a tide in the affairs of men.
Which, taken at the flood, leads on to fortune;
Omitted, all the voyage of their life
Is bound in shallows and in miseries.

In *Old Mother Riley's New Venture* (1949), when Kitty declares that Mother's hotel bedroom is fit for a film star, Mother remarks in a dreamy, wistful voice, "If I had my time over again, I'd like to be a film star." This is one of the many moments where the Riley films seem to comment ironically on the real lives of the Lucans, and Arthur must have been only too aware that he had missed just such an opportunity twenty years earlier. A fresh tide in the affairs of Lucan and McShane did eventually lead them on to fortune but, paradoxically, their life's voyage was to remain, oddly like that of the Formbys, "bound in shallows and in miseries." Or, as Arthur himself put it many years later, "My share was unhappiness and strife."

Chapter Six: New Directions and a Royal Command 1931-1939

The Stage contains no reference to an extremely important event which took place late in 1932, an event which has gone completely unnoticed and unmentioned by Lucan biographers and historians. Accounts of the Lucans' radio career state that they made their radio debut at the height of their popularity in the show *Old Mother Riley Comes to Town*. The show was broadcast live on the BBC Forces Program from the Chiswick Empire on Tuesday 13 August 1940, and eventually led to their first recorded radio series in 1941. As recently as 2009, in his discussion of the role of radio in music hall artists' transition to film, Paul Matthew St. Pierre stated that "Remarkably this cross-mediatization worked in the opposite direction as well. For instance, Arthur Lucan and Kitty McShane had starred in nine feature films in the *Old Mother Riley* series, 1936-41, before the husband and wife double-act premiered on BBC radio *in Old Mother Riley Takes the Air* in 1941."[98]

Unfortunately this is simply not true, for in reality the Lucans' radio debut had taken place long before the films, a full eight years earlier, on Friday, 19 August 1932. The evidence for this is to be found in the pages of *The Times*, which carried listings of the BBC's National and Regional programs. On that Friday night, according to *The Times*, in an hour-long "National Variety Entertainment"beginning at 8.40 p.m., "Mr. Arthur Lucan and Miss Kitty McShane will appear in a short sketch entitled *The Match-seller*." So, long before "Bridget's Night Out" had been conceived, let alone filmed, the nation had already heard Arthur's earlier sketch, with its unusual, deliberately sad and downbeat ending. "There's laughter and tears, smiles and regrets, sunshine and showers, but we must all carry on to the end."The old woman's voice fading into the night as she shuffles away must have been as tear-jerkingly effective on the radio as it undoubtedly was onstage.[99] The BBC files showing the location of the live broadcast of this program have disappeared from the BBC Written Archives at Caversham. However, when the Lucans appeared at the Tivoli Hull a week later, the *Hull Daily Mail* described them as "that well-known double act, Lucan and McShane who last week scored a hit at the Palladium."The fact that this was their West End Palladium debut, and that it was a hit is confirmed by the Palladium manager's report written on Monday, 15 August: "The first time we have had an act of this type here, but it goes very well indeed."[100] Newspaper listings of the broadcast only mention "The Match Seller," but the BBC's "program as broadcast" document, which is still at Caversham, contains the following further interesting information. "Sketch. Bridget O'Flynn with musical numbers, Sterling and King; Bridget O'Flynn, Where have you been. Belle of Barcelona." This supports my earlier contention that the Lucans must have known and performed this comedy duet, and derived their late 1920s stage name from it. "Belle of Barcelona" was a Spanish style "pasa doble" song made popular by Al Bowlly and Ray Noble's orchestra in 1931, and the Lucans may have performed it as a duet. (As we shall see shortly, the Lucans' second BBC broadcast also predates their films.)

In the light of these facts, the Lucans' appearance at the Royal Variety Performance in 1934 should perhaps be seen as not so much the beginning but the confirmation of a pre-existing rise towards national celebrity. It may well be that the success of this 1932 radio performance revived the couple's apparently flagging fortunes, and helped to bring them back, within a couple of years, from the margins to the very center of the British variety stage. At the Tivoli Hull on 30 August 1932, the *Daily Mail* reported "Chief honors go to Arthur Lucan and Kitty McShane, for what must be one of the funniest scenes presented in Hull for many a long day. We have seen them before in Hull and in consequence we marveled all the more at their ability to raise such an abundance of laughter." In September 1932 the Lucans were at the London Victoria Palace on a bill which included the Scottish comedian A. J. Power. *The Times*, on a rare kindly note reported that "the little sketch, The Old Match-seller, by Arthur Lucan and Kitty McShane, is a broad and hilarious burlesque, and A. J. Powers [*sic*] presents humor in a Scottish idiom." Michael Lyon now represented the Lucans, and was to do so almost to the bitter end.

After the Formby Christmas collaboration of 1931-1932, the Lucans renewed their links with the annual pantomime. From Christmas 1932 until their South African season in the winter of 1938, the couple toured each year in *Old Mother Hubbard*, with the exception of 1933-1934 when they toured in *Jack and the Beanstalk*, with Kitty as principal boy and Arthur as Dame. At Christmas 1932, the couple appeared in *Old Mother Hubbard* at the recently re-fur-bished Glasgow Empire, again with Power and Bendon with whom they had appeared in Glasgow pantomimes ten years earlier, and in Dublin in 1918. There exists a brief film clip from 1925 of Power and Bendon's comic routine with a pantomime horse which gives a glimpse of the kind of routine they may have performed with the Lucans.[101] In the *Edinburgh Evening News* on 13 December 1932, Arthur received an enthusiastic review for his Glasgow performance as Mother Hubbard, a review which also contained a possible fore-taste of the crockery smashing in "Bridget's Night Out."

For the children there are a grand furore of crockery 'casu-alties,' a charming fairy, broad comedy, and splendid work by performing animals . . . it was pleasing to note that both children and their elders were evidently enthusiastic about the artiste playing the name part of the show, their approbation being voiced by a small boy who, as the final curtain descended, shouted 'Good old Mother Hubbard.' A NOTABLE PERFORMANCE. If Mr. Arthur Lucan heard that small boy's praise he would assuredly know that his extraordinarily enthusiastic performance as the dame had been well worthwhile. It is certainly a long time since so joyous and energetic performance has been seen in such a role, or so much extravagant and amusing nonsense, with glimpses of pleasing pathos, have been crammed into so short a period."

This review is all the more gratifying given the fact that Arthur earned it at the Glasgow Empire, the dreaded "graveyard of English comics."

Throughout 1933 Lucan and McShane toured with "their now familiar Old Match-seller number," and the sketch received many encouraging reviews, along the lines of this one at the Empress Brixton.

Chief among those who seek to arouse hilarity are Arthur Lucan and Kitty McShane, whose Hibernian humor is always so insistent in its droll effect at Brixton. Their present offering is as funny as anything they have done, and Mr. Lucan's skill in comic character acting is pronounced; while Miss McShane has her own attractive way of seconding him.

In March, at the Finsbury Park Empire, they also presented a new sketch, "an entertaining little front cloth scena with Arthur Lucan in the role of a new nurse at a lunatic asylum, and Kitty McShane as the matron who pours cold water on the nurse's expectation of amorous adventures." Present-day good taste bids us draw a veil over this little item, except to note that here it is Kitty who, exceptionally, plays the disapproving matron and Arthur is the naughty nurse who may be related to the zany Nurse Riley who appear in *Old Mother Riley Joins Up* and *Old Mother Riley in Business*. In April they were on the bill at Brighton with Max Wall, who many years later told Michael Pointon how, through the walls of the lodgings he shared with them, he could hear Kitty "battering" her husband. When the couple returned to Hull in September, the *Daily Mail* noted the importance of the comic contrast between crabbed age and youth in their act which is now described as a "classic . . . without parallel."

It is more than a year since 'Dame' Arthur Lucan and his vivacious partner, Kitty McShane, last appeared in Hull with their 'classic' comedy act, and their re-appearance at the Tivoli Theater this week is extremely welcome. Last night's audiences were kept in an uproar by this strangely differing pair—indeed, many wisecracks were lost amid wholehearted laughter. The vast contrast between modern youth and poor old age is used to such advantage in words, and, coupled with such funny antics, that the result is a 'laughter-all-the-way' act without parallel in the variety world today.

In October "the great laughter-makers" were with their old friend Dennis Clarke at the Argyle, Birkenhead. At the end of the year at the Oldham Palace, Kitty was principal boy and Arthur was Dame Trott in *Jack and the Beanstalk*, advertised in *The Stage* as "without doubt the greatest touring pantomime ever produced, featuring Lucan and McShane, and 50 Artists, Fountains, and Flying Ballet." After Oldham the show moved to the Metropolitan Edgware Road and the Brixton Empress. This was Kitty's last appearance as a

Arthur Lucan and Kitty McShane, two Dublin artistes who will appear at the Palladium Theatre, London, on May 8.

Photo 12: Arthur and Kitty, *Irish Independent*, April 1934.

principal boy, and the couple's only appearance together in this pantomime. Arthur (alone) played Dame Trott in Gaston and Andrée's production at the Bristol Empire in 1952-1953.

In January and February 1934 the Lucans were back on the road and doing the rounds with "The Match-seller." On 19 February the Lucans were at the Palace Plymouth, and on 26 February they appeared at the Palladium where the manager's report was critical; "Arthur Lucan is a very fine 'Dame' but it is about time they presented some new material." They clearly took this advice to heart and in early April they did just that. It has been claimed that the new sketch "Bridget's Night Out" was first performed at Finsbury Park Empire. However, according to an interview with the Lucans in the *Hull Daily Mail* of 8 September 1934, the first performance was at the Holborn Empire where it was seen by the manager of the Palladium, George Black, on Whit Monday. This was clearly impossible as Whit Monday did not fall until 21 May.[102] In actual fact the Lucans were at Holborn from Monday 2 April, which was Easter Monday not Whit Monday, giving George Black ample time to see them and include them in the forthcoming Royal Command performance at the Palladium. The following week, 9-14 April at the Stratford Empire, the enthusiastic reviewer declared that "Arthur Lucan's study of an old Irishwoman is certainly among the best things in vaudeville." This was the very first review of "Bridget's Night Out" and it is amply supported by the managers' reports from Holborn, New Cross and Stratford East.

> One of the finest 'Dame' comedians in the business. Doing an excellent sketch, and gets roars of laughter from start to finish. Best he has ever done.

> A splendid broad comedy sketch. Arthur Lucan is wonderfully funny, getting shrieks of laughter out of practically nothing. Miss McShane would be better if she broadened her style.

> Lucan is an excellent dame comedian. His patter and antics create roars of laughter. He is ably assisted by Kitty McShane who is somewhat overdressed.

Then in mid-April, after almost a quarter of a century in the business, the Lucans received the telegram for which every music hall and variety artist longed:

"THEIR MAJESTIES KING GEORGE V AND QUEEN MARY COMMAND YOU TO APPEAR IN A PERFORMANCE TO BE GIVEN AT THE LONDON PALLADIUM ON 8 MAY 1934. GEORGE."

George was, of course, George Black, the impresario and manager of the Palladium, but Arthur enjoyed telling people that the telegram was signed by his old pal, George the fifth of England! Arthur must have remembered with pride that his official British debut as Arthur Lucan had been up in Carnoustie on 22 June 1911, the very day of his old pal's coronation! The roster of performers for the Royal Variety Performance was published in *The Times* on 25 April, two weeks before the show, but clearly the bringing together of the many acts (each of which had to receive royal approval) had begun weeks earlier.

The September 1934 interview in the *Hull Daily Mail* also included a curious anecdote concerning the creation of "Bridget's Night Out." This long forgotten anecdote, a version of which also appeared in the *Yorkshire Evening Post*, seems innocuous enough at first, but in the light of Max Wall's comments on "battered husbands," the story could well be a cover for something rather less amusing. It is worth comparing the two versions. First, the *Yorkshire Evening Post* of 8 September.

> At the time when they were doing their 'Match-seller sketch' . . . Arthur bought a new car, and Kitty took an immediate dislike to it; why, she did not know, except that she had a premonition that something unexpected would happen. They told me they were driving from one 'date' back to their home in London when Kitty remembered they had no meat for the dog which accompanies them on all their travels and, woman-like, began a quiet 'nag' about it. Arthur was slowing down to keep his eyes open for a butcher's shop when a tire burst, the car hit a tree—and Kitty came round to find herself lying on a slab in a butcher's shop, with meat all around her and a large piece of steak over an eye that was swelling rapidly. That accident lost them four weeks' work, but brought them their first holiday for many months. While Kitty was recovering Arthur wrote "Bridget's Night Out." And of all

the places to release them from a contract so that they could appear at the Command Performance, it was Dublin!

By the time the couple spoke to "John Humber" of the *Hull Daily Mail* at the end of the month, the anecdote had been considerably elaborated:

> Accident Leads to Fame. An accident near Grimsby which led to fame and fortune was described to me last night by Arthur Lucan and Kitty McShane, whose riotously funny domestic sketch at the Palace this week gained them a 'Royal Command' last May.
>
> In April they were motoring from Grimsby after a week's engagement, when an explosion and burst tire caused the car to skid and overturn. Miss McShane sustained a facial injury which rendered her hors de combat for a month or so and while they were convalescing at their home in London Arthur roughed out a new sketch. Their 'dates' had to be revised and it was a big test when they were given the opportunity to try out the new business so soon after the shock of the accident at no less a place than the Holborn Empire.
>
> Mr. George Black was present at the first performance on Whit Monday and along with a big audience acclaimed it as a winner. So much so that the next day he suggested it as an item for the Royal Command performance—if their Majesties approved. This followed and Hull has had the opportunity of seeing this week what caused the King and Queen to enjoy ecstasies of mirth.
>
> In private life Lucan and McShane are Mr. and Mrs. Lucan and both possess that volatile Irish temperament that has an indefinable charm. Arthur loves the quiet retreat of his suburban garden and it is here that he concocts those dame studies for which he stands unrivalled.

There are a number of oddities in this little tale. There is no record in *The Stage* of the Lucans' having visited Grimsby in early 1934, and as "Bridget's Night Out" was first given at Holborn on Monday 2

April, the accident, if there was an accident, must have taken place much earlier; as already noted, the only possible vacant weeks are in February. It seems perfectly possible that the Hull columnist (who was undoubtedly privy to unprintable gossip) is suggesting in his final paragraph that the Arthur who "loved the quiet retreat of his suburban garden" was finally goaded by Kitty's "volatile Irish temperament" into paying her back in kind, hence the black eye. The many critics who have pointed out that the Lucans' sketches were uncannily close to the reality of their lives, were even closer to the mark than they imagined.

All of Lucan and McShane's earlier sketches had needed only the simplest of staging, just a couple of props in front of the house tabs or a painted flat. "Bridget's Night Out" necessitated the building of a full stage set representing the interior of Mrs. O'Flynn's kitchen with a dresser loaded with china, a rear door through which Kitty made her entrance, and a stage left staircase. Thanks to the version of this sketch preserved in the film *Stars on Parade*, and widely available to view today, a detailed description of the set and synopsis of the action are now superfluous. A full list of the other acts in the royal program would mean little to today's general reader, and the specialist can find all the details online at the official website of the Entertainment Artistes Benevolent Fund. The event was judged by all involved to be another resounding success, and the following morning the Lucans were delighted to find that they were singled out for special mention in a newspaper review headed,

> THE KING LAUGHS HEARTILY . . . Their Majesties were particularly amused with a domestic comedy sketch by Arthur Lucan and Kitty McShane. A big laugh came from the Royal box when Arthur Lucan, dressed as an old-fashioned mother awaiting her daughter's return from a dance remarked, 'She went out last night, she isn't home yet, and now it's tomorrow. I would make myself a cup of tea if only I could find my corkscrew.'

The famous climax of this sketch involved the smashing of vast amounts of crockery which littered the Palladium stage at the end of the act. The crockery consisted of unglazed and therefore more easily smashed seconds which Arthur obtained for many years from a Stoke-on-Trent china factory.[103] The impresario George Black, who also compered the show, remembered that the Lucans' act was followed by the gentler verbal comedy of Elsie and Doris Waters, who performed in front of the closed house tabs. According to Black, poor "Gert and Daisy" were virtually inaudible above the noise made by the stagehands as they swept up the smashed crockery just behind the curtain.

Prestigious though it was, the Royal Variety Performance did not suddenly catapult the Lucans to a new level of stardom. They were already well known and appreciated all over the country, and they simply took their new sketch on the road along with "The Old Match-seller." Their old friend Dennis Clarke was so proud of his protégés that he gave them star billing in huge capital letters at the Argyle Birkenhead on 28 May. "The Royal Command Favorites LUCAN AND MCSHANE" and this remained their usual billing around the country throughout the 1930s. But in August, when they gave "The Old Match-seller" at the Palladium, the *Times'* critic was distinctly unimpressed. "There were possibilities in the sketch by Mr. Arthur Lucan and Miss Kitty McShane, *The Old Match-seller*, and it might have been quite effective had it been cut to a quarter of its length." After praising the precision of effect and competent technique of Radio New York's "American Stars of the Air" the reviewer ends with what was clearly another dig at the Lucans. "A knowledge of limitations is sometimes a valuable and an entertaining possession." The Palladium manager's report was a good deal less snooty: "'The Old Match-seller.' Had a very good reception with their old act." He mentions "their old act" because they had performed their "new act" at the Palladium on 30 July, a performance hitherto overlooked but recorded by the manager. "Robust comedy helped out by slapstick methods, cleverly worked up to a good finish."

In October when they played "The Old Match-seller" at the Holborn Empire, they were well down the bill, supporting "America's Queen of Vaudeville, Belle Baker" and Joe Loss and his Kit-Kat band. Nevertheless, the Royal Variety Performance of May 1934 represents the culmination of the Lucans' long hard slog towards full recognition by their peers in the profession; the affection of the public they had long since acquired. Dubliners first saw "Bridget's Night Out" at the Olympia Theater in October. A new high point was reached at Christmas 1934 when Arthur's original script for *Old Mother Hubbard* was premiered at the Liverpool Pavilion; according to an advertisement in *The Stage*, the pantomime broke all records, including George Formby's, before moving to the Palace at Blackpool. The Pavilion advertisement proudly boasted "The Pavilion Theater Liverpool scores again, breaking all records with 94,000 paid admissions in sixteen days with LUCAN & MCSHANE in 'Mother Hubbard.' 'There's Money besides Smoke in the North.'"

Another early radio appearance by the Lucans which has escaped critics' notice was the fiftieth radio broadcast from the Argyle Theater Birkenhead on 14 March 1935, for their old friend Dennis Clarke.[104] Over the next two years the nocturnal antics of Mrs. O'Flynn and her wayward daughter Bridget were seen in almost every theater in Britain, and the crockery smashing sketch was incorporated into the Lucan's pantomime *Old Mother Hubbard*, where critics concurred that it was not at all out of place, as the sketch clearly had its origins in a kind of pantomime "slop scene." *The Liverpool Echo* had something quite remarkable to say of Arthur's performance at the Liverpool Empire in August 1935.

> His acting was something quite outside the range of the ordi-
> nary 'dame' comedian. Mr. Lucan does not, of course, play the
> part 'straight,' but he never gets completely out of character. It
> is no small achievement thus successfully to combine what is
> in method and in effect, realistic acting with excursions into
> slapstick comedy.

When in the same year Butcher's Film Service decided to pre-serve on film some of the best of the old music hall and variety turns, the enormously popular sketch "Bridget's Night Out" was an obvious choice for inclusion in *Stars on Parade*, taking up far more running time than any other act in the film. Oswald Mitchell provided a screenplay loosely linking the disparate items, and he co-directed with Challis N. Sanderson. The sketch was filmed at the old Stoll stu-dios at Cricklewood towards the end of 1935, and the sound recordist was Lance Comfort in his first, but not last, involvement with the antics of Lucan and McShane. The completed film was released in January 1936. This is without a doubt the event which signaled the most profound change, both for good and ill, in the lives of Lucan and McShane. "Bridget's Night Out" is the first completely preserved example of Arthur's script-writing and the couple's performance style. This is often wrongly described as the first appearance of Old Mother Riley, a mistake reinforced by the opening credit "Arthur Lucan as Old Mother Riley," but since Con West did not invent the name until 1937, this must have been a later re-editing of *Stars on Parade*, added to capitalize on the new character's popularity. But Arthur was still Mrs. O'Flynn, and Kitty, as in the later film *Kathleen Mavourneen*, was still "Bridget Mary Josephine O'Flynn."

By any yardstick, "Bridget's Night Out" is a *tour de force* of stage-craft, and must have been the envy of every actor, comic or straight, who saw it at the time, and more than a few since. What makes it all the more remarkable is that it is the work of a music-hall comic and pantomime dame who, at the age of fifty, was performing for the very first time in an empty studio in front of two fixed cameras. For someone who was used to "working" an audience and riding the waves of their response, this must have been a bizarre and unnerving experience. Commenting on the sketch on YouTube, a perceptive critic points out "Mentions of this being unfunny are not taking into account that this was a stage act, filmed here with no audience. They're going through the actions as they would on stage without the interaction that would give them pace and comic timing. Also, watching on film we don't get the cues and support from the other people watching." This is particularly apparent when Mother does her bedtime strip tease to a minute and a half of total silence; in the theater this would have been punctuated with giggles and bursts of laughter, reaching a climax at the line about her uncooperative corsets—"Ooh, if only I had a spanner!"—which always brought the house down. Moreover, although the fourteen-minute sketch is technically a two-hander, the first six minutes are in reality a one-woman soliloquy which runs the gamut of emotions from fear and anxiety to anger and despair, in a way of which Winnie, in Samuel Beckett's *Happy Days*, might have been proud. Mother's genuine anxiety for her daughter's safety prompted one critic to affirm that, "Old Mother Riley [*sic*] waiting for Bridget is every mother who's ever had a daughter go out on a date." Unlike today's viewers, contemporary audiences understood that in a still morally rigid society, if a girl "fell" she could be a "fallen woman" for life, and there is more than one suggestion in the comic banter that Mother knew only too well what she was talking about!

But the climax of the sketch, the smashing of every plate in the house, always brought the house down in more ways than one, and for the "industrial classes" in the audience it seemed to provide a form of catharsis akin to symbolically breaking every rule in the book. At one point Mother is left with only the handle of a large jug in her hand, and Nigel Ellacott insists that, "The moment when he realizes, not daring to look, holding just the handle as he feels for the non-existent jug, is pure theatrical magic."

Arthur told a very funny story about the filming of "Bridget's Night Out," but the story also reveals his powers of self-control and his cleverness as an improviser. Just after Mother points out to Bridget that she went out in January and now it's March, Arthur accidentally fell backwards through the door. This was not in the script, and if one looks carefully at Arthur's face as he falls one sees genuine surprise. When he stands up he starts to "corpse" just a little but recovers and improvises with the line, "You'll pay for that! You'll pay for that!" To give Kitty McShane her due, she doesn't miss a beat with her bit of improvised dialogue, "Pay for what?" which then allows Arthur a magnificent recovery with the brilliantly appropriate lines, "Chuckin' me out of me own house! You're worse than your father ever knew how to be. *He* never chucked me out of me own house ... Perhaps he never thought of it!" They then get back on script at "Staying out till this hour of night ... I want an explanation." Although it was an accident, it looked so good, and they carried it off so well, that Oswald Mitchell decided to leave it in the film. Not only that, but it was subsequently added to the stage sketch.

Towards the end of 1935 the Lucans bought their first house, a typical 1930s semi-detached in Randall Avenue, Dollis Hill. They proudly described their new house, which Arthur said was known as "Kittykot," in an interview in the *Hull Daily Mail* in December 1935, when they opened in Arthur's pantomime, *Old Mother Hubbard* at the Palace Theater. The newspaper described them as "the famous Royal Command Artistes who are to appear as Daydream and Mother Hubbard," and published a photograph of the couple visiting Santa at the Hull Co-op's Christmas Grotto. On board the "S.S. CO-OP" Kitty is looking rather glum and Arthur has a lifebuoy slung around his neck; Arthur appears in ordinary day clothes, not always in costume, as is frequently asserted. "Arthur Lucan" said the *Daily Mail*, "with his convulsive limbs and homely apparel should be an ideal Mother Hubbard," and the pantomime's reviewer agreed heartily. The detailed cast-list in the review gives us a distant glimpse into the forgotten world of Arthur Lucan's imaginative pantomime scripts.

> If you let the season slip by without seeing "Old Mother Hubbard" at the Palace you will miss the treat of a lifetime. Whether you are a tiny tot or a gouty old grandfather you cannot help laughing at the antics of Mother Hubbard. The title role could fall on no better shoulders than those of Arthur Lucan, who lets us see that Mother Hubbard was a gay old dame, full of pep. Then there is Kitty McShane who brings distinct charm to bear in part as Daydream, Mother Hubbard's daughter. Mother Hubbard and her daughter have several tiffs, but matters reach a climax when there is a wholesale breaking of crockery in the family home. The kitchen sketch was given before the King and Queen recently, and those who see it will readily appreciate why it was such an outstanding success on the Royal Command bill.
>
> How Daydream Hubbard rose from washerwoman's daughter to Princess Snowcrest is delightfully told in twelve scenes which take us back to the days of the gnomes, elves, fairies and demons. Myrtle Kingsley makes a princely lover for Daydream, while Jimmie Pullin brings regal prestige to bear as King of Snowcrest. Alyosha Tomchinsky, Fred Raymond, Eddie Harrison and Dod Earl lend dignity and color as Fee, Fie, Foo, Fum, the King's bodyguard; Fred Brand is Wakii-Wakii (The cannibal King) and A. Binnie "Kookie" (the Cannibal King's chef).
>
> Marcelle and Sills, who act as Mother Hubbard's dog and Pongo the clown, delightfully give specialty acts, other specialties being supplied by Alexis and his Honolulu boys, a fine orchestral combination, the ten Bertram Babes and the Fourteen Maison Girls.

Whether you are looking at the local washhouse burlesque, the dazzling appointments of the King's banqueting hall, or the carnivorous savages on Treasure Island, there is always something to keep you entranced.

After a highly successful run in Hull, the show closed on 4 January and moved to Wolverhampton Hippodrome and the Liverpool Pavilion. It then transferred to the Hulme Hippodrome in Manchester, where on 30 January, it received a brief review in *The Stage*. At the end of the pantomime's two-week run at Hulme, the Lucans were listed in *The Stage* to appear in variety at the Middlesbrough Empire on Monday, 10 February. But they did not get to Middlesbrough. It was at the Hulme Hippodrome at the end of January or during the first week of February that Arthur, who at fifty-one still engaged in heavy physical knockabout, suffered serious internal injuries when he had an accidental heavy fall onstage.[105] In intense pain, he managed to finish the show (at Kitty's insistence, according to her sister Annie) but he was then rushed to hospital. At that point the names Lucan and McShane disappear from *The Stage* for over three months. Steve King was unhelpfully vague about the nature of Arthur's injuries, which he described as Arthur "unfortunately rupturing himself." There is of course no such medical condition; the colloquialism usually refers to an inguinal hernia, but such a relatively minor ailment would certainly not have required six weeks of hospitalization or a ten-week absence from the stage. Steve King's account appears to have come from Annie Carroll's rather muddled and incomplete reminiscences from later years. Her memory of the word "rupture" suggests that Arthur suffered serious internal injury. In accidents and heavy falls, any of the major internal organs can be pierced or torn (ruptured) with life-threatening consequences, resulting in death if not quickly diagnosed and treated. In view of Arthur's protracted convalescence, some such serious injury does seem likely, and Annie Carroll herself did unwittingly provide another curious clue to the gravity of Arthur's condition. In the late 1940s, when Kitty was flaunting her affair with her stage boyfriend Billy Breach, Annie declared that Arthur would have been spared much suffering if only he had died at the time of the onstage accident. Annie was a very traditional and superstitious

Irish Catholic and would never have spoken in such terms if she had not believed that Arthur's life had been in real danger back in 1936.

But Arthur did not die. After an absence of twelve weeks, he returned to the stage on Monday 4 May 1936. According to an item of "Variety Gossip" in *The Stage* on 30 April, "Following Arthur Lucan's long illness, from which he has now happily recovered, Lucan and McShane will be seen again in variety next week. They are due at the Hackney Empire on Monday." Later in May, when the couple appeared at the Holborn Empire, the reviewer noted that "Arthur Lucan gives proof of his complete recovery from his recent illness." Throughout June and July they are "at their best" at Glasgow, Blackpool, the London Palladium and Oxford, where "they presented another episode in the life of Bridget which they do so well." In August they are at Ardwick Green Manchester, from where they announce in *The Stage* the holding of auditions for the cast of their next pantomime. In September they are in Edinburgh and Birmingham, in October in Hull and New Cross, and at the Holborn Empire with Sophie Tucker. At the age of fifty-two Arthur was certainly giving proof of his resilience as an old trouper.

Yet one cannot help asking just how complete Arthur's recovery was, or wondering if he ever did fully regain all his old his agility and self-confidence. As we have already noted, the film *Stars on Parade* was released in 1936 but the sketch "Bridget's Night Out" had been filmed in 1935 some months before Arthur's accident. So it may be that this remarkable document, which is the first record preserved on film of "Lucan's boisterous energy and gift for verbal comedy" is also the first and last to show him at his physical best.[106] Sue Harper, author of *Women in British Cinema*, certainly seems to sense this when she refers to the filmed sketch as "an interesting index of Lucan's original style." Friends of the Lucans from those years told their granddaughter Marylyn (who told me) that by the time Lucan and McShane embarked on the Riley films they were already past their best. "They were still funny,' said Marylyn, "but people told me they had been even funnier!" This view is echoed by Brian Murphy and Slim Ingram, and by an online blogger, Matthew Coniam, who confirms Marylyn's view of the films; "Most people tend to ignorantly dismiss them all, but Lucan was a true comic great . . . apparently even the best of the films aren't a patch on what he was like on stage, which is usually the way."

If Arthur Lucan had in fact died in February 1936, all that would remain of him today would be the fifteen minutes of "Bridget's Night Out," "caught on film," as the history books would have told us, "shortly before his fatal accident in February 1936." In August 2012, in a letter to me in which he shared some of his own and his brother's theatrical reminiscences, the actor-director Vivyan Ellacott unknowingly put his finger on something which almost became a hideous reality. "For that classic sketch [Bridget] alone," wrote Vivyan, "Arthur Lucan deserves his place in the galaxy of the best ever comic character actors."

Vivyan Ellacott's assessment of Arthur's gifts seems to have been shared back in 1936 by producer John Argyle of Argyle Talking Pictures. He offered the Lucans a small cameo role in an Irish musical comedy, *Kathleen Mavourneen*, to be directed in the autumn at Welwyn Studios by Norman Lee. The plot of this rather convoluted but warm-hearted Irish domestic drama, which was released in January 1937, need not detain us here as the Lucans play no part in it whatsoever; they were merely one of a number of specialty acts booked to take part in a kind of *Fleadh Cheoil*, a village fair of singing and dancing, possibly included to enhance the film's appeal to Irish-American audiences when it was released in the States in 1938 (the Lucans' only successful foray into that market). It has been erroneously asserted that the film's screenplay is based on the 1890 novel *Kathleen Mavourneen* by Clara Mulholland, but the film and novel are entirely unconnected. The IMDb online database also wrongly names the Lucans' roles as Mrs. Riley and Kitty Riley. The daughter is explicitly named in the film as "Bridget Mary Josephine O'Flynn," which means that Arthur is still going by the name Mrs. O'Flynn, which he had first used in 1929. In *Kathleen Mavourneen* the Lucans took part in two separate sketches, one more successful that the other. The first seems to be an amusing adaptation of one of their stage routines, with the irate mother waiting for her flighty daughter to turn up. When she does Bridget is berated for "chasin' the men" to which she retorts "Sure, 'tis the men chase me!" Bridget asserts that her mother was never chased by men but mother claims that "one man chased me half way round the world . . . If he'd caught me he'd have killed me!" Arthur and Kitty play this scene entirely surrounded by the people of the Irish village, and they weave in and out of the laughing crowd with great natural ease and comic assurance. I believe that this little scene proved to film-makers that Arthur could handle crowds on film as well as he had been doing it in the theater for over twenty years. The second sketch involved some rather unconvincing business about Bridget having a sore leg and being unable to enter the step-dancing competition; this is brought to a merciful conclusion when mother simply steals the prize cup and runs off with it. This could have worked as a live pantomime or circus clown gag, but here it outstays its welcome.

The Lucans' 1936-1937 touring pantomime was once again Arthur's version of *Old Mother Hubbard*, "devised and staged by Lucan and McShane" at Lewisham, and including a version of "Bridget's Night Out." Kitty in the leading role of Daydream this time becomes the bride of Prince Anthracite, son of Old King Cole, another of Kitty's stage weddings, complete with "many artistic costumes." Members of the cast from the 1935-1936 *Mother Hubbard* re-joined the company and reprised their roles but Arthur also added new comic characters including "Watt Knott, Why Nott, Jack Pott and Krac Pott." Among the many musical numbers was Noel Gay's "Let's Have A Tiddley at the Milk Bar." The lavish show, with forty dancers and a ten-piece jazz band, received a long and enthusiastic review for its originality and the magnificent visual effects of the opening winter snowballing scene, the Cannibal Island, the Fairy Bower and the Palace of Gold finale. In February, after the pantomime, the Lucans took a holiday in Tangier, from where Arthur took the trouble to send a letter and photograph to an admirer.

Just a year earlier Arthur had been at death's door and the future of the act was in the balance. Now the Lucans had made one film and were hoping for another. Throughout 1937 they continued to tour with both "Bridget's Night Out" and "The Old Match-seller," but in spite of their new popularity on screen as well as stage, some critics remained unconvinced. When in March 1937 they appeared in a show called *George Ahoy* (not Formby) at the Holborn Empire, the critic of *The Times* described the show as an attempt to combine a musical comedy "with the more robust turns of the purer and simpler music-hall." He judged the attempt to be less than successful and singled out the Lucans.

> In the second half of the program, however, the scenes go on too long, and what might have been—and had every promise of being—an amusing sketch, 'The Old Match-seller,' in which Mr. Arthur Lucan and Miss Kitty McShane took part, was allowed to run down instead of being stopped at its zenith. Still, *George Ahoy* is proof that the music-hall has a great many shots left in its locker.[107]

The *Times'* critic had said almost exactly the same thing about the same sketch at the Palladium in August 1934. On his last point at least, the critic was uncannily accurate. In fact the music-hall had a most unexpected shot left in its locker, a shot which was to reverberate through the theaters and cinemas of Britain, and the furthest outposts of Empire, for another twenty years.

The Birth of Old Mother Riley

Undoubtedly encouraged by John Argyle, Butcher Hope-Bell Productions now offered Lucan and McShane a full-length film in which they would star as the mother and daughter characters they had evolved onstage and had "screen-tested" in a couple of filmed cameos. The producers of the low-budget comedy for Butcher's Films were Norman Hope-Bell and F.W. Barker, with Oswald Mitchell directing. John Argyle contributed the storyline and the screenplay was entrusted to Con West, a skilled old hand at comic writing for stage and screen and later, with Edwin Adeler, biographer of Fred Karno. West, who clearly thought very highly of Arthur, went on to work as writer, story or screenplay on no fewer than nine of the Lucan-McShane films, and to him must go the honor of having "invented" the name Old Mother Riley. West had known the Lucans onstage as Mrs. O'Flynn and her daughter Bridget, and he probably pointed out that as a film title these names would invite unwelcome comparison with the Murray and Stanley comic duet "Bridget O'Flynn" in the Lucans' repertoire. Furthermore, by a curious coincidence, just two years earlier, Dorothy Vernon, who was to play Aggie Sparks the landlady, had played the role of a Bridget O'Flynn in a film entitled *Father O'Flynn*. The possible sources for Con West's choice of the name Mother Riley and its serious cultural implications will be discussed at length in the second section of this study. The new film, simply entitled *Old Mother Riley*, was made at Cricklewood in a matter of weeks on a slender budget, and released in August 1937.

By this time, the two great working-class comics of the 1930s, Gracie Fields and George Formby (praised as the "male Gracie Fields!") had long since successfully moved from stage to film; Gracie already had eight highly popular and lucrative films to her credit, and George had six. Others who had worked with the Lucans on the variety circuit in the 1930s, including Ernie Lotinga, Will Hay and Max Miller were also enjoying successful careers in the cinema, thanks to, as John Fisher put it, "the basic social identity they shared with the bulk of their audiences . . . with their origins [and] their attitudes firmly rooted in the working class." The *British* working class that is, whether it be northern or cockney. And now, into this well-established genre of British working-class film comedy, there burst a fake Irish woman played by a man from Lincolnshire, admittedly well known and loved as a panto dame at Christmas, with a daughter played by his wife, a woman who was on the wrong side of forty and reputed in the business to be something of a harridan; and she, at least, was very, very Irish. On 21 June the *Irish Press* with evident pride announced the couple's latest success in England. Although all of Dublin must have known that Kitty McShane's husband Arthur was English, he is emphatically described (twice) as a "Dublin Man," in the news item which also contains some rather odd information.

> Items from London. Dublin Man's Distinction. Arthur Lucan, a Dublin man, who is well known on the variety stage, is the first man to take a woman's part in a full-length feature film. He plays the title role in Old Mother Riley now being made at the Stoll Studios, Cricklewood, London. The director, Oswald Mitchell, tested several leading women character actresses for the part but could not find a suitable exponent. Then he gave Mr. Lucan a test and a contract followed. Mr. Lucan has been taking women's parts in vaudeville for fifteen years.

A month later in July 1937 when the Lucans appeared at the Theater Royal in Dublin they were again described as "a Dublin pair who have made a name for themselves."

Cultural historians have discussed at great length the representation of the Irish in theater and film at this time, and the ambiguous response of the Irish themselves to this representation. James Chapman sums it up thus:

> On the one hand, caricatures of brawling drunken 'Oirishmen' were so commonplace in the 1930s that the Dublin Evening Mail could claim with some legitimacy that 'no race has suffered more at the hands of American and English film and stage productions than has ours.' However, this sort of response ignores the fact that the Irish themselves had been complicit in the creation of stereotypes and have even, in certain circumstances, celebrated them.[108]

Complicity and celebration would seem to characterize the attitude which the Irish (by and large) decided to adopt towards the imminent creation in England of Old Mother Riley. The complex issue of Old Mother Riley and her Irishness will be discussed later in greater detail. For the moment it is worth noting that for political, social, and economic reasons, the year 1937 was one of many moments in Anglo-Irish relations when the frail façade of harmless singing and dancing "Oirishness" was seriously threatened with collapse. But it was at this very same moment that perhaps the biggest piece of "Oirish" malarkey ever invented, the film *Old Mother Riley*, was launched in cinemas across Britain; and it took them by storm. So great was the unexpected popularity of this in many ways mediocre film that it was re-issued as *The Return of Old Mother Riley* and *The Original Old Mother Riley* in 1940, 1941, and yet again in 1949, albeit with a 931ft. cut. Even more remarkable was the fact that this somewhat shaky start was the beginning of a series of fifteen films, a series which outlasted the offerings of Formby, Fields and Hay, continued long after the war, and was only brought to an abrupt end by the death of Arthur in 1954, and the cancellation of Mother Riley's eagerly awaited *Trip to Mars*. Arthur himself was by no means convinced that the first film would be a hit. On 31 August he wrote rather diffidently to screenwriter Con West:

My dear Con, May I thank you for the intimation that Old Mother Riley pictures looks like being a success according to your notice in this week's *Era*. Also accept my thanks for your appreciation of my endeavor to make it so. But for your notice I might not ever have known anything at all about it.

May it mean a lot to you in your future film stories; and also help British pictures to win a little more support. Very kind regards, Yours sincerely, Arthur Lucan.[109]

It has been estimated that the first ten Riley films cost just £270,000 to produce and earned more than £780,000, the equivalent of many millions in present-day money. But the first film, with an entire budget of a couple of thousand pounds, did not make the Lucans rich overnight. Back on the variety circuit, Arthur and Kitty were still billed as Lucan and McShane, just one successful act among many on the variety bills. At Christmas 1937 they again starred as Mother and Daydream in *Old Mother Hubbard*, playing to packed houses at the Leeds Empire where their "kitchen scene" was described in *The Yorkshire Post* as "one of the cleverest things in pantomime, and deserves all the recognition it commands nightly." The Empire manager's report was somewhat sharper and made a clear distinction between the talents of Lucan and McShane. "Arthur Lucan carries the whole weight of this pantomime. Kitty McShane has a fair appearance, small voice, and is a poor dancer; good feed for Lucan." After two weeks the pantomime moved on to the Sunderland Empire and the Liverpool Pavilion. The manager at Sunderland echoed his colleague at Leeds; "Kitty McShane works efficiently with Lucan. Lucan is excellent and carries the whole show."

On 28 March 1938 the Lucans were at the top of the bill at the Empire Middlesbrough, and their photograph appeared next to their names in huge red type. The poster also announced Arthur's latest sketch. "Welcome return of the Middlesbrough favorites, ARTHUR LUCAN AND KITTY MCSHANE in their latest Comedy Scena 'The Step Washer.'" On 16 May 1938 the Lucans returned to the Palladium in a bill headed by George Formby and Vic Oliver. *The Stage* reported that "Arthur Lucan and Kitty McShane are here with their latest sketch 'The Step Washer' which causes great laughter and gives Mr. Lucan the opportunity to introduce one of those energetic and amusing dame performances of which he is so clever an exponent, and Miss McShane a chance to prove her special talent." At Finsbury Park in June Arthur received special praise in *The Stage*. "Hilarity is general during the funny sketch given with ludicrous effect by Lucan and McShane, for in 'Bridget's Night Out' there is something more than crockery-smashing, Arthur Lucan's skill as a character comedian being always notable, and Kitty McShane seconding him in her own effective way." At the beginning of August the Lucans made another hitherto unrecorded appearance at the Palladium, where the manager noted, "Very good reception. The sketch, though familiar, gets as many laughs as ever." The following week at the Liverpool Empire "working the Old Matchseller better than ever, full of laughs," Arthur is described as "a vital character comedian." On 19 September 1938, the Palladium manager again reported, "Familiar though it may be, 'Bridget's Night Out' is still getting continuous laughter."

The following week at Holborn and Stratford the managers reported, "Doing their 'Matchseller' cameo that causes roars of laughter all through. Arthur Lucan is certainly one of the best 'Dames' in the business."

"Great act, admirable talent of a clever performer, still creates excellent laughter and the usual big applause from a delighted audience."

Some performances at the Palladium and Holborn Empire had to be cancelled because of Arthur's "indisposition."

Shortly after this, work began on *Old Mother Riley in Paris*, Con West's second script for Butcher's Films, produced, and directed this time with far greater assurance, by Oswald Mitchell. Filming took place far from Paris, at Nettlefold Studios, Walton-on-Thames, and on location at Gatwick airport. *Old Mother Riley in Paris* was released in November 1938. Coming as it did at a time of great political uncertainty and public anxiety, the film provided a light-hearted take on spies (Madame Zero played by Magda Kun) and foreigners in general but especially the excitable and untrustworthy French. The film, during which Mother Riley escapes from a French prison, performs (unwillingly) a Montmartre Apache dance, and is finally decorated by the French before returning home with enormous bottles of champagne smuggled in her skirts, proved to be an even bigger box-office success than its predecessor.

At the Argyle Birkenhead in November 1938 the name Old Mother Riley was associated for the first time with the Lucans' stage act. They are described in *The Stage* as "making a big hit in 'Old Mother Riley, The Step Washer.' The comic element is uproariously funny as usual, and the touch of pathos imparted at the last moment is rendered with charm by the irresistible Kitty." The Lucans also headed the finale, "with a cameo comedy in their own amusing style." At the end of 1938, possibly because Arthur remained frail after his accident in 1936, the Lucans sailed off to South Africa where they toured in the pantomime *Aladdin*, with Arthur as the Widow Twankey and Kitty as her daughter in barely disguised versions of their stage sketches. The *Johannesburg Sunday Times* described the show as "one of the funniest pantomimes ever seen in South Africa." The couple stayed to soak up the sun until March 1939. On their return *The Stage* reported that they were "back in town, following a successful tour of South Africa. They tell us they have had a marvelous time ... and they will shortly be busy on another of the 'Old Mother Riley' series." After just two films the press already speaks of "a series."

At the New Theater Northampton in May 1939, the Lucans met a fourteen-year-old lad who ran errands for his uncle, who was the theater manager. The lad's name was Cyril Ingram. He told the Lucans that he wanted to be in show business when he grew up and Arthur wished him well. Fifteen years later Cyril (known as Slim) Ingram was Arthur's last company manager and was at his side when he collapsed in the wings at the Tivoli Theater Hull. Early in 1939 the Lucans made their third and last Riley film for Butcher's, *Old Mother Riley MP*. The film was released in August and was a huge box-office success, with Mother Riley taking the "Mother of Parliaments" by storm, a theme we shall discuss further in the second part of this study. By the time of the film's release, John Baxter had already enticed the Lucans to join him at British National Films and writer Con West came with them. It was clear to the establishment that war was rapidly approaching and that the media had a duty to remind the nation that all ranks and conditions, women included, had a role to play in the impending conflict. And so Mother Riley led the way and was among the very first comic artists to "join up." The Lucans' move to British National was even noted as far afield as

Photo 13: Old Mother Riley and her daughter Kitty, 1940. Bernie Jones

Australia, where its implications were discussed (rather belatedly) in the *Perth Sunday Times* on 17 March 1940.

Established British music hall comedians have a habit of sneaking up on the British film industry suddenly and sur-prising them. Will Hay and George Formby did it. Now it is the turn of Lucan and McShane, better known jointly as Old Mother Riley. Arthur Lucan is old Mother Riley of the halls, grey-haired, volatile, feather-bonneted beldame, with emphatic hands and collapsible feet; Kitty McShane (in private life Mrs. Lucan these 12 years [27, in fact]) is Old Mother Riley's daughter. They stand at this moment just where George Formby did three years ago. It may be up to the skies, it may be back to the halls. Old Mother Riley has made three films at a modest average cost of between £10,000 and £12,000 apiece. One of them has already booked to £33,000 worth of business, a profit calculated to make the film company laugh heartily as well. This week Old Mother Riley embarks on her biggest screen outing for a new com-pany, British National, in 'Old Mother Riley Joins Up.' The film will cost nearly £24,000, which puts her up in the Max Miller and George Formby class.

Throughout the early 1930s, theater managers' report cards show that the Lucans were earning an average of £50 per week. By 1938 this had risen to around £100. Then, thanks to the success of the films, the Lucans' rapidly improving financial situation allowed them to buy a much grander house. Late in 1939 they bought 11 Forty Lane, Wembley, a handsome double-fronted brick house on three floors with a large garden. It had an impressive double staircase which Tommy Trinder said reminded him of a Fred Astaire film. It also had a back staircase which Roy Rolland said allowed Kitty to say goodnight to you downstairs and then frighten you to death on the upstairs landing! The house was tastefully furnished, and Arthur was proud of his collections of antique furniture, fine china and oriental rugs. Kitty's sister Annie had married Bert Carroll, who had worked for the comedian Jimmy O'Shea, and the couple came to live and work at Forty Lane. For the Lucans, in spite of the war, things were looking good.

Chapter Seven: Old Mother Riley goes to War on stage screen and radio 1939-1945

Robb Wilton's most famous sketch began, "The day war broke out, my Missus said to me, she looked at me and she said, 'What good are you?'"

Britain declared war on Germany on Sunday, 3 September. The next day the Lucans were booked to appear at the Holborn Empire but all public places of entertainment were closed by order. In the course of the following two weeks, the government realized it had overreacted, and gradually cinemas and theaters were allowed to re-open; with remarkably little disruption (apart from direct bomb hits), they remained open throughout the war, helping to boost morale. Most appropriately, one of the first new films to appear after the re-opening of the cinemas was *Old Mother Riley Joins Up*.

In October 1939, at the Birmingham Hippodrome, the Lucans shared a bill with rising star Tommy Trinder who led the audience in a rousing rendition of "We're Going to Hang out the Washing on the Siegfried Line." Throughout the autumn they continued to tour "Bridget's Night Out" with the press praising "Mr. Lucan's gifts as a character actor and humorist." At Christmas they returned to a favorite haunt, the Liverpool Pavilion, with Arthur's latest panto-mime, *The Old Woman Who Lived in a Shoe*, "devised by Arthur Lucan" but "presented by KMS." The pantomime was notable for one of the earliest appearances of Jimmy Clitheroe, aged eighteen but looking eight, who went on to play Boots in the Lucans' next film, *Old Mother Riley in Society*. After praising the pantomime in general terms, *The Stage* reserved special comment for Arthur.

> Mr. Lucan as the Old Lady of the title is a host in him-self. There is no end to his fund of humor, and his efforts range over a field so wide that they include adventures in the market (where he endeavors to buy a suit for 'the youngest,' making scouse (a local delicacy) for the lodgers, taking the family to New Brighton (there are many local allusions in the show), or rising to the august heights of presiding at the

local police court. In all his work he is most ably assisted by Kitty McShane who, as a delightful Bo-Peep, captivates the dashing Robin Hood of Elsie Keen.

After receiving many glowing reviews, the show closed at the end of January 1940. The Lucans then went back on the road but no longer as one act among many on a random variety bill. The great American stage musicals of the 1940s and 1950s were preserved for posterity in memorable filmed versions; the Lucans now did the reverse—they produced the stage show of the films!

Old Mother Riley goes to the Theater

In the spring of 1940 the name Old Mother Riley at last appeared on theater bills and became the title of the Lucan's own touring show, "presented by Miss Kitty McShane." Four Riley films were doing excellent business all around the country, boosting morale with their outlandish and ramshackle mixture of slapstick, pathos and unashamedly patriotic propaganda; a fifth film was about to be released and a sixth was in preparation. For years the public had known Arthur's act with Kitty simply as Lucan and McShane. Now with their rebranding in the films their agent Michael Lyon saw that the stage act needed to capitalize on the film-star status of Old Mother Riley and her daughter Kitty, rather than Lucan and McShane. According to Slim Ingram, Lyon assured them that they could command £1,000 per week if they would make the change. This must have involved negotiation with the film companies and the writer Con West who had invented the Riley name for the first film and retained copyright of his scripts. The films and the stage show would obviously be of mutual benefit to the brand, and so at the Nottingham Empire on 18 March 1940 a completely new show was named *Old Mother Riley Comes to Nottingham*. Although the show featured many independent specialty acts, they were all drawn together by a narrative thread involving Old Mother Riley, her daughter Kitty and their friends and neighbors. Arthur's own earlier material such as the Matchseller, Bridget, and the Step Washer could of course be included, but the scripts of the films, being in copyright, were not included, apart from scenes and gags written by Arthur himself. However, the films and the stage show did have one major thing in common: Kitty had a boyfriend. Parts of the Old Match-seller sketch in which Kitty appeared as a jilted bride (not the Match-seller's daughter) were used, allowing Mother Riley to rail against the perfidy of men. But whereas in the earlier onstage act, the old woman and the jilted fiancée had gone sadly on their separate ways, now, in keeping with the plot of the films, Mother Riley's daughter Kitty gets her man, and also gets a lavish onstage wedding scene. The show concluded with Mother Riley's Swing Sisters, (a group of male musicians in drag) "conducted by Mr. Lucan in his own particular style."

The next film, *Old Mother Riley in Society*, apparently based on a story by Kitty McShane, was written in January 1940; it was shot in February and edited in March. In January, the *Kinematograph Weekly* had hinted at a remarkable development; "It is possible that in this newest feature they may be given a West End test, to see whether their particular brand of humor can appeal to West Enders in the same terrific way it appeals to the provinces and the suburbs." The film went on general release between May and July 1940, but still not in the West End. After two films in which Mother Riley was the socially and politically hyperactive heroine, audiences must have been puzzled to find her almost completely side-lined in the main plot by her daughter Kitty. Modern critics have either ignored or dismissed this film, the first Riley film to be directed by John Baxter, as rather dreary and sentimental, but at the time of its release the *Kinematograph Weekly* had no such reservations. "In the vernacular of the film itself, Arthur Lucan, alias Old Mother Riley, knows his onions, so does the director, John Baxter. That the film is a money-spinner for the industrial element is never in doubt." There is in fact a degree of subtlety in this Baxter-Riley debut which we shall explore later.

Throughout 1940, the stage show was called *Old Mother Riley Comes To—*, with the substitution of the name of the appropriate town, at Birmingham, Stratford East, New Cross, Finsbury Park, Leicester, Swansea, Hackney, Portsmouth and Norwich. At the last two venues the Lucans devoted the whole of the week's profits to the Lord Mayor's Red Cross fund, thus reinforcing Mother Riley's contribution to the war effort on both screen and stage. Given the suddenly worsening situation across Europe in May 1940, it is intriguing to read that "Mr. Lucan's policy of keeping his lines fresh with comical interpolations of topical interest is to be commended."

By August 1940 at Chiswick, perhaps to make the typesetter's job easier, the road show's title was changed simply to *Old Mother Riley Pays Us a Visit*, and under this title it ran through to Christmas.

The Lucans made another contribution to wartime propaganda at a vast open-air entertainment entitled "Rout the Rumor Rally" held in Hendon Park on Sunday, 21 July 1940. The event was organized by the Ministry of Information, whose intention was to "chase the chatter-bugs and rout the rumor-mongers" and boost morale. The program consisted of an afternoon of sketches, songs and music intended to reinforce the message that gossip and rumor prejudiced the national war effort, "careless talk costs lives." An impressive array of stars including Jack Hawkins, Jack Warner, Will Fyffe, Renée Houston, and Lucan and McShane, gave their services free of charge. Some film footage of this event has been preserved, including a clip which shows the Lucans onstage surrounded by huge crowds. Although performing as Mother Riley, Arthur is dressed in a lounge suit, contradicting the legend that he never ever performed out of costume or appeared as himself. At the same time, in June and July at Rock Studios Elstree, John Baxter was directing the sixth Riley film, *Old Mother Riley in Business*. Geoffrey Orme based the storyline for *Old Mother Riley in Business* on Con West's script for the film *The Small Man* (1935) which had also been directed by John Baxter. Baxter re-employed some of the cast from the earlier film, including Ernest Butcher, Edgar Driver, Roddy Hughes and Charles Mortimer. No commercial copy of this film is available but I have been able to view a copy just once. *Picture Show* of 21 December reported that

> This broad comedy finds that indefatigable old dame, Old Mother Riley, launching an attack on the underhand methods of some chain stores which are trying to put Village shopkeepers, including herself, out of business. There's not much story but there's plenty of fun, and Arthur Lucan's varied adventures and scrapes provide numerous opportunities for backchat and slapstick. The comedian's admirers will thoroughly enjoy it.

In the village of Willingdon, small businesses are under threat from the expansion plans of Golden Stores, a large chain whose manager wants to buy up their properties. Mrs. Riley, owner of the village general store, galvanizes the other shopkeepers into action in order to thwart the plans of Golden Stores. She sets up a pirate radio station to drum up support and broadcasts variety acts and a fake boxing match. She pushes the big boss into the river and is forced to hide in a hospital posing as a nurse. After many setbacks she eventually goes up to London and confronts the directors of Golden Stores at a board meeting. She wins the day, defeats the chain store magnates and secures the livelihood of the small village shopkeepers. The film poster shows her inspecting a line of commissionaires and addressing the Board of Directors. A rare trailer from this film shows Mother Riley driving helter-skelter past a bemused policeman in an old car festooned both inside and out with what looks like all the hardware from her shop. The clip ends as the steering wheel breaks off and the car hurtles into a hedge. One press trailer for the film confirms this: "There are some hilariously funny sequences, notably a court scene where, summoned for driving to the public danger and numerous other offences, she handles the proceedings in her own inimitable way to be let off with a small fine." Kitty as usual provides the romantic interest and falls in love with a budding young solicitor played by Cyril Chamberlain. Regrettably, most of Baxter's beloved variety turns were cut from the only print of the film I have seen; Kitty's song, "I'll Be Waiting," a charming Toytown harlequinade for children, a tap-dancing sequence by The Carlton Boys to "Alabama Jubilee," and an ensemble number probably performed by Riley and company during the pirate street broadcast.[110]

The *Western Morning News* of 17 December 1940 carried a short but amusing and perceptive review.

> The peanut and orange peel comedy of *Old Mother Riley in Business* is an excursion into the noisy good-humored atmosphere of the music hall. If Mr. Arthur Lucan sometimes puts things over with a trowel instead of sketching them in lightly with a pencil, he does it with all he has; you are left in no doubt that you ought to laugh. He *makes* these pictures.

On 18 January The *Burnley Express* reported that "The story simply teems with joyous incidents, and Lucan and McShane are on the top of their form in this scintillating and refreshing comedy.

As usual, the incorrigible dame gets into a deal of trouble, but comes through it with all her usual flair."

It is regrettable that no commercial version of this film has ever been made available, especially given the remarkably prophetic nature of its treatment of social issues which were not only close to Baxter's heart, but which have remained highly contentious to the present day; local people still campaign to prevent out-of-town supermarkets from blighting the High Street, often with far less success than Mother Riley! Lucan not only clowns but contributes to Baxter's message, as the *Kinematograph Weekly* made clear. "So well does Arthur Lucan know his stuff—with all his clowning he subtly tempers his humor with sentiment—that the wild and extravagant gags not only promote an easy continuity of laughs, but contain no little human interest. . . ." The scene of the village lad who wants to lend Mother Riley his modest legacy to save her shop from takeover is a sweetly sentimental and genuinely touching Baxter moment, and an example of the "glimpses of pleasing pathos" for which Lucan had so often been praised, even in pantomime. And given Baxter's well-known love of music hall it is not surprising to learn that "The variety trimmings, represented by a clever juvenile act and a neat and versatile concert party, [were] a box-office tit-bit."

In December 1940, *Old Mother Riley in Business* went on general release, and shooting began for the seventh film, *Old Mother Riley's Ghosts*, completed in February 1941. When *Old Mother Riley in Business* finally reached Australia in May 1945, The *Cairns Post* in Queensland shared British critics' enthusiasm.

> *Old Mother Riley in Business* is, without doubt, the funniest of the Old Mother Riley mirthmakers to arrive in Australia. Riotous comedy is the order from start to fade-out as Old Mother Riley embarks of a business career aided and abetted by Kitty McShane, and when the business is a mixed one, the background is made to order for side-splitting situations— and these abound in this laugh-a-second show.

It is also worth noting that in this film Mother Riley has gone up in the world; she is elegantly dressed, not in the latest 1940s fashions like Kitty, but in Edwardian clothes forty years out of date, another remembrance (if somewhat more up-market) of Lucy Ann Towle.

Riley appears briefly as a nurse but never as a washerwoman. She is a shrewd and quick-witted shopkeeper, and it could be argued that she has joined the ranks of the pretentious middle class she normally despises. But if she does so it is only, as she herself points out at the board meeting, in order to assert the rights of "little people" over the forces of capital and big business. Once again, the apparently zany panto dame is participating in a serious socio-political debate, and this undoubtedly contributed to her enormous popularity among the "industrial classes."

In early 1941 the Lucan-McShane stage show's title was either *Old Mother Riley Comes to Town* or *Old Mother Riley Pays Us a Visit* but the line-up was much the same. Also at this time, in order to stress the fact that the road show was live and not a film, press advertisements began to specify "personal visit of the famous film stars Lucan and McShane." When the show reached the Cheltenham Opera House on 4 March 1941, the enthusiasm of the population of this normally staid spa town exceeded all expectations. According to the *Gloucester Citizen*

> More than 10,000 people saw Arthur Lucan and Kitty McShane in 'Old Mother Riley Pays Us a Visit,' at the Opera House last week. This, Mr. Wilfred Simpson tells us, is an all-time record for the Opera House. Apart from about 50 seats at the first performance, the theater was filled to capacity at every house. On Saturday fans queued continuously from 11 o'clock in the morning until 8.15 at night. 'I have never,' says Mr. Simpson, 'heard so much laughter in the building.'

The vast and elegant Opera House designed by Frank Matcham could seat over a thousand spectators. At the Palace Leicester in March 1941, the show was called *Old Mother Riley and Her Daughter Kitty*, and this remained the title of the touring show until their very last season together in 1951-1952. To the very end, the Riley road show was largely made up of a series of variety turns but it was always bound together by the antics of Mother Riley, her sparring partner Mrs. Ginnochie, her daughter Kitty, the lodger, the doctor and, with ever-growing importance, Kitty's boyfriend.

In March *The Cinema* gave an enthusiastic bullet-point résumé of the forthcoming film, *Old Mother Riley's Ghosts*, the film in which

Arthur appeared for the only time in a male role, although critics fail to point out the fact that he had played male roles for many years onstage.

> Fluent direction puts conviction second, building up sustained succession of hilarious happenings round star's famous characterization, comic preliminaries along familiar domestic lines preceding sojourn in allegedly haunted castle. Highlights include knockabout interruption of staid board meeting, dame's infatuation for young inventor, humors of welcome to castle by dour caretaker [the genuinely Scottish John Laurie], comic chills of ghostly apparitions, and introduction of Arthur Lucan as himself, entire development featuring wealth of minor incident and hearty dialogue with many *doubles entendres*. Excellent entertainment for the masses, with outstanding stellar pull.[111]

The film went on general release in June 1941, just a matter of days after the release of an Ealing comedy with which it bore more than a passing resemblance. *The Ghost of St. Michael's*, starring Will Hay, Claude Hulbert and Charles Hawtrey, was also set in a haunted Scottish castle, and also featured John Laurie, no doubt in order to add an authentic Scottish voice of gloom and doom, long before Laurie joined the cast of *Dad's Army*. In his solitary appearance in the Riley films as a man (not as "himself" but as the character Ned Grey), Arthur, in the words of Paul Matthew St. Pierre, "turns in a daring performance, tantamount to slipping out of character." Grey is seen in the static pose of a handsome man, reminiscent of the offstage Lucan; but, as his name is meant to suggest, he is an "ineffectual and disconsolate female impersonator," whose stutter evokes our sympathy as it reveals he is also incapable of Riley's incessant gabble-talk. Professor St. Pierre concludes, "Lucan's performance as a Mother Riley imposter is his inside joke with the audience, pointing both to his actual performativity as Mother Riley and to his unique strategy of outing himself as a pantomime dame."[112]

Old Mother Riley Takes the Air

"Good evening, Mr. and Mrs. Wavelength, long, short and medium, Home and Forces and the cat's-whisker. It's me, Old Mother Riley, I'm here and I'm taking the air!"[113]

Lucan and McShane were no strangers to the BBC. As noted earlier, they had performed "The Old Match-seller" in a live radio variety show broadcast as long ago as August 1932. More recently they had taken part in shows broadcast from Chiswick Empire on 13 August 1940, and Jack Warner's "Garrison Theater" on 23 November. At the outbreak of war the BBC's Light Entertainment Department moved to Bristol, and as early as September 1939 its director Pat Hillyard and his bookings manager Arthur Brown had been discussing with Michael Lyon the possibility of the Lucans' doing a radio series. However the couple's film and stage commitments were so onerous that it was proving difficult to find suitable dates. Then there was the question of money. In July 1940 Michael Lyon asked Arthur Brown to suggest a fee, "while recognizing that you can offer them nothing in the way of remuneration which they are receiving for their Music Hall dates." In his reply, Brown suggested a fee in the region of "£60 for a series of this nature." This drew a stern rebuke from Lyon in which he put the BBC firmly in its place and made several important points of fact.

> At the outset, I think I ought to tell you the suggested fee of £60 would be quite out of the question.
>
> In order to carry out these suggested broadcasts it means that I should have to keep these artistes out of work for six weeks, and whereas their average salary from their films and road show has averaged well over £500 a week, this would be too great a sacrifice, even with the value of the remarkable publicity which, of course, I appreciate.
>
> I am afraid you do not grasp that perhaps, with the exception of Formby, that Lucan and McShane are number one box office, not only for Music Halls but for Pictures at the present moment . . . .

The BBC dithered and prevaricated for six months until Lyon told them he could wait no longer and went ahead with over six months of alternative bookings. In January he reminded Pat Hillyard that the Lucans' "average salary from Film and Music Hall engagements during the last year was in the neighborhood of £750 per week, so that will give you some idea." Lyon had a point. In 1941, £3,000 per month was an astronomical sum of money. The website measuringworth.com gives the following guide for the relative value of £1,000:

> For the value of a £1,000 of Income or Wealth, in 1941 there are three choices. In 2013 the relative historic standard of living value of that income or wealth is £43,210. The economic status value of that income or wealth is £138,500, and the economic power value of that income or wealth is £183,000.

Formby and the Lucans were among the very few in British show business who could command such sums.

Finally, in March 1941, a deal was struck. Lucan and McShane would record a series of eight shows with guest stars, in front of live audiences at the County Cinema in Bangor North Wales, where the Light Entertainment Department had just been re-located after being bombed out of Bristol in 1940. Arthur was to write the original comedy scripts for *Old Mother Riley Takes the Air*, assisted by Harry Alan Towers, a lad of twenty who was at the beginning of a long and colorful career in the entertainment industry. The Lucans were to receive £125 for each 45-minute show, a total of £1,000, and the series was to be directed by Tom Ronald. Arthur and Kitty announced they would appear in full costume and make-up, and Arthur insisted on learning his part because, as he put it, "How can I be that wild Old Mother Riley if I have to hold a script in my hand all the time?" The show was scheduled for recording in the space of two weeks from 8 June, between the end of the stage show *Old Mother Riley* and the shooting of their next film, due to begin on 23 June. The schedule proved to be rather too tight and was eventually revised to general satisfaction when the BBC offered the Lucans a further six shows after their next film.

However when they returned to Bangor in early August after shooting *Old Mother Riley's Circus*, the Lucans discovered that without consulting them the BBC had moved two recording sessions to the Grand Theater Llandudno. Both Arthur and Kitty were furious, and in spite of much pleading and cajoling, they stood their ground and categorically refused to compromise. Sharp tongues in the BBC management hinted that they were scared of the more sophisticated Llandudno audiences, but they in turn insisted on their loyalty to their existing Bangor audiences. They also pointed to the massive inconvenience of travel in the blackout (they had just been bombed out of one theater), and the fact that they were both tired from touring and filming. Arthur might also have revealed that his career as a performer had more or less begun with the Musical Cliftons at Llandudno, so fear of Llandudno audiences was not a plausible reason. Producer Tom Ronald took the Lucans' side against the management. He wrote to Pat Hillyard, concluding,

> After all they've been through this year their health isn't too good and it would ease the situation if all the broadcasts could be from the County Cinema. I've never seen two more hardworking and conscientious artists than Lucan and McShane. They both spend long hours in their hotel, writing and rewriting scripts to get the best of their work, and it does seem such a shame that we should lose two good artists over a question of studio allocation.

The Lucans won the day, and the whole series of *Old Mother Riley Takes the Air* was recorded in Bangor, ending on Saturday 20 September.

From September 1941 onwards, a detailed and uniquely reliable eye-witness record of the day-to-day making of the two Bangor radio series was preserved in the diaries and letters of Tom Ronald's new secretary Sybil Rowse. Sybil had moved from the BBC at Bristol in time to work on the last three September 1941 recordings; she remained with Ronald until the end of the second series in 1942, and her diaries and frequent letters to her mother and sister provide a delightfully sharp insight and uncensored view of the daily hazards of working with Lucan and McShane on "these hilarious, rowdy, quarrelsome, difficult shows."[114] Sybil summed up her most abiding memory of Arthur as,

> A dear artistic man whom we loved; I always looked on him as a genius. Always so delicately funny, yet sad too; your real, marvelous comedian . . . Such a dear and much-bullied man. But as a couple they were absolutely unthinkable... Every

moment of rehearsal was dodgy and rows over everything would blow up, and down as quickly, Kitty being Irish, stentorian, touchy, noisy, commanding etc., etc. No-one ever realized what agonies we all had to go through to get those shows on. Tom's divine tact and gentleness were marvelous and somehow we got through. We only had two small dressing rooms backstage, up a stone staircase with iron banisters. Arthur would have one with his trunk full of authentic old-lady clothes, all sent or donated by real old ladies, he told me. Kitty had to have the other, and the whole secret of the performance, as far as possible, was to keep them apart. So, to help Tom, I would Keep Kitty happy chatting and ironing her pretty dresses (in the absurd Kitty-young-girl-style) and zipping her up, etc., while Tom would keep Arthur entertained right next door.

The following excerpts from Sybil's candid private letters and diaries need little comment:

Saturday 6 Sept. 41
Terrific shemozzle all day over Old Mother Riley. Marvelous show with a huge audience. It was grand to be mixed up with a musical show again with lights and noise and crowds, and I adored it. We nearly didn't have a show as poor Arthur, a perfect lamb and almost a genius, had got tiddly the night before for the first time in his life—the doctor has told him that any alcohol is poison to him as he is so excitable anyway—and naughty Clay Keyes and Bobby Howes enticed him away with champagne and liqueurs and kept him up till 5.00 a.m. He was desperately ill and felt ghastly and couldn't rehearse till after lunch, and Kitty was furious with her frantic Irish temper and stormed at him and bullied the poor pet. He is so sweet and good and tried to do his best. Kitty is a real vixen who suddenly goes all sweet and all over everyone and no-one knows what she will do or say next. She didn't know whether to storm or cry or sing or feel humiliated and tried 'em all. Oh, she is a scream and acting all the time!

We had a marvelous show in the end and Mother Riley and Kitty played up and dressed up and the audience adored it and shrieked with joy.

Saturday 13 September 41
'Old Mother Haybag.' Much less fun than last Saturday. K. McShane is a real virago! Arthur is a dear but Kitty needs a lot of tactful handling!

Saturday 20 September 41
Old Mother Riley Usual rows between Kitty and everyone."

On 27 September after the first series of recordings, Sybil Rowse married and became Mrs. Dickinson. She and Tom Ronald were soon plunged into preparing an 80-minute Christmas Day live special, *Old Mother Riley's Christmas Party* ("The world's biggest all-round headache" wrote Sybil) scheduled to be broadcast from Bangor.

The Gramophone

From around this time theater posters often featured the words "Personal Appearance of your Stage, Radio and Screen Favorites." Lucan and McShane had conquered the media of film and radio, but there remained one more "modern" and highly popular entertainment medium, the gramophone, and they now added it to the list of their conquests. In the midst of their busy 1941 schedule, in July and August they made four 78 rpm gramophone records (eight sides) for Columbia records. Fortunately all of these have survived and can be heard today in excellent CD transfers. The recordings are made up of five sketches written by Arthur; *Old Mother Riley's Past*;[115] *Old Mother Riley in the Police Force*;[116] *Old Mother Riley on the Farm*;[117] *Old Mother Riley's Budget*, and *Old Mother Riley takes her Medicine*.[118] The sketch *Old Mother Riley in the Police Force* contains one of the rare examples of Riley having anything positive to say about the police, and then only because of the war; women had a duty to join the force because "The men have gone from it and we must go to it!" Similarly, the skit *Old Mother Riley on the Farm* is clearly an allusion of the trials and tribulations of "townie" girls in the Women's Land Army; when Kitty offers her mother a bucket to milk the cow, mother retorts, "You don't milk a cow with a bucket, you use a spanner!" But mostly the sketches are pure escapism and verbal fantasy, with occasional references to wartime conditions, such as "A married woman's Home Guard—the rolling pin!"

The survival of these sketches is particularly important given the fact that almost nothing remains in print of Arthur's material for the two major radio series which were being written and recorded at the very same time. Although both radio series were recorded, only one episode from the second series seems to have survived in the BBC's sound archives. There is evidence that some of the radio and gramophone material overlapped; a snatch of dialogue from one gramophone record was re-used in a film script in 1945, and at least one gramophone sketch was based on one of the routines from the road show. Scripts from both the radio and stage sketches appear to have been among the material burned by Kitty in 1948, so these five gramophone sketches are valuable examples of the kind of material Arthur was writing in the 1940s without the help of screenwriters.[119]

Throughout the autumn of 1941 the show *Old Mother Riley and Her Daughter Kitty* continued its progress around a country now reeling under the dreadful effects of blackouts, bombing, evacuation and, perhaps worst of all, the rationing of food, clothing and many other commodities. Theaters had become dangerous places; the Argyle at Birkenhead, where Dennis Clarke had given the Lucans one of their earliest bookings, was destroyed by a direct hit in September 1940, and in London, Drury Lane and the Poplar Hippodrome were also hit in 1940. Having narrowly missed losing their scenery and costumes at the Palace Plymouth, and at the Metropole Bootle, the Lucans lost everything after the second house at South Shields on 9 April 1941. *The Shields Gazette* reported "Old Mother Riley pays us a visit. It's a Yell. A riot of laughter. You have never seen a funnier show," and the theater played to capacity business for three nights. But on the Wednesday night, mercifully after the show, during a sustained attack on the North-East coast by Nazi "moonlight raiders" some 6,000 incendiary bombs and high explosives rained down on the town, and the Queen's was gutted, almost taking the Lucans with it. The couple would have gone up with all their props but because of a blazing row they had left the theater unusually early after the show and were cowering in a shelter further down Mile End Road. The Lucans' future BBC producer and friend Tom Ronald might also have perished with them in South Shields, as that week was one of the dates Michael Lyon suggested he might visit them on tour. The Queen's was no provincial flea-pit, and its loss was a huge blow. Local historian Mike Todd has written,

> The Queen's was capable of seating an audience of 2400, and with a stage that was 40ft by 40ft. The main entrance was marble, with granite columns and a mosaic floor. The staircase to the circle was a particularly grand affair, with steps of marble and a large mahogany handrail. Inside the auditorium were modern and luxurious tip-up chairs, and there was a lot of red plush in varying shades. It was hailed by building experts and theatrical entrepreneurs from all over the country as 'standing alongside the finest and most up-to-date in the country.'

When the public learned that Arthur had lost all his costumes he was inundated with parcels containing skirts, shawls and bonnets from old ladies all over the country.

The Tivoli at Grimsby was bombed out in the summer of 1943, and as late as January 1945 the Ilford Hippodrome was hit by a V2 rocket during *Robinson Crusoe*, injuring Renée Houston and a teenage dance troupe. All around the country, live performers were important morale-raisers and they were admired for running the same deadly risks as the audiences who night after night braved the bombs and the blackout to see them. John Ward's memories of the Wolverhampton Hippodrome in wartime catch the mood perfectly:

> During the blitz, a bomb exploding near a London theater had dislodged a crystal chandelier and sent it hurtling down on the audience, killing and injuring several people. Consequently, all other theaters immediately removed their chandeliers and replaced them with something less dangerous. In the case of the Hippodrome this was a single light bulb on a short length of cable. You can imagine how dim and dismal this made the place appear. Plush curtains grown heavy with dust and grimy stucco nymphs and cherubs, their gilt long since tarnished, added to the general dinginess. Once the lights went down, all the frustration of waiting in

long queues for meagre rations, of racking brains for ways to turn those rations into appetizing meals, of being woken at night by shrieking sirens and scuttling to cold damper shelters, receded. Patrons suddenly found themselves in another world, a fantasy world where dogs rode tricycles, musicians coaxed exquisite melodies out of carpenter's saws, and attractive young women, cut in half, miraculously came together again. Dark and anonymous, the theater provided a welcome antidote to the times.

John Ward also had a clear memory of the Lucans at "the Hippo," or at least of Kitty:

The stage door was just down the street from us and to amuse ourselves we tried to recognize performers as they arrived. It was a near impossible task. Dressed just like everyone else and without makeup they would have passed as ordinary people. We could tell Wee Georgie Wood easily enough, but would never have recognized Arthur Lucan (Old Mother Riley) if he hadn't been accompanied by his wife, Kitty McShane; dressed up to the nines in a fur coat and wearing enough make up to keep the [Women's] Land Army happy, she could not possibly have been anyone else.

In November 1941 the eighth Riley film, *Old Mother Riley's Circus*, was released. It was the very last film of the prolific veteran director Thomas Bentley, himself an ex-music-hall performer, and its heart-warming story, with a roll-call of real circus artistes, painted a nostalgic picture of the "big top" and the ups and downs of the travelling circus life. Perhaps quite deliberately, the film offered a momentary respite from the horrors of war. Arthur's versatility in characterization is well displayed in this film in which, while remaining Mother Riley throughout, he successively portrays the down-and-out ex-music-hall artist, Maggie O'Hara, who proves to be circus-girl Kitty's long-lost mother; the hoity-toity Countess Wax-Vesta ("A match for any one of you!") who saves the circus from closure; the fortune-teller, Gypsy Wye, who hoodwinks the bailiff; and an agile ring-master who can beat the clowns at their own game. Riley is on punning form; 'To think I used to have my own carriage, and now I'm cleaning out the stalls." "The Sultan wanted to make me his Sultana . . . Yes, his current wife!" Contemporary social and political issues are not entirely absent, but are woven in with great subtlety, like this oblique compliment from Bentley to John Baxter. In the scene where Riley, as the fallen music-hall star Maggie O'Hara, is busking outside a cinema, the film which the well-heeled patrons are queuing to see is John Baxter's recently released *Love on the Dole*, a film the Board of Censors had earlier forbidden him to make. A little later, when Riley, now the cinema's floor-washer, is called to the manager's office to be reprimanded, the scene begins with a lingering close-up of the manager's desk on which lies a poster for Baxter's 1941 film, *The Common Touch*, which Baxter dedicated to "the humble people of our great Cities whose courage and endurance has gained for us all, the admiration and support of the free countries of the world." These deliberately committed, even provocative, intertextual references to working-class solidarity would have been instantly recognized and understood by the original audiences, but they are largely lost on modern critics. This film also contains Lucan's longest and most amusing "lah-di-dah" impersonation. His scenes as the Countess Wax-Vesta reveal the depth and extent of his attention to interpretative detail. When Riley enters as the Countess, her entire posture and carriage are completely transformed. Riley's hunched shoulders are thrown back and her drooping head is held aloft; her elbows, normally close to her sides, are lifted and spread wide in elegant and airy gestures. Even the waddle-walk is replaced by an elegant dancer's gait. What makes this even more remarkable is the fact that as soon as the fake Countess leaves the bailiff's presence, Riley's tight arms and waddle-walk return, even when she is walking out of camera shot. An internet critic who is no fan of the Lucan films was at least forced to concede, "More impressively, Lucan does a scene in which Old Mother Riley disguises herself as a counterfeit countess. To his credit, in this sequence Lucan actually seems to be playing a completely different female impersonation from his Mother Riley turn." Finally, the fake Countess Wax-Vesta of the 1941 film bears more than a passing visual resemblance to the image of the Countess of Alagazam on the front page of the 1904 sheet music. The Countess in *Old Mother Riley's Circus* is surely descended from Arthur's Countess of Alagazam sketch of 1911-1912.

As 1941 drew to a close, it was widely noticed in the business (and even by schoolboys like John Ward at the Wolverhampton "Hippo") that, in the midst of much frugality and community spirit, Kitty was having "a good war" in the sense that she was splashing out her new-found wealth on every kind of indulgence and luxury. One of her indulgences went by the name of Alex Harland. He and Kitty had played Mr. and Mrs. Daydream in a sketch called "Married Bliss and Blisters," with Arthur as Daphne the maid. Harland was also playing the best man in the show's wedding scene, but Kitty seems to have thought of promoting him to bridegroom. She insisted to Tom Ronald that Harland must be in the forthcoming Christmas radio show, and Sybil was to organize accommodation for him in Bangor. In the end, so many guest artistes refused to leave London that the live broadcast of *Old Mother Riley's Christmas Party* was re-located to the Monseigneur, a 400-seater News Theater in Oxford Street, which had opened in 1939. A slightly sour note was struck by the BBC's Controller of Programs, who insisted that Tom Ronald should write to Michael Lyon demanding a clean script for this Christmas Day family show, with "no vulgarity or innuendos of any sort." Lyon was incensed by this and he replied that as "Arthur's mentality is much too high" to need such a reminder, he was not prepared to give one. Instead he suggested that Ronald himself could point out anything he deemed inappropriate. The show was another resounding success, with guests including Billy Bennett, Dorothy Carless, Geraldo and his orchestra, and Tommy Trinder who later recalled a party given by the Lucans at Forty Lane where the buffet was so magnificent that "you'd never have thought there was a war on." On New Year's Eve, Ronald sent a telegram; "EVERYONE DELIGHTED WITH CHRISTMAS SHOW. LOVE, TOM."

After Christmas, "Old Mother Haybag" as Tom Ronald affectionately called Arthur, and the "real vixen" as Sybil called Kitty, set out on another long and arduous nationwide tour. But Arthur was taken ill onstage at Chiswick and on 19 February 1942 *The Stage* reported that,

> Owing to the sudden illness of Arthur Lucan who was due to appear at the Hackney Empire this week in 'Old Mother Riley,' a variety company was booked. Over the telephone

yesterday (Wednesday) Kitty McShane told us that Mr. Lucan was better after a rest and would resume his engagements at the Shepherd's Bush Empire next week.

In fact the names Lucan and McShane did not re-appear in *The Stage* until 6 April at the Empress Brixton, a total absence of seven weeks. Some six years after Arthur's major accident, this was a worrying development that would be repeated several times throughout the 1940s.

On 7 May 1942 *The Stage* advertised a new radio show. "A new ten weeks' series, written by Arthur Lucan and produced by Tom Ronald, 'Old Mother Riley and her daughter Kitty' will return to the microphone on Saturday nights, starting on 23 May." But on 5 May Sybil Rowse had written to her family explaining that the start of new BBC series was to be delayed.

> You will no doubt be amused to hear that *Old Mother Riley* has had to be postponed for a fortnight and should now start on 6 June, all because Kitty has thrown a temperament and banged into a nursing home. The doctor says 'sheer hysteria.' She was annoyed because Arthur was ordered to rest and not her! Et cetera . . . Silly old cow.

Sybil was grateful for the extra time to prepare for the series,

> which Tom and I always consider our biggest headache! We usually discuss booking ourselves rooms at the nearest nursing home, into which we may need to retire the moment the series is finished! Maybe Kitty overheard us some time and tried it on herself. She is an old B. if ever there was one. The funny part is we've heard today that she thought Arthur couldn't possibly carry on without her but he, never having had such a wonderful break in his life, *did* with an understudy with great success, so Kitty, livid, flew back to work at once! This all goes to show . . . .

The Lucans returned to Bangor at the end of May to begin work on the series of ten 30-minute broadcasts, and Sybil was inundated with "heaps of stencils, mountains of scripts needing hours of typing." Kitty was becoming more and more involved in the scriptwriting, constantly chopping, changing and re-writing, to Sybil's utter despair. Once again Sybil's chatty, informative and often very funny diaries and letters home provide an array of details which have not survived in any other format; as far as the dry memos of the BBC's Caversham Archives are concerned, this witty, perceptive and articulate young woman might never have existed.

27 May 42
Fixed hairdressing appointment for Kitty McShane but doubt if it will suit Milady ...

5 June 42
Arthur gave me a pretty little pale green pottery vase he had bought for me at Ann's café near Moelfre (which he kept calling 'Peg's Pantry'). He filled it with ivy and other leaves and a few flowers he had picked off the BBC rockery, and carried it in so carefully and presented it to me with most graceful gestures.

5 June 42.
Do listen to Old Mother Riley tomorrow at 8.15. Kitty and Arthur are in great spirits (hope it lasts) and the script is very amusing. In the final scene (providing the costumes arrive today by train) Arthur, Kitty, and big fat Joan Young will be wearing bogus ATS uniform. Kitty and Joan have to be very smart whereas Arthur's is to be a badly-fitting comedy one! You will probably be able to tell by the audience reaction whether the costumes have turned up or not.

Tom will be at the side of the stage wearing tails and a red carnation. Young Michael Lynd, the compère is a great big jolly boy, awfully enthusiastic about everything in the world— about 22. [After the series Kitty kidnapped him for the road show and the next Old Mother Riley film.] There will be a big chorus and Billy Ternant's augmented dance band and a huge audience of some 700 or more. All the public tickets were mopped up a fortnight ago, we hear! All day we shall be rehearsing frantically and in between whiles Kitty will be backstage in her dressing room ironing frilly frocks which she loves to wear—she usually wears two or three during one program! [And this was a radio program!] She hasn't brought the agent, the manager, the maid and the maid's mother this time so maybe I shall have to help iron among many other cooking and bottle-washing jobs.

Another long interruption while Kitty calls on me to discuss ration books and have the costumes arrived and will I ring Joan Young and must she give the Castle Hotel her soap ration and Arthur didn't ought to do this and that, did he, etc. So now, for a while, I must bid you au revoir and make for my train. I had awful visions of not catching it when Kitty popped in! She is great fun but what an old B. Ask Betty [Sybil's sister] what an old B is. I hardly know except that I know one when I see one!"

[The apparently harmless send-up of the women's army corps, the ATS, attracted some very sharp criticism from the authorities to which we shall return in our discussion of the wartime films.]

10 June 42
Such a busy week. Dear old Tom gets so wrapped up in Kitty and Arthur and leaves every bit of routine to me. This week is more peaceful and I have somewhat regained my savoir faire! All Sunday I felt really whacked. Kitty is a real old cow, though Arthur is always sweet. Occasionally, however, he tells Kitty what he thinks of her in no uncertain terms.

18 June 42
I was so tired last night having typed the whole of *Old Mother Riley* till nearly 9.00 p.m., Kitty is being a big headache as usual, always throwing temperaments (theatrical term for stinking tempers) or feeling ill and by Saturday night the whole cast is usually on pins and a mass of nerves, poor dears. It all worries Tom to death as he isn't the man to deal effectively with difficult old cows and he gets insomnia and whatnot and takes Metatone. [a 'nerve tonic' not methadone!]

26 June 42

Do listen to Old Mother Riley this week and have a good private laugh to yourself over the second sketch between 'her' and naughty Kitty! It will remind you so much of the arguments you have with Old B. [Sybil's mother and sister Betty]. Kitty grumbles about her washing etc., and poor Old Mother Riley goes all resigned and says daughters don't realize what poor old mum has to get through in an inconvenient house, etc.

I really had to laugh as I typed it last night. Arthur (Old Mother Riley) writes it all himself and absolutely gets inside the 'ordinary person.' The general public simply love it! I worked out some figures last week which show that our listening audience is nearly EIGHT MILLION for this program! And that's a good deal smaller than last year owing to various wartime factors, no doubt.

P.S. Today is only Friday! Maybe dear Kitty will have torn up and rewritten the show by tomorrow night. All Bangor set for tremendous ARP exercises [Air Raid Precautions]. We are having gas released all over Bangor tomorrow so let's hope she gets done for!

(But nothing much happened at our end of the town.)

4 July 42

Old Mother Riley 5. They nearly came to blows over the morning and afternoon rehearsals. Kitty is quite impossible. Splendid audience, including a party of Free French sailors to whom Tom made a special speech in French.

1 August 42

A rather hectic and atmospheric day in which Kitty and Arthur were just difficult all along! Very nearly a revolution just before the curtain went up as Arthur refused to dress and did the whole show in a lounge suit and glasses. Kitty tried to faint and have hysterics with horror and temper(ament) but it didn't come off very well so she did her part and the show was O.K. for sound. Poor Tom nearly had kittens.

8 August 42

Busy but pleasant day for the final show in the *Old Mother Riley* series and everything went off smoothly for once. It was my swansong and my final show too. Kitty gave me a 'wedding present' afterwards [£5] which was most acceptable."

I think Sybil put "wedding present" in commas because she had already been married for a whole year before Kitty, ever economical when it came to others, combined wedding present and farewell gratuity into one. At the end of the series Sybil, now Mrs. Dickinson, left the BBC and returned to London with her husband, but thankfully not before she had left a unique, fascinating and unexpurgated record of looking after this "absolutely unthinkable" couple who were "endless trouble." Sybil transcribed these notes from her original letters and diaries in 1979 and, after various additions and corrections, she added in the margin, "The present ms. is accurate and more to be taken as gospel." Sybil's account allows a number of brief glimpses into the content of the sketches, the recordings of which have all been lost with the exception of the first show of the second series, which Arthur opened with one of his trademark greetings. "Good evening blackguards, bodyguards, coal yards and fire guards, it's me, Mother Riley, just blown in for a breath of fresh air! How's everybody?"

And so Sybil and the Lucans went their separate ways, but among Sybil's notes there is one more interesting and important snippet of information to which we shall return: "Kitty used to tell me she bought diamonds rather than *more* property . . . a jolly good idea in those risky days and so easily and safely stored in the bank." (my italics.) Clever Sybil hit the nail right on the head! Before buying 11 Forty Lane in 1939, the Lucans' notepaper in 1937 was headed 46 Randall Avenue, Dollis Hill, which would seem to be "Kittykot," the new house they mentioned in an interview at Christmas 1935. They also appear to have owned a house two miles away at Craven Park in Harlesden which was let as two flats, and, according to their son Donald, another property in the countryside south of London. At some point toward the end of the war Kitty bought 20 South Molton Street where she set up her disastrously loss-making beauty parlor; she also had a flat above the shop where she lived permanently after the sale of 11 Forty Lane. She perhaps thought that, should it ever become necessary, diamonds would be easier to conceal than a portfolio of properties. Her financial prospects must have seemed even more secure when, in a poll of exhibitors organized by the *Motion Picture Herald*, the Lucans were voted Britain's third top money-making stars for 1942, after George Formby and Leslie Howard. At some point in 1942 the Lucans made a short film for the Ministry of Information; it was part of a series of fourteen shorts concerning fuel rationing, something poor old Mother Riley of Ration Row knew a great deal about. The film is preserved in the archives of the Imperial War Museum's All Saints Annex in Austral Street, London.

Shortly after leaving Bangor the Lucans embarked on the ninth Riley film, *Old Mother Riley Detective*, produced by John Baxter at Elstree for British National Films, and directed by Lance Comfort. This was one of a number of film comedies at this time dealing with rationing and racketeers, and the film's working title was *Old Mother Riley Cleans Up*, a title also used in 1942 for Elsie and Doris Waters' film on a similar theme, *Gert and Daisy Clean Up*.

Brian McFarlane records that on its release in January 1943 *Old Mother Riley Detective* was hailed by *Kinematograph Weekly* as "One of Arthur Lucan's and the series' best efforts." *Today's Cinema* called it "a sure-fire follow-up to previous Mother Riley successes," and praised its "animated direction." The *Motion Picture Herald* took a more patronizing stance, relegating it to "that brand of backstreet comedy which aims at the lowest common denominator of audience appeal." If this critic actually saw the film he must have slept through patriotic scenes concerning the Ministry of Food and fair rationing for all, the unmasking of black marketeers and the role of women in the struggle. *Old Mother Riley Detective* ushered in what proved to be the most dazzlingly successful year of the Lucans' career so far, but it was also the year that saw the beginning of the end of their life as a couple.

"O Danny Boy . . ."

On 11 February 1943 *The Stage* noted that *Old Mother Riley* "opens a London season at the New Cross Empire this week." For three months the show toured the London suburban theaters (never once straying "oop North!") proving that Michael Lyon's initial confidence in the drawing power of Mother Riley's name was not misplaced.

On 6 May 1943 *The Stage* carried the following remarkable news: "Michael Lyon tells us that the Syndicate offices have informed him that on their visit to the Metropolitan last week Arthur Lucan and Kitty McShane in the 'Old Mother Riley' road show broke existing takings records for the theater."

But now, at the height of their public fame, the Lucans' private life, which for years had been going from bad to worse, took a turn from which it never recovered. "Best man" Alex Harland, who wasn't really interested in Kitty's attentions, was replaced in the show, and in Kitty's affections, by a singer named William Breach, who most definitely was.

Before meeting the Lucans, William Breach had had a long and initially promising career as a light comedian and tenor vocalist, "Singing songs you'll love to hear" in revue and variety. In 1924, the *Aberdeen Journal* had described him as "a successful young tenor who sings with feeling and good taste," and in 1927 the same paper reported that "William Breach is a promising young tenor who is quickly forging ahead in his studies." In November 1930 the *Evening Telegraph* of Dundee reported that "As a juvenile lead, William Breach is excellent and makes a splendid 'lover' for the young leading lady, his duets with Ettie Howard being very pleasing." One of his best reviews came at the Hull Palace Theater in 1931. "William Breach [is] one of the finest tenors heard in vaudeville. His singing simply brought down the house and, and if time had permitted, the audience would gladly have heard more of him."

But Breach's early promise did not lead on to a solo career such as that of Eric Randolph, who had toured so successfully with the Lucans. Reviews, such as this one at Exeter in 1938, became more perfunctory; "William Breach sings several songs in acceptable fashion," and Breach increasingly found work in vocal duos and ensembles.

Steve King asserts, wrongly, that it was during 1944 that Kitty took up with "a smart young man," from a male vocal quartet in the road show, and King repeatedly claims that "Billy Bleach," as he calls him, was younger than Kitty; "He was younger than Kitty and was a married man with a family . . . Here she was, madly in love with someone much younger than herself . . ."

William Breach was indeed a married man with a family, but he was most certainly not younger than Kitty. Born in 1892, he was five years older than Kitty, and was already past fifty when he caught her eye. He appeared for the first time under his own name in Lucan and McShane programs as early as 18 February 1943, when the advertisement for the show at Golders Green Hippodrome lists "Arthur Lucan, Kitty McShane, William Breach" and others. Unless Breach had already found particular favor with Miss McShane and her productions, his name would most certainly not have been given such sudden prominence, and he may well have joined the road show in late 1942. He appeared just one more time under his own name, in an Edinburgh cast list in July 1943, after which Kitty decided to rename him as Willer Neal, partly because Arthur joked that people were calling him "Bleach," but also because any lover of Kitty McShane surely needed a more elegant and romantic name.

Before Breach joined the company, the Mother Riley stage show already included a boyfriend, a best man, and a wedding scene. Now that Willer Neal was featured singing romantic duets with Kitty, he took over the role of bridegroom from Norman Williams and was given the name Danny Boy. But whereas the wedding scene had always been at the end of the first half of the show, it now became the grand finale. This onstage wedding finale, which was even seen at the Palladium in December 1943, became in effect a shameless public announcement of the beginning of a twenty-year affair between Kitty McShane and Billy Breach, an affair which ended only with Billy's death in Kitty's South Molton Street flat in December 1963.

As further proof that William Breach must have found favor in Kitty's eyes by the end of 1942 at the latest, he also appeared under his own name in the cast of *Old Mother Riley Overseas*, the tenth film in the *Old Mother Riley* series, released in December 1943 but cast almost a year earlier. After the change of stage name, Billy Breach appeared as Willer Neal in the remaining four Riley films in which Kitty also featured, singing onscreen duets with his mistress as Arthur looked helplessly on. To the annoyance and incomprehension of many, Kitty now insisted on taking up more and more of the stage show (and the final radio series) with duets with Danny Boy, including "I'll String Along with You," "Galway Bay" and "I'll take you home again, Kathleen," the last two of which later featured in the film *Old Mother Riley's New Venture* (1949). Some contemporary commentators have claimed that Arthur acquiesced passively in all this, and that, as Roy Rolland put it many years later, "he condoned it." This is surely an oversimplification of something more complex and too intimate to be explained away so lightly; in reality, Arthur had little choice in the matter, and he surely did not "condone" the severe beating which, according to Annie Carroll, Breach gave him in his own house, a house in which he was rapidly becoming a fearful and intimidated lodger.

The view that the shy, nervous and sensitive Arthur was well aware that a profound change was now taking place in his private life would seem to be supported by an apparently insignificant event which took place in faraway Lincolnshire. There, on 8 August 1943, with money sent by her brother, Arthur's eldest sister, Annie Butler, purchased the exclusive burial rights to the grave of Lucy Ann Towle in Horncastle Road cemetery. Lucy had died seventeen years earlier in November 1927, and her unpurchased grave had remained unmarked, and probably overgrown. Purchase gave the grave-owner the right to erect a memorial, and this seems to have been Arthur's sole intention in purchasing the grave, as the high water-table in the Boston cemetery precluded any further burials in the same plot. At the dizzy height of the Lucans' fame and fortune, it would be odd if mere coincidence were the main cause for Arthur's feeling a strong need, after so many years, to seek out and honor his mother's last resting-place. Although Arthur must have known that his father was buried close by, and may even have attended his funeral in 1895, he did not buy or mark his father's grave. Lucy Ann Towle's simple and dignified memorial consists of a kerb-surround within which lies a stone slab inscribed with the words,

> Lucy Ann Towle
> Buried on 7 November 1927
> Erected in Remembrance
> By her sons and daughters

In this inscription, Arthur does not seek to highlight his own exceptional wealth or status, but rather preferred to include himself simply among the sons and daughters as part of the Towle family. He had left that family long ago, taking the names Clifton and Lucan. Now it was as if he felt a psychological and emotional need to make some kind of visible gesture of gratitude or reparation towards the mother, aspects of whose odd and quirky character he had lampooned so successfully for years. Perhaps, in what could be seen as propitiatory magical thinking, he hoped that this symbolic act of filial piety might somehow make all well again in the present. But like some grisly fairy tale worthy of the Brothers Grimm, telling of a ghostly mother-in-law's revenge, Arthur's wife was now becoming as grotesque a caricature as his dead mother had been long ago!

Worse still, in an uncanny example of life imitating art, the maternal melodrama played out from the very first of the Riley films was becoming a bizarre reality. As Francis King put it, "This stage situation was merely a comic travesty of a tragic real-life one." Although Kitty was legally Mrs. Kathleen Towle, she now made it clear beyond doubt that the marriage was over in every meaningful sense bar one—the money. But at the pinnacle of their material success in public, the Lucans could not simply walk away from a private relationship which was growing daily more poisoned and destructive because, in their professional lives, both had become equally imprisoned in the popular and lucrative stage act they had built up over more than twenty years. During those years, Arthur had retreated ever more deeply into the brilliant but strangely surreal and depersonalized role of the widowed dame. In Alfred de Musset's play *Lorenzaccio*, when the hero is told that all sicknesses, even vice, may be cured he replies, "It is too late. I have become accustomed to the task. I wore the mask as a costume but now it has stuck to my skin." This seems chillingly to sum up Arthur's predicament. When preparing his play *On Your Way, Riley*, Alan Plater remarked flippantly but perceptively that "it is tempting to see Lucan's need to dress up as an Irish washerwoman as a psychological need springing from every trauma known to cut-price analysis." Indeed, one may well ask, what is one to do when one's wife and darling daughter starts to turn into the evil stepmother, who said (after his death) that she often had to "mother him"?

But Kitty's predicament was no less bizarre.

A rather stout woman approaching fifty, by all accounts utterly egocentric, immature and unstable, much given to foul tempers and foul language, and whose talent was "wafer-thin," this reluctant mother of an almost thirty-year-old son was still disguised in what Sybil Rowse had called "the absurd Kitty-young-girl-style frilly frocks." The vast sums of money the couple were earning allowed her to indulge the fantasies with which she kept the truth of age at bay, but however much she liked to delude herself and others, it was only as Arthur Lucan's sidekick that she could hope to keep the money, the contracts, and the compliments, rolling in. The aging Kitty was just as trapped in the role of the "dainty maid" as Arthur was in the weeds of the dame; but whereas Mother Riley, like whiskey, got better with age ("The older I get the better I like it!"), every passing year made Kitty a more garish travesty of what she had once been; she was becoming, in Francis King's words, "pathetic and macabre." "To look at Old Mother Riley," wrote John Fisher, "was to observe the height of the grotesque, a quality which the formidable old harridan was always head over heels to emphasize herself." Sadly, as Kitty's age and over-indulgence took their toll, the same became daily more true of the darling daughter in her ridiculous frilly frocks. And yet, as Riley had said with palpably genuine feeling in *Old Mother Riley Joins Up*, "That's my daughter. She's all I've got in the world. I've scraped and saved all these years so that she could have a chance in life." Paradoxically, for this very reason, the worse things got, the more this "unthinkable couple" still clung to each other in a way which no outsider could ever quite fathom; after thirty years they couldn't bear to be together, and couldn't manage to be apart. And so, on stage, screen, and radio, the show rolled on willy-nilly, with Willer Neal in tow!

So great was Riley's drawing power at this time that a couple of pale imitations appeared briefly. In the early 1940s Lancashire born Jack Sherwin was working on the variety circuit as a patter comedian and saxophonist and advertised himself as "the only comic to have understudied for Arthur Lucan as Old Mother Riley." Dressed as a poor old woman but with garish clown-like stage make-up, he had a topical routine dealing with shopping, rationing and various other war-time issues. This apparently led to him being billed as "The Old Mother Riley of the North." Sherwin's billing is interesting in that it not only underscores the popularity of the original and her wartime topicality, but also provides another refutation of the critics' erroneous classification of the real Mother Riley as a creature of the North.[120] In July 1943 another comedy couple offered "Mother Kelly, no relation or resemblance to Mother Riley," and Robb and Dobb were advertised as "t'other Mother Riley." In December at Finsbury

Park, Anna Rogers was applauded for her "clever mimicry of Lucan and McShane."

At the beginning of 1943, the Lucans, leading stars of British stage, screen, radio and gramophone, fully expected to be invited to make a new series of Mother Riley broadcasts, but the BBC's Written Archives at Caversham reveal that there were now reservations about giving them the prime Saturday night spot. In January, J.E.C. Langham in an internal Memo explained that it was felt that "Old Mother Riley like ITMA does not have general appeal, both programs have audiences of those who are 100% in favor but at the same time there are large numbers of other listeners who are equally strongly against." For this reason Langham concluded that a new series would be possible, on condition that it went out on a different evening. In the end nothing came of the project, but the Lucans did appear in five one-off radio shows during 1943. The fourth of these was *The Happidrome*. This enormously popular and long-running show was broadcast live on Sunday evenings from the Grand Theater Llandudno to an audience of war workers and service personnel. Harry Korris as Mr. Lovejoy was the proprietor of the imaginary theater of the show's title, aided and abetted by his Stage Manager Ernie Ramsbottom, and gormless Enoch the call boy. For almost seven years all the major stars of variety made guest appearances on this show. The Lucans' turn came on 26 September when, to Kitty's intense annoyance, her final song was faded out because they had overrun their allotted airtime by eight minutes. Kitty was so miffed that she ordered Michael Lyon to make an official complaint to the BBC, but she got very short shrift, prompting one of her few recorded funny lines. From then on, she declared, she would call the show *The Miserydrome*.

When the latest film, *Old Mother Riley Overseas*, was released in December 1943, it proved to belong to the genre of "good, clean, silly fun," a farrago of utter nonsense calculated to provide another antidote to the darkness of war. At the very moment when the German U-boats' threat to Britain's lifeline of shipping convoys was at last receding, Mother Riley follows Kitty and her boyfriend to Portugal in Barnacle Bill's rickety old boat, a move which would have been viewed as tasteless and insensitive one year earlier. Once again, one of the most striking, and neglected, features of the film is the transformation of Mother Riley the scruffy washerwoman into a series of lah-di-dah female stereotypes. In a Lisbon concert hall, wearing an elegant black dress and with her head swathed in a flowing mantilla, she is mistaken for the late-running piano soloist, Madame Juanita. Rising absurdly to the occasion, she sweeps onto the stage and gives a magnificent rendering of Beethoven's fifth piano Concerto, *The Emperor*. In this long scene, containing almost the whole of the concerto's first movement, the camera cuts between the London Symphony Orchestra, the conductor, the hands of a genuine concert pianist, and long shots of "Madame Juanita" twiddling at the keyboard, and looking so pleased with herself that to this day in biographical notes on Arthur Lucan one can read that "he was a magnificent pianist!" A little later, at an elegant Portuguese seaside resort, Mother is transformed into a bathing belle in mop cap and frilly costume, while the soundtrack comments wryly with the tunes "Oh! I Do Like to Be Beside the Seaside!" and "Hello, Who's Your Lady Friend?" But she soon reverts to type, comes to blows with the lady crook who is trying to seduce Kitty's boyfriend, and dumps her into the Lido. There then follows an interesting and amusing scene which harks back to Plautus, Shakespeare and *The Comedy of Errors*. For the voyage home, Mother changes clothes yet again, this time donning an elegant outfit with a striped short cape. Before the voyage from Portugal to England (via Argentina!), the crooks plan to kidnap and imprison Kitty on the ship, and the wily female crook, played by Hungarian Magda Kun in her second Riley film, disguises herself as "the old Riley woman" in order to lure Kitty into the trap. The plot works and, once on board ship, the two Rileys in identical striped outfits narrowly miss each other as they appear and reappear in the bar, to the utter consternation of the bartender, who is confused when one Riley angrily refuses the drink which the other Riley had taken moments earlier. Seeing that the second Riley has a different male escort the barman tells his friend, "I've seen some fast workers on this ship in my time, but this old woman beats the lot!" When Mother Riley spots her fake double on deck she says to the captain, "Take a look at that old woman sitting there and tell me if it's me!" Magda Kun does a clever impression of Riley, and whereas in the *Old Mother Riley's Ghosts* impersonation episode we had a man (Arthur Lucan) impersonating a man (Ned Grey) impersonating a woman

(Mother Riley), now we have a woman (Magda Kun) impersonating a man (Arthur) impersonating a woman (Riley)! Gender lines in Lucan's absurd comedies have become so blurred and irrelevant that by the end of 1943 it almost seems as if everybody wanted to be Old Mother Riley!

The Lucans' last broadcast of 1943 was part of a rather more serious and significant contribution to the war effort. On 8 November the BBC devoted all its evening programs to Britain's ally Russia, whose people had suffered death and destruction on a massive scale during the German invasion. The programs were devised as

> A tribute to Russia's National Day (7 November) and to the prodigious part the Russian people are playing in the war against Nazi Germany. At 7.35 p.m. on the Forces wavelength there is 'Factory Floor Show,' a variety program given before an audience of factory workers. Artists include Lucan and McShane, Bertha Willmott and Malcolm McEachern with Leonard Henry as Master of Ceremonies and music by the BBC Revue Chorus and Orchestra directed by Jack Payne. As a prologue to 'Factory Floor Show' there will be a broadcast from a factory making Hurricanes, and the epilogue comes from a factory where tanks for the Russian front are rolling off the line.

Finally, as 1943 drew to a close, the Lucans crowned their seemingly universal popularity with an appearance at the Palladium in the heart of a West End which had for so long proved resistant to their charms. However, if the review in *The Times* of George Black's show *Look Who's Here!* is to be believed, that resistance was far from conquered. After briefly presenting the stars of the first part of the show, including Binnie Hale and Cyril Fletcher, the reviewer concludes,

> These are among the stimulating influences; but after the interval there are no more of them. Mr. Arthur Lucan as Old Mother Riley, and his company, who have won great popularity on the air, take charge of the stage, and for the rest of the evening the entertainment sprawls at its ease, sporting with jokes which evidently die as hard as Old Mother Riley herself.

Photo 14: Kitty's stage wedding to Willer Neal, late 1940s. Steve King

The Stage described the Lucan's program rather more kindly as "An Irish burlesque in three scenes entitled 'The Tearing of the Green.' The humor is of a popular nature rather than West End or international. The scenes are An Irish Village, Mother Riley's Cottage, and The Wedding." The Bridegroom was of course Willer Neal.

Cyril Fletcher has a more balanced and interesting account of the very same show in his 1978 memoir, *Nice One Cyril*. In spite of his own discomfiture, Fletcher paid generous tribute to the Lucans and their comic style, so different from his own:

It was a rather odd bill. Lucan and McShane, with excerpts from their many 'Old Mother Riley and her Daughter Kitty' road-show successes, took up the second half of the program, and I and a rather quietly artistic bill . . . were in the first. Our part of the audience did not like Lucan and McShane, and Lucan and McShane, as a very good strong visual comedy duo who filled every single provincial music hall and cinema for years with their road show revues and films, drew in an audience who hated our half of the show. Oil did not mix with water. George Black therefore decided to mingle the two halves of the show. I was moved into the second half. This was in a way flattering, but for my act it was a disaster. I had to follow a boisterous sketch of talk and visual comedy with not a note of music which went on for a hilarious twenty-five minutes . . . After such rough and tumble as Arthur Lucan and Kitty McShane had perpetrated for nearly half an hour, it was a little difficult to get a laugh out of suggesting some happening when the audience had seen it take place before their very eyes in a sketch a few moments earlier. (pp. 56-57.)

Fletcher was referring to his "Odd Ode," which told the tale, in polite verse, of a girl who had scorched her bottom; but moments earlier the audience had seen the real thing when Kitty pushed Mother onto the kitchen stove and Mother ran shrieking around the stage of the Palladium with her skirts on fire. Fortunately, a further account of this Palladium performance has survived, and its quality eclipses the grudging jibes of the *Times'* anonymous critic.

Ivor Brown had joined *The Observer* as drama critic in 1929 and was soon widely regarded as the most influential and insightful drama critic in the British press. In 1939 he was appointed professor of drama in the Royal Society of Literature, and in August 1943 he became editor of *The Observer* but continued to write on Shakespeare and the theater. His memorable review of Arthur Lucan appeared in *The Observer* on 5 December 1943:

The [Tommy] Trinders and [Max] Millers of our day are men of attack. They have the essential energy and so, in his own way, has Mr. Arthur Lucan, endeared to the public as old Mother Riley, now sharing with Kitty McShane and their company,

half an imposing bill at the Palladium. The BBC has given a
wonderful leg-up to the garrulous and volatile Dame of Mr.
Lucan's manufacture, whom I remember in much humbler
circumstances. But, once conquer the listeners and the top-
of-the-bill is yours ... Now, though Old Mother Riley is a far
from inventive creation, she does, by sheer energy, dominate
the Palladium program with its greater names and subtler
wits. She is simply the eternal 'old faggot' of the music-hall
tradition, the screaming, abusive, back-chatting, unquench-
able harridan. Energy, energy, energy. As thin as a wire, she is
certainly a live wire, too, and sets the sparks flying. At death's
door, she can make rings round the doctor [played by Willer
Neal]; never was moribundity so agile as this skipping queen
of penury and jollity. Throw in the kind of blarney that the
music hall believes to be Irish, and you have the Riley Sports
Model, 1943. It certainly covers the ground.

The Riley was a prestigious British brand of motor cars, and Old
Mother Riley was rapidly becoming an equally prestigious pseudo-
Irish and truly British institution.

In April 1944, when the Riley show was at Brixton, there was a
rather odd item in the "Variety Gossip" column in *The Stage*. After
discussing "A Starry Night" at the Prince of Wales Theater, where
Vivien Leigh, Laurence Olivier, David Niven and Will Hay had
turned up to congratulate the comedian Sid Field on his latest success in *Strike it Again*, the columnist makes a link to the Lucans with
a touch of bathos, as if moving from the sublime to the grotesque!
"From the West End to Brixton where, at the Empress, Arthur Lucan
and Kitty McShane were doing capacity business with their new 'Old
Mother Riley' revue. Arthur was full of praise for Kitty and Kitty
all the time paying compliments to Arthur. It was good to see these
superb artists in an excellent show." Within the entertainment business, the Lucans' horrendous arguments and their shaky private life
were by now common knowledge, and one cannot help wondering if
this apparently sugary little aside was not in fact meant sarcastically.

In Brighton, a new sketch was introduced in June, "dealing with
that delectable dame's adventures in the ATS." This was probably
based on the sketch mentioned in Sybil Rowse's letters, which had

earned the disapproval of the authorities. Mother Riley has now become such a fixture that little is recorded in the press beyond the fact that, as at Reading in September, "she is paying her annual visit here. In the person of Arthur Lucan she is a lovable old lady . . . ." Throughout 1944 the re-vamped Old Mother Riley road show continued to roll just like a "Riley Sports Model" all around the country. The Lucans also made six radio broadcasts in the course of the year, including three episodes of *Workers' Playtime*, the lunchtime entertainment for factory workers, broadcast "from a factory canteen somewhere in Britain."

After a gap of almost two years, British National agreed to a new film, *Old Mother Riley at Home*. It was filmed in December 1944 and released in May 1945 just as the war in Europe came to an end. This was the second film to feature Billy Breach, but the first under his new name of Willer Neal. It was also the first in which he played Kitty's boyfriend Bill.

> Kitty, furious at her mother's rough treatment of Bill, her latest boyfriend, leaves home and goes to live with her friend Mary. Mother Riley goes to the hotel where Kitty is employed with the intention of begging her daughter to return home, but creates such a scene that not only is she herself thrown out by the police but Kitty is discharged by the manager. Bill then finds Kitty a job as hostess at a gambling den in the country. Accompanied by Dan, her lodger, who is in love with Kitty, Mother Riley sets out for the gambling den in order to warn her daughter that Bill is no good. She is discovered and chased by Bill and mistakenly gives the alarm for a police raid. In the resulting commotion, Dan seizes the opportunity to give Bill the hiding he deserves, and to Mother Riley's great satisfaction Kitty decides that Dan, after all, is the worthier suitor.[121]

The scriptwriters came dangerously close to the truth when they made Billy Breach a villain whose real intention was to exploit Kitty for his own ends! After the fight between Bill and Mother Riley, which must have felt very strange to the two men who were at loggerheads over Kitty in real life, Kitty is rescued from danger, but not before the film stops dead in its tracks for a particularly nauseating duet between the "young lovers" who croon "Let's Pretend We're Sweethearts," "while farm girls rake hay and a bored-looking horse stands by on what is obviously a studio set."[122] The lovers in question were fifty-two and forty-eight years old. Many believed that this rather uneven offering must surely signal the end of the Riley film series, and for four years this appeared to be the case.

Still, Arthur soldiered on. In March 1945 at Chiswick, Mother Riley's ATS sketch was described as "a vastly amusing creation which has a plentiful supply of original observation on army life and conduct," another reminder of the much praised topicality of Arthur's material. In the same review there is yet another reference to Kitty's frocks; "The Wedding Scene, with Kitty dressed in the most striking wedding gown, telling the Old Match-seller about her mournful love affair and being rewarded with much caustic comment by the Old Lady." This is the original Match-seller sketch which they had been performing since the 1920s, but as we noted earlier, now given an eventual happy ending with Kitty's marriage to Willer Neal. Before that on the same bill "we have Lucan's celebrated impersonation of Old Mother Riley as an exceedingly difficult invalid, with Willer Neal playing the much tried doctor." This was the scene Ivor Brown had admired in his *Observer* review of 1943; "At death's door, she can make rings round the doctor; never was moribundity so agile as this skipping queen of penury and jollity."

As the *Hull Daily Mail* had reported years earlier, Old Mother Riley continued to appeal to young and old alike, now on screen as well as on stage. During the war, the actor-director Vivyan Ellacott was growing up in his mother's grocery shop in Swansea, just a few yards from the Empire Theater. Each Monday the cast of the latest show would be obliged to sign on at the shop in order to obtain their meagre food rations for the week. This led directly to young Vivyan's first taste of show business, and of Old Mother Riley.

It didn't do any harm for the resident staff at the Empire to be on good terms with my Mum—free tickets every Monday for the shows—and welcoming her 'cute little boy' (me!!!), regularly to come and stand in the wings during the first houses and watch the show. I was a kind of backstage 'mascot.' And naturally, since my Mum knew I was being safely looked after backstage for the odd hour or so, she could help out with the extra eggs or the occasional extra bit of butter, and so on! Accordingly I watched every show at the Swansea Empire, week after week. I saw Lucan and McShane perform at the Empire and I remember thinking Old Mother Riley was the funniest thing I had ever seen. Then the next day I remember Arthur Lucan coming into my mother's grocery shop and being told this was Old Mother Riley. Because he was not wearing the Old Mother Riley costume I refused to believe it.[123]

Not far from Swansea at the very same moment, the writer Leslie Thomas was growing up in Newport. In his second volume of autobiography, *In My Wildest Dreams*, he recalled his love of comedians at the local Empire Theater. But of all the theater's "funny ladies" Thomas declared that

The funniest lady to me was a man, Arthur Lucan, the knobby, bulbous nosed old Mother Riley ... "Oh Mrs. Stonochy!" [*sic*] Mother Riley used to howl, rolling up her sleeves preparing for an Irish fight. When they came to the Empire in Newport the street and those around were besieged with people trying to get into the theater.[124]

In 1943, at the age of twelve, Thomas lost both parents and was sent to a Dr. Barnardo home in Kingston upon Thames. Even there, nothing could dim his love for Lucan and McShane.

I would sit in the gods in the Empire on Saturday afternoon, forever entranced by comedians, singers, jugglers and magicians. My heart lifted when I saw that Old Mother Riley and Her Daughter Kitty were to top the bill. I could scarcely wait until Saturday but when it arrived some misdemeanor had been committed in the home and no one was allowed out. This time I made a break for it, climbing over the fence and haring down Kingston hill. I sat up in the dimness, next to the cherubs carved on the roof of the Empire, watching my music hall idols and engulfed with guilty pleasure. I was not caught, either.[125]

Growing up during the war in Edinburgh, the distinguished actor Ian Richardson contracted a love of Mother Riley which he was to display years later to the delight or bewilderment of his fellow actors. After Richardson's death in 2007, fellow actor Brian Blessed recalled their working together in 1972 on the film of the musical *The Man from La Mancha* in which Ian played and sang the role of the priest.

He loved imitating Old Mother Riley from her films. They were very comical films and Ian would imitate her brilliantly. He would drop his jaw and his face would contort into Old Mother Riley and this sophisticated actor would turn into a ridiculous comedian. In between scenes he would become Old Mother Riley (and sometimes forget to come out of character when filming).[126]

Just what Richardson's co-stars, Peter O'Toole and Sophia Loren made of this, Brian Blessed does not record; but Richardson was a highly intelligent and perceptive actor, and his imitation of Arthur Lucan was surely the tribute of one sophisticated actor to another sophisticated actor, albeit one disguised as "a ridiculous comedian."

In complete contrast to the rather patrician Richardson, the committed left-wing, working-class actor Ricky Tomlinson also acknowledged his love of Old Mother Riley and her central role in launching his career shortly after the war. Rather surprisingly, as a lad Rick hated cowboy films and secretly yearned for something gentler.

Sometimes I'd sneak around the corner and see a romance or a comedy, but I couldn't tell anyone. As with my writing, the lads wouldn't have understood. That's how I discovered the Old Mother Riley films. Arthur Lucan and his wife Kitty McShane were the biggest box-office stars of their day. Lucan would dress up in a frock and play Old Mother Riley, a gossipy Irish washerwoman, while Kitty played the headstrong daughter. I laughed until the tears ran down my cheeks. Inspired by these films, I convinced a mate of mine, Davey Steele, that we should put on a show for the neighborhood kids and charge them a penny at the door. I walked the streets banging on a metal drum to publicise the show, while Davey hung a sack for the curtain in the loft over his garage. The audience were literally packed to the rafters as I donned one of Mam's frocks and did my own version of Old Mother Riley. This was my first experience of acting . . . it wasn't a bravura performance but none of the kids asked for their money back . . . I've been improvising ever since.[127]

There are many more accounts of the respect and affection which Old Ma Riley commanded among her fans both young and old during these years. One of my favorite oddities is a letter to the bandleader Henry Hall from the twelve-year-old Birmingham schoolboy Kenneth Tynan; one of the great theater critic's earliest surviving letters is a plea for the "honor" of receiving the autographs of "Lucan and McShane, and other famous artists." Most intriguingly, Mother Riley seems to have instilled into many a talented young lad a desire to enter the profession in which the crazy dame had her being. For that, at least, her critics should be grateful.

Chapter Eight:
A Hollow Victory, 1945-1951

Throughout 1945, amid the victory celebrations, the Riley road show, now in its sixth year, continued to tour the length and breadth of the country, ending the year in the London suburban theaters. There is no record of a Lucan-McShane pantomime in December 1945; in fact *The Stage* contains hardly a mention of the couple for several months, apart from the artists' cards inserted by one of the show's variety acts, the harp and 'cello duo The Hayes Sisters. Throughout February the duo list themselves as members of the Lucan-McShane company but give their home address until the end of the month, when they give their next addresses as the theaters at Northampton, Peterborough and Ipswich. *The Stage* also lists Charles Meek as musical director of "Lucan and McShane's new show," which seems to support the view that the whole company had been "resting" for some considerable time.

In September 1945, Michael Lyon, perhaps because he knew there was no prospect of a pantomime, had written to the BBC, mentioning the volume of the Lucans' fan mail and hoping to set up a new series of broadcasts, as the couple would be free from November to February. On a memo to Michael Standing, Director of Variety, Arthur Brown scribbled, "Are you interested?" Beneath this, Standing simply scribbled "No thanks." When Lyon suggests further discussions, Standing wrote to him saying there was no point to discussions "as we don't want a series." And that was the end of that.

Perhaps another reason for the hitherto unexplained "resting" over Christmas is to be found in the state of Arthur's health. *The Stage* reported from the Kingston Empire in the last week of March 1946 that Arthur was again taken ill and was replaced by the new understudy George Beck. "Disappointment was voiced when the announcement was made," but Kitty and Willer Neal were on good form, as were "the very fine costumes worn by the principals and supporting cast." The reviewer added, perhaps a touch acidly given that clothes rationing was far from over, "The wardrobe, in fact, plays a large part in the lively production."

The show moved on without Arthur and was at Finsbury Park Empire when Kitty's mother Kate McShane died in Dublin on 11 April 1946. There seems to have been no call for the following week so it is possible that Kitty went to Dublin for the funeral. Less than two months later on 2 June 1946 Kitty's father Daniel McShane died and was laid to rest alongside his wife in Glasnevin cemetery. Daddy's little girl, who still dressed up every night with the ringlets and frills she had first worn forty years earlier, was now an orphan. No account survives of Kitty's reaction to this news, but the road show trundled on until the end of the year, moving week after week through every major town and city from Brighton to Edinburgh and all points in between. The Lucans returned to the Bristol Hippodrome for the week of 19 August and the advertisements in the *Western Daily Press* reveal that part of the show was also broadcast on radio; 'Broadcast Wednesday, 21 August, 8.30-9.00.' This is another radio broadcast (the third) which to the best of my knowledge has never before been documented. At the Sheffield Empire in October the show is advertised in the program as 'An entirely new production' and patrons, most of whom would have been hoarding coupons in the hope of buying some winter clothes were also informed that "Miss McShane's Dresses and Girls' Modern Dresses by Cubbitt and Manger, South Molton Street, London W. The Girls' first and Last Scene Dresses by Chas. Fox, London. All Wardrobe under the personal supervision of Miss Maisie Munroe." Kitty McShane, now Daddy's little orphan in the frilly frock, seemed to be hell-bent on presenting ever more lavish wardrobes in the midst of post-war austerity, but since April 1945 the Lucans had had no new film commitments and they made just two one-off radio broadcasts (25 July and 21 August) in the whole of 1946. For a couple of post-war years, it was principally the road show that kept them going.

The contrast between Miss McShane's lavish wardrobes both on and off stage and screen, and the reality of life for the girls who queued to see her, is well brought out in a hilarious anecdote told to me in 2013 by a Leicester woman, Heather Sills. Heather's grandmother, Gladys Staton, was born and brought up in Stoke-on-Trent. Like every other teenage girl during the war, she had very few clothes, and no luxury items such as nylons. Many women have told the story of how they would stain their legs with a weak solution of gravy browning, and draw a "seam" up the back with an eyebrow pencil, but none with more disastrous results than Gladys. One Saturday night she went with her friends to see one of the Old Mother Riley films. As she stood in the queue outside the cinema, a passing mongrel took a sniff at Gladys's legs and decided they were a doggie treat meant for him. To her horror he greedily licked and slurped from her legs as much gravy browning as he could until desperate Gladys, by now the laughing stock of the whole queue, finally persuaded some of the lads who were enjoying the show to chase the dog away. That night, the poor girl must have gazed at Kitty's frills with even more envy than usual!

Through early 1947 the show revisited all the familiar theaters, and in March 1947 at Finsbury Park, it was again announced as a new production; however, as critics pointed out, the frocks may have been new but the central act remained the same, except that Kitty and Billy were taking up more time with their "song scena" and Arthur was marginalized. In June 1947 *The Stage* announced that both Arthur and Kitty were to take "a well-deserved seven-week holiday" and would be replaced in the show by understudies George Beck and Eileen Ogle. Perhaps significantly, Willer Neal was also absent from the show and may have been sharing the holiday. When all three returned to the show, Arthur was taken ill several times in October and was again replaced by George Beck. The supposed seven-week holiday (including Willer Neal) and Arthur's recurring illnesses would seem to mask some deeper disruption in the lives of the Lucans, and it is highly likely that they were in the throes of a potential separation caused by Kitty's affair with Billy, common knowledge in the business but concealed, for a little longer at least, from their adoring fans. This hypothesis is supported by the fact that as early as September the management of the Bristol Hippodrome announced that "to the joy of many Bristolians, Arthur Lucan (Old Mother Riley) would be starring in that year's pantomime."[128] On 6 November *The Stage* confirmed that the Bristol Hippodrome panto-mime starring Arthur Lucan was to be *The Babes in the Wood*. There is no reference of any kind to Kitty McShane in advance notices, advertisements or cast lists, and throughout the winter months her name did not appear in *The Stage* in any other context. This seems to be the very first time since their earliest pantomimes, apart from documented illnesses, that Lucan and McShane did not perform together. Arthur's solo appearance at Bristol has hitherto gone unremarked, but it is important because it pre-dates by five years what is normally accepted as Arthur's first going solo in 1952. Kitty had played Maid Marian almost thirty years earlier but had stopped playing principal boys in the 1930s; now aged fifty, she would certainly not have taken kindly to being excluded and replaced by younger and prettier leading boys and girls. Arthur, however, must have relished the opportunity to escape from endless marital rows, and from playing second fiddle in his own house to Billy Breach.

Among the few pleasures left to the tired and aging Arthur, and by all accounts the one he still enjoyed most, was to share the stage (and the green room) with a bevy of bright young women, and that is exactly what was on offer at Bristol in Lynwood Robert's production for Prince Littler of *Babes in the Wood*, with "Arthur Lucan as Old Mother Riley, the Babes' Nurse." The pantomime opened on Christmas Eve. Jean Adrienne, who played Robin Hood and received star billing with Arthur, was widely acknowledged to be one of the finest pantomime principal boys of the 1930s and 1940s. In her obituary in *The Stage* in 1994 Geoffrey Guy wrote that "Jean had a lovely warm personality, deep velvet voice, a perfect figure and was an exquisite dancer." She was in fact a classically trained dancer, and in her youth had toured with the company of Anna Pavlova. In 2012, musical star Sheila Mathews, one of Britain's highest-paid pantomime Principal Boys for more than 40 years, told *The Call Boy* editor Geoff Bowden that "Jean Adrienne was the best principal boy I ever saw and whenever I played 'boy' I modelled the role on Jean." Valerie Lawson, who played Maid Marian, was noted for her exceptionally pretty singing voice, and she went on a year later to play the lead in a long tour of Vivian Ellis's hit musical *Bless the Bride*. Jeanne Goddard and Josephine Anne were Arthur's "lovable babes," Carol Lane played Will Scarlet, Rita Baker was the Spirit of the Glade and Bert Platt was Baron Cul-de-Sac. Arthur was mentioned by name in several reviews, and was clearly not being impersonated by an understudy. Arthur's old understudy, George Beck, was playing the dame in *Dick Whittington* at the Pavilion in Liverpool, where he sang the same new comedy song as Arthur at Bristol, "O Where is

My Sunday Potato?" Roy Rolland, who had not yet joined the Lucans' company, was appearing in pantomime at Clacton.

A Bristol reviewer for *The Stage* in January 1948 called *Babes in the Wood* "a pantomime which promises to have a long run, for its ingredients are spectacle, fun and laughter," and a review in the *Western Daily Press* noted that "such is the pantomime spirit prevailing that parents feel unashamed when endeavoring to create more noise in pantomimic songs than their children. Good, clean, wholesome fun is provided, as expected, by Arthur Lucan as the nurse." Alas, the promised long run until 14 March was tragically cut short, as the history pages of the Bristol Hippodrome website explain:

FIRE! FIRE! Having survived the war unscathed, during which time the theater contributed enormously to the morale of Bristolians with a continuous run of first-rate entertainment, it was a tragic irony when, less than three years after the war ended, a disastrous fire broke out and almost destroyed it. The annual pantomime was *Babes in the Wood* and at approximately 1 p.m. on 16 Monday fire broke out backstage and within minutes had spread from the flies and enveloped the stage. Thirty-foot high flames gutted the entire rear portion of the theater, but the auditorium and roof were saved after a frantic battle by the Fire Brigade. The conflagration was halted, almost miraculously it seemed, at the orchestra pit, and the damage sustained in the auditorium was caused chiefly by smoke and water. No definite cause of the fire was established and the investigation committee concluded that the most likely cause was *a cigarette or match carelessly discarded by some unknown person immediately before leaving the theater.* (my italics)

Kitty McShane's name has never been formally associated with this fire; after all, she was not in the company with Arthur. But could that "unknown person" have been Kitty McShane? A re-examination of certain pieces of evidence suggests that this shocking hypothesis is more than a vague possibility. Steve King does in fact mention a row between Arthur and Kitty which he says took place when *Going Gay* was at the Bristol Hippodrome, after which "a mysterious fire occurred at the theater, causing sufficient damage to ensure that the show would be unable to go on the following night." I cannot find any mention, either in *The Stage* or in the very complete Bristol Hippodrome performance archive, of the shows *Going Gay* (1952-53) or *Old Mother Riley in Paris* (1954), and Slim Ingram assured me that neither show visited the Bristol Hippodrome. Lucan and McShane had appeared at the Hippodrome, five times in the 1920s, and just once in the 1930s. *Old Mother Riley and Her Daughter Kitty* played there in 1946 and 1947, but after that the names Lucan and McShane never again appear in the archives of the Bristol Hippodrome.

Arthur did return to Bristol one more time, again without Kitty. At the end of the 1952 tour of *Going Gay* he was given star billing in Gaston and Andrée's pantomime *Jack and the Beanstalk* at the Bristol New Empire. The argument King reported apparently concerned the ownership of the name Old Mother Riley, and Kitty must have been enraged to discover that "Arthur Lucan–Old Mother Riley" had featured on the 1952 Bristol pantomime posters above *Jack and the Beanstalk*, and in far bigger type. But there is no record of Kitty visiting the Bristol New Empire pantomime or of any cancellation there due to fire. This is borne out by the company manager Slim Ingram, who told me in a conversation in April 2012 that Kitty definitely did not come to the Bristol Empire pantomime. On a more sinister note, during the tour of *Going Gay*, when Kitty had taken to following and stalking Arthur, Slim was convinced that at the Colchester Playhouse in November 1952, some rubbish bins immediately behind the theater had been deliberately set on fire. To the consternation of the cast and audience, smoke began to rise through the stage floor and the fire brigade arrived, halted the show and evacuated the theater. Back in his dressing room, as Arthur took off his putty nose he said to Slim, 'You'd have blamed that on our Kitty if she wasn't in London.' But when they got back to their hotel, Kitty was waiting for them in the foyer. Far from Slim's suspicion seeming outlandish, Arthur's remark suggests that he already knew his wife was capable of arson. Was it mere coincidence that this fire was started at a time (late 1952) when Kitty must have known that Arthur was about to return in pantomime to Bristol, the scene of the 1948 conflagration? This was just one of many dangerous and irrational antics with which the increasingly deranged and drunken Kitty blighted the last few years of Arthur's life.

Steve King's version of the Bristol anecdote would appear to be a conflation or confusion of two, or even more, separate incidents. But its very existence, once the dates and facts are adjusted and corrected, definitely serves to increase the dreadful though utterly plausible possibility that an enraged and jealous Kitty, who seems not to have been working anywhere in January 1948 and was feeling neglected and left out, had in fact visited Arthur in Bristol during *Babes in the Wood*. She may have come at the week-end primarily to indulge her favorite pastime of collecting money, perhaps staying over on the Sunday when Arthur wasn't working just to torment him, by keeping him away from his "babes."

Kitty's own flagrant adultery did not prevent her constant attempts to spoil any bit of romance which came Arthur's way. Slim Ingram remembered that a couple of years later Arthur made a secret detour *via Bristol* (to Wolverhampton!) in order to give flowers to a girlfriend. Unlike Kitty and Billy, poor Arthur had to camouflage his canoodling to prevent trouble; Kitty regularly fired chorus girls who got too close to Arthur. Alan Mackinnon, whose mother Molly Braithwaite came from a theatrical family and was working with Hylda Baker at this time, wrote to me,

> I do remember one other thing my mother told me, and that was that Kitty used to watch Arthur with extra care if any of the young ladies in the cast seemed to catch his eye and that many a young chorus girl suddenly found that her contract (if any) was not renewed if she showed any interest in Arthur or he in her.

Other people recalled that Kitty chased one poor chorus girl through a house and down the street, and another was threatened with a gun on a railway platform! As the years went on, and Kitty's affair with Billy had become common knowledge, her irrational jealousy and vindictive behavior actually got worse rather than better. And at Bristol she was not even permanently on hand to "to watch Arthur with extra care."

The nightmare scenario of Kitty's involvement in the 1948 Bristol fire is fully supported by Slim Ingram who was told, presumably by Arthur himself, that Kitty had indeed been in Bristol and present in the Hippodrome theater at the crucial moment. In 2002 at the

Covent Garden Theater Museum, Slim recalled a persistent rumor from the theater world of 1948:

Arthur was engaged to play the Dame at the Bristol Hippodrome. Kitty was not in the production but she was on the scene. She came down to Bristol in her Studebaker with her chauffeur. In the afternoon the theater was locked and nobody was allowed backstage, and it was said that Kitty was the last person to leave the stage door before it was locked. Very shortly afterwards a fire gutted the entire backstage area. But it was never ever proved that it was Kitty's doing. This rumor was doing the rounds among stage management but was of course never discussed outside the profession.

Given Slim's testimony, repeated verbatim to me in September 2012, it seems to me not only possible but quite likely that on the morning of Monday, 16 February, after another row about money or Arthur's "girls," Kitty may have worked herself up into one of those rages, described by Boscombe theater manager Roy Denton, in which she was convinced she was the wronged or aggrieved party. At lunchtime, after leaving the Hippodrome by the stage door in Denmark Street, she was driven back to London, leaving in her wake a devastated Hippodrome which had escaped the Blitz but not the wrath of Kitty McShane.

This is largely speculation, of course, but to support it we have Slim Ingram's report of the Bristol rumor, Steve King's mention of Kitty and a fire at Bristol Hippodrome (clearly a garbled version of Slim's anecdote), and Slim Ingram's suspicious fire at Colchester. To this day there is no other really satisfactory explanation for what might have caused the 1948 Bristol fire. Mercifully no-one died or was seriously injured, but the entire staff of the theater was out of work for almost a year during re-building. The costumes and sets for *Babes in the Wood*, which one critic said were among the most beautiful he had ever seen, were completely destroyed. The panto-mime closed prematurely, and Arthur's pleasant and argument-free collaboration with the "lovable babes" Jeanne and Josephine, the dashing" Jean Adrienne and the "charming" Valerie Lawson came to an abrupt and unexpected end. And all because of "a cigarette or match carelessly discarded by some unknown person immediately before leaving the theater ...."

If indeed Kitty was involved, Arthur would almost certainly have suspected her, but had he denounced her she might well have been tried for arson and received a prison sentence, which would only have served to make his own already wretched situation even worse. In the words of Max Wall he was, and had been for some time, "a battered husband," and around this time, according to Kitty's sister Annie, Billy Breach also gave Arthur a beating at the house in Forty Lane. Arthur, gentle and quiet at the best of times, was now totally cowed into submission. Or so Kitty thought. The announcement of the couple's extended holiday in the second half of 1947, when they were replaced by understudies George Beck and Eileen Ogle, seems to have been a cover-up for their first major split. Then, to Kitty's intense annoyance, Arthur actually had the nerve to get himself a solo engagement without the woman who thought she ran his life both on and off the stage. Kitty must have been seized by a panic she had not felt since her position was threatened by Bert Arnold in 1926. Her next bizarre reaction provides further smoke for the fires of suspicion which surrounded her, for it was around this time in 1948 that in fit of rage she resorted to a cruel and heartless act of pyromania; she burned all the couple's scripts, photograph albums and press cuttings, at least all those she could lay her hands on. By a strange irony, Kitty's father Dan had been a fire officer who specialized in extinguishing fires in the theater.

But Arthur was not entirely or always the passive victim of Kitty's machinations. In December 2012, in an unexpected postscript to the Bristol fire, I was introduced to Mrs. Miriam Kite from Bristol. As Miriam Rose she had appeared, aged sixteen, as a singer and dancer in Peggy Barnes's troupe in the 1947-1948 production of *Babes in the Wood*. In a letter to the *Bristol Post*, and in several long telephone conversations with me, Miriam recalled that the day after the fire Arthur, not as helpless or lacking in initiative as critics have claimed, offered to take the Peggy Barnes girls into the Lucan-McShane road show.

Peggy Barnes was choreographer for the pantomime, a lovely lady. We were her girls and it was through her that I started my stage career, answering her advert for dancers in 1946.

We were in our eighth week of the pantomime when the fire started. The morning after the fire I went to the theater to find the stage and back wall completely gutted, also the orchestra pit and first few rows of the stalls. I stood on the wrecked stage and the *Evening Post* took my photo for the paper. There was a meeting of the cast the next day and Arthur Lucan 'Old Mother Riley' chose some of us Bristol girls for his No.1 touring show. The names of the girls I remember were: Jean, Margaret, Doreen, Jane, Yvonne, Hazel, Brenda, Barbara, sisters Katy and Edith, and me, Miriam.

So Kitty could not totally deprive Arthur of his "babes" but seems to have been obliged to take them into the 1948 Riley road show, where she could at least keep a closer eye on them, and on Arthur, the Mother Goose who was still laying golden eggs for KMS productions. Miriam Rose was with the show throughout 1948 and remembered Kitty as cold, distant and domineering.

Kitty was by now rather stout and we were all young and pretty so she seems to have been jealous of us. In the show's opening scene as 'The Dancing Colleens,' we all had to wear our hair knotted up under our headscarves while she showed off her shoulder-length hair. Arthur was very sweet but also rather shy, almost bashful. He didn't normally travel by train with us on Sundays but just once, for some reason he did, and when we were changing trains at Crewe we saw him on the platform. The girls crowded round him and begged him to come to the refreshment room for a cup of tea. He hesitated and said 'I don't really think I should,' as if he was scared. But Kitty wasn't there to boss him so we persuaded him to join us. He seemed relieved to get away and soon forgot all about her. We all laughed and joked and he had us in stitches!

The knotted headscarves of the Dancing Colleens are very visible in *Old Mother Riley's New Venture*, behind Kitty with her flowing locks.

Miriam, like so many others, also told me that Kitty truly believed, in spite of her very modest talents, that she was the star of the show that culminated in her mock wedding to her real boyfriend. She was often loud and argumentative and was haughty and bossy; this was in stark contrast to the title of the show's opening number, "The Annual Outing" with its subtitle "In the Spirit of Good Fellowship and Harmony." Miriam remembered that everything seemed to be labelled "By permission of Miss Kitty McShane."

My copy of the program from the Empire Swindon in May 1948, compared with another from October 1946, shows that the main scenes had not evolved over the years; only the variety acts changed as exasperated artistes came and went. The opening "Annual Outing" included Riley's neighbor and sparring partner Mrs. Ginnochie, a travesty role, with understudy George E. Beck as her son. The second Riley scene in the first half was called "Fireworks by Gaslight," with Kitty late home as in "Bridget's Night Out." In the second half there was a "Morning after the Dance" scene in Mother Riley's kitchen which included Danny Boy (Willer Neal) and the lodger. The grand finale "Kitty's Night Out" included Willer Neal as the Bridegroom and George E. Beck as Mother Riley's Old Flame. According to Miriam, the atmosphere in the company was far from harmonious, and by Christmas 1948 she had had enough. So she went back to Bristol where she danced in the pantomime that re-opened the restored Hippodrome, the theater which had almost burned down the day Kitty McShane left town in February 1948. In December 1948, Lucan, McShane and Willer Neal appeared in the pantomime *The Old Woman Who Lived in a Shoe* at Chatham and New Cross. The Lucans repeated this pantomime for four more years, and it was to be the very last show in which they appeared together. Arthur's old understudy, George Beck, left the 1948 company for Christmas and was far away in Rotherham, playing the dame in *Babes in the Wood*, and not much help in case of Arthur's drunken incapacity.

Throughout the late 1940s, when he was not medically unwell, Arthur as Old Mother Riley was on the road, touring with "daughter and boy-friend" and making money for McShane Productions, most of which went to support the lavish, chauffeur-driven lifestyle of Kitty and Billy, while Arthur took the bus or walked home after the show to his single hotel bedroom. At the New Cross Empire in April 1948, post-war austerity had even robbed Arthur of real plates to smash. "Mother Riley must now throw tin plates about owing to the crockery shortage. The laughter is by no means rationed, however, and there is still that rapid and effective change from humor to pathos . . . ." Sadly the pathos was all too real. And yet in spite of Arthur's growing weariness and disillusionment in real life, he managed to keep up appearances in a show which culminated in the twice-nightly onstage wedding of Kitty and Billy.

But behind the scenes all was far from sweetness and light. The variety artist Molly Braithwaite, who also observed the couple at close quarters, put her finger on a major reason for Kitty's irrational anxiety. "It was pretty well common knowledge amongst people in the know in those days that all Arthur was to Kitty was a meal ticket and there was no way she would have let him go." Molly also noted this as a point of resemblance between Kitty and George Formby's wife Beryl. "There was the same fierce protection of her meal ticket in the case of Kitty McShane who probably quite rightly felt that she would end up with nothing if she let Arthur get away. Both wives would have done anything to secure their positions." In an interview Tommy Trinder once said that Beryl Formby's attitude to George was, "Well, here's the gold mine, I'm not going to let anybody else take their pick and shovel there." But the major difference between Kitty and Beryl was that Beryl's constant vigilance and unswerving loyalty to her husband made Formby so rich that in his will he left the equivalent of millions in today's money, whereas when Kitty had finished with Arthur he was penniless.

The young singer-actress Betty Driver, later of *Coronation Street* fame, who by now had appeared a number of times on the same bill as Lucan and McShane, recalled in her memoirs that Beryl Formby once told her that her (Betty's) mother Nellie Driver, Beryl herself, and Kitty McShane were the three most hated women in British show business. Betty Driver's own opinion of Kitty was equally negative. "She was a hard woman who browbeat the sweet old man [Arthur] until she ruined him. She had the biggest head and thought of herself as the star. Whenever I played with them in theaters I was always amazed to see she took the star dressing-room." Betty Astell, the wife of comedian Cyril Fletcher, was interviewed by Michael Pointon shortly before her death in 2005. She recalled working with the Lucans in the 1940s.

Photo 15: Billy Breach (Willer Neal), Kitty and Arthur, late 1940s. Steve King

The man was really a puppet. She ran every aspect of their lives, in and out of the theater, on and off the stage. I've never seen anything like it, a bit like George Formby's wife, another Beryl Formby. But in Lucan and McShane he came alive when he was the character. That was the only time he was alive; otherwise he was just a piece of flesh and blood. It was a very, very odd relationship. He was a great performer, frightfully funny. But she was a horrible woman.

Another observer at this time corroborates Max Wall's impression of Arthur as the battered husband. "Arthur Lucan I adored. He was genuinely hopeless. I never saw him without a scratch or a bruise. She (Kitty McShane) was very abusive, the worst kind of bog Celtic."

In a publicity photograph from 1943 (the year Billy Breach became Kitty's lover) Arthur's right eye is clearly swollen and closed. The comedian Arthur Askey, who knew the couple well, also referred to Kitty's reputation for violence. Discussing Beryl Formby's hold over George he said: "There was no doubt as to who was boss. Almost the same situation as poor Arthur Lucan with the harridan Kitty McShane, though not quite as physical."[129]

Kitty watched Arthur like a hawk and kept him "under the thumb" as Molly Braithwaite put it, but not from any real concern or regard for his health or happiness. At times her behavior verged on the deranged. Roy Denton was manager of the Boscombe Hippodrome and the nearby Chine Hotel and remembered many bizarre episodes. Although Kitty and Billy now shared a room, Kitty would go on the rampage through the hotel late at night, looking for Arthur.

> She used to drink a little, well, perhaps a little more than a little, but she used to get into that state in which she really was feeling angry, angry, angry over Arthur. . . for some reason or other, and she used to lose control, and she'd be going up and down the corridors of the hotel banging on the doors. 'I want Arthur Lucan! Arthur Lucan! He's my husband, Arthur Lucan! I'm Kitty McShane, I want Arthur Lucan!' In fact she was hysterical, and it frightened Arthur to death, because he was a timid little man. There'd been so much trouble that he used to change his room every night to get away from her.

Roy Denton recalled that in those days, at the end of every week he would hand Kitty McShane over £1,000 in cash (around £18,000 in 2014) and she would give Arthur £30. On one occasion she even refused to give him that, and Denton told of finding a distressed Arthur in his dressing room refusing to go on. "I've given that woman everything and now she won't even give me thirty quid!" Roy promised to lend him thirty pounds until Kitty got over her tantrum, and moments later Arthur went onstage to perform with his "darling daughter."

There are many accounts of Kitty throwing things at people, but just once it seems that someone hit back at her. In an interview with Rob Cope in 2004, Sue Pollard revealed another charming Kitty anecdote which must date from the post-war period.

> I did get a huge mail bag from [the TV comedy series] *You Rang, M'Lord?* One lady wrote to say that she'd been in service some fifty odd years ago and she was cleaning the room of Kitty McShane, the stage daughter of Old Mother Riley, the great variety comic. She spied some face cream on the dressing table and because she was only sixteen dipped her finger in it and put a bit on her face. Anyway, the next day Kitty McShane sent for her and shouted 'How dare you touch my make-up!' and slapped her across the face. The upshot of

it was that this woman's mother was furious and went to see Kitty and ended up slapping the stage star across the face before walking triumphantly out.[130]

Arthur Lucan was getting older and more tired, but Mother Riley's status was by now legendary. Back in November 1946, when the latest version of the road show came to the Hippodrome, *The Manchester Guardian* had reported that

> The more a Lucan-McShane show changes the more it remains the same thing. Its foundation is always that comic creation which Arthur Lucan has made so well known in the variety theater, Old Mother Riley. There are many dame comedians but none quite like Arthur Lucan. He is as high-spirited and as full of robust nonsense as ever and as appealing to all save those who are too hopelessly stiff to unbend.[131]

Arthur's special status was more fully confirmed in March 1947 when a critic reviewing the show at Shepherd's Bush declared,

"Arthur Lucan has made the loquacious and inexhaustible Mother Riley, a classical figure in the world of variety, a perfect model of dame characterization and laughter-making. As Kitty of the piece, Miss McShane adequately portrays the wayward daughter, and Willer Neal cuts a fine figure as the lover." At the New Cross Empire in April 1948 the critic declared that "Arthur Lucan's Mother Riley is a classic of the music-hall and the act can be seen again and again without losing its effect. He always succeeds in being up to date and topical." On the subject of topicality, as recently as August 2013, an internet blogger rescued an example of just such an "up to date and topical" sketch from total oblivion, and his résumé of the sketch saw in the late 1940s reveals the extent to which Mother Riley was still widely viewed as an irrepressible spokesperson for the impoverished working class. I quote an article from the blog of "The Cynical Tendency," entitled "Fiscal Policy and old Mother Riley," in which he recalls "Old Mother Riley Economics" as practiced by "the famous, and much loved, music hall turn of Arthur Lucan and Kitty McShane:"

I saw them live on stage a time or two, and part of the act was to relate to difficulties and hazards of the ordinary people, with the lack of money at the end of the week being a constant theme. This sketch I recall from the late 1940s offered many people the most rational explanation of the economic policy of Sir Stafford Cripps at the time, and perhaps made more sense. They were concerned with the economics of reality, but this sketch did not make it into any film, for obvious reasons given the period and the grip of the film censors:

Old Mother Riley and Kitty are in their kitchen.

Kitty–Mother, we haven't any money and its only Tuesday.

Old Mother Riley–I don't know where it all goes.

Kitty–You've been buying rum again.

Old Mother Riley–I haven't had a drop since Mafeking Night.

Kitty–When was that?

Old Mother Riley–Yesterday, oops, a long time ago.

Kitty–How can we get some money for food, the light and the rent?

Old Mother Riley–There is some washing to do.

Kitty–Mother, it's our own washing, how can we get paid to do that?

Old Mother Riley–The man next door will give it to me.

Kitty–Why would he want to do that?

Old Mother Riley (looking coy)–Well I make his tea for him when his wife's out.

Kitty–What does she think about that?

Old Mother Riley advances down stage, flaps her skirts, leers at the audience, and says—She says it saves her all the trouble!

Kitty–Oh mother, mother, exits.

Old Mother Riley pours herself a cup of tea, takes a rum bottle from behind the sink, shakes her head and puts it back. Knock on door, Old Mother Riley says 'Come in,' a small man with a large hat, which he removes to show he is bald, and carrying a notebook and satchel enters. He is the rent man, and everyone knows it. He tells Old Mother Riley she is behind on the rent, and there is then a long diatribe of nonsense, at the end of which he demands the rent again.

Another knock, another man, carrying a bucket, obviously the window cleaner, he wants his money, another comedy routine. Another knock, another man, now the milkman, also wanting payment. Old Mother Riley flaps about fussing, and while the men begin to argue with each other dips her hand into the satchel to take out some money. She then tells the men to line up, and goes to the milkman, puts money in his right hand, tells him to transfer it to his left, and pass it on to the window cleaner, who then passes it onto the rent man, who puts it into his satchel. Old Mother Riley now tells them they have all been paid and to get out. The rent man looks in his satchel and realizes he has been conned. An arm waving loud argument starts that degenerates into a bout of major slapstick that wrecks the kitchen. When Old Mother Riley finally sits on the rent man he pulls out a police whistle and blows. In those days rent men always carried police whistles, and the policeman was usually nearby. A Police Officer rushes in, Old Mother Riley claims she has been attacked for her money, picking up the satchel, and the men have tarnished her virtue, feigning a dramatic swoon. The men are arrested and marched out. Old Mother Riley pours another cup of tea, and sits down.

Kitty returns and sees the ruined kitchen.

Kitty–Mother, mother, what have you done?

Old Mother Riley–I've just tidied up dear.

Old Mother Riley drains her cup takes money from the satchel and gives it to Kitty, telling her to go and get some groceries. Kitty leaves, Old Mother Riley goes to the sink cupboard, gets out the rum, fills the cup, and then goes forward to toast the audience. Curtain.[132]

The "wayward daughter" and her "fine figure of a lover" now decided they were worthy of a radio series of their own, with a bit of Mother Riley thrown in. On 10 May 1948, Tom Ronald wrote to Ronald Waldman, Assistant Head of Variety.

Lucan and McShane are very anxious to come back in a series and are free for broadcasting at the end of June . . . These two have not been on the air for some time, and in spite of headaches at Bangor, I would be perfectly willing to shoulder them again. They have got older and wiser. There's no doubt about it they were very popular. I suggest a show of not longer than half an hour and a maximum of one song from her 'lovely daughter.' This they would agree to.

On 13 May it was agreed that "The Light Program will place a series of six Lucan and McShane programs on Mondays, 7.30-8.00 p.m., beginning Monday 20 September." The recording of six 30-minute episodes of Old Mother Riley and her Daughter Kitty' was to begin on 12 July at the Paris Cinema. The Lucans' fee was £100 per program and Billy Breach (aka Willer Neal) who was included at Kitty's insistence was to receive £20 per show. Along with a new scriptwriter Ronnie Taylor, Kitty took a major hand in writing the scripts, claiming that Arthur was not well enough. She also ensured that Arthur's role was minimized to make time for her duets with Billy. But Tom Ronald, who had produced their earlier highly successful radio series and had been genuinely fond of the couple, was deeply disappointed with these latest scripts, largely a rehash of old material, and he was saddened by the changes he had noticed in Arthur over the eight years of their friendship. His frank view of the series is contained in a letter he wrote some time later to Michael

Lyon. "Arthur was completely under their thumb [Kitty and Billy] and his personality over the air failed to project." One amusing incident, probably the only one, from this series, is recorded in the files at Caversham. When giving instructions for pre-broadcast editing, Tom Ronald wrote, "There is a bit of editing to be done on SLO35559 . . . During the first few speeches with Roger the Lodger at the beginning of the program, Arthur Lucan went a bit haywire and talked about 'warming the lodger's sausage.' This sounded filthy. Perhaps you would play this over and cut the offending bit out." I can't help wondering if this gaffe wasn't a Freudian slip or Arthur's howl of despair about his own predicament as lodger in his own house.

When the road show returned to Manchester in October 1948 the *Guardian* reviewer wrote of the Lucans, "They do not take up new parts, but who would have them do so? They have become identified with the characters they have made so popular beyond all possibility of change." As we have already noted, this was frighteningly true in a way which the reviewer had probably not intended!

But for one less impressionable, or perhaps more perceptive, observer, the years were now visibly beginning to take their toll. The novelist Francis King was for many years a book reviewer and theater critic for *The Telegraph*. In his 1969 review for *The Listener* of Margery Baker's Thames TV documentary on the Lucans, he recalled his own memory of seeing the couple onstage.

> On the only occasion, in the 1940s, when I saw Arthur Lucan and his wife, Kitty McShane, on the stage, their act struck me, in spite of their fame, as both pathetic and macabre. Lucan, an animated hairpin accoutered in bonnet, black bombazine skirt reaching to bony ankles and a pair of elastic-sided boots, played the 'lovable' (i.e. peculiarly unlovely and even repellent) Old Mother Riley to the Kitty, all puff-sleeves, frills and shoulder-length hair, of his middle-aged wife.

In this review entitled "Shabby Treatment," Francis King admits that he had not expected much of the Lucan television documentary. "The two surprises of a dreary ten days were an appearance by Anthony Burgess . . . and *Applause, Applause* (Thames TV) a documentary, seemingly unpromising in subject, about the music-hall duo Old Mother Riley and her 'daughter' Kitty." But King goes on to reveal his fascination with this sad blend of the pathetic and the macabre. His review, and the excellent Thames documentary directed by Margery Baker, are among the earliest, and sharpest, accounts of the tragi-comic complexity of the Lucan-McShane phenomenon.

Kitty, everyone who appeared on the program seemed to agree, was a bitch with little talent. Arthur was a quiet, retiring man, never happier than when he could relax alone after a performance with a bottle of brandy. A constant theme of their inept sketches—Arthur Lucan wrote them—was Old Mother Riley's anxiety for her Kitty: the girl was not back in the early hours; she has taken up with an unsuitable boyfriend; she was leading a rackety and godless life. Kitty would threaten to leave home forever; mother and daughter would scream at each other; then, sobbing, they would fall into each other's arms. This program demonstrated how this stage situation was merely a comic travesty of a tragic real-life one in which Kitty took lovers—one actually shared their house with them—pretended that her son was her brother, in order to conceal her age, publicly insulted Arthur, made scenes in restaurants and bullied her fellow performers; and in which Lucan, ever-suffering and ever-loving, took pleasure in abasing himself before her.

Francis King also saw that the story cried out to be dramatized. "A wonderful film could be made of this story: what a chance for one of our theatrical knights to play Old Mother Riley!" Ten years later, in 1980, Brian Murphy and Maureen Lipman played Arthur and Kitty in Alan Plater's stage play *On Your Way Riley!* But the bio-pic still cries out to be made!

By 1949 it seemed clear that the series of films by music hall to cinema crossover comedians had run its course. Max Miller's last film was released in 1942, and Will Hay's last film in 1943; neither Gracie Fields nor the Lucans has made a film since 1945, and George Formby's 1946 *George in Civvy Street* was his parting shot. It therefore came as something of a surprise when it was announced in 1949 that Lucan and McShane were to make a new film, *Old Mother Riley's New Venture*, for Harry Reynolds Productions and the Renown Pictures Corporation, directed by John Harlow with John Gilling.

This in fact proved to be the first of a trio of films distributed by Renown between 1949 and 1951. One cannot pretend that these are great works of cinematic art; they are, as Halliwell put it "ramshackle," with flimsy plots, digressions, jerky transitions, and the inevitable hold-ups for Kitty to sing, now often in duets with her real-life boyfriend. Kitty's ever more voluminous frills can no longer disguise the fact that she is no colleen but a heavy fifty-two-year-old matron, still engaged in unconvincing girlish flirtations. As one internet critic put it, "Alas, no amount of puffed sleeves, hair ribbons, or cabin doors disguising an expanding waistline, could detract from the fact that by the time of this film Miss McShane was 51, and far from being a dainty young Irish colleen!" Yet in spite of all that, thanks almost entirely to Arthur's undiminished performing skills, all three films have moments of clever or absurd dialogue, and set-piece sequences of hilarious comedy or unexpected pathos.

Old Mother Riley's New Venture was released in July 1949 and was successful enough to gain a re-release in 1953.

> Following a distressing series of robberies, the proprietor of a hotel decides to go on holiday, and puts Mrs. Riley, a dishwasher, in charge. After the 'Hula' diamond belonging to an Eastern potentate is stolen, Mrs. Riley is suspected of theft and is arrested by the police. After escaping from jail, she catches the real thieves, and Kitty marries the proprietor's son (Billy Breach/Willer Neal). The film ends with a custard pie fight which includes a shot of the director shouting 'Give me more!' And he gets it![133]

Once again, the film has barely got going before the upwardly mobile washerwoman exchanges her widow's weeds for the finery of a hotel manageress, and later for a prisoner's uniform. Reinforcing my assertion that the Lucans' lives and films are strangely intertwined, I noticed that an external shot of the beauty parlor to which Kitty takes her mother for titivation is, in fact, a shot of Kitty's heavily loss-making salon at 20 South Molton Street.

Theater posters for the road show now grandly announced "Personal appearance of your stage, radio and screen favorites," but it wasn't always as personal as expected. In October 1949, Arthur was taken ill during the first house at the Chiswick Empire and was rushed to the West Middlesex Hospital where he underwent an operation for the removal of his prostate. During his long convalescence his place was taken by Roy Rolland, the new understudy who had replaced George Beck earlier in the year. It was during these years of illness that Rolland frequently stood in for Arthur, not, as is often claimed, during Arthur's last two seasons. And on posters all around the country, Willer Neal as Danny Boy was now receiving second billing, his name as prominent as those of Lucan and McShane.

The next film, *Old Mother Riley Headmistress*, was produced for Grand National Pictures by Harry Reynolds. John Harlow directed with John Gilling, and old faithful Con West was back on the script. The film was released in May 1950 around the same time as a much more polished comedy vehicle for Alastair Sim, Margaret Rutherford, and the young Joyce Grenfell, *The Happiest Days of Your Life*. In the 1950 annual poll in the *Motion Picture Herald*, British film exhibitors voted Alastair Sim equal eighth with Margaret Rutherford among the top ten local stars at the box office, and discussing the career of Patricia Owens one critic wrote 'She appeared in *The Happiest Days of Your Life*, one of the funniest movies ever made in England; she also appeared in the abysmal *Old Mother Riley Headmistress*.' I strongly disagree with both of these judgements. Even with its starry cast, *The Happiest Days of Your Life* is formulaic and rather predictable, and in spite of its title it evokes little nostalgia for a lost age; *Carry on Teacher*, for instance, is often much funnier, and its characters more likeable. *Old Mother Riley Headmistress* is clearly not in the same league and has its undeniable faults, but it also has its moments, with Mother Riley once again discarding her laundry scrubs, this time for academic mortar and gown. She inherits the laundry in which she formerly worked and mortgages it in order to buy the school where Kitty the music teacher has just been sacked. With her inimitable mixture of verbal dexterity and physical absurdity (and vice versa) Headmistress Riley presides at sports and speech day, and foils the plans of a gang of crooked property developers.

As with some of the other Riley films, such as *Old Mother Riley MP*, *Old Mother Riley Joins Up*, *Old Mother Riley's Ghosts* and *Old Mother Riley Detective*, I believe *Old Mother Riley Headmistress* may actually have been conceived partly as a spoof or send-up of a genre of which a more serious example was in production at the time, and it should thus be seen and judged as an absurd parody, aimed as much at children as adults. And yet, with the passage of time, this film has even acquired a curiously touching charm, thanks in part to the refined singing of the much-loved Luton Girls' Choir, immaculately dressed in identical frocks of *exactly* the same length, a period piece of early 1950s visual and vocal nostalgia. And Mother Riley still contrives to give her broad slapstick an edge of social comment. The hoity-toity Lady Meersham ("Stick that in yer pipe and smoke it Lady Meersham!") is revealed to be a cockney parvenue; later, when the school catches fire, Riley rescues her tins of rationed food, a commodity which doesn't appear to trouble the well fed pupils of Rutherford and Sim. The incorrigible side of Riley is also still there. When trying to balance the books Kitty asks, "Now, where's the ledger?" to which Riley the gambler replies, "At Doncaster of course!" There is also an element of pantomime surrealism, with a talking statue, a dancing piano, and a transformation "wipe" in the closing shot from laundry to railway platform where Kitty hopes for a "Flying Scotsman" and Mother longs for an "Irish Mail." Sadly for Kitty, because Billy Breach was among the dastardly crooks, there could be no white wedding or frilly frock.

Old Mother Riley Headmistress was also a baptism of fire for the young continuity assistant Angela Allen who survived the ordeal of her first experience as head script supervisor to become one of the finest in the business. Apart from the Lucans' non-stop arguing on and off the set, Angela revealed another difficult aspect of working with them.

> I did three films as an assistant and then they said, 'You can go out on your own.' My very first picture was *Old Mother Riley* and I thought after day one, that's it, give up, because they could never do the same thing twice, never say the same thing twice, and I was crying. All the crew said to me, 'Don't worry, they're like this all the time. Nobody can tell them. We'll help you through it. Don't get upset.' So I survived that.[134]

In the last Riley film, *Mother Riley Meets the Vampire*, Bela Lugosi was similarly put out by Arthur's fondness for ad-libbing and departing from the written script.

At some point in 1950, Headmistress Riley changed back into her washerwoman's scrubs for a very different film. Wallace Publicity made a short (300 feet) publicity film for Lever Brothers called "Signs of the Times." The British Film Institute in their catalogue archive of Music Hall Related Films describes it as an "Advert for Persil starring Arthur Lucan and Kitty McShane in their music hall and cinema roles as Old Mother Riley and her daughter." At that time it was probably true that Mother Riley was the most famous washerwoman in the world, or at least in the British Empire.

It was also in 1950 that Jack Whiteley (of the legendary Whiteley circus family) and his wife Pauline joined the Riley road show with their comedy double act as Le White and Simone (sometimes Simonne), "scraping a living on two violins" and xylophones, while performing acrobatics. Jack first summed up his memories for Steve King.

> Miss McShane as everyone had to call her gave the impression that she was an astute business woman. She was also hard-hearted, and had no respect for other people's feelings. At times she would be sweet and very kind, but more often than not she was a bad tempered evil woman, who thrived on terrifying the living daylights out of people with that commanding cool voice of hers. One was never quite sure when she would explode.

In 1992, in his memoir *Rings and Curtains*, Jack's fuller account of life with the Lucans corroborated Betty Astell's impressions and added further important insights and anecdotes. The Whiteley's first day at rehearsal was unforgettable:

> Arthur Lucan was known as one of the nicest people in the business, but the same could never be said of Kitty McShane, who had a reputation for being difficult, to put it mildly. In fact she was known as an absolute terror ... At once we spotted Arthur sitting alone in a corner. Before we could greet him, Kitty swept up to us and announced, like a sergeant-major in the barrack-room, 'I'm Kitty McShane. All you've heard about me is true, and sometimes I'm even worse.' We were never even introduced to Arthur.[135]

During one week when an actor was taken ill, Jack was thrown, without rehearsal, into the part of Mother Riley's old flame Barnacle Bill. Jack received an excellent review for this in the press, in spite of the fact that Kitty kept hissing audibly from the wings, "We're running late, make him cut!" He ignored her and was severely reprimanded. "Remember, in future when I give an order I expect it to be obeyed." On another occasion Pauline, who was Kitty's understudy, was also promoted at short notice. "Pauline's opportunity came when Kitty threw one of her tantrums, chucked a teapot at somebody's head and promptly passed out. Pauline was far slimmer than Kitty and needed to be pinned into her costumes."

In the midst of these onstage and offstage dramas, Arthur continued to attract remarkably positive reviews, such as this one for "that dear old lady" in the ever-loyal *Hull Daily Mail* in November 1950. "Arthur Lucan's creation is unquestionably perennial in its appeal. Old Mother Riley has a broad, generous humor that penetrates the most staid theatergoer. His fantastic character has the gusto of a Dickensian creation." As Christmas 1950 approached, the Whiteleys were invited to stay on and play the children in the pantomime *The Old Woman Who Lived in a Shoe* at Boscombe Hippodrome, where manager Roy Denton gave such a lurid account of Kitty's offstage tantrums. The Whiteley's daughter Annette, who was almost five, joined her parents at Boscombe, but their landlady refused to babysit, so in spite of Miss McShane's strict ban on children and pets, they were obliged to bring little Annette to rehearsals. Something happened during one rehearsal which Jack Whiteley considered to be very strange and revealing.

"One morning, Kitty asked suddenly, 'Whose child is that?' She knew perfectly well. She'd seen us walking out with her." In spite of her ban, Kitty seemed oddly impressed, somehow touched by the presence of the well-behaved child who politely told her she was Annette Whiteley. Perhaps it was Kitty's awareness that Annette had been fostered just as she had fostered her only son—but never went back to collect him; or perhaps it was Annette's resemblance to a precocious little Dublin girl from long ago, which partly caused what happened next.

At this point an extraordinary transformation came over Kitty. It was something we were never able to account for fully. All at once we were allocated our own dressing room …which meant we could bed Annette down there when the evening performance was in progress … She also enjoyed the remarkable privilege of having *carte blanche* to enter Miss McShane's dressing room any time she liked.

At Kitty's party on Christmas Day, Annette was treated as the guest of honor. Kitty ordered the show manager to "Go and get a doll." The manager protested that all the shops were closed but Kitty told him to get hold of the theater owner Frederick Butterworth (F.J. Butterworth, known as "the Guv'nor") who would be able to rouse a local shopkeeper. Sure enough, Annette got her doll and was thereafter included in the matinee performances for a fee of five shillings, joining other children onstage in the latest hit song "All I Want for Christmas Is My Two Front Teeth." Jack Whiteley was not alone in noticing Kitty's sudden kindness to children. Even the *Stage* reviewer, who must have been familiar with Kitty's low tolerance of children remarked, "At the Hippodrome, Boscombe, Arthur Lucan as the Old Woman, manages her rebellious family [including Jack, Pauline and Roy Rolland] with considerable humor, and Kitty McShane makes things bright and merry and specially endears herself to the children."

After the pantomime season, the Whiteleys were persuaded, rather reluctantly, to stay on in the Riley road show. "We agreed to give it a try, but before long life was back to normal in the Lucan and McShane circus, with Kitty in the wings telling Arthur to drop dead in loud stage whispers. The aggression and abrasiveness were more than we could stand." They stuck it until May, gave two weeks' notice and left the show. This sort of thing now happened so often that Kitty began to offer bonuses to chorus girls who were willing to stay for a second season, a detail borne out by the memories of an online blogger:

Another person I used to know worked in the chorus for the Lucan and McShane Company. He said that Kitty was a vile person, who would inspect their hands and teeth before curtain up and really tear in to them if things didn't meet her approval. The only time they conversed with Lucan and

McShane, other than in the script, was when they were getting paid. Apparently, if you stayed for a second season, your money went up, as people were constantly leaving the show, mostly on account of her.

But in his concluding remarks on the Lucans, Jack Whiteley showed remarkable perspicacity and an awareness of another, hidden side of Kitty McShane.

Kitty McShane has hardly received the best press in the annals of show business, and it is difficult to think kindly of her. Perhaps it would be most charitable, as we take our leave of Lucan and McShane, to remember the time when, for a brief spell, Kitty showed kindness and generosity to our child—an incident that maybe indicated what tragic wounds must have lain beneath her hardness.

Jack could not have known of a very old photograph of Kitty McShane in Dublin, still, like his Annette, little more than a child with ringlets and frills, and clutching a doll . . . . But Arthur may have noticed, remembered, and understood the hidden sadness of the woman who, in spite of everything, he still called "my Kitty." In the light of this incident at Boscombe, it is interesting to note that in the new road show in March 1951, Kitty progressed for the first and only time "from courtship to the christening of her new baby," Willer Neal's baby! The reviewer at Finsbury Park added that Arthur's "clowning receives an added force from his unusual pathos; and even when he jumps right outside character and goes all out for knockabout, he has the audience's laughter and sympathy." He needed their sympathy more than they could possibly have imagined!

The last film in which Lucan and McShane appeared together, *Old Mother Riley's Jungle Treasure*, was released in March 1951. Its working title had been *Old Mother Riley Queen of the Cannibals* and there are trade posters bearing this title. It would be more accurate to say that the Lucans "appeared to appear" together because in reality their interminable quarrels had by this time become so intolerable that George Minter decided to film all their scenes separately and edit them later, a fact that accounts for the rather strange atmosphere in many scenes in which Mother and Kitty seem to be talking not to each other but to someone just over each other's shoulder. In spite of that, the film holds together pretty well as a kids' matinee adventure story. An online critic at IMDb summarizes the plot:

> Many years after burying his treasure and concealing a map in his bedstead, the ghost of Captain Morgan seems to take a shine to mother Riley who is working in a failing antiques shop. He shows her where to find the map for the treasure which is also sought by the descendants of a rival gang who smash up the shop. The shop is sold and the new owner, a Yorkshire man (from Manchester!) and his son played by Billy Breach, invite Mrs. Riley and her daughter to set out for the South Seas ('which looks suspiciously like Walton-on-Thames and is inhabited by stock footage of lions, tigers and penguins') to recover the hoard. After the usual adventures and some odd encounters, including an ex-Etonian tribal chief, Mrs. Riley finds the treasure and is made a native queen. Kitty, as usual, gets her man.

A couple of online critics have expressed anachronistic indignation about what they take to be racist elements in the film, but they fail entirely to understand that the whole point of the old-Etonian tribal chief is to undermine and lampoon stereotypical received views of "revolting natives." It may even be a subtle way of pointing out that Etonians are themselves a tribe apart with habits no less odd as those ascribed to the "natives." A less neurotic online critic wrote, "This is a delightful little romp from Arthur Lucan and his wife Kitty, along with a notable appearance from Peter Butterworth, who later went on to appear in some of the long-running British 'Carry-On' films." Another critic on the IMDb website takes the film, and his own critical faculties, far too seriously but is worth quoting as a typical example of an adult taking a real sledgehammer to crack a pantomime nut.

> The funniest (and most racist) line occurs when villainess Estelle refers to the natives as 'Kentucky minstrels.' There are also some jokes that only British audiences will get. [Who else did he think it was aimed at?] The pilot of Mother Riley's plane is named Prang. (RAF slang for a crash landing.) We hear references to scoring a century at Marylebone Cricket

Club, Man. Utd. beating Arsenal, post-war rationing, and a young man expecting a call-up for national service. [And why not?] The ghost of Morgan the pirate, last seen in that antiques shop, has no difficulty materializing on the Caribbean island at the climax [isn't that precisely what ghosts are good at?], when Mother Riley and her friends are about to get burned at the stake. Which would make them the only things well done in this bad comedy. Ooh, matron! Considering how many dark-skinned natives are on offer here (some of them played by white actors in body paint), there is much less racism and unga-bunga than I'd expected. One of the white men in Mother Riley's expedition (supposedly the good guys) hopes to encounter some natives so that he can force them to work as porters. The convenient gimmick that rescues Old Mother Riley from the natives is obvious a mile off, and the ending is anticlimactic. Distressingly, at least two of the male characters in this movie express romantic affection for Old Mother Riley . . . even though Lucan's drag performance doesn't remotely resemble a biological woman!

One can only wonder at this critic's distress at the bizarre notion that Lucan might have had any intention of resembling "a biological woman!" Not a word here of irony, parody, lampoon, send-up or spoof. Did he think he was reviewing *Heart of Darkness* or *The African Queen*? Luckily, the reviewer does find one redeeming feature. "On the plus side, late in this film the natives perform a very impressive display of rapid athletic movement that's either an authentic African folk dance or an extremely convincing imitation of one. More for that dancing than anything else, I'll rate this movie 2 points out of 10."[136]

I like the geographical and lazily racist implications of the "natives" doing an "authentic African folk dance" on a supposed "Caribbean island," but let it pass!

Given the widely reported breakdown of civilized relations on the set of *Old Mother Riley's Jungle Treasure*, it comes as a surprise to learn that the Lucans now asked Michael Lyon to write to BBC producer Tom Ronald in order to explore the possibility of another radio series. Lyon wrote to Ronald on 23 April 1951 and, probably to counteract the rumors of strife emerging from the film studios, assured him that "I have been having a chat with your old friends ... and everything in the garden is lovely so if you have any suggestions at all I would be glad to hear, as I promised them I would contact you today." But just a week before he received this letter, Ronald had had lunch with Arthur, and his reply to Lyon contains further proof that, after a first attempt at Bristol back in 1947, Arthur was again trying to break free:

27 April 1951.

My Dear Michael,

Many thanks for your letter, the contents of which amaze me. Arthur Lucan and I lunched together the other day, during which he definitely told me that he was breaking away from Kitty and wanting to start on his own, and now you tell me that everything in the garden is lovely. The question that exercises my mind is, for how long will the garden remain lovely? Weeds grow so quickly. As you know, I am very fond of them both but Old Mother Riley is Old Mother Riley and in my view should not be subservient to Kitty and Bill. In the last series we did Arthur was completely under their thumb and his personality over the air failed to project. I think Arthur Lucan is a very funny man and I would like to use him in my Festival Music Hall, provided it is not three minutes of Arthur and the rest being taken up with Kitty and Billy singing.

Perhaps you would be kind enough to clarify this position for me before I do anything about it, and also treat this letter as confidential. Frankly, between ourselves, the BBC will not wear these songs from Kitty but look on Arthur as a great comedian.

Mike Lyon's reply to Ronald on 30 April was headed "STRICTLY PRIVATE" and was devastatingly frank. "I absolutely agree with every word you say. This, you must know, I have been fighting for years ... Candidly I think the last couple of broadcasts have been disgraceful, because of what you refer to." But Lyon insists that much of the blame lay with Ronald and his BBC colleagues for not vetting the scripts more closely or protesting loudly enough, and he urges them to do so in future. "This, to my mind, is the way to deal with this young person." The young person seems to be a reference to Willer Neal, as elsewhere Lyon refers to Kitty as "her Ladyship."

Tom Ronald wrote again on 2 May, defending his BBC colleagues, pointing out that for the last series, "Ronnie Taylor did the script, and very well . . . but Madam would insist on going back on all the old material they had been working for many years." Arthur was happy with Taylor but "Kitty would have none of it" in spite of the fact that "Ronnie Taylor has gone from strength to strength; he writes all Norman Evans' material and Al Reid's as well." Michael Lyon made two more tentative enquiries in May and June but, to the annoyance of "her Ladyship," the whole project was quietly shelved, and the Lucans' long association with the BBC had come to an end. By now, the couple were not even capable of recording film dialogue in the same studio on the same day, and in the business it was becoming increasingly clear that the days of Lucan and McShane were numbered.

Nothing further was ever heard from the BBC and the Riley road show dragged itself painfully but valiantly through the last year of its existence, with Willer Neal's name on the bills, as at Finsbury Park in February 1951, continuing to receive prominent second billing. In spite of all the ups-and-downs, an eleven-year run of Old Mother Riley shows in the days before blockbuster musicals was still by any standard a considerable theatrical achievement. Arthur's insertion of topical or local material got him into trouble with Arsenal football fans in March 1951. The writer and broadcaster Brian Glanville tells the story, which concerns Jack Kelsey, a goalkeeper who made an inauspicious start to his Arsenal football career by conceding five goals to Charlton Athletic at Highbury.

> The following week, up the road from Highbury at the old Finsbury Park Empire—a bastion of variety—Old Mother Riley and Kitty McShane were playing. At one point they brought on a bedraggled figure. 'Arsenal's new goalkeeper' said Arthur Lucan. Arsenal complained and the scene was dropped.[137]

Toward the end of 1951, the producer George Minter seemed determined to come to the aid of Arthur whose financial and marital predicament was now common knowledge. In footsteps of Abbott and Costello, but without the help of Kitty, Old Mother Riley was scheduled to meet a Vampire to be played by Bela Lugosi. As Richard Anthony Baker wickedly put it, "One horrific figure was replaced by another." On 15 September, 1951 The *London Evening News* reported,

> Old Mother Riley is making the social grade. Some time ago, Arthur Lucan was given a lot more money to spend on his films. This has made them even more popular at the box-office. For the first time Kitty McShane will not be in the film. Frightened of vampires? Now the old lady is to have a Hollywood star for team-mate. None other than the fearsome Bela Lugosi! *Mother Riley meets the Vampire* is the title. They begin to haunt each other next month.

After appearing in the last Old Mother Riley road show with Kitty and Willer Neal at the Leeds Empire in October 1951, Arthur went alone to Nettlefold Studios in November to film *Mother Riley Meets the Vampire*. Excluded from this film by her intolerable and unpredictable behavior, an angry, jealous and resentful Kitty insisted on coming almost daily to the studios and tormenting Arthur, to such an extent that he finally begged director George Minter to bar her from entering the premises. But Renown Films seem to have had complete faith in Lucan without McShane because they offered Arthur yet another film—an odd way to treat a man who some have asserted was a hopeless alcoholic. On 13 December 1951 *Kinematograph Weekly* revealed that, "Another Mother Riley is also scheduled, 'Mother Riley's Trip to Mars,' which will be a broad comedy satire on the present atom bomb experiments and rocket trips to the moon." On 20 December it was again announced as "a roaring satire on the space travel age." It was not the absence of Kitty which brought the Riley film series to an end, but Arthur's untimely death.

After filming with a rather bewildered Bela Lugosi, Arthur re-joined Kitty and they worked together for the very last time in the pantomime *The Old Woman Who Lived in a Shoe*, at the Grand Theater in Southampton. Here, whatever the detractors of Arthur Lucan may have claimed or insinuated, neither his older nor his

younger understudy could have come to his aid if he had been inca-
pable through drink of doing a second house; George Beck, "at one
time understudy to Old Mother Riley," was playing Mrs. Tickle in
Goldilocks at Cambridge, and Roy Rolland was appearing in *Dick
Whittington* at the Peterborough Embassy. When *The Old Woman
Who Lived in a Shoe* closed on 26 January 1952, so did the joint careers
of Lucan and McShane. After forty long years, "The Dame and the
Dainty Maid" would never again appear together on stage or screen.

Mother Riley Meets the Vampire was released in July 1952, and
over the years it has attracted very mixed reviews. Given the desperate circumstances of its conception and execution it is little short of
a miracle that it is as good in some parts as it is ramshackle in others.
When, because of Bela Lugosi, the film was released in America as
My Son the Vampire, audiences and critics alike seemed incapable
of comprehending the odd ragbag to which British audiences had
been responding joyfully since 1937. But more recently, cult producer Richard Gordon who had worked on the film with Lucan
and Lugosi was asked, shortly before his death in 2011, about audience reaction to a showing of *Mother Riley Meets the Vampire* at the
Manchester Festival of Fantastic Films. The cynical reviewer did not
get the answer he clearly expected.

Q: At a recent Festival of Fantastic Films in England, *Mother
Riley Meets the Vampire* was shown with you in attendance.
What was the reaction? When it was over, was there an open
eye in the house?

R. GORDON: When it was shown at that festival in
Manchester, England, I have to admit that it was the big hit
of the festival ... It was the hit of the festival, and when I was
doing my interviews, everybody wanted to talk about *Mother
Riley Meets the Vampire* [laughs] nobody wanted to talk about
Boris Karloff or any of the other pictures that I made. I was
a big hero for *Mother Riley Meets the Vampire*. So when you
ask 'Was there an open eye in the house,' very much so—they
applauded it wildly![138]

In 2013, Lucan and Lugosi found two new champions in the
"people's playwright," Patrick Prior, and the biographer, critic, and

prize-winning journalist Roger Lewis. Prior's two-hander *The Vampire and Mrs. Riley*, given its première at the Yvonne Arnaud Theater in Guildford in November 2013, imaginatively reconstructed the relationship between the two fading stars during the making of *Mother Riley Meets the Vampire*. Roger Lewis's prize-winning 2014 essay "Freaks," contains a poignant and perceptive view of the coming together of two "disturbingly ambivalent creatures." I am grateful to Roger Lewis for allowing me to reproduce the following lines from his essay:

> In *Mother Riley Meets the Vampire*, horror and comedy finally come together—though the sinister and disturbing dimension of comedy had been apparent in Lucan from the beginning . . . What you do notice is Lugosi's musical voice—lilting and rasping, foreign, obviously, and exotic—and he brings with him the suggestion of strange landscapes, of Hungary and Transylvania, wolves and frozen forests. Lucan's Old Mother Riley, too, is suggestive of her background, in the mildewy chill of boarding houses, and when she and Lugosi meet, there is a kind of accord between them, an affinity or tenderness. Though the initial appeal of the dreadful film is frankly bizarre and almost voyeuristic: to see the desperation of two fallen sozzled artistes at the end of their careers, artistes who might be forgiven for giving up on the roots of life.
>
> In the way they play their big scene together, Lucan and Lugosi approach the sublime. Old Mother Riley begins warily. 'I must be going now,' she says. 'You see, I left a bit of scrag end on to simmer.' But soon she's caving in to Von Housen's charm and blandishments, skipping with a feather duster about the castle, complete with its secret passageways. 'I'll just give it a quick flick,' she says. It's as if she's found true love. Lugosi and Lucan transcend the junk script, the music hall frivolity, the piffle of popular entertainment, and as actors show the confidence their famous characters feel in being themselves, their natural awareness and familiarity. The vampire and the transvestite, both disturbingly ambivalent creatures when you think about it (the one half-dead and half-alive, the other half-man and half-woman), enter

each other's loneliness. There seems to be a link between their psychological nature and activities and the confusion of what is going on around them. You expect Old Mother Riley to be bickering and pitiless, trapped in a room with the Undead, but there's a romantic mournfulness. As pale and dry as straw, she seems to have no weight or color, as if she is already fading before our eyes. Lugosi, meanwhile, is all East European heaviness, lugubriousness, with his white face and strong glistening stained black teeth. It's fleeting, this sequence—a midnight moment. But enough for us to glimpse or sense the lonely pathos of injured spirits.[139]

Chapter Nine:
"Unhappiness and Strife" 1951-1964
Going Gay 1952-1953

All those who observed the Lucans in public were convinced that Arthur was so firmly under Kitty's thumb that his talk of leaving her and striking out alone was an idle pipedream, and that he was so weak and shy he would not or could not do it. But by the end of 1951 he was not only desperately unhappy but he was desperately broke. Kitty and Billy had been living it up as a couple at Forty Lane since 1949 at the latest, and Arthur, in his own home, was tolerated in the spare room like Roger the Lodger. But incredibly, Arthur was far from finished, and late in January 1952 he went to the office of his old friend and agent Michael Lyon in the Haymarket and had a long chat with Betty Jacoby (who was Mrs. Lyon). Little did he suspect that the last chapter of his show business life was waiting for him in the next room.

James Gaston and Rosemary Andrée had had a long stage career as specialty dancers, even appearing in the 1920s at the *Folies Bergère* in Paris. They were also very successful producers of touring variety shows and now, late in their career, this had become their full-time occupation. Their company manager in 1952 was Slim Ingram, who told me in 2012 of his vivid memory of how Arthur came to be part of the Gaston and Andrée Company.

> We were finishing a tour of a show called *Exotic Nights*, and we were looking for top-class acts for a new show, so we went to our agent Michael Lyon's office in the Haymarket where we also met Betty Jacoby. In the course of the conversation they mentioned a number of possible acts, and then someone said, 'Oh yes, and Arthur Lucan is looking for something.' The state of the Lucan-McShane ménage à trois both on and off the stage was common knowledge in the business, and it would be no exaggeration to say that whereas Arthur was well liked, Kitty was universally loathed. I'll never forget how, as soon as they said 'Arthur Lucan,' the three of us threw up our

hands and shrieked 'No, no, no!' We were of course thinking that they meant both Lucan and McShane, as we knew they had just finished a pantomime together at Southampton, *The Old Woman Who Lived in a Shoe*, but Betty said, 'Arthur has left Kitty, he wants to go solo.' This time we all thought, 'Oh yes, we've heard that one before!' But Betty then said, 'As a matter of fact he's in the other office at this very moment. Would you like to have a word with him?' Well, we did, and before the end of the day he was signed up as top of the bill, Arthur Lucan as Old Mother Riley in a new show to be called *Going Gay*. He would write his own material and his wages were to be thirty pounds per week. We were all a bit stunned to think that this man, a legend as he really was, would be a mere employee of our company; but he turned up, we rehearsed, and we opened at the Swindon Empire on 25 February 1952. Roy Rolland, who had been Arthur's understudy for several years, was also taken on at £17. 10s per week, excellent money for those days. I remember all these figures because I paid the wages. It can't have been a bad show because, with a break for pantomime, *Going Gay* ran for nearly two years.

But back at 11 Forty Lane things were going from bad to worse. Kitty McShane of "KMS Productions," who had claimed to be such an astute businesswoman, was forced to admit that not only had she neglected to settle the company's bills but she had squandered vast sums of the Lucans' joint wealth on buying beauty salons and hairdressing parlors, and on maintaining the conspicuously lavish life style she enjoyed with her boyfriend Billy Breach, aka Willer Neal. On top of all that, income tax arrears were building up. Arthur was legally responsible for all these debts but he was almost destitute, and his financial advisors told him that if he could not stall payments until the next film brought in new funds his only way out would be to declare himself bankrupt. Thus it was that Arthur was effectively pushed out of his own home and had to carry on working and living from hand to mouth, while continuing to support his spendthrift wife, who kept very quiet about her diamonds and several other properties she owned in London and the countryside. It has been suggested that Arthur may have been exaggerating his predicament in order to gain sympathy from his friends and creditors or, a little later, from the Official Receiver and the courts. But I can now show quite categorically that this was simply not the case.

Arthur had always been close to his son Donald; shortly after Donald's graduation in medicine from Trinity College Dublin (Arthur was present but Kitty stayed away) at a time when the Lucans were among the highest earners in show business, Arthur had promised his son £20,000 to "set him up" and allow him to do research in tropical medicine rather than enter general practice. In an act of incomprehensible meanness which deeply hurt Arthur and infuriated Donald, Kitty, who held the purse-strings, changed her mind and categorically refused to pay up.[140] Arthur had continued to hope that he might be able somehow to help his son, who was now working as a GP in Blackheath, but whose situation at this time was also rather precarious. In 1938, when Donald was still a very junior and impecunious doctor in Dublin, he had married Eileen Ladkin, but shortly after the birth of their first child, his wife, as flighty as his own mother, left him, leaving baby Marylyn in his care; Donald came to work in London during the war and married again in 1949. Now in 1952 he was awaiting the arrival of his second child, while still contributing to the upkeep of his first wife and daughter. Not only had Kitty fleeced her husband but she stubbornly refused her son any financial help. Arthur kept in regular touch with Donald, and Roy Rolland remembered meeting them together on many occasions. From now on to the end, both father and son saw themselves not so much as the family of Kitty McShane but as her defrauded victims.

This background information helps to make sense of some aspects of the following letter from Arthur to Donald, which I publish here for the very first time by kind permission of Donald's widow, Mrs. Joan Towle. What needs little comment or clarification is the heart-rending honesty with which Arthur reveals privately to his only son the awful depths to which he has been reduced by a "Someone" he cannot even bring himself to name; he twice alludes to "Someone" where he could have said "my wife," "your mother," or just "Kitty." But his reference to a "certain letter that I have at the solicitor's" and Donald's awareness of it, also reveal that Arthur was not the childish and gullible pawn Kitty made him out to be, but was actively trying to extricate himself, possibly even by legal means, from the mess into which his wife's profligacy and duplicity had plunged him. Here is the letter which Arthur wrote to Donald, probably on Sunday, 24 February 1952, the week before the opening of *Going Gay*; the bitter irony of the show's title speaks for itself:

Dear Don,

Here is a short letter—now don't get worried about it.

I shall have to send you what I promised you in instalments, if possible. You know I am going to work and might I suggest that Someone may try and stop me. You may know something about it as you told me to keep a certain letter that I have at the solicitors.

I am not going to work because I like it. I've got to work, otherwise I'll starve. I've got no money or assets. But I should have. But I let Someone have the whole of the profits of a life's work. My share was unhappiness and strife, and more to come.

We shall see what will happen this coming week.

Bless you and yours,

Arthur

I am (Please God) playing Empire Swindon this week.

This abject letter, from one of the greatest actors in British music hall, variety and film comedy, clearly implies that Kitty was trying, possibly even by legal means, to prevent Arthur from working without her permission, or, if he did work, to forbid him the use of the name Old Mother Riley. Her efforts were unsuccessful and *Going Gay* duly opened at Swindon without impediment. Gaston and Andrée took on Roy Rolland as Arthur's understudy, and the Lucans' former dresser Maisie Munro who had had "personal supervision of Miss McShane's wardrobe," was taken on as Arthur's dresser, a role she fulfilled until the night he died.

When Kitty, now sidelined and ostracized, realized that Arthur had been engaged to top the bill as Old Mother Riley in a variety show which was receiving excellent reviews, she was beside herself with a mixture of rage and wounded pride. Thus began a saga that was truly more "pathetic and macabre" than anything Francis King had seen in the 1940s. The ITV producer Margery Baker clearly understood that "to Arthur in those last years, when he dared to go on tour without her, she was as cruel as only a frightened child can be." Unemployed, and frequently the worse for drink, Kitty now took to following the show *Going Gay* around the country and stalking Arthur. Roy Rolland recalled, "She visited us in nearly every town we went to, and if she wasn't visiting then she was in London phoning us. Her phone bill must have been colossal. Arthur never answered the calls but then he'd get a sixteen-page telegram, full of unprintable nonsense." One of many grotesque and frightening incidents took place when the show reached the Metropolitan Edgware Road in August 1952. It seems highly likely that what happened was unleashed by Kitty's reading her own name in the following review in *The Stage*.

> 'Going Gay' offers great scope to Arthur Lucan in his still-fresh character of 'Old Mother Riley.' The vivacious Kitty McShane is missing from the partnership, and the familiar mother-and-daughter contretemps are now replaced by broader sketches of rather less plot-content . . . There is no doubt that [Arthur Lucan's] burlesque characterization and energetic personality are the main factors in keeping this show alive.

Kitty found out that although she was missing from the show, Arthur had in fact retained one of their oldest two-hander sketches, "The Old Match-seller" in which, since 1924, Kitty had played the jilted bride. Arthur had taught the role to a bright young actress Gale Douglas, and they played the sketch at a key moment in *Going Gay*, immediately before the grand finale.

One night, Kitty, who by now was barred from many theaters across the country, managed to make her way into the Metropolitan and down to the very front of the stalls. When she saw pretty young Gale Douglas usurping *her* role, *her* frilly wedding frock and, in spite of everything, *her* Arthur, she could no longer contain herself. In the sketch, the Match-seller says, "I know my husband loved me because he said he would die for me!" The bride asks exactly what words the husband had used and the Match-seller replies, to roars of laughter, "He said, 'One day I'll swing for you!'" The sketch was played well downstage with just a bench in front of a painted cloth, and the forestage at the Met (which Kitty knew well) could be reached from steps under the side boxes. At this very point she ran onto the stage, pushed Gale Douglas roughly to one side and shouted, "And I'll fucking swing for you!" As she did so she swung her heavy crocodile handbag and hit Arthur across the face. The audience, thinking for a moment that this was a new gag, laughed and applauded, but as Arthur fell back onto the bench with blood trickling down his face, the laughter stopped and the stage crew went into action. Slim Ingram (who told me all this in September 2012) was in prompt corner, and stage manager Ellis Ashton (for some reason wearing red trousers!) was in the opposite wing. They both raced onstage, Ellis grabbed Kitty and dragged her off to one side while Slim hauled Arthur, Gale and the bench into the opposite wing, while gesturing frantically to the M.D. The band struck up, the front cloth rose, and the company went hurriedly into "Au Revoir, Until We Meet Again," the jolly finale during which all the acts walked down center stage to take their bow. Arthur came down last and Slim remembered being shocked as Arthur pulled off his wig and putty nose to reveal—for the first time ever onstage—the battered husband of Kitty McShane. In spite of all this, Arthur insisted that the drunken Kitty be rescued from the street where the staff had thrown her, and had her brought to his dressing room. Slim remembered that after calming Kitty and sending her home, Arthur retreated for the night to the Savage Club, the one civilized hideaway where for many years he had found sanctuary, understanding and respect.

On a happier note, a brief clip of film survives showing Arthur in his element, judging a beauty contest on 31 July 1952 when *Going Gay* was at Weston-super-Mare. Arthur in costume as Mother Riley was filmed judging the line-up of bathing beauties in swimsuits and then climbing onto the rostrum to give Jean Murphy, the winner, a garland of flowers and a very big kiss. Also during this tour, avid theatergoer Barry Davies remembered seeing Arthur at Wolverhampton and Dudley; "I met him at the Royal Pier in 1952 after he had split up with Kitty McShane. You wouldn't recognize him off the stage without his wig, but he was a devil for the women; he tried to make a few passes at my sister." There are many stories, none serious or improper, of Arthur's affectionate dalliance with chorus girls. In one of his more infuriating TV interviews, Roy Rolland said, "I could go into very intimate details if I wished . . . and say there's nothing said about Arthur's girlfriends . . . You see it was more or less on a mutual basis." He then coyly changed the subject. Arthur obviously loved the company of young women but this never seemed to pose a threat to his almost incomprehensible loyalty to Kitty.

Kitty continued to stalk Arthur and the *Going Gay* production throughout 1952 and 1953. Roy Rolland told, with great relish, of an incident during a performance, when Kitty positioned herself conspicuously in the stalls and commanded the attention of everyone onstage. By now she had so often threatened to shoot Arthur that when she rummaged in her large handbag the terrified actors feared the worst. Instead of a gun, with a theatrical flourish she produced a silk scarf, but the sketch, and the actors, had already "died the death." Another member of the cast, Kenneth Earle, had a vivid memory of a further incident involving the woman he called "Lucan's tormentor." "One day she caught up with the show and when Lucan was on stage, she stood up in the center stalls to let forth a stream of invective against him. Gaston and Andrée made it clear to all further theater managers that the woman was never to be allowed in again."

A much nastier incident took place in an elegant London restaurant where Arthur was dining with Jimmy Gaston, Rosemary Andrée, Slim Ingram and other company members. As Slim remembered it, Kitty appeared at the door of the restaurant "the worse for wear" and produced a gun. Years later, Rosemary Andrée, speaking to ITV producer Margery Baker for her 1969 documentary *Applause! Applause!* could still recall the sudden change that came over Arthur.

One particular night we were having dinner, he was quite happy that night, gay, enjoying himself, and suddenly I happened to glance up and I saw Arthur's face change completely, in fact it was almost like a rabbit and a snake. I turned my head round, there was Kitty. She marched in and I believe she had the old Irish gardener with her. So anyway, she sat down at the table and we tried to be polite, we didn't want to make a scene if it was not going to be necessary, asked her to have something to eat. So then she started on Arthur, a terrible quarrel blew up, a terrible scene in the restaurant, and we thought, well, something's got to be done about this. Either we'll be thrown out or she'll come to blows with Arthur and there'll be something dreadful happen. So we tried to call the manager and tell him quietly to get the police and ask her to leave. Well, the police arrived and stood at the door, and of course, when she saw them she got up and went fairly quietly, and Arthur got up too and said 'We must see her to the door.' Always the gentleman. So we got to the door, a taxi was waiting, she'd had the taxi waiting about an hour, and she was just about to step into the taxi when she had an afterthought, and she turned round and gave Arthur the most terrific wallop across the face. He staggered a bit, stood there slightly bowed, and she got into the taxi and drove away. We both looked at him, my partner Gaston and I, and Gaston said to him, 'Arthur, I'm surprised at you! Why didn't you give her one back?' He said [here Rosemary imitated Arthur's plaintive voice] 'How could I? She's my Kitty, the woman I love. . .'

Rosemary Andrée's account of this scene was sanitized for television; in Slim Ingram's equally eye-witness version there was a great deal more loud-mouthed drunken business and foul language. When Margery Baker visited Donald Towle in St. Austell in 1968, she must have discussed the above interview with him because in a letter thanking him for his help and hospitality she adds, "And thank you for confirming the 'snake and rabbit' angle." Donald had confirmed what many others, including Jack Whiteley and Roy Rolland had witnessed; Kitty would fix her hapless victims with an unnerving, almost demented stare, behavior suggestive of some form of personality disorder. That stare can be seen in a couple of Kitty's earliest photographs. Margery Baker's script for her documentary clearly shows her sensitive understanding of the Lucans' strange and fatal misalliance in which some part of both partners had failed to grow up.

Although as a performer she was never more than mediocre, Arthur adored her just the same, and he adored her like this; the little Irish colleen he had married. The Kitty he loved never grew up. She refused to grow up. She even passed off their son as her brother. And this pathological fear of growing old led her from first to last to cling to her little girl dresses, frills and puff-sleeves . . . And to Arthur in those last years, when he dared to go on tour without her, she was as cruel as only a frightened child can be.

The "frightened child" could indeed be cruel and malicious, but at times Arthur was genuinely afraid of this malevolent creature, to the point where the "frightened little man" as Roy Denton had called him, actually sought police protection. Roy Rolland told with great relish and hilarity the absurd story of the odd couple seeking police protection when, in July 1952, Kitty threatened in one of her five-page telegrams to come down to the Swansea Empire and pull off Arthur's nose. To the bemused and incredulous police officer on duty Arthur explained "We're two Old Mother Rileys. I'm Mother Riley and he's Mother Riley, my understudy. It's about my wife. She's threatening to pull me nose off." What today seems to be a very funny story was just one of a series of ghastly events which left Arthur genuinely worried that Kitty might really do something dangerous. She had already struck him violently onstage, and the threat to his putty nose had a symbolic significance; it was the only artificial aid which Arthur used in order to become Mother Riley, and damaging it in public might destroy the much-loved illusion. Surely nothing less than genuine fear would have induced a pair of rather odd-looking thespians to go the police station and brave the sniggers of the unsympathetic Swansea constabulary, as they told what must have seemed their rather ridiculous story. "In the end," said Roy Rolland, "Arthur pushed me out into the street, saying 'Come on! You see, you've got to be murdered before they'll do anything!'"[141]

There was yet another aspect of Kitty's temperament that was deeply offensive and not at all childlike. Slim Ingram told me in 2012 of an incident which he had refused to reveal for over fifty years because for a long time he had considered it just too gross for polite consumption. As we have seen, during the run of *Going Gay*

Kitty would descend unannounced on theaters around the country in order to harangue and torment Arthur. On one occasion, around the time when she had taken to calling Arthur a "poof," she came into his dressing room in a nastier mood than usual. Slim was there and, to his extreme embarrassment, Kitty began to taunt Arthur about his supposed lack of virility. Arthur tried as usual to ignore her but this only seemed to exacerbate her need to be offensive. Slim remembered that on an outing into the countryside that week Arthur had picked a bunch of wildflowers and in the absence of a vase had put them in a milk bottle. Suddenly to Slim's utter disgust, Kitty shouted "You see that milk bottle? Well, that's nothing compared to the size of Billy's prick!" Arthur carried on removing his make-up as if nothing had been said, but he later told Slim how humiliated he felt, but also confused and bewildered, trying to understand why the woman he had loved and supported for so long felt such an insane urge to keep hurting him, rather than just leaving him alone.

In August 1952 the management of the Bristol New Empire "announced to the joy of many Bristolians that Arthur Lucan (Old Mother Riley) would be starring in that year's pantomime." The bills announced proudly "SENSATIONAL PANTOMIME ENGAGEMENT! ARTHUR LUCAN OLD MOTHER RILEY." The last name was in huge red capitals. Gaston and Andrée's production of *Jack and the Beanstalk*, "A Gigantic Laughter Pantomime for Children up to the Age of Eighty" opened on Boxing Day and featured most of the *Going Gay* company, with the notable exception of Roy Rolland whose name appears nowhere in the bills, programs or reviews. This would have been simply unthinkable if, as one has been led to believe, Arthur was by now usually too sozzled to do the second house. The pantomime received excellent reviews and, considering the emotional and financial strain on Arthur at this time, he masked his weariness so well that one critic reported, "As for Arthur Lucan, all that need be said is that he is on the top of his form, as expressive and funny as ever." The critics and the public were unanimous in their praise, and far from being the jaded old drunk of the anti-Lucan black legend, Arthur was the toast of Bristol throughout a grueling seven-week "record-breaking run" without an understudy.

Terry Hallett takes up the story:

There was no lack of numbers to see the opening of the pantomime, 'Jack and the Beanstalk' on 26 December, one of three major Christmas shows in Bristol that season. Old Mother Riley was undoubtedly the star attraction, and 'she' dominated the production. One impressed critic wrote: "This is the best Empire pantomime I have ever seen. They have done wonders with the stage, and they have dressed the production lavishly." The pantomime set a post-war business record for the Empire, and manager Kenneth Miles confirmed on 14 January that evening performances for the remainder of the seven weeks run, due to end on 14 February, were likely to be sell-outs. Arthur Lucan's engagement had proved to be even more popular than expected.[142]

As in 1948, the choreographer was Peggy Barnes with her "Little Alvettes, Bristol's own Tiny Tots." The young singer Malcolm Thomas, who later gained fame as Malcolm Vaughan, joined the cast (at £17. 10s. per week), and had particularly fond memories of Arthur.

The star was one Malcolm came to regard with affection: Arthur Lucan. Malcolm became very fond of Arthur (who called him 'Chookey'). They would often have tea together and Arthur would give Malcolm valuable tips on comedy timing. In the dressing room Malcolm would watch in fascination as Arthur applied the face make-up for his character of Old Mother Riley.[143]

In the light of our discussion of events in 1948 at the Hippodrome, it is worth noting that, as Slim Ingram assured me, this time Kitty did not dare show her face in Bristol.

Back in September 1952, given the fact that Arthur had been touring in *Going Gay* for over six months, readers of *The Stage* must have been puzzled by the following announcement. "LUCAN AND MCSHANE. Old Mother Riley and her daughter Kitty will be starting their spring tour in March. Complete with new show. All enquiries to Kitty McShane, 20 South Molton Street, W1." The heading "Lucan and McShane" rather than "KMS productions" suggests that Kitty genuinely had hopes of luring Arthur back into the act. But in spite of her alternate raging and pleading, Arthur remained firmly committed to Gaston and Andrée. So, in March 1953, Arthur's pre-1949 understudy George E. Beck, who had recently played a very Lucanesque Old Mother Hubbard at Cheltenham, was hired by Kitty to play Mother Riley, not Roy Rolland, as many have claimed, as he was still understudy to Arthur in *Going Gay*. Willer Neal again played the boyfriend Danny Boy, and Kitty's new show was called, rather ominously, *With My Shillelagh Under My Arm*. The poster featured Kitty's name and photograph (from years ago) inside a large green shamrock, with smaller print underneath, "Old Mother Riley's daughter." Although George E. Beck played Mother Riley in the show he was not billed as such on posters, as has also been claimed, but simply as "The Great Little Comedian." The supporting company included the Four Delisles, Eddie Williams, Brandon and Hilliard, Peter Brothers, Nancy Gregory and the Ten Shillelagh Girls. It is interesting to note that neither Kitty's *Shillelagh* nor Arthur's *Going Gay* contained a reference to Old Mother Riley in the show's actual title, but the *Going Gay* poster did feature the words "Arthur Lucan–Old Mother Riley" in bold capitals above the title and, to make things even more explicit, in smaller print below "Old Mother Riley" were the words "IN PERSON."

With My Shillelagh Under My Arm seems to have had a brief and not very noteworthy run, and was almost certainly responsible for piling up more of the debts with which KMS Productions finally forced Arthur into bankruptcy. *The Stage* lists the show at the Ipswich Hippodrome on 4 May, hot on the heels of *Going Gay*. In May it toured to the Grand Theater Doncaster, the West Bromwich Plaza and finally the Portsmouth Empire where it was followed in June by *Going Gay*. I have found just one further booking for *Shillelagh*, at the Oldham Empire in the first week of June. The show must have folded shortly thereafter because Kitty's co-star George E. Beck announced in *The Stage* in late July that he was "vacant for revue or road show, also unexpectedly vacant for pantomime."

Slim Ingram told me a story from this period concerning Kitty and Frank Randle, which he also told Philip and David Williams for their book on Frank, *Wired to the Moon*. With their permission I reproduce their version of the tale.

While doing the rounds of London's variety theaters Randle found time to visit Kitty McShane who herself was appearing locally. Now split from her partner and husband Arthur Lucan, alias Old Mother Riley, McShane had begun performing with an alternative 'Old Mother Riley.' Slim Ingram, friend of Arthur Lucan and also his tour manager in the 1950s, recounted an intriguing story which he remembered well. Randle had gone to see Kitty at one of her London dates. Once backstage the pair soon ended up drinking heavily, not just after the show but also while it was ongoing with Kitty going back and forth between stage and dressing room. Shortly before completing her performance and now quite visibly under the influence, she announced to the audience that she would in future be presenting a brand new act with a another partner. Amidst murmurings from the audience she went on to say, 'I would like to introduce him to you now, please ladies and gentlemen welcome my new partner... Frank Randle.' Instantly the audience joined as one in loud applause as an intoxicated Randle staggered on stage to take his bow. From both artistes at that moment in time it may well have been their intention to team up together. However, in the cold light of day—no doubt the very next day, after effects of the alcohol had worn off, reality obviously dawned. Nothing ever came of this and it was never mentioned again. Of similar temperament and both with a liking for the bottle, one could only imagine what a nightmare of a partnership that one would have been.[144]

But when Slim re-told the story to me in September 2012, he added another ghastly (or hilarious) detail. "After Kitty brought Frank onstage, and the drunken pair had taken their bow, they tried to sing 'There's No Business Like Show Business.' They staggered and slurred and forgot the words until in utter exasperation the stage manager ordered that the curtain be brought down to cut them off in full flow!"

Although Kitty sometimes stayed in the flat at 20 South Molton Street, she was still firmly ensconced at 11 Forty Lane, which she used as her official residence when applying for registration as a theatrical employer in March 1953. Again according to Slim Ingram, with whom Arthur spent much of his last two years, Arthur hardly ever returned to the house on Forty Lane, but lived more or less "out of brown paper carrier bags." However Kitty would occasionally have an upsurge of feeling, and on one such occasion Arthur and Slim were invited to have Sunday lunch with Kitty and Billy, and to stay at Forty Lane. Lunch passed off quite peacefully, and then Arthur and Slim retired to their rooms to read the Sunday papers, leaving Kitty and Billy drinking. After a while, fuelled by drink, Kitty flew into one of the demented rages, of which poor Arthur was always both the subject and the object. Suddenly, she pounded up the stairs, flung open the bedroom doors and with a torrent of abuse ordered a bewildered Arthur and Slim to "get out of my effing house!" As Slim remembered it she helped them on their way by hurling their belongings into the street, including a Roberts portable radio of which Arthur was very proud. (I think this may have been the portable radio which had had a walk-on part in *Old Mother Riley's Jungle Treasure.*)

Slim recalled, "As night fell we sat in a daze on a grass verge trying to work out what had sparked things off, with poor Arthur checking to see if his radio had survived the blitz." Once again, the Savage Club came to the rescue. It was probably an incident such as this which prompted the following memory on an internet discussion site. "One of our former neighbors used to live next-door to them in Wembley Park many years ago. She said Arthur was a nice little man, but Kitty was absolutely awful." And yet the gossips later talked of "Alcoholic Arthur," who in reality was performing twice nightly all around the country to keep his wife's creditors from his door! There are many well documented stories of embarrassing drunken episodes involving Kitty, but not one authenticated account of this sort concerning Arthur. The Lucans' eldest granddaughter Marylyn remembered that as a young girl, "Whenever I saw my grandmother she always seemed to be a bit tipsy, whereas my grandfather never was." Arthur was no abstainer, and certainly enjoyed a drink or two, but there is not a single rumor of his ever having made a spectacle of himself in public, except on the legitimate comic stage. Slim Ingram remembered that on tour Arthur tippled from miniature gin bottles; miniatures were probably all he could afford by then. Slim used to say to him, "Why don't you drink whisky Arthur? You know gin makes you sad." Arthur simply replied, "Because I'm sad already, chuck!"

In May 1953 *Going Gay* was at the Wood Green Empire. Arthur, barely a year before his death, was growing increasingly old, sad, and tired, but given his dreadful personal situation he was obliged to soldier grimly on. Yet in spite of this, the critic for *The Stage* who reviewed the performance at Wood Green, still caught something of the uncanny appeal of Arthur's comic alter ego, a true archetype, transcending and effacing the offstage weakness and frailty its creator. The critic begins by lamenting the fact that "sound radio and the gramophone record have made the purely vocal artist pre-eminent" to the detriment of "those acts dependent on visual effects." Such acts, he speculates, may be helped in the future by the growth of television. He then turns to Arthur, and gives him one of the finest, and most perceptive, reviews he ever received.

There is an exception however, and that exception, in the person of Arthur Lucan, is delighting audiences at Wood Green this week. It may be objected that Mr. Lucan should be included in the ranks of the comedians but, in fact, this clever artist, who hides a sensitive, intelligent talent behind the irate exterior of Old Mother Riley is a good deal more than that. For although he is extremely amusing in the vein of simple humor that he chooses to pursue, that alone is not sufficient to explain the success that attends his efforts, and one must look further into the brilliant characterization that has completely submerged the identity of the man beneath the bonnet. Old Mother Riley is at once so real and so fantastic that her mere presence is a source of endless delight, and although on this occasion her activities seem more aimless than usual and supported by no distinction of dialogue, the affectionate response she arouses is quite unmistakably genuine.

"A sensitive, intelligent talent ... brilliant ... at once so real and so fantastic ... affectionate response ...." These views were reiterated time and again by so many of those who knew Arthur and saw him perform even in those final seasons. The actor Brian Murphy, who as a boy saw the show at this time, recalled that Arthur somehow seemed to fill the entire stage with his vital presence. Slim Ingram told me that Arthur loved to work as far downstage as he could, darting about just behind the footlights with as little as possible between him and the sea of delighted faces in the auditorium. A review at Finsbury Park back in January 1942 had spoken of the gales of laughter as Old Mother Riley "visits the audience." Arthur was old enough to remember that George Formby senior had made a habit of jumping down from the stage between numbers and chatting with people in the audience. In July 1953, the *Hastings and St. Leonards Observer* echoed the fulsome praise of the Wood Green critic, and his review firmly contradicts those who have claimed that without Kitty Arthur's act had lost its luster.

> 'Going Gay,' the Gaston and Andrée production featuring Arthur Lucan as Old Mother Riley, supported by a versatile company, provides a first-class opening to the summer season of live shows at the Regal Theater, St. Leonards, this week. Arthur Lucan's famous character, which has been a favorite for almost a generation, comes up as fresh as ever in some uproariously funny numbers, and ensures that the show lives up to its name . . . Numbers like 'Old Mother Riley Goes West,' featuring the whole company, with acrobatic dancing by Dot and Maureen, are full of sparkle and color.

Far from losing his touch, as Arthur's obituary in *The Times* put it, "he recognized early that he had created a popular character, and as the years passed by he developed it and rounded it off with a sure touch which time could not wither nor custom stale." David Kenton, the director of Anglia TV's 1980 Lucan documentary concluded that to the end, "The public wanted to see Lucan, not Kitty McShane. He was the key figure and without him there was nothing. Everyone loved him. Both on the stage and in real life he had a tremendously warm personality. There was no malice in him."

But neither time nor custom could protect Arthur from Kitty's profligacy or his creditors, and in August 1953, Old Mother Riley, who had won a couple of resounding onscreen victories in the dock, was summoned as plain Arthur Towle to appear in very different circumstances in the Bankruptcy Court in Carey Street. The

Legal Notices in *The Times* on 22 August included the following announcement:

In the High Court of Justice in Bankruptcy. No 441 of 1953. Re Arthur Towle, otherwise known As Arthur Lucan of 11, Forty Lane, Wembley, in the county of Middlesex, Variety Artist, (under receiving order dated 13 August 1953). First Meeting of Creditors, 28th August, 1953 at 11.30 a.m. Public Examination 20th October 1953, at 11.00 a.m. both to be held at Bankruptcy Buildings, Carey Street, London W.C.2 F.W. Cresswell, Senior Official Receiver.

At the meeting of creditors which followed, the Receiver reported that Arthur (who was excused attendance because *Going Gay* was playing in Exeter) had assets of only £2,866, but that "he was doing all he could to make a contribution out of his earnings towards his liabilities." A first Public Examination was held on 20 October 1953. Slim Ingram accompanied Arthur and remembered it as "the saddest day of Arthur's career, the day we went to Carey Street." It would also seem that *Going Gay* did not play that week. The Public Examination in the Bankruptcy Court was fixed for 9 March 1954, and for the next six months Arthur was haunted by anxiety, often asking members of the company what would become of him, and wondering if he might go to prison. And through all this, as company manager Slim Ingram confirmed to me, Arthur continued to send what money he could to Kitty, and she continued to send him ten-page telegrams filled with drunken insults, and threats to shoot him, knife him, or pull off his nose.

When in December 1953 *Going Gay* finally closed after its long and successful nation-wide run, the company went into pantomime at Folkestone and Swindon.[145] It was at Folkestone Pleasure Gardens (not really "oop North!") that Arthur received his very last glowing review in *The Stage* as a pantomime dame—the first had been for *Cinderella* in Paisley in 1912.

Gaston and Andrée's Productions' presentation of 'Old Mother Hubbard' at the Pleasure Gardens is lavishly produced and excellently staged. It provides Arthur Lucan with ample scope for the type of comedy with which he has

delighted the public for many years. He makes Old Mother
Hubbard a lively, skittish old harridan, not averse to a little
romance even at her age, and with sprightliness that takes the
show along at a cracking pace. And her small beady eyes are
alternately dancing with fun or aslant with a knowledgeable
cunning.

Over forty years on from Arthur's first pantomime, the enthusiastic reviewer at Folkestone could have had no idea that Arthur had
recently written to his son, "I am not going to work because I like it.
I've got to work, otherwise I'll starve. I've got no money or assets. But
I should have . . . ." Unlike the previous year, Roy Rolland remained
with the company, not as understudy but playing "an attractive squire's
daughter, a remarkable example of female impersonation." This was
also the very last time he worked with Arthur Lucan.

In the break between his last pantomime and his last show,
Arthur was photographed with Kitty for the very last time when, on
22 February 1954, he accompanied her to the High Court. The verso
of the photograph states that it was taken when they attended the

Photo 16: The last photograph of Arthur and Kitty, 22 February, 1954.
John Fisher

Chancery Division of the High Court to settle Kitty's dispute over receipts from *Old Mother Riley's Jungle Treasure*. Kitty had wanted her share paid directly into her separate bank account but it was ruled that the film contract was valid only in the joint name of Lucan and McShane. In the bleak offstage photograph, just three months before Arthur's death, the effects of the years of "unhappiness and strife," not to mention the effects of desperate recourse to the bottle, are clearly etched on the faces of the sad ex-couple. If life together had become intolerable, it seems that life apart was little better, and this last photograph allows us, in the words of Roger Lewis "to glimpse or sense the lonely pathos of injured spirits."

After two sell-out pantomimes and the long and successful run of *Going Gay*, Gaston and Andrée were more than happy to devise a new show with Arthur as the star. But just one week before the show was due to open Arthur had to keep another appointment at the London Bankruptcy Court on Tuesday 9 March. The report of the proceedings in *The Times* contained one further ignominy. Arthur was described as "Mr. Towle, of no fixed address, but formerly of Forty Lane, Wembley, Middlesex." He agreed that he probably owed the Inland Revenue £15,000 and that "at the moment they were claiming £10,051, mainly in respect of surtax." The rest of the report makes embarrassing and pathetic reading, with Arthur clearly unwilling or unable to state the plain truth of his wife's central role in his ruin.

Questioned by the Assistant Official Receiver, Mr. Towle said he had been in the theatrical profession since he left school. In 1913 he married, and he and his wife then did an act together, 'Old Mother Riley and her daughter Kitty.' They also made several films together. At first he looked after the money but later his wife took over.

'Did she give you an allowance?'

'A pound here and a pound there.'

'If your wife said she gave you £50 to £100 a week what would you say to that?'

'I would have to say no.'

Mr. Towle agreed that his wife paid the living expenses and the hotel expenses.

In 1946 or 1947, Mr. Towle agreed, his wife bought a beauty parlor on which he contended she lost about £30,000 or £40,000. He said she also unsuccessfully invested in property and other businesses. After 1951 he decided to carry on the act alone as he thought his wife wished to look after her business interests. He said that since 1951 he had paid her about three-quarters of his income. Normally he earned over £100 a week and he was prepared to continue paying a percentage to his trustee. In the interests of his creditors he was willing to go back on the stage with his wife as a double act. In that way the debts could probably be paid more quickly. The examination was adjourned until 25 May.

One week after this humiliating experience, far from going back on the stage with his wife, Arthur opened in *Old Mother Riley Goes to Paris* at the New Theater Cambridge. The poster for the show featured Arthur's name at the top of the bill, "Arthur Lucan in his latest and greatest comedy success," and a cartoon of Mother Riley wrapping herself around the Eiffel Tower. As a last gesture of friendship and solidarity with an old friend, Con West, the man who had created the name Old Mother Riley in 1937, provided the book for the new show by giving Gaston and Andrée permission to use his script from the 1938 film *Old Mother Riley in Paris* as the narrative thread around which the show's various acts would be woven. Once again Kitty was furious, but Con West's gesture effectively gave the lie to her erroneous claims to owning the rights to everything to do with Old Mother Riley. The show's fourteen scenes each had a title which referred to an episode in the film, beginning on Paradise Row and moving via a hospital ward and the Customs Office at Calais to an all singing and dancing first half finale at Le Moulin Rouge, Paris. After the interval the scene moves from the Boulevards to a prison cell when Mother Riley is arrested as a spy. After her rescue and return to the Hotel Magnifique, an Apache Den in Montmartre is the scene for the re-creation of one of the funniest scenes in the 1938 film. Mother Riley mistakes the "danse apache" for a violent lovers' altercation, and when she challenges the French bully he promptly sweeps her up like a rag doll and does a hilarious spoof dance with her. That was all very well in 1938 when Arthur was a lad of 53 and still remarkably agile for his years. Now 67, he was old and tired; the voice still worked and the eyes still sparkled with the adrenalin of live performance, but he was far too physically debilitated to be flung around in an energetic *pas de deux*.

What has never before been reported is the fact that Arthur was not flung around at all! Slim Ingram told me in September 2012 that Arthur never once performed the dance scene. So concerned was the whole company for Arthur's health that it was Slim, disguised as Mother Riley (not even the nominal understudy Frank Seton), who after a quick twirl behind a flat emerged to be flung twice nightly around the stage. All ended happily and the grand finale brought the whole company back home to Paradise Row. In the 1938 film *Old Mother Riley in Paris*, Mother of course had a daughter, but in the 1954 stage show she acquired a son, Pat Riley, played by Jimmy Grant, who later had a career in folk music. On learning of this substitution, Kitty flew into a rage not unlike her reaction two years earlier when she found out that Gale Douglas had replaced her as the jilted bride. She created an unpleasant scene during which she again made the tasteless and ridiculous claim that Arthur was a "poof" who took Jimmy on board because he "fancied" him. Arthur of course had no such proclivities, nor did he have a say in the show's casting; and besides, Jimmy's wife was among the dancers. To the abiding disgust of Donald Towle and many others, Kitty had already used the "poof" jibe in an attempt to justify her moving in with Billy Breach, and eventually pushing Arthur out of his own house.

After opening at the New Theater Cambridge on 15 March, *Old Mother Riley in Paris* moved on to Peterborough. From there, on the following Sunday morning, en route for West Hartlepool, Slim Ingram drove Arthur "home" to Boston for what proved to be the last time. In April the show was at the Pavilion Liverpool where the press reported that "Arthur Lucan, as diverting as ever, provides many laughs." With a generosity of spirit that was widely acknowledged in the business, one of Arthur's last public pronouncements was a "plug" for the younger generation. On 6 May *The Stage* reported that "Arthur Lucan is proud of Jimmy Grant his latest vocalist discovery, currently appearing as his son Pat at Wigan Hippodrome.

'Jimmy'll go places,' he vouches."[146] From Wigan *Old Mother Riley in Paris* moved to the Theater Royal Barnsley on 10 May, and the week passed without incident. At the end of the week, on Saturday 15 May, a couple of older fans, "Arthur's Ladies" as they were affectionately known, came to meet him backstage and presented him with a box of Nestlé chocolates. Still in costume, Arthur happily agreed to be photographed, the very last photograph to be taken of Arthur Towle/Arthur Lucan/Old Mother Riley, a copy of which Slim Ingram gave to me when I said goodbye to him in September 2012. As Arthur poses for his last photo call, laughing happily between the two sisters, Minnie Chappell and Sally Porter, with their hairnets and owlish NHS glasses, it is actually difficult to be sure which dame is the caricature! Just as a second generation of children now loved him, so too did the last of that generation of working-class women who had known two world wars, factory work and domestic drudgery without labor-saving appliances; a world of mass conformity in environment and expectation, especially for ordinary women; a world of identical houses with coal fires and outside lavatories; a world in which domineering and sometimes physically abusive husbands were seen as the norm, with little protection from anything vaguely resembling "women's rights." To paraphrase Sue Harper, Arthur's old ladies' enjoyment of, and sense of complicity in, the anarchy and bad behavior of Mother Riley was their vicarious "just reward for a long life of conformity." All that, and Arthur Lucan's part in it, were now coming to an end.

On Sunday 16 May Slim Ingram drove Arthur from Barnsley to Hull in his Hillman Minx. Arthur stayed at the Royal Station Hotel; by an ironic twist of fate, two weeks after Arthur's one-night stay, Laurel and Hardy stayed there before their last sea voyage back to Los Angeles and Hollywood, the very destination which Lew Lake had predicted for Lucan and Arnold in the 1920s. On Sunday evening Arthur gave his last interview to a *Hull Daily Mail* reporter who wrote, "I was impressed with his devotion to show business. This was not merely a job to him but a part of his life which he loved fervently. He was a grand old trouper who never failed to respond to the maxim that 'the show must go on.' *Even when he was ill he never spared himself and rarely called on his understudy.*" In retrospect, that last sentence (which I have italicised) seems to me to reveal an

Photo 17: The last photograph. Arthur and two of his "Ladies," Barnsley,
Saturday, 15 May, 1954. Slim Ingram

uncanny premonition, and an attempt by Arthur to counter the black legend which he suspected would be peddled when he could longer defend himself.

Arthur's next appearance in the Bankruptcy Court was now only a week away and he was clearly very worried. Slim remembered two unusual things about Monday 17 May when the show was due to open at the Tivoli. "Arthur came into the theater far earlier than usual. In the afternoon I was painting some rostra when to my surprise Arthur wandered onto the stage, already half-dressed. He also did something which I had never known him do before. He went round the dressing rooms and chatted to most of the cast." As the overture began for the first house at 6.15 p.m. Arthur stood beside Slim in the wings ready for his entrance. Slim was in prompt corner but as he himself told me, because of the lack of space in the wings at the Tivoli, prompt corner was not stage left as is normal but stage right, to the left as seen by the audience. Slim reminded Arthur to beware of the Tivoli's unusually steep trough just behind the footlights and Arthur said "OK, chuck." Those were his last words. As the singers and dancers finished the opening number, Ellis Ashton playing the mayor announced the entrance of Mother Riley from her cottage.

At that moment Slim, who had turned away to give a cue, heard a groan and a thud, and when he looked back Arthur had collapsed and was lying behind the flat. Slim at once gave the emergency signal for the house tabs to close, and the whole cast quickly realized that something was very wrong. Jack Le White's dreadful premonition had finally come true; "So many times we had heard Kitty telling Arthur to drop dead in her reverberating stage whisper. In the end, that is what he did." As John Fisher put it, "It is a chilling epitaph."[147]

While Ellis Ashton went out front and announced to the audience that due to a technical hitch the show would re-start in a few minutes, Slim Ingram and senior electrician Roland Watson carried Arthur to his dressing room, and Slim called Frank Seton to get changed. This should not have been a problem for a man who, as we noted earlier, was reputed to have stood in for Arthur on a regular basis. Indeed, according to one account, "Arthur Lucan had frequently missed performances during this tour—so frequently that sometimes announcements were never made, and Frank would go on, playing to an audience who would be unaware that it wasn't the real Old Mother Riley . . . Very often the other members of the company would be unaware that Arthur was off until they realized it was Frank in his place. Arthur's drinking problems were heavy: he was more likely to be off for a second show on a twice-nightly schedule."[148] All of this is a complete fabrication. In 2002, with disarming honesty, Frank Seton at last tried to put the record straight and correct this travesty of the truth. In an interview filmed live at the Theater Museum in Covent Garden he insisted that he had *never once* dressed, or made up, as Mother Riley before that fateful night.[149] As Seton himself said later "You can't really take over a part like Old Mother Riley. It is entirely Lucan's own characterisation. You just can't mimic him."

For these reasons, the ten minutes following Arthur's collapse must have been ghastly for all concerned. Frank was given Arthur's boots and told by the dresser Maisie Munro to "put them on the wrong feet, it will help you with the walk." He then quickly made up and was helped into Arthur's second change costume, and the show began all over again. The cast had their jobs to do, so Maisie was left alone with Arthur. Frank Seton remembered (or liked to believe) that when he left the dressing room Arthur was still breathing, but when he returned after his first scene Arthur's face had been covered, and it was clear to everyone that he was dead. The full awfulness of the old theatrical adage that "the show must go on" was lived out that night in the Tivoli, as brightly-costumed characters rushed grimly onstage and, according to the *Daily Mail*, "The pretty chorus line crowded down the stairs, some of them choking back sobs, and danced gaily onto the stage."

Back in the number one dressing room, Arthur's devoted dresser, Maisie Munro, wept as she removed Arthur's wig and putty nose, and waited for the City Coroner, Dr. Philip Science, who arrived, and, "while the chorus line tapped through routines and peals of laughter swept the stage," he officially pronounced Arthur Lucan to be dead. Frank Seton, helped by the whole company, staggered heroically through the first house; but the same cruel theatrical adage demanded that the whole show must go on again for the second house at 8:25pm. As Leoncavallo's operatic clown Pagliaccio sings in his famous aria, *"La gente paga, e rider vuole qua ...* The people pay to be here, and they want to laugh." Arthur Lucan, like Pagliaccio, had understood the sad predicament of the clown throughout the ages; laughter in the midst of tears. "If Harlequin should steal your Columbine, Laugh, Clown, and the crowd will cheer." But before Leoncavallo, W. S. Gilbert had given similar sentiments to his jester, Jack Point, oddly even more applicable to Arthur.

> Though your wife ran away with a soldier that day,
> And took with her your trifle of money;
> Bless your heart, they don't mind,
> They're exceedingly kind,
> They don't blame you—as long as you're funny![150]

As the crowd streamed out at the end of the first house, many whispered to the waiting queue, "That's not Mother Riley onstage!" Rumors of Arthur's death were circulating before the end of the second house. At the end of the first house Slim Ingram had a number of grim phone calls to make. Firstly he called Kitty, and he vividly recalled for me the bizarre opening of their conversation. When he told her that Arthur had died there was a long pause and then she shouted "You fucking bastard!" Slim said that he at first thought she was addressing him, "but then I realized she was talking to Arthur not me!" The often repeated story that when Kitty was told that Arthur had died she said "Where?" and when told Hull she said "Typical!" is completely untrue. She already knew exactly where he was and later claimed, with brazen mendacity, that she had been preparing to come to Hull two days later to celebrate her birthday with him. Kitty seems to have phoned the theater several times later in the evening and early the next day. In 1982 Roland Watson shared his memories of that night with Nigel Ellacott. Nigel's brother Vivyan kindly sent me the following notes:

> Kitty's reaction shocked them. She demanded that the body be left where it was, and that the dressing room should be locked and no one be allowed to enter until she got there. She said that none of his property was to be touched or removed, and she mentioned particularly the contents of his wallet. She said she knew exactly how much money he would have and she would expect that amount of money to be there when she arrived. This was considered to be deeply insulting to both the Stage Managers and staff at the theater. Mr. Watson explained that it would not be possible to keep the door locked, in any event the doctor would be arriving any minute, and he was not sure what would happen if the doctor issued a death certificate.
>
> At this point Kitty McShane tried to insist that Arthur's death was to be kept absolutely secret. No one was to be informed. Not even the cast. They should say that Arthur was ill. Frank was to be instructed to cover him as usual for the rest of the week, and she would try and arrange for a local undertaker to take the body out later that night, and to keep his death a secret. Eventually this message was relayed to Frank in the interval, and he and the Stage Manager agreed that what Kitty McShane was asking was quite impossible. Because she had expressed no sadness, but had instantly concerned herself about the money, they thought she must be hoping to cover up the death until the end of the week so she could collect the full money for Arthur's appearance, and not a much reduced sum or even a cancellation if word got out. Neither Frank Seton nor Roland Watson elaborated further on what happened that night; certainly Frank played

the second show, and a doctor arrived. Frank suspected the body was taken away that night by an undertaker. However, the news of Arthur's death had spread round the entire company, so there was no possibility whatsoever of keeping the news secret.

In actual fact, Kitty had no say whatever in the running of the Gaston and Andrée company, and had even been banned by the producers from visiting theaters where the show was playing. In the course of the evening Slim also rang Gaston and Andrée, who agreed that he should contact Roy Rolland and ask him to replace Arthur. Luckily Roy was "resting" at home in Rhyl and he was able to travel to Hull the following morning, but not with Kitty as some have claimed. He arrived at lunchtime and Slim spent the afternoon taking him through the show and adapting it to the sketches Roy knew best. Roy went on that night and for the rest of the week, but Slim Ingram told me he didn't have an easy time of it as, good though he was, audiences could be heard murmuring, "That's not Arthur Lucan, Arthur's dead!"

Kitty arrived from London later in the day. When she was told that Arthur's dressing room was locked, and realizing she wasn't welcome in the theater, she fired off a torrent of foul language that shocked even the hardened senior electrician Roland Watson. She sent for Roy to call on her at her hotel, and Roy felt that "she was genuinely upset." Perhaps it was because he told her that Arthur had left him his boots, to which Kitty replied, "Well, shall we say it is Miss McShane giving them to you." There were rumors that Kitty originally intended to have Arthur buried in London, but this would have involved immediate financial outlay, something she had not done for him in life for a very long time. So she settled for a Hull funeral, where everything could be put on account, and eventually paid for by Dr. Donald Towle.

No inquest was deemed necessary, and the Hull Coroner, Dr. Philip Science, performed a post-mortem examination on Tuesday, 18 May. He certified Arthur's death to be the result of "a, Cerebral hemorrhage, b, Arterio-sclerosis, c, Chronic Interstitial Nephritis." The chronic nephritis was almost certainly a long-term legacy of childhood scarlet fever. Nowhere was alcohol mentioned as even a subsidiary contributing factor.

Arthur's obituary appeared in *The Times* on Wednesday 19 May. It contained the usual misinformation about "The North" but was otherwise perceptive and sympathetic.

Mr. Arthur Towle, known professionally as Arthur Lucan, whose death at the age of 67 was briefly reported in our later editions yesterday, for long delighted large audiences, particularly in Yorkshire and Lancashire, with his perennially entertaining impersonation of 'Mother Riley.'

Belonging, as he did, to the old school of knock-about comedians, he recognized early that he had created a popular character, and as the years passed by developed it and rounded it off with a sure touch which time could not wither nor custom stale. He had been in the theatrical profession since he left school, and in 1913 he married and he and his wife began a double act which in those days was called 'Old Mother Riley and her Daughter Kitty,' or 'Lucan and McShane.'

The homely adventures of the naive 'mother' and her sophisticated daughter, spiced with a salty Irish flavor, were favorites not only on the boards but on the air as well and it was only a matter of time, in 1937, in fact, for the cinema companies to realize the possibilities of the act. The many films of the pair in various situations were great successes. The partnership broke up after the last war and Mr. Towle carried on alone, keeping alive the fame of the endearing, bemused old woman, who seemed to those who laughed at her antics to enjoy an existence of her own.

The Manchester Guardian, more eloquently than *The Times*, not only captured something of Riley's larger than life "existence of her own," but also evoked the darker undercurrents in Lucan's creation.

Old Mother Riley was, in her prime, one of the most formidable beldames on the stage. Lucan had a lean hungry look, a sweeping disorderliness, a garrulous incoherence which kept the stage humming; his old hag was realistic up to a point, and then she climbed a beanstalk and rode off on a broomstick;

or was it that she kept alive something of the real squalor of a harsher vanished age? There was some pretense of Irishry, but it was the Irish of the Scotland Road, Liverpool, rather than of Dublin or Galway; the words might distantly recall Kilkenny, but the eager, bony face and the appalling black bonnet were a descant on our own deformity, at which we laughed with the shadow of a shudder.[151]

On 18 May Donald Towle received the following letter from Arthur's old friend and fellow performer, the highly literate comedian Gillie Potter, creator of the saga of the village of Hogsnorton for BBC radio.[152]

Five Mile Cottage, Highgate, N.6
18/5/1954

Dear Dr. Towle,

Please permit an old friend of his to say how deeply the passing of your Father under so sad a set of circumstances has affected him.

Accept his heartfelt sympathy with you all in your sorrow.

Yours sincerely,
Gillie Potter

Another old friend and colleague from the years of variety, Wee Georgie Wood, writing in *The Stage* one week after the funeral, managed by subtle understatement to express far more than he actually said.

It would have gladdened Arthur Lucan to have heard the tributes from the V.A.F., but most of all the eulogies of his brother 'Savages' and the staff of the Savage Club, where he often stayed. Some of us who were closest to Arthur noticed, no matter what troubles beset him, that he had praise for all that Rosemary Andrée and Jimmie Gaston had done to help him. That's all I want to say, but it isn't all I am feeling about the passing of a great performer.

Readers of *The Stage* will have known exactly what he meant. But perhaps the most unashamedly poignant tribute to Arthur's passing is one I read on an internet blog. A chap who was just a boy in 1954 recalled something he witnessed at a children's Saturday cinema matinee shortly after Arthur's death.[153]

It was only a few months after Lucan's death when one of his films came up on Saturday Morning Pictures. Most of us knew what had happened, and the film being shown ended with Old Mother Riley being in bed and about to go to sleep. He was shown getting comfortable under the bed clothes as the film ended, and a lot of the kids were crying . . . .

Chapter Ten: Funeral Games

The *Hull Daily Mail* announced on Wednesday 19 May (which happened to be Kitty's birthday) that Arthur was to be buried in Hull, and that evening Roy Rolland paid a tribute to him from the stage of the Tivoli Theater at the end of the second house. Kitty had no role in the company but she now played the role of Arthur's grieving widow for all it was worth, although she was careful not to spend any money. Roy Rolland remembered being taken by Kitty to view the body at Annison's chapel of rest on the corner of Witham and Great Union Street, in a vast listed building still standing today. Roy felt she was making a "production" of it and said he wouldn't have been surprised to see dancing girls appear. Kitty had placed a large crucifix on Arthur's chest, "to keep him down" said Roy, and had scattered spring flowers over him "as if thrown from a great height." Roy remarked on her Irish pronunciation ("Artur, Irish like, she never said Arthur") as Kitty addressed the body of her late husband. "Well Artur, forty years, we've been together all those years, and you old bugger, you leave me for two, and where has it got you?" Arthur's corpse should surely have answered, "The Court of Bankruptcy, you old bugger!"

Arthur's funeral, which was not at all the low-key affair some have made it out to be, took place on the afternoon of Friday 21 May. Rather appropriately for the creator of the "Irish" Old Mother Riley, the Requiem Mass was celebrated in the Catholic church of St. Patrick on Spring Street, just down the road and round the corner from the Tivoli Theater.[154] The celebrant at Mass was the parish priest Fr. Charles Clifford, assisted by Fr. Ryan. The *Daily Mail* reported that there was a large congregation in church, and that large crowds had also gathered outside. Kitty played the role of chief mourner, accompanied by Billy Breach, giving his own name to reporters and described in the press as "Miss McShane's manager." Dr. Donald Towle and his second wife, Maureen, were also present, along with Maisie Munro, Arthur's dresser. From Boston came Arthur's sisters, Annie and Kate, brothers George and Tom, and several nieces and nephews. The entire cast and crew of the Riley show were in church and at the graveside, some as representatives of the Variety Artists' Federation, the Water Rats, and British Equity, along with the staff of both the Tivoli and Palace theaters where Lucan and McShane had worked so many times over the years. After Mass, the cortege made its way, "like a royal procession" according to Slim Ingram, through city center streets lined with fans; Tom Towle recalled that his brother's cortege "stopped the "traffic" as it made its way out to Hull's Eastern Cemetery. Thanks to the *Daily Mail* reporter who recorded names as people left the cemetery, it is clear that in addition to the Towle family members and the theater companies, there were over a hundred other people at the graveside, making a total in excess of one hundred and fifty mourners, gathered to lay Arthur to rest. The *Hull Daily Mail* reported that "Many people were in tears at the interment of Arthur Lucan (Old Mother Riley) at Eastern Cemetery, Hull, this afternoon, as the coffin was lowered and his stage clothes were thrown on top."

Many of the names recorded by the reporter were of women, members of the faithful fan club of "Arthur's Ladies." The Tivoli Theater's senior electrician Roland Watson remembered that "Arthur's Ladies were out in force, a crowd of elderly women who went to see the Tivoli shows and Arthur in particular." These ladies had always taken a rather dim view of Kitty, and when they saw her on the arm of "Danny Boy" Breach, who was now well known to be her "fancy man," they were visibly annoyed. According to Watson, "the ladies took umbrage and were already muttering before Kitty approached the coffin and dumped the costume into the grave." Roland Watson is also the source of the most reliable account of this graveside incident, which has been hitherto inadequately reported. When Kitty, following an old show business tradition, threw the costume into the grave, it has been claimed that she hissed the word "Bastard!" Roland Watson's version far better captures the instantly recognizable McShane tone of voice, as remembered by Jack Whiteley. Kitty's parting shot to the man who had given her (in his own words) "the whole of the profits of a life's work" was in fact, "Lie there, y'aul bastard!" Then, in keeping with the utterly incomprehensible symbiosis that was Lucan and McShane, she dropped a single red rose into the grave before walking away for the last time, from her husband, her "mummy darling, jewel of the whole wide world," and forty years of "fruitful misalliance."

On Tuesday 25 May 1954, four days after his funeral, Arthur had been due to appear at the London Bankruptcy Court; instead several not unrelated events took place. On Wednesday 26 May, the "News in Brief" section of *The Times* carried the following announcement: "The public examination of Mr. Arthur Towle—Arthur Lucan the music hall comedian—was formally closed at London Bankruptcy Court yesterday, the Registrar being informed that Mr. Towle died at Hull on 17 May." Arthur's personal debts as a bankrupt died with him and were not inherited by the widow who was, in fact, mostly responsible for them. Roy Rolland claimed that when Arthur first thought of going solo around 1950 he said he thought he could raise capital by selling the big house at 11 Forty Lane. But in reality he must have forgotten, or possibly not even been aware, that the house was not owned by him but by "Mrs. Kathleen Towle." As late as 2011, Richard Anthony Baker was under the impression that "In August 1953, Arthur was made bankrupt and was forced to sell his home." However, things were not that simple. The *Stage Yearbook* for 1954 shows that Kitty was still firmly in possession; she is listed as "Miss Kitty McShane, 11 Forty Lane, Wembley, Middx. (Tel. Arnold 5470)." Not even the phone had been cut off.

In 2012, Mrs. Urvashi Chudasama, the present owner of the house, which is now a nursing home, was kind enough to obtain and send me a copy of the Land Registry for the relevant years. This clearly shows that on the very day on which *The Times* reported the closing of Arthur's bankruptcy hearing, 25 May 1954, H.M. Land Registry recorded the fact that the Title Absolute of 11 Forty Lane, Wembley, passed from its owner, not Arthur, but Mrs. Kathleen Towle, and was registered to the Royal National Institute for the Deaf on payment of £7,500, all of which went to Kitty.[155] This did not prevent her from pleading poverty when it came to paying for Arthur's funeral and gravestone; the bills were eventually settled by Donald Towle. In the same week following the funeral, Kitty gave a press interview. In what Anthony Slide has called "an exhibition of extraordinary hypocrisy, superior to her performances on film," she said of Arthur, "He was a wonderful man, but like a child in many things. He needed mothering and I often had to bully him. Life was never quiet for us, but he was a darling. I was going up to Hull last week because he asked me. He planned a celebration for my birthday. Instead I went to his funeral."[156] When I asked Slim Ingram if there was any truth in Kitty's claim about a birthday visit to Hull, he assured me that this was most unlikely, to put it mildly; in fact he replied in one word. "Bollocks!"

Over the years Kitty had got it into her head that her production company somehow owned the rights not only to Arthur himself but to the character of Old Mother Riley. Arthur's letter to his son Donald in 1952 had seemed to suggest that she might try resorting to the law to prevent his using the name without her consent. In the weeks following Arthur's death she appears to have made similar claims against the Gaston and Andrée show. That would provide the only satisfactory explanation for a rather ominous advertisement placed by Con West in *The Stage* in June 1954.

TO WHOM IT MAY CONCERN/ The Title, Story and Book of the Revusical Comedy OLD MOTHER RILEY IN PARIS /Were originated and written by CON WEST who owns /The full Copyright /The Title has now been changed to PARADISE ROW TO PARIS /And the Script is leased on license to GASTON AND ANDREE /Who have the SOLE RIGHTS to perform this show.

Any hope Kitty may have had of cashing in or making another comeback seems to have been firmly quashed by what can only be interpreted as a very public put-down by one of Arthur's many loyal friends, the man who had invented the name Old Mother Riley, and had been involved in nine of the films.

Donald Towle's relationship with his mother, distant at the best of times, became even more fraught after Arthur's death. Contrary to popular legends, Arthur's grave did not lie unmarked for years, nor was his gravestone paid for by public subscription, or Les Dawson. Shortly after the funeral, Arthur's son Donald ordered a headstone for his father's grave, but when Kitty found this out she decided to interfere. In July 1954 she wrote to Annison's Funeral Directors in Hull:

Dear Mr. Richardson, With reference to the stone that my son ordered for my husband's grave, I do not wish to have the normal inscription upon the stone; instead I would like the following: ARTHUR LUCAN, BETTER KNOWN AND LOVED BY MILLIONS OF CHILDREN AS OLD MOTHER RILEY. DON'T CRY AS YOU PASS BY BUT SAY A LITTLE PRAYER. Would you please see that this is carried out correctly. Sincerely, Kathleen Towle.

Mr. Richardson wrote to Donald saying, "As you placed the order for the stone in the first instance, I await your instructions." Donald's reply barely conceals his distaste. "Dear Mr. Richardson, As Mother requested you to include those vulgar little lines, I think we should do as she wishes. My father died with debts in excess of £14,000, so I would suggest that you send the balance of payments to me. Yours faithfully, Donald Towle."

In January 1955 Donald finally settled the bill for his father's gravestone in Hull, in spite of the fact that his own financial position was very precarious. He had remarried in 1949 and now had a three-year-old daughter, as well as a divorced first wife and their thirteen-year-old daughter to support. He had come to feel trapped in NHS general practice, which he had entered only when his mother refused the promised financial help for further post-graduate study, at a time when the Lucans were among the highest earners in British show business. In spite of Kitty's ostentatious life-style, Donald simply could not believe that his mother had squandered the equivalent of millions in today's money in the space of a few short years.

One surviving letter, shown to me by Donald's widow, Joan, indicates that in early 1955 he was trying to dig deeper into the whole sorry business of the financial ruin of his father. Before reproducing the letter, some preliminary remarks will help to place it more clearly in context.

The letter was written to Donald Towle on 19 March 1955 by Jill Denman, shortly after a meeting with Donald and his family at his house and practice, Lee Park Lodge, in Blackheath. Although Jill did not know Donald well, the tone and content of the letter make it clear that Arthur had often spoken to her with concern and affection for his son. Both Jill and her friend Alan Aitcheson were close and trusted friends of Arthur, and they acted as custodians for Arthur's personal documents and memorabilia. Alan Aitcheson seems to have been safeguarding sensitive legal and financial papers which Arthur may have needed at his court appearances in 1954. This would account for Arthur's "asking for all the other papers shortly before he died." Jill Denman is clearly of the opinion that it was deeply regrettable that Arthur's sudden death allowed all of these sensitive documents to fall into Kitty's hands, the obvious implication being that she would use and abuse them to her own best advantage, regardless of the truth. The fact that serious financial matters were under discussion is supported by the next sentence in which Jill advises Donald to consult Arthur's "accountant and friend, in whom he confided all his financial worries." The letter so far paints a picture of an Arthur Lucan totally different from the childish incompetent regularly described by Kitty in the press. It seems clear that with the help of some of Arthur's trusted confidantes, Donald was trying to ascertain whether anything could be done to force Kitty to reveal the true extent of the Lucan-McShane monies and properties which she may have held concealed in her own name, and against which Donald felt he had a claim. The view that Donald was preparing to take some kind of legal action against his mother is supported by Arthur's earlier letter to his son in March 1952, when Arthur said that Kitty might try to prevent him from working and that "you [Donald] may know something about it as you told me to keep a certain letter that I have at the solicitors." Both father and son had been hoping that Donald might one day benefit from a full inventory and realization of the Lucan-McShane assets, but Kitty's "unfortunate" acquisition of Arthur's private papers put an end to those hopes. Kitty was free to re-organize or destroy documents to her own best advantage, and after the death of his father Donald Towle received nothing of "the profits of a life's work."

With her letter, Jill sent Donald an early photograph that Arthur had given her for safe keeping. She also mentioned other things of Arthur's (alas, unspecified!) still stored with her parents in Devon, to save them from another Kitty conflagration. The seriously embittered and adversarial nature of the relationship between Donald and his mother is brought home chillingly in Jill's final paragraph, which alludes to Donald's "great difficulties and distress of mind," and ends with the words, "You will find that Arthur had many true friends, *all of whom would be on your side*" (my italics). Here is the letter in full:[157]

20 Onslow Gardens, Kensington, S.W. 7, 19 March 1955.

Dear Donald,

I hope you and your wife will excuse my using your Christian name, but having heard Arthur call you this for many years, I find it hard to use 'Dr. Towle' instead.

I have phoned my friend Alan Aitchison, and will send him your address so that he can get in touch with you. He thinks that he only has some telegrams left, as Arthur asked for all the other papers shortly before he died, so these, will unfortunately now be in Kitty's possession.

Arthur's accountant and friend in whom he confided all his financial worries is Mr. [Leonard Frederick] Gould of Edward, Blinkthorn, Lyon and Co. of Queen Victoria Street, E.C.4. I think you will find Mr. Gould very pleasant (I've met him) and he will be able to explain the financial position as it is at present. (I suggest you say that Arthur himself had given you the address, not me!!)

I cannot at the moment find the surnames of your two cousins, as they are married now but I can find these, as I have a cutting with the names on it, but I think it must be in Devon (which is my parents' home.)

I thought you might like the enclosed, all I have here I'm afraid. The photo of Arthur as a boy was taken when he was twelve, and in fancy dress in which he used to sing in a Concert Party on a boat which crossed the Bristol Channel— the cigarette is only paper—or so he used to tell me![158]

I should like to say again, in writing this time, that if there is anything that I can do to help you, in your great difficulties and distress of mind, please never hesitate to ask me or Alan. We will both do what we can to help you and your wife and

family. You will find that Arthur had many true friends, all
of whom would be on your side.

I hope I may have the pleasure of seeing you and your wife
(and sweet baby Susan) again soon.

Kindest regards,
Yours very sincerely,
Jill Denman

I have been unable to find any further information about Jill
Denman or Alan Aitcheson, but what I do know is that Donald's
efforts came to nothing, and the following year his mother made
a gratuitous reference in the press to the cost of his education at
Trinity College Dublin, while pleading poverty for herself. Kitty's
self-pitying article in the *Sunday Dispatch* on 26 October 1956, must
have destroyed any last vestige of family feeling between mother and
son and contributed even further to what Jill Denman called "your
great difficulties and distress of mind."

The full-page piece by Kitty McShane was headed "From £30,000
a year to a Widow's Pension"with the sub-heading, "That's where the
money goes."With breath-taking effrontery, Kitty asked, "Where has
all the money gone? Has it been fast cars, rich living, champagne for
breakfast and lavish parties?" For anyone who knew her, the answer
to all of those questions could only have been, "Yes, yes, yes, and yes!"
She claimed that Arthur's death "not only widowed me, but took
away my income. The act died with my husband. And after his death,
his bills came to me. I have settled them all now."This was a scandalous misrepresentation of the facts and it must have caused real anger
and resentment among the many people, including Donald Towle,
Jill Denman, Slim Ingram, Michael Lyon and Betty Jacoby, James
Gaston and Rosemary Andrée, who had watched Arthur slaving to
the end to send Kitty his wages from the road show while she sat
in London with her boyfriend, or hurled drunken abuse in public at
her long-suffering husband. I quote Richard Anthony Baker's curt
summary of the remaining points Kitty made in the *Sunday Dispatch*:

Kitty maintained the last bill she had to pay was for £350
[£5,500 in today's money]. That was an account with British

Railways for transporting their scenery and props around Britain. Kitty said she had managed to reduce the debt to £39 13s 3d [£635], money she could just not raise. In the nick of time the debt was settled and she avoided being sent to prison: all balderdash.[159]

It was indeed balderdash. The last time British Railways had transported anything for Lucan and McShane was in December 1951 at the very latest, and Roy Denton, manager of the Boscombe Hippodrome, recalled that in those days, at the end of every week he would hand Kitty McShane over £1,000 in cash. There may have been bills dating that far back but that merely raises the question, why didn't Miss McShane of KMS Productions, "the business one" as Ellis Ashton called her, pay them from the money which was still rolling in when the Lucans split up definitively in January 1952? It seems far more likely that many of the bills came from her short-lived solo tour in May-June 1953, bills for which Arthur was in no way responsible. What Kitty failed to mention was the fact that her beauty parlor alone had made a loss of at least £30,000 by 1954. The reliable academic-based website measuringworth.com gives the following relative values for the £30,000 in 1950.

If you want to compare the value of a £30,000 Income or Wealth in 1950 there are three choices. In 2013 the relative historic standard of living value of that income or wealth is £896,900; the economic status value of that income or wealth is £2,818,000; the economic power value of that income or wealth is £3,571,000.

"The whole of the profits of a life's work . . . ." Just how Kitty McShane, without any help from Arthur, managed to lose a fortune of this magnitude, remains to this day a sore point with Donald Towle's descendants.

Not content with tormenting Arthur in life, after his death, while claiming that "he was a lovely man," Kitty actually helped to elaborate and perpetuate the cruel and unjust travesty of "Alcoholic Arthur," and "Keep him in Kitty," which was sadly recalled as a matter of fact in Geoff Mellor's brief biographical entry for Lucan in *They Made Us Laugh*. One of the most egregious examples of the success of

Kitty's damning her dead husband with faint praise is contained in the interviews which Ellis Ashton gave for the two Lucan television documentaries in 1980. Ashton by this time was a distinguished figure on every committee in the world of variety theater but this did not prevent him from talking complete nonsense. In spite of his apparently knowledgeable pontificating, he had never in fact worked with Lucan and McShane, and as he only started in stage management and as a comic feed in the very late 1940s, he may not even have seen their act. He first worked with Arthur on *Going Gay* in March 1952 after the Lucans had split up, and, like the rest of the company, all he knew of Kitty McShane at that time was the stalking and the drunken rages. But distance seems to have strangely altered Ashton's powers of recall:

> The same as Leighton and Johnson or Morecambe and Wise, they were a wonderful team. But you did not appreciate Kitty, you see you only appreciated the funny one, but the feed, the straight man or woman, you took for granted. But you see Kitty was the business one, she arranged all their engagements. She was a hard taskmaster. She knew what would get a laugh and what wouldn't. She knew how to time a laugh, but you did not appreciate her point at all. And because of course, as Arthur had been known to take a drink occasionally, she nevertheless had to keep him in check, and by virtue of this, by virtue of her protecting him, more or less a mother figure, she often fell foul of people, because the back stage people said, 'Arthur's a lovely old soul but that old bag there...'[160]

Much of what Ashton had to say in 1980 sounds suspiciously like the version of reality which Kitty herself had started to propagate in the week after Arthur's funeral; "He needed mothering and I often had to bully him. Life was never quiet for us, but he was a darling." As for Kitty's ability to time a joke and get a laugh, one only has to watch her on film to see that, as one internet critic put it, "Arthur shows his accomplished timing with both dialogue and slapstick ... Kitty McShane couldn't deliver a line if she'd been a postman."[161] As a friend of mine put it, "Kitty? Time a laugh? She couldn't time an egg!"

Later in the 1980 interview Ashton goers into the realm of pure fiction when he speaks of the Lucan-McShane act being barred from theaters. This simply did not happen, and Ashton could not possibly have been unaware of the fact that it was only Kitty the stalker who was barred by managements from entering theaters where Arthur was playing.

In order to forget his troubles with Kitty, you see, he did sometimes take to the bottle. And so there were some very violent rows, as you will have heard possibly. Which was a shame because it meant in this sense that some of the theaters barred them, and they would no longer take them back, even though they were such a big draw, nevertheless some theaters said, 'We've had enough of them, we're not putting up with them anymore, they're not working here again.'

Ashton then goes on to contradict the main thrust of his earlier statements. "They say the course of true love never did run smooth, and eventually Arthur felt he'd had enough, and he went out with the *Going Gay* show for Gaston and Andrée." Surely, according to Ashton's logic, this should have been the other way round, with a drunken unemployable Arthur and a resurgent Miss McShane? It is worth pointing out that when, back in 1968, Ashton was interviewed by Margery Baker, he confined himself to verifiable facts and did not offer any of the misleading views he expressed in the 1980 documentary. Company manager Slim Ingram was also interviewed by Margery Baker in 1968 but did not take part in either of the two later documentaries. When I asked him in 2012 his opinion of the later Ashton interview his remarks were mostly unprintable. It is also worth noting that Donald Towle had died in 1975; had he been alive he would almost certainly have taken exception to Ashton's remarks concerning his father and would have been justified in demanding a retraction and correction.

In 1958, four years after Arthur's death, Kitty decided that the act hadn't, after all, died with her husband. Once again, as Slim Ingram put it, she "heard the call of the greasepaint" and resurrected the act. *The Stage* announced that "Kitty McShane is to revive the 'Old Mother Riley' sketches in which she was partnered by Arthur Lucan, who died in 1954. The new Mother Riley will be Roy Rowland [Rolland], Arthur Lucan's former understudy. The opening date for the revival of 'Bridget's Night Out' is set for 17 March at the

Metropolitan." Again, contrary to many accepted accounts, this is the one and only time Kitty (alone) employed Rolland to play Riley, four years after Arthur's death. *The Stage* carried a photograph of Kitty with Roy in costume as Riley, and Willer Neal as "the lodger." The brief review of *The Blarney Rock Show* reported that "Returning to the stage after an absence of five years, Kitty McShane was given a heart-touching warmth of welcome." But the reviewer also wondered what "the youngsters, attracted by the 'rock' part of the show's title, made of the over-long dialogue." A couple of very glamorous publicity photographs of Kitty were taken at this time, showing her expertly made up, with a modern short hairstyle, and decked in the furs, hats and fashions she still adored. The comeback was short-lived, but almost to the end Kitty kept her "card" in *The Stage*; "Kitty McShane, Old Mother Riley, all comms. 20 South Molton St." But by now "comms," money, and even time itself, were running out.

Kitty made one last comeback, again at the Metropolitan Edgware Road. In 1962 it was announced that the theater was to be demolished. It had opened in 1862 and was magnificently remodeled by Frank Matcham in 1897. The night club owner Murray Goldstein was saddened by the Metropolitan's impending demise.

> Every star of the music hall had played there so I was espe-
> cially sentimental about it . . . I leased the theater from
> Granada for six consecutive Thursday evenings to showcase
> the talents of some of the stars of variety's heyday. I chose to
> overlook the inescapable fact that variety theaters were being
> demolished because variety was dead. But I have no regrets.[162]

These stars of yesteryear, including "two-ton" Tessie O'Shea and Vic Oliver, played to very small audiences, and on the final Thursday a pea-souper fog descended on London, and Randolph Sutton sang "Mother Kelly's Doorstep" to an audience of twenty people in a theater that could seat almost three thousand. Murray wrote of Kitty, "Sadly, Kitty was by now an alcoholic and this show was her swan song." Even more sadly, Kitty apparently managed to conclude her swan song by falling down the backstage stairs.

During Kitty's remaining few years, relative poverty was at last beginning to catch up with her. Donald Towle told his daughter Marylyn that whenever his mother was short of cash she would

Photo 18: Kitty's revival at the Metropolitan, Edgware Road, March, 1958. Mrs.
Joan Towle

take to her jeweler a piece of her diamond jewelry, the diamonds she
had boasted about to Sybil Rowse back in 1941-1942; the jeweler
would buy a stone or two and replace it with paste, thus allowing
Miss McShane to keep up appearances. She also sold off, bit-by-bit,
the collection of fine antique furniture, china and glass with which
Arthur had filled the house at Forty Lane.

Both Billy and Kitty spent much of their last year in an alcoholic haze, and by the end of 1963 it was obvious that Billy was very ill. He died on 19 December of cancer of the bladder, not in the Middlesex Hospital, as previously reported, but, as Slim Ingram revealed to me in September 2012, at Kitty's flat in South Molton Street. According to Slim Ingram, he and Arthur's former dresser Maisie Munro were at the flat on the night Billy died, and all had been having pre-Christmas drinks. Kitty's sister Annie returned from Dublin and was met at Euston station by a distraught Kitty who, according to Annie, was "dressed in an old dark green tweed skirt which was badly stained and creased, and an old fur coat that had seen better days. Her hair was unwashed and her make-up was a mess." Back at the flat, it became clear as the evening wore on that Billy was in serious pain and distress and should have been taken to hospital, but both he and Kitty had been drinking very heavily and Kitty became obstreperous and refused to allow it. When Billy became unconscious Annie and Slim were so worried that he might be dying that they called the police. When the police arrived Billy was in fact pronounced dead. Slim remembered that the police wanted Kitty to give a statement but by now she too had passed out in her bedroom and it was impossible to rouse her. Billy's body was not removed to the morgue at the Middlesex Hospital until the early hours of the morning. His death was registered later the same day, not by Kitty but by Billy's daughter, M. Hemment of Bonnington Square, Lambeth. His profession was entered on the certificate as "variety artiste (retired)" and his address as 20 South Molton Street.

When Kitty came round that morning she had to be told what had happened, and Slim remembered that when they prepared to go to view the body Kitty emerged from her bedroom dressed all in black. At the mortuary, when asked if she was related to the deceased she replied, "I was his mistress!" Annie Carroll told the story of the mortuary attendant's shocked "double-take" on hearing Kitty address the corpse. "You bastard! Fancy dying the week before Christmas!" This is very reminiscent of what she had said on the telephone to Slim Ingram on being told of the death of Arthur; "You fucking bastard!" Her husband's death on 17 May 1954 had spoiled her birthday on 19 May, and now her lover's death had ruined her Christmas! What has never been told before is Slim's clear memory that the distraught

Kitty also grabbed Billy's body by the throat and said, "You promised I could go first!"

In fact Kitty survived Billy by less than four months. She died alone in the South Molton Street flat on 24 March 1964. Neighbors alerted the police that Miss McShane had not been seen and they telephoned Kitty's son, Dr. Donald Towle. The call was taken by Donald's wife Joan, who agreed to identify Kitty's body, knowing, as she told me, that her husband would not have wanted to do so. Kitty had not died in bed but lay fully clothed on the floor where she had collapsed. Joan remembered that "the body was lying in an odd position, face down with the arms outstretched in front as if praying." The Police did not turn the body over, or ask Joan to look at Kitty's face, as the identity of the body seemed perfectly clear. In a memoir in *Film History*, the film buff Peter Jewell recalled hearing at the time of "the lonely death of Kitty McShane, surrounded by empty gin bottles, near where we lived at the time. We thought, if only we had known . . . ."[163]

At the inquest on Mrs. Kathleen Towle, the pathologist's report was disturbing. He found advanced cirrhosis of the liver, but along with the high levels of alcohol present in the body he also found an unusual and exceptionally high amount of aspirin. According to Marylyn and Joan Towle, who were both present, it seemed clear that the coroner would have been entitled to return a verdict of suicide. This was still a terrible stigma, and as the Church considered suicide a mortal sin, Kitty might have been denied a Catholic funeral or burial. However, as Marylyn put it, "The pathologist was very kind and made it sound as though the aspirin was not the crucial factor, so the coroner was able to avoid a verdict of suicide. But everyone present clearly thought that the real verdict should have been suicide." Nevertheless, the actual verdict recorded on the death certificate is stark enough; "Chronic alcoholic poisoning/chronic alcoholism."

Donald Towle began to make arrangements for his mother's funeral, most of which he left in the hands of Kitty's sisters, Auntie Biddy, now Mrs. Bridget Gallagher of Blackheath, and Annie Carroll who prepared to come over from Dublin for the Requiem Mass which, according to Slim Ingram, was held in Notting Hill.[164] Arrangements were slightly complicated by the fact that Kitty had died two days before Good Friday, which was still formally observed as both a religious feast and a Bank Holiday, and was followed by another Bank Holiday on the Monday.

Donald was distressed but he was also angry. Throughout his life he had been on affectionate terms with his father but his relationship with his mother had been at best lukewarm and strained, at worst non-existent. This was exacerbated after Arthur's death by Kitty's heavy drinking, her unwillingness to reveal to Donald the true state of his father's financial affairs, and her increasingly offensive attitude and behavior towards Donald and his family, including his children. Kitty had always used foul language, but even this was now turning more grossly offensive. On a number of occasions, the Police had had to be called to Donald's surgery at Lee Park Lodge in Blackheath to remove Kitty, who was deemed to be causing a breach of the peace; she was, as Joan Towle put it, "the worse for wear and demanding money." Eventually she became offensive beyond belief, as Joan told me in 2012:

> On a cold day late in 1963, I answered the doorbell at Lee Park Lodge and found Kitty on the doorstep. She was wrapped in a long dark coat and a broad-brimmed hat, and was clearly 'under the weather.' As instructed by Donald, I told her he was out and prepared to close the door. At that point Kitty flew into one of her rages, and with much cursing she shouted at me, 'Tell my fucking son that I look forward to reading in *The Times* that his fucking children [Marylyn and Suzanne] have been found floating face down in the Thames!'

After this last hideous outburst of grandmotherly venom, Donald gave instructions that the doorbell was never again to be answered if his mother was seen approaching the house.

Donald's true mother-figure had been his grandmother, Kate McShane, who had died in Dublin in 1946. As Donald's eldest daughter Marylyn put it, "Kitty did not have a single maternal bone in her whole body." For these and other reasons which Donald confided only to his close family, he could not bring himself to mourn Kitty as his mother, or even to attend her funeral. While he went to his surgery as usual, his wife Joan and his eldest daughter Marylyn, in whom Kitty had never taken the slightest interest, and who had never visited her grandparents' house in Forty Lane, agreed to attend the funeral together. Donald's second daughter Suzanne was only twelve at this time, and Donald and Joan's first daughter Katherine was barely two months old. However, Joan and Marylyn did not go to church for the Requiem Mass in Notting Hill. Instead they drove to the gates of the cemetery at the appointed time and waited there to join the handful of mourners at the graveside. The entire funeral party consisted of a priest, two Towles, two of Kitty's sisters and a couple of their children, and not a single soul from the theater world. On the day of the funeral the weather, according to *The Times* was 'Dull, with outbreaks of rain, sleet or snow over high ground; fresh to strong N. E. Wind; very cold. Maximum temp. 41F (5C).'

To this day, neither Joan nor Marylyn can remember the location of the cemetery where Kitty was buried, except that it was "somewhere north of the river." What little they did remember of the ceremony itself added a sad and grotesque note to the end of what had become a rather sad and grotesque life. Because icy rain had been pouring down for most of the day, the priest had come suitably shod. From under his solemn black vestments his big Wellington boots protruded so incongruously that Joan and Marylyn both got the giggles. They managed to control themselves, but when after the committal the priest handed round a container of holy water for the mourners to sprinkle into the grave, Marylyn inexplicably got the giggles again. She afterwards told Joan that she had been doing some ironing earlier in the day and had used an identical plastic water-sprinkler on her clothes. After the burial, Joan and Marylyn and the few mourners came back into town, and they sat talking for a while, as the rain continued to fall outside. Then the McShanes and the Towles said their last farewells, and Annie Carroll returned to Dublin where Kitty's brief obituary in the *Irish Independent* may have jogged a few memories; but far more space was given to an appreciation of another alcoholic, the playwright Brendan Behan, who had died a few days earlier.

Marylyn Towle helped her father to clear Kitty's effects from the South Molton Street flat, and remembered that very little remained of the antique furniture, carpets and porcelain which she herself had never seen, but knew that Arthur had lovingly collected. "Kitty had sold the best things off bit by bit over the years, and there literally were orange boxes among the jumble and the gin bottles, and there was hardly any food in the house." Of the hundreds of thousands of pounds, millions in today's money, which his parents had earned in their heyday, there was nothing left to come to Donald; everything had been swallowed up by Kitty's fatal mixture of greed and incompetence. Arthur Towle was only officially released from bankruptcy on 9 April 1964, ten years after his own death and a fortnight after Kitty's. On hearing this news Donald must have again recalled, or even re-read with bitterness, the letter his father had sent him twelve years earlier, a letter he kept until his own death in 1975. "I let Someone have the whole of the profits of a life's work. My share was unhappiness and strife, and more to come." Donald of course knew that 'Someone' meant his own mother.

On 1 June, Administration was granted to "Donald Daniel Towle, doctor of medicine." The amount of Kitty's will was published in *The Times* in June 1964. "Towle, Mrs. Kathleen—Kitty McShane, the variety artiste—of South Molton Street, W. (Gross, £3,400) £530." After bills and expenses had been paid, all that remained for Donald of the astronomical earnings of Lucan and McShane was a few hundred pounds, barely enough in 1964 to buy a modest Ford Cortina car. Back in 1954, after endless phone calls from Kitty, who pleaded poverty and had the effrontery to blame it on the cost of Donald's education, Donald had paid for the stone on his father's grave in Hull. His mother's grave he left unmarked, and to this day it remains unlocated. It was time to forget, and to move on.

Shortly thereafter Donald and Joan Towle moved to Par near St. Austell, where their two children grew up. Both "Dr. and Mrs. Donald Towle" quickly became prominent and highly respected figures in the local community. Donald was County Surgeon for St. John Ambulance and Joan became a J.P. They lived in a large, elegant house called Rosehill, surrounded by leafy gardens and a high stone wall. Donald was still so short of money that the house was bought by his father-in-law, the distinguished child psychiatrist Robert Freeland Barbour, whose profession perhaps gave him a sympathetic insight into the psyche of the son of Kitty McShane, because life for the Towles, although apparently now more agreeable on the surface, was not always a bed of roses. Donald was in many ways as complex and contradictory as the parents from whom he had inherited certain recognizable traits of personality. He could be loveable and funny like his father, and like his father he loved to collect antiques. But he also suffered from darker mood swings, when he felt needy and vulnerable, convinced that he had been an unwanted child, "a mistake," as he himself put it; given that he was a close confidante of his father, he may well have had solid grounds for believing this. At such times he did not go in for histrionic outbursts of temper like his mother, but would lock himself away for hours in his study at Lee Park Lodge, and later in the sitting room at Rosehill, drinking quietly and listening to classical music.

It was at Rosehill in 1969 that ITV producer Margery Baker managed to persuade him to grant her an interview for her documentary, *Applause! Applause!* Their brief correspondence (kindly lent to me by Joan Towle) shows that they hit it off, and for the first and last time, Donald unburdened himself to an outsider on the subject of his parents, especially his mother; but he asked not to be mentioned in the credits, and he thereafter refused to help prospective biographers, to the end of his life finding the subject too distressing. As a child he had never been part of a genuinely stable family unit and he found it difficult to create one in his own adult life. He was well aware that he could be wayward and "difficult," and he once confided that he wished he were different or better, regretting the strains he placed on all his close relationships. He had an irrational fear of death, which he personified in a letter to Joan as "that horrid man *Thanatos*," who seemed at times to accompany him like an uninvited, invisible companion, making him wonder if he was quite sane. This constant tension may well have shortened his life. He told his eldest daughter Marylyn that he "would never make old bones," and remarked to his wife Joan that he would not live to be sixty. His premonition proved all too accurate. On 10 January 1975, at the age of 59, while out on a home visit, he had a stroke at the wheel of his car, and died a month later. Donald was apparently the only fruit of the real-life union of Lucan and McShane; but there were rumors. Eileen Oldfield, a dancer in "Madame Clarke's Twelve Parisienne Maids" in Liverpool in the 1930s, maintained to her dying day that her eldest son, born in 1931, was the result of a brief affair with Arthur Lucan.[165]

Ellis Ashton's pious memorial notice for Kitty McShane in *The Stage* had contained the line "Reunited with Arthur at last." A clairvoyant medium's account of any such reunion might have proved interesting! But in literal terms the remains of Arthur and Kitty were never physically reunited in death. In Hull's Eastern Cemetery,

Arthur's grave, which was given a new headstone in 2006, remains a much-frequented place of pilgrimage for his many admirers. They regularly leave flowers and messages on anniversaries, and make a detour to see the original gravestone which, at the request of local people, was re-erected nearby and now stands all alone at the center of the cloister garden between the cemetery chapels. Back in Hull town center, many of them go to the Orchard Café on the site of the demolished Tivoli Theater in Paragon Street. There they can admire a small display of photographs and old theater posters, and a bronze bust of Arthur by local sculptor Martin Wolverston, which was unveiled by Danny La Rue in 1986. The bust disappeared for a time in 2010 but was quickly found and replaced by popular demand.

Far away, somewhere in an unidentified London cemetery, Kitty McShane lies in an unmarked grave, alone and unvisited. This cruelly eloquent contrast remains to this day as a symbolic witness and poignant testimony to the genius of Arthur Lucan . . . and the sadness of Kitty McShane. A fatal misalliance.

PART TWO
THE OLD MOTHER RILEY
FILMS 1937-1952

Chapter Eleven: "Tiddlywinked by a Gasman." Arthur Lucan and the Comedy of Language.

When Con West began his screenplay for the first Mother Riley film, Arthur Lucan had already been writing for the stage for almost twenty years. Henry Desborough remembered that during their time with Gilbert Payne in Carnoustie, around 1912, Arthur had developed a sketch based on the antics of the zany Countess of Alagazam. This nonsense song which, as we have seen, is full of strikingly outlandish comic images of a kind that were to feature prominently in Arthur's later scripts, reveals Arthur's early love of verbal fantasy, nonsense and the language of the absurd. By 1917 Arthur was judged capable of writing a pantomime for the Queen's Theater, and his *Little Jack Horner* was a huge success, "written and produced by Arthur Lucan and acknowledged by the management to be the best Panto put on for years." In Galway in March 1918, the press announced "a sketch entitled 'The Billposter,' written by Mr. A. Lucan, who will take part in it." In December 1918 Arthur scored another personal triumph at the Queen's with *Little Red Riding Hood*, advertised as "show, lyrics and original songs written and produced by Arthur Lucan." By 1919, Arthur had written "Come Over," the first of his many mother-daughter sketches, and set out on what was to be a forty-year career of comic scriptwriting.

The creation of Old Mother Riley in 1937 was, in many ways, merely a transposition to the screen of a character, Mrs. O'Flynn, who already had a vibrant stage life and language of her own, entirely scripted by Arthur Lucan. The filmed sketch "Bridget's Night Out," with its original script, makes it clear that much of Mother Riley's later comic language and verbal fantasy was almost certainly as much the work of Arthur Lucan as it was that of the credited scriptwriters, and this fact is acknowledged in the films' credits under "additional material by Arthur Lucan." Little survives in print of Arthur's enormous written output, but the scripts for "Bridget's Night Out" and the four Columbia gramophone records make it possible to trace a broad outline of what constituted Arthur's highly idiosyncratic verbal comic style.

The first, and perhaps most surprising, thing to be stressed is the fact that Arthur's comic Dame, the "garrulous Malaprop" who "did violence to the language," was the creation of someone who was, according to those who knew him well, a highly literate and articulate man, possessed of a broad general culture which informs and underlies his creation in a way that has never been adequately pointed out. What Jane Moody said of Dan Leno holds equally true for Lucan. "Leno's Dames . . . spoke in a form of inconsequential chatter. This cleverly captured the rhythms of ordinary speech, while opening up chasms of lunacy, one absurdity on top of another. Just like Lewis Carroll and Edward Lear, Leno revelled in the ludicrous logic of nonsense . . . ." "The Countess of Alagazam" first signalled Lucan's affinity with the nonsense poets Carroll and Lear, and there are also many moments in his work which seem to come closer to Surrealism or the Theater of the Absurd. Lucan's scripts reveal a powerful awareness of the pathetic or grotesque incongruities lurking in everyday situations, and he developed a highly idiosyncratic verbal style to communicate his comic vision.

But where, one might ask, did a Lincolnshire lad who received only the most basic primary education, acquire this alleged cultural baggage? I firmly believe, as I said in chapter one, that the Musical Cliftons must take most of the credit for educating Arthur. The Cliftons were accomplished musicians as well as actors, and during the seven years Arthur claimed he spent with them, he gained the richer knowledge and appreciation of language, literature, and the arts in general, to which he clearly aspired back in Boston as the office boy who sold programmes and swept the stage by night. Like all aspiring actors, he also watched and learned from his elders, copying their gags and business, and reshaping them as his own. His brief but close association with the Latonas in the mid-1920s also allowed him to share the reminiscences of performers who had worked with all the music hall greats, including Leno, Robey, Tilley and Forde, and to learn from their experiences. But the most important thing which cannot easily be learned, timing, Arthur seems to have possessed as a natural gift that never deserted him. As critics often point out when discussing Les Dawson, to appear to play the piano badly on stage

452848

CPPO492.

08000 321129

01243 321129.

642181

one must in fact possess a very solid technique, and the same is true
of Arthur Lucan and language, for behind his gabble talk and his
countless malapropisms and non-sequiturs, a very sharp, controlling
mind was at work. A brief but representative sample of verbal tropes
and techniques used by Arthur shows that he had a sound grasp of
many of the devices of literary rhetoric. The American writer E.B.
White once wrote that "analyzing humor is like dissecting a frog. Few
people are interested and the frog dies of it." Nevertheless, Lucan's
admirers will, I feel sure, instantly know how to bring the following
dry list back to life with examples to be found in Arthur's own scripts,
beginning with "Bridget's Night Out," and the Columbia recordings:

Simile. Not stale clichés but revitalised outlandish
comparisons.

Paronomasia. Punning wordplay, including homophonic or
homographic puns.

Accumulatio. The piling up of repeated phrases or parts of
speech.

Enumeratio. Listing parts, causes, effects, or consequences to
make a point more forcibly.

Anaphora. Repetition of the same word or words at the
beginning of successive phrases.

Hyperbole. Deliberate exaggeration for emphasis or comic
effect.

Litotes. Understatement, the counterpart of Hyperbole.

Hypophora. Asking questions and then proceeding to answer
them, usually at some length.

Assonance and Alliteration. The patterned repetition of similar vowels or consonants.

Aposiopesis. Stopping abruptly and leaving a statement
unfinished.

Paraprosdokian. A surprising or unexpected ending to a list or series of phrases (often allied to Bathos.)

An excellent example of these last two tropes is found in *Old Mother Riley Headmistress*. Mother goes into a long and serious explanation of how they will juggle the laundry finances in order to purchase the school, but her convincing list ends with, "...And then we'll do the bank, and then we'll do a bunk!"

Arthur's use of these devices always quickly leaves the realms of rational discourse and takes off into flights of absurd verbal fantasy akin to surrealist poetry. The title of the radio series *Old Mother Riley Takes the Air*, with its pun on "the air," leads to further radio-themed verbal nonsense; "Good evening, Mr. and Mrs. Wavelength, long, short and medium, Home and Forces and the cat's-whisker. It's me, Old Mother Riley, I'm here and I'm taking the air!" Even more complex is another radio greeting; "Good evening blackguards, bodyguards, coal yards and fire guards, it's me, Mother Riley, just blown in for a breath of fresh air! How's everybody?" This is a clever blend of assonance and alliteration, and free word association based on absurd couplings of sound and sense, like one of the Old Match-seller's earliest recorded quips: "All men before wedlock should be padlocked!" The absurdity of language is often highlighted by the way in which Riley frequently says something which seems grammatically or syntactically correct but in fact contains a paradox or logical impossibility:

"I've been sitting there since yesterday, waiting for her to come home tonight, and now it's tomorrow."

"I'd make a cup of tea if I could find me corkscrew."

"One o'clock, three times!"

"Take a look at that old woman sitting there and tell me if it's me!"

"That's different. I married your father—you want to marry a stranger!"

A rich source of verbal comedy is found in Riley's constant veering, often within a phrase, between literal and figurative language, or the concrete and the abstract use of words and expressions.

Of Riley and her husband; "We might have had a few words in bed, but we never fell out."

"I've got my health—I often wish somebody else had it."

"Am I in? No, I'm out! Me liver's come up and put me lights out!" "You'll be charged with contempt." "I don't care if I'm charged with the Light Brigade!"

"So there, Lady Meersham [Meerschaum]. Put that in your pipe and smoke it!"

Perhaps Riley's favorites ploy is when she can mix all these various tropes together in one of the inimitable lists which often almost have the rhythms and cadences of comic verse.

"I wonder where she is, I wonder where she's gone, I wonder who she's with, I wonder what she's doing, I wonder what time it is; I hope she's all right."

"Don't know whether it's daytime, nighttime, half-time, summer time, early closing or next Wednesday."

"I spent my childhood, my womanhood, my motherhood, my widowhood, my . . . falsehood in a museum."

"I met him by the pale moon, I was engaged by the new moon, I got married on the full moon, and I lost him on the honeymoon."

Another stylistic trait is Riley's liking for tripartite patterns. She is so poor that all she can expect is "scraps from the butcher, a sour look from the milkman, and raspberries from the greengrocer." The word "wink" undergoes some amusing and suggestive transformations when the gasman threatens to "tiddlywink" Riley if she keeps putting tiddlywinks in the gas meter. "Oh daughter, I wonder what it feels like to be tiddlywinked! I've been hoodwinked by the coalman, I've been winked at by the milkman, but I've never been tiddlywinked by a gasman!" This was about as risqué as Mother Riley ever got, and it allowed her quips to be enjoyed by kids and adults in equal measure, without the need for prurient nudging and winking.

But for all her merciless mangling of the language, whenever Riley wants to she can be exceptionally eloquent, often as a parody of "high-falutin" diction, the kind of class-based send-up that always seemed to delight the inarticulate masses. Here is Riley's account of her husband's proposal of marriage:

> He took hold of my hand, he gazed into my eyes, and with a voice choking with emotion he said to me , 'Daphne,' he said, 'After deep consideration and due meditation of the reputation you hold in this nation, I've a strong inclination

to change my situation so that you may become my relation. If my inclination meets with your approbation, it will be a strong foundation for a new and rising generation.

Riley can also be eloquent in deadly earnest, defending herself in the dock, on the hustings, or in the House of Commons, but her oratory is always leavened by puns and malapropisms. Her eloquence and absurdity come gloriously together in her definition of an alibi. "An alibi is proving that you weren't where you were when you committed the crime that you never committed at all when you did it!"

There is one more source of humor in Lucan's scripts which has never been discussed or even noticed, and that is his unusually rich range of cultural references. These references are particularly fascinating because they would have been completely lost, and therefore wasted, on children. We have already noted the racing and betting images which would have had a broad appeal to ordinary working adults; but the "intertextual" allusions to which I now refer were not only aimed at adult audiences, but at those with enough cultural sophistication to recognize the source of the allusion and thus enjoy the joke.

In "Bridget's Night Out," after bewailing Bridget's indifference to her plight, Mrs. O'Flynn says, "If she doesn't come home soon, I know I shall have a nervous breakdown. I shall have a total eclipse. It's my nerves . . ."

There had been no total eclipse visible in England since 1734, so Lucan was not referencing some recent topical fact. The link between nervous breakdown and the words "total eclipse" make most sense in the context of Milton's poem "Samson Agonistes," where the lines are almost shockingly relevant to Mrs. Flynn's predicament.

Within doors, or without, still as a fool,
In power of others, never in my own—
Scarce half I seem to live, dead more than half.
O dark, dark, dark, amid the blaze of noon,
Irrecoverably dark, total eclipse
Without all hope of day!"

In *Old Mother Riley in Paris*, bewailing her ill-treatment by her wayward daughter, Mother Riley cries, "O how sharper than a serpent's thingummy it is to have a thankless child." Although garbled, this is of course a parody of King Lear's bitter railing against his ungrateful daughters;

> Let it stamp wrinkles in her brow of youth,
> With cadent tears fret channels in her cheeks,
> Turn all her mother's pains and benefits
> To laughter and contempt, that she may feel
> How sharper than a serpent's tooth it is
> To have a thankless child! *King Lear* Act 1, scene 4.

In *Old Mother Riley's New Venture*, when Mother Riley is called to the manager's office, she looks back at Kitty from the doorway and declaims with mock resignation, "It is a far better thingummy I do than I. . . ." This is of course a spoof on Sydney Carton's inner monologue as he goes to the guillotine at the end of Dickens' *A Tale of Two Cities*; but it was also the tear-jerking final speech in John Harvey-Martin's record-breaking stage adaptation, *The Only Way*, which Arthur must have seen as a lad. Tom Towle remembered that Arthur's boyhood dream was to emulate Harvey-Martin; sadly this was about as close as he ever came, which gives added poignancy to Riley's remark to Kitty a little later in the same film; "If I had my time over again, I'd like to be a film star." In the same film there is a passing reference to the title of a rather grim film dealing with combat neurosis and schizophrenia. When Riley is placed under a hair-dryer she asks, "What's this? *Mine own Executioner?*" The "A" Certificate film noir of that name could have meant nothing to children, and so was another allusion for well-informed adults, some of whom might even have recognized the words as a quotation from John Donne's meditation on the self-destructive power of the mind. The same is true of Riley's coy reference to the romantic comedy *A Girl Must Live* (1939) in *Old Mother Riley in Business*.

By a very circuitous, but I believe plausible route, another inter-textual reference links the young Arthur Lucan, Rudyard Kipling, and an Irish-American nonsense song from 1876, "Arrah! Patrick Mind the Baby!" In *Old Mother Riley's New Venture*, Arthur and Kitty dance and sing (in harmony) "Patrick Mind the Baby!" as they move their belongings in an old pram. This brief scene has all the hallmarks of one of the many (often gratuitous) pantomime routines they wove into their films; it would have fitted perfectly into Arthur's Liverpool production of *Old Mother Hubbard* at the point when Mother took her whole brood, including the infants, on a day trip to New Brighton. When writing that script, Arthur may have remembered reading Kipling's story collection *Stalky and Co.* during the long winters spent with the Cliftons.

The story "Slaves of the Lamp" would have appealed enormously back then to the young man who already loved pantomime and its attendant absurdities. In the schoolboy yarn, Stalky and his school friends are rehearsing the pantomime, *Aladdin*.

Dick was Aladdin, stage-manager, ballet-master, half the orchestra, and largely librettist, for the 'book' had been rewritten and filled with local allusions. The pantomime was to be given next week, in the down-stairs study occupied by Aladdin, Abanazar, and the Emperor of China. The Slave of the Lamp, with the Princess Badroulbadour and the Widow Twankay, owned Number Five study across the same landing, so that the company could be easily assembled. The floor shook to the stamp-and-go of the ballet, while Aladdin, in pink cotton tights, a blue and tinsel jacket, and a plumed hat, banged alternately on the piano and his banjo . . . 'What about the last song, though?' said the Emperor, a tallish, fair-headed boy with a ghost of a mustache, at which he pulled manfully. 'We need a rousing old tune.'" Stalky, Slave of the Lamp, hummed "a catchy music-hall tune." "Dick Four cocked his head critically, and squinted down a large red nose. 'Once more and I can pick it up,' he said, strumming. 'Sing the words.'

'Arrah, Patsy, mind the baby! Arrah, Patsy, mind the child! Wrap him in an overcoat, he's surely going wild! Arrah, Patsy, mind the baby! Just you mind the child awhile! He'll kick and bite and cry all night! Arrah, Patsy, mind the child!' 'Rippin! Oh, rippin!' said Dick Four. 'Only we shan't have any piano on the night. We must work it with the banjoes—play an' dance at the same time.'

This American song was never particularly popular in Ireland, so I believe that the original inspiration for its inclusion in *Old Mother Riley's New Venture* goes back, via Arthur's pantomime scripts, to his youthful reading of Kipling's "Slave of the Lamp."

Perhaps Arthur Lucan's most complex intertextual allusion (no speculation here at all) is to be found in "Bridget's Night Out." As Mrs. O'Flynn undresses for bed, she says, "I'll get pneumonia; I've got all the symphonies already." Then, half way through her striptease, she strikes a very particular pose and says, "I'm frozen stiff! Ooh, I've gone all September Morn-ish." The significance of this is lost on modern audiences, but it would have been instantly identified at the time as a reference to a notorious painting, *Matinée de Septembre* or *September Morn*, by the French painter Paul Chabas; the painting depicts a young girl standing naked at the edge of a lake as the sun rises. In 1913, the painting caused a scandal when it arrived in the United States for exhibition. Anthony Comstock, founder of the New York Society for the Suppression of Vice, condemned it as obscene saying, "There's too little morning and too much maid." In the immediate wake of the controversy, reproductions and parodies of the painting proliferated; postcards, prints, bottle openers, pins, and pennants all appeared bearing different versions of Chabas's painting, which for years remained a soft porn icon. Lucan's audience would have recognized his pose as a visual parody of the young woman, particularly as there were grotesque postcards circulating showing a naked old crone in the same pose, entitled "September Midnight." But Lucan is almost certainly making one further intertextual allusion here, namely to the fact that Charlie Chaplin had struck the very same *September Morn* pose (also in his underwear!) in *The Cure* in 1917, at the height of the scandal.[166]

For far too long, critics seem to have forgotten that the garrulous, semi-literate old harridan was Mrs. O'Flynn then Daphne Riley, whereas Arthur Lucan was a gifted writer of comedy, widely admired by peers and contemporaries of the caliber of Gillie Potter and Ivor Brown, for the many witty and inventive scripts which they knew and loved, and we have lost. Until 1968, all British theater scripts, comic or tragic, had to be submitted for clearance to the Office of the Lord Chamberlain. Scripts were then archived by the British Library. Much of Arthur's written material therefore exists, both here and on microfilm at BBC Caversham, but I leave the task of locating and studying it to a younger, more energetic researcher.

Chapter Twelve: "What Creature is this?" The Creation of Old Mother Riley

The character who made her first appearance in the 1937 film which bore her name was created by the bringing together of a number of disparate strands from a remarkable variety of sources, each of which contributed something to the complex and at times confusing persona. The unravelling of these strands may dispel the confusion and lead to a better understanding of how Con West helped Arthur Lucan to create one of the great British comic archetypes of the twentieth century.

The Lucans' first appearance in a narrative film, as opposed to the filmed sketch in *Stars on Parade*, 1936, was in *Kathleen Mavourneen*, a film which Ruth Barton situates in the very particular context of a cycle of sentimental and nostalgic Irish "ballad films."

> Entrenched as they are in working-class traditions of parlor entertainment and the music hall sing-along, these films may be placed in what Peter Bailey has termed a "culture of consolation." *Father O'Flynn* (1935), *Kathleen Mavourneen* (1937), *Mountains O'Mourne* (1938) and *My Irish Molly* (1938) respond, through song and performance, to two overlapping drives within British society at that moment. They address, on the one hand, the massive working-class Irish immigrant population who had settled in urban areas such as Liverpool in the wake of a series of famines in the nineteenth century and earlier, and whose numbers were constantly being added to, as the economy of the Irish Free State stagnated. They also played to a general sense of nostalgia for an idealized rural simplicity and sense of rootedness.[167]

But Ruth Barton goes on to show that, unlike these ballad films, the Riley films have relatively little to do with the immigrants' nostalgic yearning for Irish hearth and home.

> If the ballad films are reluctant to admit the possibilities of assimilation, the popular variety hall husband and wife duo

of Arthur Lucan and Kitty McShane were defined by it. In immediate pre- and post-war Britain, their Old Mother Riley stage act was one of the staples of the variety circuit ... Lucan was English and little of his act was identifiably Irish; at the same time the films discreetly proclaimed their ethnic affiliations through devices such as the inclusion of shamrocks in the titles. Only in occasional films such as *Old Mother Riley's New Venture* ... in which 'McShane and an unidentified tenor [Billy Breach aka Willer Neal] perform well-known Irish ballads,' was her ostensible ethnicity cited. Although McShane retains her Irish accent, their stage personae suggest a high degree of assimilation ... Films such as the Lucan/McShane cycle disavow their Irishness by emphasizing its artificiality—Lucan, as his audience well knew, was no more Irish than he was a washerwoman. By virtue of ignoring the political strand of the Irish ballad in favor of the love song, these films negotiated a space for Irishness within popular British culture that seems to have appealed to immigrants and non-immigrants alike.[168]

But in some ways that potential "space for Irishness," indeed the very nature of its supposed Irishness, were as contentious then as they have been in more recent history. It has proved to be notoriously difficult to "ignore the political strand" of even the most innocuous of British-Irish cultural relations, especially during the war. In the Britain of 1937, in spite of several jolly "Oirish" films such as *Kathleen Mavourneen* and *Father O'Flynn*, Ireland was not really the "flavor of the month." Éamon de Valera, who had escaped execution in the 1916 Dublin Rising because of his American passport, had come to power with his Fianna Fáil party in 1932, vowing to transform the Irish Free State into a Republic outside the Commonwealth. De Valera's vision of an Ireland of "Gaelic-speaking maidens dancing at the crossroads," was a pious fantasy and Lance Pettitt speaks of "the considerable economic, social and cultural difficulties that beset the southern state: limited economic power, high unemployment, poor social welfare provisions, social conservatism and, above all, cultural insularity."[169] Given this harsh reality, emigration, principally to Britain, continued unabated up to and throughout the war, and this meant that there was an Irish audience for "Irish films" in Britain, almost as big as in Ireland itself.

We have already noted that when Con West set to work on what was to become the first Riley film, Lucan and McShane were still known as Mrs. O'Flynn and her daughter Bridget. Indeed, in their first film, *Kathleen Mavourneen*, mother, still Mrs. O'Flynn, addresses her daughter as Bridget Mary Josephine O'Flynn. One hardly needs to point out that these names are unequivocally Irish. The trouble was that they were *too* identifiably Irish for the heterogeneous British audiences Con West needed to please. In the first place the name Bridget O'Flynn would still have recalled the American mother-daughter comedy duet, "Bridget O'Flynn, Where've Ya Been?" which we have already discussed. West might be accused of plagiarism or, at the very least, the public might have been led to expect a screen version of the music hall duet, which was not at all what he had in mind. The Bridget O'Flynn of the comic duets was a very Americanized young woman, whereas Kitty still sounded like a recent immigrant to Britain from Dublin (not at all "Liverpool Irish" as some have suggested.)

The American-Irish links also had other, less pleasant, connotations which could have invited unflattering comparison with the status of Irish immigrants in 1930s Britain. Throughout the late nineteenth and early twentieth century, large numbers of young Irish men and, more unusually for Europe, even larger numbers of single women, had emigrated to America. The story of their slow and painful assimilation has been analyzed elsewhere, but the one point which concerns us here is the fact that many young Irish women in America were employed in domestic service, so many in fact that some middle-class families did not even take the trouble to learn the name of their latest Irish maid, calling her simply by the generic appellation *"the Bridget."*[170] While the British masses may still have been largely unaware of this, in the wake of the "Bridget" songs in America, insulting "thick Bridget" jokes soon crossed the Atlantic and the name came to have the same demeaning and negative associations as "Paddy" or "Mick." William Williams, in his exhaustive study of the comic stereotypes of Paddy and Bridget in songs on the American vaudeville stage, has pointed out that "the very sound of native Irish names" invited ridicule. Along with certain forenames, Irish surnames became shorthand for all the negative attributes of the Irish racial stereotype. Much of what Williams has to say was equally true in Britain which had eagerly imported the Bridget O'Flynn duets.

In effect the Gaelic surnames became an advertisement for comedy. Songs with titles such as 'Mike McCarthy's Wake,' 'McGonigle's Led Astray,' 'Reagan's Evening Out,' 'Let Her Go Gallagher,' 'Murphy's Boarding House,' and any song featuring the name 'McGinty' carried the promise of comedy.[171]

While Williams acknowledges the existence of songs dealing with Irish pride and patriotism, he nonetheless concludes that "Only African Americans suffered from a more demeaning stereotype."[172] Christopher Dowd has also noted the sinister connotations of comic "Irish" surnames.

American audiences became acquainted with the stage Irishmen through early British dramas . . . comic fools named MacBuffle, O'Balderdash, O'Blunder, MacBrogue, MacTawdry, O'Trigger and O'Whack . . . they could appear civilized but were really violent, illogical savages at their core.[173]

Maureen Waters' study of *The Comic Irishman* on the stage and in the literature of Britain and Ireland offers further disconcerting examples of these ingrained racial and cultural stereotypes.[174]

Con West clearly wanted to divest his characters of any such offensively pejorative associations, and to do so he needed to find a less aggressively Irish surname, preferably lacking the particles O, Mc or Mac. In Britain and Ireland, there was a popular song by Percy French from 1912 which contained the name Riley; "Come Back Paddy Riley to Ballyjamesduff," and although this probably sounded to English ears like another comic invention, it was in fact based on a real person and a real place. However, by a curiously circuitous route, the name Riley also had far more positive connotations for the British, and Con West was undoubtedly aware of this.

The expression "living the life of Reilly/Riley," suggestive of a life of ease and contentment, dates from the First World War. It was commonly used by American servicemen, and was copied by their

British counterparts in the trenches. The original American expression referred to a popular song, "Is That Mr. Reilly?" written in 1883 by Pat Rooney, an American vaudeville comedian, singer and Irish impersonator. The song's bragging hero Terence O'Reilly describes, with the typical immigrant's wishful thinking, how things will be in America when he strikes it rich. Here are the first verse and chorus.

"I'm Terence O'Reilly, I'm a man of renown,
I'm a thoroughbred to the backbone.
I'm related to O'Connor, my mother was Queen
Of China, ten miles from Athlone.
But if they'd let me be, I'd have Ireland free;
On the railroads you would pay no fare.
I'd have the United States under my thumb,
And I'd sleep in the President's chair.

Is that Mister Reilly, can anyone tell?
Is that Mister Reilly that owns the hotel?
Well, if that's Mister Reilly they speak of so highly,
Upon me soul, Reilly, you're doing quite well."

In October 1915 *The Star and Sentinel* of Gettysburg reported that

The song heard just now wherever the Tommies are gathered together is nothing else than our old favorite, 'Is This Mr. Reilly They Speak of So Highly?' Several months ago it became a craze with the English soldiers and has quite displaced *It's a Long Way to Tipperary* as the soldiers' favorite. British publishers in search of the rights were surprised to discover that it was actually American. How it got into the trenches of northern France one can only guess.[175]

Con West, the biographer of Fred Karno and his wartime "barmy army," may well have known and sung the song himself during the war to the tune "Sweet Betsy of Pike"/ "The Old Orange Flute" (West was twenty-four in 1914). My contention that this is where West hit upon the name is given weight by the fact that in the first film, one of old Mother Riley's cockney neighbors sings a song, not only to the very same tune but with almost the same lyrics and rhymes as the American song from the trenches. And he sings it not in a hotel but in the elegant Mayfair mansion where Mother Riley is a guest, and "doing quite well!"

"Are you Mother Riley that comes from the dell?
Are you Mother Riley they speak of so well?
If you're Mother Riley they speak of so highly,
Then blimey O Riley you are looking well."

I believe this constitutes a clear acknowledgement from Con West of the origin of Old Mother Riley's name. The first Riley film's opening credits were accompanied by the very same Irish tune, making all the old "Tommies" in the cinema instantly feel a very nostalgic and *British* affection for the "Riley they speak of so highly" before she had even appeared.

The "Old Mother" part of Riley's name could be interpreted in several ways. In popular British speech it was often used disrespectfully for any older lower-class woman, especially a widow. But after a century of Irish emigration, the sentimentalised image of the beloved old mother was powerfully present in the popular culture of the Irish diaspora throughout the English-speaking world. The classic tear-jerker, "Mother Machree" was written in America in 1910, and following its success there was a spate of songs with old Irish mothers in their titles. The great Irish tenor John McCormack made the definitive recording;

"There's a spot in my heart which no colleen may own.
There's a depth in my soul, never sounded or known;
There's a place in my memory, my life, that you fill,
No other can take it, no one ever will."

This is the song of a male emigrant for his gentle Mother Machree left behind in the old country, but Con West's Mother Riley was determined never to be left behind anywhere, and so she immediately set about exploding the stereotype of the sweet and passive Irish Mother. However she did have one trait partly in common with the "Machrees." William Shannon pointed out that Irish working-class fathers often died early, leaving the mother, "as the children's only link to the happier days of the past and the symbol of the family's will to survive. . . The widow woman thereby became a classic figure in the

Irish community."[176] Mother Riley gave a new and in many ways less
sentimental dimension to Irish stereotypes, including motherhood
and widowhood, and, as James Chapman put it, "For British cinema
audiences, Arthur Lucan's comic washerwoman 'Old Mother Riley'
was probably the most familiar screen image of Irishness in the 1930s
and 1940s."That really should read "screen image of Stage-Irishness,"
because Kitty must in fact have been the most familiar image of
authentic Irishness on British film screens at that time; Kitty's particular appeal to certain sections of the Irish community in Britain
will be discussed further on.

But the name Old Mother Riley was also an important signal
to all those who had followed Arthur Lucan's onstage career that
he was not about to sever his links with pantomime; Old Mother
Goose, Old Mother Hubbard, Old Mother Riley. One observer saw
clearly the provenance of this unusual new film star; "It was as if
Arthur Lucan took the Widow Twankey in Christmas Panto and
turned it into a lifelong year-round career."[177] And when, in the first
film, Mother Riley drank from the spout of a teapot and splattered
blancmange all over a Bishop, cinema audiences knew that she was
still the sloppy old pantomime dame some of them had loved for
over twenty years! "Excessive" Irishness was further effaced when
the Rileys revealed their forenames. Daughter was no longer Bridget
Mary Josephine O'Flynn but plain Kitty Riley, and mother has now
became Daphne Snowdrop Bluebell, revealing beyond all doubt that
she was indeed a pantomime dame and that her Irishness was of the
strangest, but most unthreatening kind. Here then is another utterly
unusual feature of Mother Riley. Never before (or since) has a pantomime dame been the eponymous star of a film, let alone a major
series of fifteen films. Indeed, it may well be that some of the most
crucial elements in the success of the Riley character are paradoxically
the most bizarre and unlikely. Precisely because Old Mother Riley is
a pantomime dame, and as such is, of course, traditionally played by
a man as a grotesque and parodic figure, she is a larger-than-life but
two-dimensional comic charade, frequently involved in slapstick and
strenuous physical comedy including the "slop scenes."

The late professor Jane Moody of the University of York, in her
summing up of Dan Leno's particular contribution to the role of the

dame, highlights an aspect which applies equally to Arthur Lucan's serio-comic creation:

> With Dan Leno at the end of the 19th century, the center of comic gravity shifts away from the Clown and toward an unexpected star: a careworn mother, haggard and a bit of a gossip, struggling to cope in this unfriendly world. Pantomime crystallises around the story of a dysfunctional family and that strange, eccentric figure of the Dame. Dan Leno was the celebrated music hall performer who created this garrulous, working-class woman. Dames had existed in pantomime before Leno, but they were usually unbelievable, ridiculous characters. Slowly, Leno began to domesticate the Dame and to imagine her as a mother, facing problems which he and his audiences knew all too well: poverty, unemployment and abandonment. A small thin man, with an odd wistful face, and a husky voice, he was said to have 'the saddest eyes in the world.' What he brought to the Dame was a talent for impersonating the absurd dilemmas of ordinary people, from waiters and railway guards to downtrodden women. What emerged was a lovelorn older woman, facing adversity with a kind of desperate fun.[178]

Lucan, more than any other performer, was able to follow Leno into the twentieth century, and perhaps even surpass him. Jane Moody wrote, "Leno created a Dame whose theatrical power comes from the locking together of our sympathy and our laughter. His women were intensely human characters, living in a chaotic world full of disastrous mishaps." Every word of this might equally be applied to Arthur Lucan.

In the last resort, the dame belonged in the unselfconscious world of childhood and fairy tale, an upside-down world which scorns common sense in favor of magic, mystery and mayhem! As we have seen, Arthur Lucan had been a successful dame performer in this demanding pantomime tradition, a "weird and comical mother," since before the Great War, and as such he already had a huge following among children throughout Britain and Ireland. Parents in 1937 may even have remembered that in their own childhood, Arthur Lucan as the Widow Twankey in *Aladdin* in 1919 had played a widowed

Chinese washerwoman before he became famous as an Irish one! Thus, aspects of character and speech, which might have been considered offensive if viewed primarily as mock-Chinese or mock-Irish, were acceptable in a pantomime dame who is mock-everything; as Jane Moody put it, "Pantomime's absurdity depends on us enjoying this pretence. Pantomime self-consciously disorganises the ordinary world and releases us to participate in its magic."

To complain then, as some critics have, that *Old Mother Riley* films are naive or childish is like complaining that water is wet! In film after film, every time Mother gives chase or is chased, ends up on the floor or suspended in mid-air, upside down, covered in flour or water or both, and then just gets up and carries on, contemporary audiences knew they were in the familiar and reassuring world of pantomime slop scenes, and the censors knew that nothing dangerous could happen, or so they thought. For years the public had already enjoyed this relationship with Lucan. Every Christmas they had interacted with him live onstage as the pantomime Dame, commiserating with her lot or booing, whistling and heckling, singing along or shouting encouragement from up in the gods. When at last they saw Riley onscreen, they already knew her, loved her, and, importantly, they knew what to expect from her; rarely were they disappointed.

In Lucan's last film, *Mother Riley Meets the Vampire*, he makes one last reference to his pantomime and music hall roots when he sings Leslie Sarony's 1929 nonsense song, "I Lift Up My Finger And I Say Tweet-Tweet, Shush-Shush, Now-Now, Come-Come!" with the young Hattie Jacques and Dandy Nichols as his backing group. In spite of this film's "baggy plot and aging stars Lucan and Lugosi both past their prime," one internet critic partly exonerates the film on the grounds of this very song.

This number, which looks as if it was rehearsed for all of two minutes, is totally charming and announces that the film is nothing but a kiddies' pantomime. On this level, it's hard to see why the film has such a bad reputation. It has a few laughs, and you can find plenty of more amateurish stuff on children's TV today.

At a technical level, the aging Lucan performs this piece with beautifully appropriate gestures and facial expressions but, forty years on, his low, husky voice is a sad remnant of the light lyric tenor of "Archie Mashington," the debonair dude of 1911. The internet critic understood that traditional pantomime routines are the key to a number of scenes that adults today find problematic or silly; such scenes were aimed at children and were meant to be silly! Every Riley film contains scenes and routines which audiences expected of the pantomime dame, and many of these scenes, when understood and viewed in their appropriate context, are still funny. Even the arbitrary hold-ups in many films to allow Kitty to sing can find their justification (just) in the pantomime sing-song tradition in which Lucan and McShane had been working for twenty-five years. The particularly broad appeal of Lucan in pantomime is a perfect illustration of Anne Varty's assertion that, as in Victorian pantomime, from which Arthur himself had started out in 1895, "The carnivalesque suspension of convention and law liberates the imagination. The children in the pantomime audience could enter a magical world of infinite possibility, while the adults were invited to escape into a world of anarchy and subversion."[179] This could almost serve as a definition of the unique world of Old Mother Riley.

The other major source of the Riley character is of course the Music Hall. Lucan was just one of many film performers whose roots also lay in music hall and variety, and this aspect has been more fully documented and discussed by the critics. Just a couple of points need to be stressed. Arthur was perfectly capable of learning a script but, in common with many comedians in the rowdy music hall tradition from which modern "stand-up" comedy derives, he still loved to extemporize according to the whim of the moment or the mood of the crowd. Like John Blakeley's team of gifted lunatics at Mancunian Films, Arthur knew what to do when the script simply said "BUS" (business); but this was not always welcomed or understood by other film companies or directors. Brian McFarlane suggests that Lance Comfort wondered what had hit him when he first directed Arthur in *Old Mother Riley Detective*. And so did poor Angela Allen, the young script supervisor who wept on the set of *Old Mother Riley Headmistress*. Richard Gordon reported that Bela Lugosi was similarly thrown and annoyed by Arthur's ad-libbing, but McFarlane understood the tradition from which Lucan came: "Though Lucan was probably director proof, the film opens with Comfort's customary speed ... and he allows Lucan to have his/her head with often very funny results." McFarlane then makes a point which is very apposite to music hall performative: "Perhaps it is a valuable element in a film maker's 'disposition' to know when to let a particular collaborator have room to move. The dialogue, some of it provided by Lucan, is fast, outrageous, wildly punning, innuendo-ridden."[180] This is an excellent précis of the most exciting qualities of a good music hall comedian, and McFarlane goes on the make another exceptionally important point about music hall and performative. "Lucan plays [Riley] as a music hall turn, often seeming to bypass the plot to address the audience directly." This ability to "look through" the camera, a legacy of the music hall performer's rapport with his audience, was a gift Lucan shared with silent screen comedians, most notably Charlie Chaplin, whose early career was remarkably similar to Arthur's own. It is worth noting that when the "talkies" took over, Arthur was already in his late forties, and he was familiar with the miming techniques of silent cinema, which his later films suggest he may even have copied in his stage performances. Instances of Mother Riley speaking or looking "through" the camera could fill a whole chapter, and Lucan, like Chaplin, used this technique as a comic demolition of the conventions of film, but also at times to achieve a rare degree of poignant and seemingly personal communication with his public.

Probably the longest and most scholarly treatment of the Riley films, both in general and with special reference to their music hall origins, is to be found in Paul Matthew St. Pierre's recent *Music Hall Mimesis in British Film*.[181] Not only does this excellent study do Arthur Lucan the courtesy of taking him seriously as a performing artist, it also goes further than any previous study in analyzing the structure and significance of his performance on film; extensive examples are meticulously dissected with reference to critical theory, to film, theater, and performance studies, including biosemiotic theory and body performance poetics. Professor St. Pierre, with frequent references to both Charlie Chaplin and Arthur Lucan, discusses

> how music hall artists play their film roles by performing their bodies, specifically in the instances of slapstick, knockabout, and pantomime comedians for whom how they comport their bodies is crucial, and ... other music hall artists such as

living statue performers, acrobats and dancers, whose performance space *is* the body.

Much of Professor St. Pierre's original and illuminating analysis
of Lucan's art is to be found in his chapter on "Screening Pantomime
Dames and Principal Boys," but is by no means confined there, and
the most striking thing about the volume as far as Lucan is concerned
is the frequent comparison and unmistakable kinship St. Pierre estab-
lishes between Lucan and Charlie Chaplin, both of whom were
formed in the same British music hall tradition. St. Pierre's study is
now indispensable to a fully contextualized historical understanding
of Arthur Lucan's stage and screen persona, and its links to other
performers who crossed from music hall to silent, and later, sound
film. I have already mentioned Chaplin's 1914 film *A Busy Day*, in
which he plays an unruly wife who ends up, like Lucan in his last
film, floundering in the harbor. Paul Matthew St. Pierre's comments
on Chaplin include not only a reference to Lucan but also a number
of implied parallels which deserve to be quoted in full.

As a pantomime dame, Chaplin exhibits the appearance of
a woman and some women's mannerisms, such as foreshort-
ening the arms by holding his upper arms close to his body,
pointing the forearms upward, and bending the wrists, in
the manner of Arthur Lucan as Old Mother Riley. Chaplin's
clean-shaven face, modest make-up, understated costume,
albeit with oversized boots, and coy, prancing, and knockabout
mannerisms do not conspire to conceal his male gender.[182]

Professor St. Pierre's remarks serve as a reminder that exceptional
physical dexterity, closely related to circus-style acrobatics, was a hall-
mark of the music-hall tradition from which both Chaplin and Lucan
emerged. From the very beginning of Lucan's career, critics stressed
his remarkable agility; at the London Alhambra in 1925 the reviewer
of the sketch "Come Over" spoke of "Mr. Lucan as a very funny and
unexpectedly agile old dame," and as late as 1943 Ivor Brown declared
admiringly that "never was moribundity so agile as this skipping queen
of penury and jollity." Indeed, in Arthur's very last pantomime in 1953
he was still able to create, at the very least, the impression of "a lively,
skittish old harridan ... with a sprightliness that takes the show along

at a cracking pace. And her small beady eyes are alternately dancing with fun or aslant with a knowledgeable cunning."

The Riley films all contain examples of Arthur's highly idiosyncratic physical performance style but, as we have already noted, by the time his film career began, Arthur was already in his fifties, an age at which most physical acts would be thinking of hanging up their leotards. More importantly, only one short sketch, "Bridget's Night Out," was filmed before Arthur's life-threatening accident in February 1936, which makes it all the more remarkable that the strenuous tumbles and pratfalls, the "wide acrobatic movements, tremendous but controlled waving of the arms, gesticulating with large, delicate and expressive hands"were the work of a slightly built, frail, middle-aged man in rather indifferent health. Arthur's antics can be viewed at leisure in the films, but several examples of the "superanimated, rubber-limbed rag doll" call for special mention. All of them form what might be called Lucan's physical paralanguage, through which his body constantly reinforces or subverts his verbal language. It is worth recalling that in his very first British tour in 1911, as Archie Mashington in Gilbert Payne's musical comedy *The Honeymoon*, Arthur was required to sing and dance, and many of his early reviews mention his dancing. He somehow managed to retain something of his youthful agility well into old age. Jeffrey Richard's memorable description of Riley the "rubber-limbed rag doll" was echoed by Sue Harper, with an interesting twist: "Her body language is jerky: her arms flail, her head bobs, her legs swivel. Like a comic character from Dickens her body has lost coherence and rebels against itself." In 1950 the *Hull Daily Mail* made a similar observation; "His fantastic character has the gusto of a Dickensian creation." Here are four of Lucan's most idiosyncratic routines:

The Comic Entrechat.

This move is often performed when Riley is angry and aroused and preparing to go into battle. Her emotions seem to flood from her brain into her body, causing her to spring into the air like a jack-in-the-box; while airborne she performs scissor-like movements with her legs, and sometimes clicks her heels together in mid-air.

Windmill Legs.

This move is performed seated in a chair and is also performed when Mother Riley is overcome with forms of extreme emotion, such as bafflement or frustration, often accompanied with words such as "Would you believe that?" Riley lifts her body slightly from the chair and then, supported by her hands on the armrests, appears to twirl her legs rapidly in complete circles. Although audiences throughout the country must have seen Arthur do this onstage many times, it was first captured on film in "Bridget's Night Out." The move was copied many years later by the comedian Kenny Everett in his role as the scatty starlet, Cupid Stunt.

Climbing the invisible rope.

This illusion is well known in the repertory of mime-artists, but it is extremely difficult to do well. It is loosely related to moves known as kip-up, or kipping-up, used in martial arts and break dancing. Arthur's version was a particularly difficult variation, demanding not just the illusion of a "point fixe" which is in fact thin air, but also immense strength and muscular control—if you don't believe me, try it! Old Mother Riley falls or is knocked flat onto her back. Her lower legs are bent under her from the knee, and her feet are under her buttocks. From this supine position, using only her unsupported muscles, she draws herself to a fully upright standing position by appearing to pull strenuously on a rope which is in fact not there. Arthur performed this move near the opening of the very first Riley film, another signal to his fans that this was still the Mrs. O'Flynn who had undoubtedly performed the move many times onstage. He did it again in *Old Mother Riley's Circus.*

The Rubber Leg.

In the course of her frenzied physical exertions, Mother Riley was frequently injured, and the injury was invariably sustained by her left leg. She would then perform a wonderful stagger across the stage or screen while howling "Ooh, me leg!" Her left knee joint would suddenly seem to be made of rubber, appearing to defy the laws of human physiology and capable of collapsing and bending in any and every possible direction. At the height of her agony she would often use a horse-racing analogy, "I shall have to be shot, or scratched!" Moments later the serious injury was forgotten and the show carried on. This move was also first filmed in "Bridget's Night Out," which Sue Harper perceptively referred to as "an interesting index of Lucan's original style."

These four trademark moves principally concern the lower body, but a last general word needs to be said concerning Arthur's hand and arm movements. Mother Riley had an immense repertoire, one is tempted to say vocabulary, of expressive hand and arm gestures with which she punctuated and enriched her every verbal utterance. These gestures ranged from the grotesque and comic to the poignant and pathetic; rolling up her sleeves and baring her fists, making emphatic patterns with her hands and forearms like an Egyptian wall-painting; clasping hands above her head like a boxing champ; or wringing her hands in despair and dabbing her tears with a corner of her grubby shawl. Many of her gestures were so stylized, almost choreographed, as to be virtually impossible to copy, which has not, to this day, prevented admirers from trying. The perceptive critic Roger Lewis recently wrote,

To watch the material today is to be struck not by grossness or coarseness, as one might expect, but by an odd kind a beauty. Old Mother Riley is in constant motion: arms, fists, elbows, knees, wrists, like a dancer. Robert Helpmann comes to mind. She's pale and wispy, emanating wistfulness not sourness. In her bonnet with the elastic chin-strap, the ribbons, the shawl, the clogs, her chief attribute is speed."[183]

Youngsters watching her for the first time today, often wonder if she's "on speed!"

The First Film: *Old Mother Riley* (1937)

When the first Riley film opened with a scene between Old Mother Riley and her daughter on the Thames Embankment, cinema audiences must have realized at once that this was none other than the widowed Old Match-seller they had known and loved in the music halls for over ten years. They also quickly understood that the former jilted bride was now a flower seller, and that Bridget O'Flynn of the famous "Night Out" had now become Kitty Riley. But Lucan's contributions from his Match-seller script to the serious aspects of the plot were probably more extensive and important to the film's success than hitherto realized. Given that *Old Mother Riley* (1937) was the first of a remarkable series, it deserves to be examined in some detail. Trinity College Dublin Film and TV Research website summarizes the plot.

> William Briggs, a wealthy match manufacturer, leaves his money to his widow, and only son Edwin, on condition that they invite the first street Match-seller they encounter selling Briggs' matches to live with them as a guest for at least six months. Should the guest leave for any reason whatever, the money is to go to Briggs' sister, Matilda Lawson, and her husband, Captain Lawson. The first Match-seller encountered turns out to be a strange old woman known as Old Mother Riley. When taken into the Briggs' Mayfair residence and informed that she is to be given a comfortable home, the astonished Mrs. Riley at first suspects that there is a catch somewhere and asks who has she to murder. After being reassured, Mrs. Riley makes the stipulation that her daughter Kitty, a flower seller, should come and live with her. Strange and embarrassing incidents occur, but Mrs. Briggs is desperately anxious not to lose her guests and the Lawsons become alarmed. They conspire with the butler to stage a fake robbery, and manage to make it look as if Mrs. Riley is the thief. When the case comes to court Mrs. Riley is unsatisfied with the way her counsel is conducting her defence, takes the law into her own hands, and shows up the conspiracy. The film ends with the wedding of Kitty and Edwin.

This rather creaky plot hinges on a number of well-worn but perhaps comforting narrative clichés. The theme of the test or trial in order to win success is common to both myth and fairy tale. The reading of a will has echoes of more serious dramas. The theft of jewelry and wrongful accusation are also commonplace themes with overtones of class war. Finally, the courtroom scene, a regular feature of more serious films, is used to good effect at the climax, and the wedding of a happy couple rounds off proceedings in time-honored fairy-tale style. This film has never been commercially available in a modern format and I suspect that even some of the enthusiastic accounts of it offered by critics may be based on secondary sources. When I viewed the film at the BFI in July 2012, I at first felt slightly disappointed that it moved rather jerkily from one rather stilted set piece to the next. The main "Mayfair" characters, the Briggs and their butler, the Lawsons and the bishop, seemed to be predictable stereotypes of the stuffy middle class as viewed by the "industrial" classes who were to be the film's audience. By way of contrast there were several scenes of (presumably East End) working-class life involving Mother Riley's erstwhile neighbors. The two utterly disparate groups are thrown together by Mother Riley and Kitty, who move between two worlds thanks to the artificial demands of the plot. This clash of classes and cultures is vividly dramatized in an amusing scene when the Riley's East End ex-landlady Aggie Sparks and her lodgers take a donkey and cart up to Mayfair and hold a jolly "knees-up" in the Briggs' drawing room, while in the dining room the family sits through an embarrassing dinner. Several scenes seemed at first to be completely extraneous to the action, merely providing a pretext for a few more of Arthur's gags or an interlude of high society dancing. The gratuitous inclusion of one unsympathetic female American, a "gold-digger" who is seen off by Mother Riley, strikes an odd note in this English comedy, and other characters' self-conscious use of a number of verbal Americanisms was also rather bizarre. The dialogue at times moved slowly, almost tentatively, as if finding its way and still uncertain of its register or genre. Even Mother Riley at times declaims rather ponderously, and over-articulates as if still trying to reach the gods in some vast provincial theater. Rachael Low claims that the film is "taken at a terrific pace" but that is not always the case, and there are a couple of irrelevant scenes that hold up the action; for instance, the scene between Mrs. Briggs and Mrs. Riley and the following scene with the maid on the butler's lap seem particularly irrelevant.

In the light of all this I was briefly baffled by the fact that the film was such an enormous box-office success and led to the making of five more Riley films before the end of 1940: *Old Mother Riley in Paris* (November 1938); *Old Mother Riley MP* (August 1939); *Old Mother*

Riley Joins Up (November 1939); *Old Mother Riley in Society* (April 1940); *Old Mother Riley in Business* (September 1940). But if one reflects on these titles, their dates and their phenomenal box-office earnings, it soon becomes clear that the adoption of an anachronistic and patronizing critical stance entirely misses the point. Instead, as soon as one attempts to understand the *contemporary* reception of Old Mother Riley, to re-situate the films (in the pioneering footsteps of Rachael Low) in their time and place, their social and political context, things immediately become clearer and much more interesting.

In his *The Age of the Dream Palace*, Jeffrey Richards opens his chapter on lower-class films with a useful reminder:

The broad division of society into upper, middle and lower classes, each with its own internal divisions and groupings ... was widely recognized in the 1930s and governed the nation's attitude and outlook on an official and an unofficial level. The cinema both perpetuated and reflected this state of affairs. But it also prompted an attitude of consensus, of harmony and sympathetic understanding between the existing classes as the way forward.

Richards discusses how in the pre-war years Gracie Fields became the very embodiment of that consensus, almost canonized as a secular proletarian Britannia, and he notes that working-class cinema audiences instinctively preferred stars who hailed from a background with which they could identify. As Peter Miles and Malcolm Smith also point out, this usually meant the comic world of the music hall with its "culture of consolation," in which "contemporary experience was re-contextualized, replaced in a well-known and ideologically neutral terrain where it still remained an expression of working-class identity but, just as importantly, where it was not an expression of class friction."[184] In resolutely upbeat films where everything "turns out nice again," characters such as Formby and Fields were allowed a limited license to transgress the stable class bounds imposed by society, on the condition that harmony and consensus eventually prevailed. In plainer language, cheeky chappies of both sexes could be naughty so long as they ended up toeing the establishment line.

In the wake of John Fisher and Rachael Low, Jeffrey Richards, who was writing in 1984 when Mother Riley had almost faded from cultural memory, was among the first to insist on the ground-breaking nature of Old Mother Riley's character:

But there was one continuing character with a rather sharper edge than most, Old Mother Riley . . . the central character in fifteen films made between 1937 and 1952. Cheaply produced on rudimentary sets, with functional direction and dismal supporting casts, the films adopt a genuinely populist stance and provide a comic heroine of titanic dimensions, exaggerated admittedly but rooted in truth. Old Mother Riley, the Irish washerwoman with apron, shawl, old black dress and poke bonnet is the inextinguishable life force of the slums, a veritable *Brünnhilde* of the back streets. A garrulous Malaprop, vituperative and combative, she has an unforgettable physical presence. She is breast-beating, arm-waving, finger-pointing, hand-flourishing, elbow-stretching, knee-bending, sleeve-rolling, superanimated, rubber-limbed rag doll. Hers is truly a case of body language gone berserk, but it is an outward and visible sign of her refusal to be cowed or to conform.[185]

It is gratifying to note that more recent critics have adopted and reinforced the judgment of Low, Fisher and Richards. In 2000, David Sutton reiterated the view that

It is certainly true that Lucan's [Old Mother Riley] is one of the great, indomitable comic creations of the age; she is unrepentantly working-class, completely at ease with herself, and the humor of the films is always on her side in her transgressions of middle-class propriety; her inability, or refusal, to conform, constantly reveals such restraint and decorum for the carefully constructed system of conventions that it is.[186]

Nowhere near all the elements of these perceptive analyses were present in the first Riley film, but in spite of its defects, the potential of the Riley phenomenon was somehow glimpsed by writers and directors from the outset and was enough, coupled with a healthy box-office, to convince them that there was a huge market for the further antics of this "animated hairpin."

Nor were the supporting casts always as "dismal" as Richards claims. A motley parade of quite distinguished actors found its way through the Riley films, including Martita Hunt (before she played Miss Havisham), Magda Kuhn, Chili Bouchier, Bruce Seton, John Stuart and Torin Thatcher. In the John Baxter films there was a sad roll call of unemployed ex-music-hall artists fallen on hard times, including Edgar Driver and Dorothy Vernon, actors who John Baxter often literally rescued from the dole queues for his crowd scenes, and to whom he gave food hampers at Christmas.[187] In the last films there was a happier roll call of the next generation of comic actors; John le Mesurier, Peter Butterworth, Richard Wattis, Hattie Jacques, Dandy Nichols, and Dora Bryan. Philip Gillett, in *The British Working Class in Postwar Film*, quite rightly sees that class does offer one angle for serious analysis of the Riley films, but he also notes the view of Andy Medhurst that

The Riley films offered perhaps the most honest solution to the problem of reconciling variety traditions and generic credibility: don't bother. The public that liked the act on stage would pay to come and see it on film, and it was the mass paying public that these films were made for. Fretting over their narrative flaws and absence of psychological credibility is, in the final analysis, a waste of time.

Gillett objects that, "Though it is hard to disagree with Medhurst's conclusion, his approach does pre-empt serious consideration of the films." This was perhaps not Medhurst's intention, and in the light of his most recent work it seems more likely that all he wanted to pre-empt was the excessive taxonomical "fretting" of academics. However, what Medhurst calls "narrative flaws and absence of psychological credibility" may actually have much to be said in their defence. Compare what Robert Knopf has to say about those sequences in the Buster Keaton films, when the object of the chase is lost and "we have no idea where Buster is headed."

To my mind, these climactic sequences are the most exhilarating in all of Keaton's work, precisely because in these moments Keaton leaves behind all concern for narrative. It is as if narrative has allowed him to accumulate enough velocity to veer off onto a trajectory all his own, and this trajectory, which scholars have frequently mistaken for the narrative line, is precisely the opposite: a visual line that transcends the narrative through its excess. For these sequences—seen most clearly, oddly enough, when shown as clips in the various documentaries about Keaton—are primarily gags, not comic events.[188]

This passage, almost *verbatim*, could apply equally to some of the funniest moments in the Riley films. Although just occasionally the lurch into a Riley "gag" scene feels contrived, it still remains interesting as a film record of Arthur Lucan's earlier stage performance style. In the very first Old Mother Riley film, the Briggs family was obliged by the terms of a will to give shelter to a common Match-seller; little did they realize they had taken in *a pantomime dame*. There is gleeful dramatic irony here because every kid in the cinema in 1937 knew something which the Briggs were not supposed to be able to see! And this is the truly clever catch, which Con West and later John Baxter exploited to such good effect. If Mother Riley (as a character) is not, in the everyday sense, *real*, then, unlike Gracie Fields or George Formby in their various incarnations, she does not have to conform to conventional *reality*. As an eccentric, "one that deviates markedly from an established norm, especially a person of odd or unconventional behavior," Riley is under no compunction at the close of play (the pun is intended) to return to the center, to consensus. In other words, she can get away with murder! When offered luxury lodgings with the Briggs, she perceptively remarks, "What's the catch? Who do I have to murder?" All she has to murder is conventional propriety, and in the film's set pieces she does this to perfection.

"Absence of psychological credibility" is in fact one of the hallmarks of her absurd and outlandish persona. She thumps a policeman at the beginning and again at the end of the film. She discusses her flatulence at table, loudly slurps her soup, and flings blancmange over a Bishop. In a rarely mentioned scene, Riley casts off her washerwoman's scrubs and becomes the first of a series of *grandes dames*. In order to help Edwin Briggs outwit an American gold-digger, Riley impersonates his mother, Mrs. Briggs, and goes off to a night club "dressed to the nines." In this sequence Lucan, in double-drag, brilliantly plays a role within a role, using a completely different vocal register and body language. As a parody of a rich middle-class lady, she is oddly more stylish and attractive than the real Mrs. Briggs. (This double-travesty was something Lucan frequently enjoyed doing, but like much else he did, it has received little comment.) During the night, after Riley's triumphant return from the night club, the greedy and malevolent Colonel Lawson and his wife frame her, and she is arrested for the theft of "my jewels" (or "may joo-ills" as posh Mrs. Lawson pronounces it); by now the audience is totally on the side of this ill-used working woman, abused by rich toffee-nosed snobs and their fawning lackey the butler.

The ensuing court scene with Mother Riley in the dock is a *tour de force*, in which the poor but honest lower orders triumph symbolically over the leering and conspiratorial upper-class Lawsons. The scene begins with an apparently defeated Riley pleading "I'm a poor old woman." But as the faked circumstantial evidence piles up against her, her fighting spirit and sharp tongue return, and Lucan's voice, manner and language are suddenly transformed. When Riley's defence counsel pleads for leniency, she finally explodes.

"Leniency? Leniency?" she shrieks. "I want Justice!" Rachael Low accurately notes that "her anger is both funny and understandable . . . She shows blarney, cunning and aggression, darting malevolently and triumphantly about in the witness box." When her exasperated counsel withdraws from the case she refuses to concede, begging the judge to allow her to recall the witnesses. She appears on the surface to cajole the crusty old judge when she flatters him by comparing him to Solomon and saying, "You've got a kind face." But old Tommies from 1914-1918 in contemporary cinema audiences must have smirked as they completed, *sotto voce*, the lines from their wartime ditty, "Greetings to the Sergeant."

> "You've got a kind face, you old bastard,
> You ought to be bloody well shot!
> You ought to be tied to a gun-wheel,
> And left there to bloody well rot!"

Having won over the judge, who clearly hadn't served in the trenches, she now transforms herself into Old Mother Riley Q.C. In a brilliant parody of a forensic cross-examination, she utterly discredits

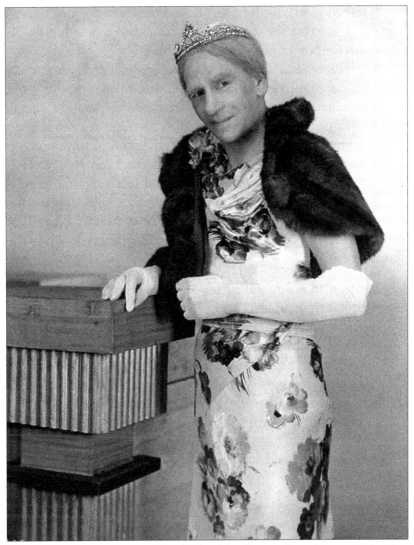

Photo 19: Old Mother Riley disguised as Mrs. Briggs. Pre-release publicity for *Old Mother Riley* (1937).

the perjured witnesses and is invited by the old bastard (sorry, the judge) to sum up:"Now, Mrs. Riley, just address the jury in your own words."

She begins in a light, conciliatory manner, with a few comic touches.

"Dear Mr. and Mrs. Jury, my learned friends of the jury, I'm sure you will agree that the case is just as plain as the nose on his face (points to the lawyer for the prosecution)."

She recapitulates the terms of the Briggs' will and how Captain and Mrs. Lawson conspired against her with the butler who "hated me like a sausage hates a frying pan." Then, as the "poor old woman" delivers her peroration, there is again a sudden and dramatic change of tone. From this point on there is no question of pantomime or parody. Lucan the character actor plays it absolutely straight as an eloquent indictment of society's cruelty and indifference to those at the bottom of the heap. Film director John Baxter, at a time when he was still forbidden to make *Love on the Dole*, must have heard and watched with envy the actor who could make the transition to this touching climax.

My learned enemy called me a parasite . . . Do you know what it is to stand in a street on a long winter's day, with the cold rain beating into your face like the lash of a whip, your own little stock of matches soaked through and unfit for sale? And when you are nearly dropping with fatigue, to wend your way home . . . Home? One room in a back alley, no fire, no light, no food! To throw yourself down on the bundle of rags I call a bed and pray for sleep, that I may forget my misery." [Pointing to the Lawsons] "*They* are the parachutes! They're the ones you should put behind bars, and I don't mean saloon bars either!

I'm not asking you to set me free for myself. I'm asking you for my daughter's sake. All my life I've prayed that she would meet someone who would be kind to her; someone who would give her the good things that have been denied me in this world. I'm glad to say she has met someone. Oh! I shall be proud to be the grandmother of his children! I shall be happy to take them on my knee and change their—positions! It's for their sake, my dear friends, for their sake and theirs alone, I ask you to set me free.

Compared to other great courtroom pleadings on film, this speech may be no great shakes of rhetoric. And yet, as she stands alone, framed in the dock by a fixed camera, Lucan/Riley delivers it with such nuanced conviction that she succeeds in investing it alternately with flashes of barbed humor and real pathos, culminating in a quite unexpectedly poignant plea, not for herself but for her future grandchildren. Part of this speech must surely have been based on the Match-seller sketch, and its evocation of the "bitter experiences of poverty" which had earned Arthur rounds of applause in theaters back in the 1920s.

The "not guilty" verdict that follows comes at exactly the right psychological moment in film terms to provide the required emotional release, as Riley vaults out of the high dock (at the age of fifty-two) and re-joins her East End pals in a reprise of their Mayfair knees-up around the courtroom. Finally, with Kitty in her frilly frock as the bride of Edwin Briggs, the film could have ended with wedding bells, but it doesn't. Instead, outside the church, Riley reasserts her working-class solidarity by giving twenty pounds (in 1937!) to a passing Match-seller, and then, having (again) thumped a policeman with the Match-seller's tray, she is chased off into the sunset, ready to fight another day. This repeated visual image from the film's opening scene is a neat symbolic framing of the whole action. Contemporary cinemagoers recalled that this classic happy chase ending was greeted with cheers and roars of approval. At the age of fifty-two Arthur Lucan had become Old Mother Riley, and a new working-class cinema icon was born. As for Kitty, apart from modelling several of the frilly frocks her mother had secured for her ("And you'll buy my daughter some pretty dresses?"), her role in this first film is really rather marginal and passive, and at no point does she attempt to sing!

Jeffrey Richards rightly states that the film's humor "is not based on making [Riley] seem out of place, uncomfortable or intimidated, it is with her all the way in deflating pomposity, subverting all the rules of middle-class decorum and triumphing in her anarchy." Professor Richard's final remark, coupled with my earlier thoughts on the unreality of the dame, leads me to demur when he continues "But she does so within a framework which makes it clear that society as presently structured is basically sound. The judge is fair, the courts are just, the Briggs are decent people, and Kitty marries their son." Had this film (or any other) dared *overtly* to suggest otherwise (a corrupt British judiciary?) it would most certainly not have received a certificate from the censors, let alone the "U" certificate which made it suitable viewing for children. Instead, Riley's anarchic refusal to acquiesce and re-integrate is adumbrated more subtly, through symbols, imagery and coded language, all of which go straight under the noses and over the heads of the literal-minded and po-faced censors, who saw only a grotesque middle-aged man in drag who should have known better than to make an ass of himself in ways to which a properly constituted British male would never deign to stoop! But audiences loved her, and late in Lucan's career, in May 1953 at Wood Green Empire, the reviewer perfectly caught the public mood which for years had never wavered: "Old Mother Riley is at once so real and so fantastic that her mere presence is a source of endless delight."

Chapter Thirteen: Maternal Melodrama; from the Old Brown Hen to the Lone Ranger

In *Old Mother Riley in Society* (1940) there is an incidental and yet crucial scene in which the homeless Riley is briefly employed as a housekeeper-nanny. The woman of the house makes it clear that the children are not her own, but are some of the million children evacuated from London at the outbreak of war in 1939. Many children from the slums were dirty, lousy and undernourished, and were often only grudgingly accommodated by the shocked middle classes in the relatively prosperous provinces. Evelyn Waugh's novel *Put Out More Flags* (1942) includes a billeting officer taking bribes from householders wanting to avoid awful child evacuees. Here, the haughty female householder represents starchy bourgeois respectability coupled with unpatriotic meanness and a suggestion of barrenness. The proletarian and impoverished Riley, who is already tired after her long walk from the station, is deeply deferential to her employer but unlike her she clearly loves children. Two children come home at tea-time, and Riley then tries to send away five more, until she realizes that all seven are billeted in the house. The presence of so many children further serves to underline the sadness of Riley's own severance from her only child. After tea, she gathers the children round the blazing fire and tells them a bedtime story which in fact proves to be the poignant tale of Old Mother Riley's own predicament and, in an odd way, that of Arthur Lucan and Kitty McShane. As the story begins background music is heard, and *pathos* is very effectively heightened by *melos*. The television producer Margery Baker, who made the first documentary on Lucan and McShane for Thames Television in 1969, very perceptively chose to end her program with this scene, commenting simply, "... and this is the whole story."

> Old Mother Riley–Once upon a time there was an old hen who had a very fine chick. She was very proud of it and she didn't want the chick to grow up into an old hen like herself. So she asked the fairies to change her chick into a peacock.

Child–And did the fairies grant her wish?

Old Mother Riley–Yes they did, and the chick became a peacock.

Child–Was the old hen happy?

Old Mother Riley–She was, but she was sad too.

Child–How could she be happy and sad too?

Old Mother Riley–Because she got her wish but lost her chick.

Child–When the chick became a peacock did she fly away?

Old Mother Riley–Well, not exactly, but when the old hen saw her chick with its fine friends, *she* went away, because she knew that if she stayed the other peacocks would laugh at her chick and they'd say, 'You're not a proper peacock. Your mother's just a silly old hen.'

Child–And did the chick miss her mother?

Old Mother Riley–I hope so my dear, I hope so.

Child–But why didn't the old hen go to the fairies and ask them to change the peacock back into a chick again?

Old Mother Riley–Because it warmed her heart to know that her chick was a peacock.

Child–Even if she never saw her again?

Old Mother Riley–Even if she never saw her again. . .

This fairy tale is also a remarkably precise enunciation of a major theme of early twentieth-century cinema, so precise in fact that it seems the writers (including Kitty McShane, who is credited with the original story) must have been consciously aware of its implications, not just in its immediate context but in relation to the Riley films in general. Theorists and critics have labelled this theme "the maternal melodrama," and in her discussion of its significance, the writer Mary Ann Doane borrows Christian Viviani's concise definition of the genre.

In a study of the maternal melodrama from 1930 to 1939, Christian Viviani isolates the thematic matrix of the form. Although this thematic matrix is modified or inflected in various ways by particular films, all of the texts bring into play the contradictory position of the mother within a patriarchal society:

"A woman is separated from her child, falls from her social class and founders in disgrace. The child grows up in respectability and enters established society where [she] stands for progress. . . The mother watches the social rise of her child from afar; she cannot risk jeopardizing [her] fortunes by contamination with her own bad repute. Chance draws them together again, and the partial or total rehabilitation of the mother is accomplished, often through a cathartic trial scene."

The scenario of "watching the child from afar" thus constitutes itself as a privileged tableau of the genre . . . and the films tend to establish an intimate relationship between the problems of the mother and issues of social class and/or economic status. The price to be paid for the child's social success is the mother's descent into anonymity.

These quotations from Mary Ann Doane and Christian Viviani are taken from a discussion of the film *Stella Dallas*, both the 1925 silent version with Belle Bennett, whose performance Arthur and Kitty must have known well, and King Vidor's recent 1937 remake; but down to the smallest detail they could apply to *Old Mother Riley in Society* in particular, and *grosso modo* to all the Riley films in general. Brian McFarlane sees *Old Mother Riley in Society* as "in line with John Baxter's naive populism, but it is not very funny and it is surely absurd to try to whip up Stella Dallas-style pathos for a mother played by a man in drag."

Marcia Landy also asserts that the Riley films are "a parody" of female melodramas, but the reality is more complex. Although David Sutton rightly sees the films as "essentially showcases for

Lucan's remarkable performances" he does note that "the elements of melodrama, the emphasis on female emotion and mother/daughter relationship were carried over into the [films]."[189] Scriptwriters of the caliber of Con West were aware of these undercurrents and, possibly encouraged by Arthur and/or Kitty, wove intertextual references into more than one film. For instance, in *Old Mother Riley's Circus*, Mother says protectively to Kitty's would-be suitor, "I suppose you're wondering how an old tabby cat like me came to have a Persian kitten." In a more negative vein, in *Old Mother Riley Goes to Paris*, when Kitty is being difficult, pathos and Shakespearean parody are mingled as mother throws up her hands and expostulates, "O how sharper than a serpent's thingummy it is to have a thankless child."

Pathos and parody might seem like oil and water, and yet when it comes to "pathos for a mother played by a man in drag," many distinguished critics have insisted that this was indeed something which Arthur Lucan was able to evoke superbly and, at moments, to an almost uncanny degree of authentic emotion. At the same time, the *Aladdin* pantomime sequence in *Old Mother Riley in Society* is in fact one of the most hilarious episodes in the whole Riley series.

Kitty McShane's "original story" for this film seems to reveal, no doubt unintentionally, a great deal about Kitty's view of herself and her at times "oil and water" relationship with Arthur, both on and off the set. We have seen how from the time of her earliest performances Kitty was encouraged to believe that she was quite exceptionally beautiful and talented, ("Isn't she gorgeous" said a Dublin advert back in 1919). All her early photographs show her lavishly dressed in the "frilly frocks" which later became almost an obsession. In one of the photographs she reclines invitingly on a chaise longue in a seductive pose that is troublingly reminiscent of portraits and photographs of courtesans. In another photograph the heavily made-up Kitty smiles archly at a doll, not cradled but held at arm's length. Far from evoking a desire for maternity, this image suggests a narcissistic sensibility frozen in a spoiled childhood. A third photograph from these early years show Kitty's hair arranged in enormous ringlets, again reminiscent of a Victorian china doll. For a time after meeting Arthur she discarded this "Baby Jane Hudson" image, straightened her hair and was photographed in a pose in which could almost be mistaken for Mary Pickford.

After humble beginnings in Dublin, marriage to a talented English actor, a beauty contest prize and a "world tour," all made Kitty feel destined for some kind of stardom in the theater. It didn't quite work out like that. Instead, with ever-increasing disappointment, resentment (and waistline), she had spent over twenty years in the shadow of a pantomime Dame. When at last the films came along, in the words of Teddy Booth, who worked for the Lucans' agent Michael Lyon, "The success of their first film had gone to her head." But the camera was also brutally honest in revealing what one critic called "Kitty's extraordinary image of herself as the perpetual schoolgirl."[190] Another critic was even blunter; "The running conceit of McShane's character is that Kitty is supposed to be extremely gorgeous. She was mildly pretty in the earlier films, but less so later … especially when the camera catches her in profile so we can see her nose in all its glory."[191] In fact the critics were often as brutal as the camera. George Melly remembered being taken as a child to see Lucan and McShane in pantomime at the Liverpool Pavilion. He later wrote that Kitty was "never beautiful and with the passage of the years increasingly less so. She was apparently a drunken termagant who made Lucan's life a hell."[192] This view is repeated in Brian McFarlane's *Encyclopedia of British Film*. "In film after film, audiences were asked to believe that otherwise normal men wanted to make off with Kitty. This, in view of her very modest personal appeal (and even more modest singing voice) was a stretch." *In Magill's Survey of Cinema*, Anthony Slide calls her "an unattractive, dowdy, slightly plump actress with no acting or singing ability, but who insists on doing both, and who always ends the films in the arms of the handsome leading man."

John Reid's judgment on Kitty in his book *Films Famous, Fanciful, Frolicsome & Fantastic* is devastating. In *Old Mother Riley's New Venture* "far too much footage is devoted to Kitty McShane, who must rank as one of the most unphotogenic heroines in film history. She's a lousy actress to boot." Discussing the same film, another critic, Elkan Allen speaks of "the utterly resistible daughter Kitty chasing men, who in real life would not even have been aware of her existence." Allen was not aware that Willer Neal, Kitty's boyfriend in this film, was in fact her boyfriend in real life. Of all the critics, Anthony Slide is the most damning. "Without question, McShane was one of the ugliest women ever to appear on British screens."

Whether or not Kitty was aware at the time of opinions and attitudes such as these one cannot say for certain, but it seems very likely that much of her bizarre behavior, her rages and mood swings were a defensive reaction against acknowledging just such a negative perception of self. As she grew older, her role as the pretty young daughter did not, and the exaggerated make-up, the fur coats and frilly frocks increasingly functioned as a double camouflage, both for her ageing body and her wounded feelings. This notion of disguise, masking her reality just as Arthur's wig and bonnet masked his, made their act a double travesty, with several critics joking that it was hard to decide which of the two was most "in drag." For John Fisher, thanks to her "props" Kitty "embodied a gushing glamour, artificial, theatrical, and with a hint of the fairground. By itself the personality would have been cloying, the speech too affected, but in performance both were admirably counter-balanced;"[193] and Kitty's kitsch provided a contrast with and context for the acerbic effervescence of Arthur.

I simply cannot agree with Alan Plater's intellectualized view of Kitty's frilly frock syndrome: "My instinct is that Kitty's taste for over-dressing indicated an ironic self-awareness of the bizarre pretense she was obliged to take part in, spiced with the bravura sod-them-all attitude that she employed, in public and in private, throughout her life."[194] As I hope I have shown, Kitty's "frilly frock" syndrome long predated the Riley films and had nothing to do with irony. Her role in the recurring maternal melodrama, some of which must have been scripted at her imperious command, was in reality, *for her*, a deeply serious work of psychic compensation. The endless procession of suitors from a higher social class, the clothes, the jewels, grand houses, hotels and restaurants, exotic holidays, and, above all that supreme archetype of the frilly frock, the wedding gown, all of this was for Kitty, the deadly earnest wish fulfilment fantasy of a hurt and spoilt child with a kind of Cinderella complex; in spite of appearances to the contrary, she *was* a princess and she *would* go to the ball!

In Lucan's 1924 "Match-seller" sketch, Kitty was resplendent in a frilly wedding gown but played a jilted bride. As we have already seen, this was modified in the first Riley film, and later on stage, to give Kitty an ersatz emotional satisfaction she seems never to have received in life. Sybil Rowse observed in 1941 that offstage Kitty never stopped acting, in the most negative sense of the word, whereas in the films, and also for ten years as Willer Neal's bride in the touring Riley stage show, she was not so much acting, as rather clumsily living out the dream scenarios of a pathetically damaged secret self. At this time Kitty's son Donald had already graduated in medicine from Trinity College Dublin, was married and about to make Kitty a grandmother. But the film Kitty has no children; in fact nowhere in the entire Mother Riley film series does she progress beyond the wedding dress to the maternity smock (she did it once on stage in 1951 as we have already noted), and in a bizarre twist in *Old Mother Riley Joins Up*, she even usurps her real son Donald's qualifications, telling her new beau that she is about to qualify as a doctor. And it was only because of her symbiotic co-existence with the genius of Arthur Lucan that she was allowed to get away with it all. As we noted earlier, Margery Baker, who had the benefit of Donald Towle's unique insight, maintained that

> Arthur adored her just the same, and he adored her like this; the little Irish colleen he had married. The Kitty he loved never grew up. She refused to grow up. She even passed off their son as her brother. And this pathological fear of growing old led her from first to last to cling to her little girl dresses, frills and puff-sleeves . . . .

Not only did Arthur allow "his Kitty" to get away with it, he protected and encouraged her until at last her toxic blend of pretension, ingratitude and scandalous financial rapaciousness left him as bankrupt and homeless as he had been when he set out at the turn of the century. Even to the end, according to his last stage manager, Slim Ingram, and others, Arthur still loved Kitty and never spoke ill of her in public. As a young man, Richard Gordon had been involved in the production of *Mother Riley Meets the Vampire*. It was he who confirmed that Arthur asked George Minter to bar Kitty from the studio "because Lucan didn't want her around harassing him in her usual manner." But Gordon added, "I heard all these stories about her from other people—Lucan never said anything." In a strange way, the tensions and conflicts of their private lives seem to have contributed at first to the success of the partnership on stage and in film. It gave their interactions a sharper, more dangerous edge which corrected any excessive tendency towards mawkishness, although from the start sentimentality was there in buckets because it was still not a forbidden zone; Lucan, like Chaplin, understood that audiences enjoyed tears as much as laughter. In fact Lucan comes close to Chaplin in unashamedly daring to exploit a gamut of "sentimental" emotions beyond the accepted comfort zones of most British actors.

Old Mother Riley in Society is the one film in which Riley has no real cause to fight for, and no-one to fight with. Apart from her glorious onstage pantomime fiasco near the beginning, she never gets physical, no bendy legs, no pratfalls, no shadow-boxing. True to the maternal melodrama, she sinks ever deeper into John Baxter's territory, until at last she is literally in the doss house, while Kitty and her upper-class husband wine and dine in splendor, in the restaurant where Riley is washing dishes in the kitchen and salvaging scraps from the diners' plates. When, thanks to the kind-hearted roughneck Tug Mulligan, Riley is restored to her family, there is a reconciliation scene at Riley's bedside, where all the main characters have gathered, including Jimmy Clitheroe in his first screen role as Boots. This threatens to sink the whole film beneath a tidal wave of schmaltz, but two small comic touches save the day. The Morgans, Kitty's in-laws, reveal that they are not real toffs but made their money "in sausages." Sausages are vulgar, comic-phallic, circus clown and Punch and Judy props, and this totally deflates Kitty's supposed social ascension. Then Mother Riley gets her revenge on the fawning lackeys of the upper classes when she orders Nugent the butler to drink her nasty medicine for her. In Riley's oddball version of the maternal melodrama, the Old Brown Hen sometimes strikes back with "a smack in the gob!" Or she would, "If I wasn't a lady!"

The theme of the mother watching her chick from afar recurs many times in the Riley films. In Old Mother Riley in Society it is of course evoked in the tale of the Old Brown Hen but it is also powerfully present in the first half of the film when Riley watches proudly from the wings as Kitty, having been catapulted into the role of principal boy, is onstage alone for the first time, singing a touching ballad, "No Matter Where You Are." Riley's place in the darkened wings is as significant as the place of Barbara Stanwyck in the dark, rainy street at the end of Stella Dallas, watching her daughter's wedding through the frame/proscenium of the brightly lit window. Incidentally, one year later in *Old Mother Riley's Circus* (not directed by John Baxter) there is an amusing echo of Barbara Stanwyck being moved on by a policeman at the end of *Stella Dallas*. The destitute Riley is singing "Meet Me Tonight in Dreamland" outside a cinema showing (most appropriately) Baxter's *Love on the Dole*, but whereas Stanwyck compliantly moves on, Riley fights back, as she does whenever policemen try to move her anywhere! A sad and rather gruesome instance of the mother as onlooker occurs many years later in *Old Mother Riley's New Venture* (1949). Mother and Kitty have organized a St. Patrick's night party at which Kitty, heavily but unsuccessfully disguised beneath layers of frills as the young colleen she had once been, entertains the hotel guests (through clouds of cigarette smoke!) by singing "Galway Bay." Her lover Willer Neal is dressed as Danny Boy as in the touring Riley stage show, and he serenades Kitty with "I'll Take You Home Again Kathleen," which is precisely what he was doing off-screen. During this spectacle of ostentatious cuckoldry, the camera cuts away to Mother Riley, undoubtedly shot separately, but apparently watching them from the shadows, moved to tears and dabbing her eyes with her shawl.

In the five films involving William Breach/Willer Neal, the Old Brown Hen's loss of her chick was not play-acting but a hideous reality. Kitty's wedding scene at the end of the first film in 1937 also became part of the Old Mother Riley touring show throughout the 1940s, with Kitty wearing an enormous frilly white wedding gown, an item of profound symbolic significance at the best of times but especially in wartime, and something which she certainly did not have at her real-life marriage to Arthur back in 1913. Roy Rolland, Arthur's understudy at the end of the 1940s, remembered many years later that one of his jobs on tour was to make a new wedding bouquet of fresh flowers for Kitty every week, in spite of an old theatrical superstition forbidding the use of fresh flowers onstage. A new bouquet was needed because, according to Rolland, after the playing of the "Wedding March," Kitty would fling carnations into the audience. This may not be the only reason. In any other show, artificial flowers from props would have sufficed, but being odorless and made of paper they would have reminded Kitty that all this was merely play-acting. There exists a copy of the "wedding photograph" of Kitty and Billy signed "To Roy" from the couple. Life and make-believe became so hopelessly confused that Anthony Slide appeared to be under the impression that this was Arthur and Kitty's real wedding photograph.[195]

By now Willer Neal was with Kitty in the number one dressing room (and the number one bedroom at Forty Lane) and Arthur was pushed out. In real life Arthur Lucan had become the Old Brown Hen who had lost her chick, and in real life there was to be no redemption or tender reconciliation. Given all this, it is difficult not to view Kitty's belated introduction of the onstage christening of Willer Neal's child in 1951 as the tasteless nadir of her psychological delusions. "Absurd, Stella Dallas-style pathos?" Perhaps, but every night for ten years, framed in the lighted window of the stage or the screen, Arthur Lucan/Old Mother Riley had looked on from the side-lines as his/her wife-daughter-chick left him for Danny Boy, soon widely known as her "fancy man."

We have seen that the thematic matrix of the maternal melo-drama or "Tale of the Old Brown Hen" is to be found, albeit at times in self-consciously parodic form, in every Old Mother Riley film apart from, for obvious reasons, *Mother Riley meets the Vampire*. But it is normally complemented and counterbalanced by another thematic matrix belonging to a different genre, one with which it does not normally co-exist, namely that of the principal protagonist as heroic underdog, a brave loner or outsider, fighting for the rights of the downtrodden, the voiceless and the oppressed. This role was normally a male preserve, incarnated by performers as different as Chaplin and Formby, playing the "little man" up against brutes and bullies; another category within the genre was made up of brave sher-iffs or lone avenging outsiders in Westerns, and noble stiff-upper-lip Sir Galahad types in heroic quest films. But Mother Riley, the Dame who shatters the boundaries of polite gender role-assignment with her "smack in the gob," is always at her funniest and most effective in precisely this guise. She may ride into town on a bicycle, in an old car, pushing a pram or a wheelbarrow, or even parachute in from an airplane; all these are her trusty steeds, like Don Quixote's Rocinante. But by the time she leaves town, a wrong will have been righted, a criminal brought to justice, snobbery and pretension will have been exposed and deflated, and darling daughter Kitty will have got her man, and another frilly frock. This aspect of Riley's multi-faceted persona was clearly recognized by the critic who wrote, "Old Mother Riley in films and comics strips—for many years she was featured in a weekly called *Film Fun*—is as much an institution in Britain as is Superman in America. The goals of both are much the same."[196]

The most representative films for this genre are the first *Old Mother Riley*, *Old Mother Riley in Paris*, *Old Mother Riley Joins Up*, *Old Mother Riley MP*, *Old Mother Riley Detective*, and above all *Old Mother Riley in Business*. It is in these films that Riley is most convincingly portrayed as "the champion of the underdog, a hater of shams, a Valkyrie of the backstreets," and as a "screechy-voiced virago . . . shaking her scrawny fist at the world in defence of the downtrodden." And, as she goes into battle, as if to acknowledge that she is straying into a genre normally reserved for men, "she" deliberately parodies the belligerent physical body language traditionally associated with aggressive male heroes and champion boxers; limbering up in her corner with knee-bends, rolling up sleeves, ducking and weaving and waving her fists. Here Riley mocks the cinema's stereotypically gendered pantheon of masculine heroes, and she does it by playing mock "butch," the very antithesis of the strategy adopted by quasi-feminine "little man" underdogs from Chaplin and Formby to Norman Wisdom.

Mother Riley also invaded and conquered what had been, until relatively recently, another ferociously male preserve; The House of Commons. The very first woman MP, the Irish Countess Constance Markiewicz, did not take her seat at Westminster, but the stage-Irish Countess of Alagazam (aka Old Mother Riley MP) most certainly did! The following account of this highly significant event was written by Professor Steven Fielding, who has kindly allowed me to reproduce it here:

> In 1939, the same year United States Senator Jefferson Smith [in Frank Capra's *Mr. Smith Goes to Washington*] exposed the corrupt political machine that ran his home state, a poor single mother named Riley joined the British Cabinet. Hers had been a dramatic rise: before being elected as an independent MP she had languished on the dole. On first entering the House of Commons, Riley attacked a measure supported

by all MPs to reduce government spending by closing public parks. Such amenities were, she announced, the 'poor people's gardens,' the only chance most had to enjoy unpolluted air. During this peroration Riley widened her sights and asserted the 'Englishman's birthright to work,' concluding dramatically: 'Everyone shall be employed!' A press campaign followed that catapulted the new MP into government where she immediately introduced legislation to abolish unemployment. The bane of the 1930s was set to become a thing of the past.

Heady stuff indeed, but Fielding goes on to contrast the reception of the two films:

There are many parallels with that other 'outsider', young Jefferson Smith, the protagonist in *auteur* Frank Capra's Academy Award winning *Mr. Smith Goes to Washington*, also released in 1939. Capra's film also benefited from a Washington premiere attended by members of Congress and generated international critical comment. Riley's audience, being predominantly northern and working class, her film received hardly any press attention. As a result, and unlike *Mr. Smith*, *Old Mother Riley MP* remains languishing in obscurity. There are possibly sound artistic reasons: there is no doubt which is the better produced movie, and it's not Riley's. However, while *Mr. Smith* has generated much debate about its political message, *Old Mother Riley MP*'s very similar critique of the unrepresentative nature of representative democracy has never been discussed.

Professor Fielding himself made amends for this neglect in the paper he gave on "Old Mother Riley and Politics" at the Lucan day at the London Cinema Museum in October 2013. His comments also appear in his new book, *A State of Play: British Politics on Screen, Stage and Page, from Anthony Trollope to The Thick of It*, published by Bloomsbury Academic in April 2014.

Because they thought they were dealing with a harmless pantomime dame, the censors in 1939, preoccupied with graver matters, passed without murmur Mother Riley's election hustings speech, which is in fact a serious and eloquent indictment of inequality of opportunity for women, years before the feminist movement said the same thing. The glittering prospects Riley evokes for the working-class baby boy in her arms are reduced to just Red Cross Nurse when she is told the baby is in fact a girl. One cannot help wondering if a certain Margaret Hilda Roberts saw this film in a cinema in Grantham and got ideas . . .

When Mother Riley reaches Parliament, her totally serious and eloquent speech in defence of open green spaces for working people could have been delivered at a Green Party conference sixty years later in 1998 almost without altering a word. She is overruled by the Speaker and ordered to leave the chamber. At this point Lucan first adopts his humble, crestfallen and defeated manner, and prepares to leave quietly. Then suddenly, as if at the flick of a switch, the body language changes completely, and Riley the defiant virago takes on the world of pompous male politicians; by the end of the scene she is bobbing and weaving around the chamber to roars of approval, hands clasped above her head as if she has just won a boxing match by a knockout! In a way which demands further study, political issues are subtly woven into almost every Riley film, and long after Arthur's death the perception of Mother Riley as a champion of the underdog was at the root of a violently partisan political debate in the chamber of the Greater London Council in 1975, when it was proposed to erect a blue plaque at the Lucans' house in Forty Lane, Wembley. The Labor administration had been arguing for some time that blue plaques should commemorate all walks of life, not just grandees, and the debate was recorded in *New Society*:

The issue came to a head over the decision to commemorate the creator of Old Mother Riley, Arthur Lucan; and it all showed how deep cultural politics go. The Conservatives said Arthur Lucan was a second-rate female impersonator. Labor replied that if Lucan did not have any standing in Chelsea and Kensington, it was very different in the Labor boroughs. There, Arthur Lucan was a figure in working class folklore, and Old Mother Riley was still entertaining the mums and kids. Blue plaques, they said, were also for the man in the street.[197]

In an online review of the Renown re-issue on DVD of *Old Mother Riley MP*, a critic wrote,

The plot is simple (like you were expecting *War and Peace!*). Mrs. Riley and her daughter are unfairly sacked from their jobs in the local laundry. When Mrs. Riley learns that her ex-boss is going to knock down the neighborhood, she decides to run for Parliament in order to stop him. Despite a bit of skullduggery on the part of her opponent, she triumphs. Her impassioned speeches propel her to a Cabinet position where she secures the repayment of a foreign loan which is put towards providing full employment. Put like that, the film seems like one of those earnest, politically-committed, realist pictures that get the critics raving. But that reckons without the glorious character that is Old Mother Riley . . . The character of Old Mother Riley is an unruly mixture of malapropisms, frenzied gestures and slapstick. She inhabits a world of slums, poverty and domestic violence. In these films women have minimal expectations and set roles, but she is able to transcend them. She'll claim to be a poor frail woman, but then set about a gang of thugs with her umbrella. When a sailor is stopped from telling a mucky joke because a "lady" is present, she says "don't mind me, I expect I've heard it." The character provides the energy that keeps this rackety vehicle going. Kitty, on the other hand, is already surplus to requirements. She has a handful of lines, none of them convincingly delivered; and, if we're going to be uncharitable, looks more like a drag act than her mother. No wonder she was permanently annoyed. By any reasonable definition, this is not a good film. But the character is so watchable, so wonderfully manic, you enjoy the film despite its faults.[198]

That last sentence could apply most of the films.

Another of the subversive forms taken by Mother Riley's insubordination is her almost total lack of respect for the police. The benign British bobby, a role perfected not many years later by Elsie and Doris Waters' brother, Jack Warner, is noticeably absent from the films, and his place is taken by a bunch of rather bumbling oafs, at times reminiscent of the Keystone Kops or a Gilbert and Sullivan chorus, all of them utterly incapable of subduing Riley, either physically or verbally. In *Old Mother Riley Detective*, Riley says to the one clever and likeable officer, Detective Inspector Cole, "You may be a merry old soul, but I wish you'd tell your fiddlers to keep their hands off me!" At the beginning and the end of the first film, Riley hits a policeman with a tray of matches and is chased. She physically fights with police officers in *Old Mother Riley in Paris, Old Mother Riley Detective* and *Mother Riley meets the Vampire*. In two films she is arrested, imprisoned, and breaks out of jail. Even when not actually fighting, she refuses to be cowed; in *Old Mother Riley in Society* she breaks up a brawl without police help and then sends a nosey policeman on his way; In *Old Mother Riley Joins Up* she orders a constable to inflate her bicycle tire saying "You've got a mechanical face," and in *Old Mother Riley's Circus* she reminds an impertinent officer that she has known better days, and promises to turn her batteries off so he can't arrest her for "Assault and Battery." In *Old Mother Riley in Business*, a horrified constable is left gasping and speechless at the roadside as Riley thunders past at the wheel of an old banger which is festooned both inside and out with brooms, buckets, mops and clothes lines from her village shop. Although arrested and charged with dangerous driving, she gets off almost scot free, mocking the police and the courts of law.

By the time the police arrive at any scene, Mother Riley has usually done her own detective work and "cleaned up" without their help, and one is left with the cumulative impression of a certain working-class mistrust bordering on hostility towards policemen who bear little resemblance to the reassuring figure of Dixon of Dock Green. When Bridget O'Flynn says, "If you strike me I'll call the police!" Mother replies, "Don't bother, I don't want any help!" Less frequently but equally subversively, judges, lawyers and doctors receive similarly disrespectful treatment, a bizarre point of contact between Mother Riley and the great comic playwright Molière!

In a more deliberately music-hall comic episode, in *Old Mother Riley in Paris* Mother Riley's noble intervention on behalf of the oppressed turns out to be utterly inappropriate, and a glorious excuse for Arthur's rubber-limbed antics. Mother's misunderstanding of the mock-brutality of the "danse apache" in a Montmartre nightclub leads her to challenge the male dancer, only to be swept up into a magnificently acrobatic parody of the dance; deliberately echoing a similar scene in Charlie Chaplin's *City Lights* (and danced to the same music!) Cinemagoers would also have been familiar with a spectacular "danse apache" in the film *Charlie Chan in Paris* from 1935. In fact, Riley's apache dance may well be a salute to something of a recurring gag in British comic films at the time, partly sending up the elegant dancing couples of musical comedy on both sides of the Atlantic. Cicely Courtneidge had performed an energetic apache dance in *Aunt Sally* (1933); Gracie Fields did it in *Queen of Hearts* (1936), both women displaying more energy, and underwear, than was usual for the time; The Crazy Gang had a go in *Okay for Sound* (1937) and Frank Randle later did a grotesque parody in *Somewhere in Camp* (1942).

Even in the films where Riley the successful fighter is mostly to the fore, the innate pathos of the maternal melodrama remains present by implication, because Kitty, the chick who becomes a peacock-bride at the end of every film and stage show, is forever on the point of leaving behind the old brown hen who "got her wish but lost her chick." But this unusual hen never wallows in melodramatic passivity for long, and she soon reverts to her fighting stage-Irish and quasi-male-gendered hero-persona, perfectly captured in her rhetorical question to the "merry old soul" Inspector Cole: "Did you ever see a rat get away from an Irish terrier?"

Feminist critics insist that only in the wake of Simone de Beauvoir was the myth of the idyllic mother-daughter relationship exploded and problematized; but long before the publication of *Le Deuxième Sexe* in 1949, Lucan and McShane as Mother and Bridget (later Kitty) had for years been exploding and problematizing their unique onstage version of the maternal melodrama.

Chapter Fourteen: "I Can Take it!" Old Mother Riley Wins the War

Old Mother Riley's key role in the sustaining of civilian morale on the home front during the Second World War has never been properly analyzed or evaluated.[199] Indeed, until relatively recently, as Neil Rattigan has pointed out, critics of British wartime cinema focused on a very partial selection of "quality" films to the exclusion of everything else, arguing that

> British wartime film was defined by the qualities of a carefully selected group of particular films, the cream of the films. . . *In Which We Serve, The Next of Kin, The Way Ahead, We Dive at Dawn, The Demi-Paradise*, and a handful of others . . . Nothing whatever is made of the far more numerous run-of-the-mill wartime productions such as the 'Old Mother Riley' series of films . . . Nor indeed is there mention of the other comedies such as those featuring Britain's most popular box-office star, George Formby. . . .[200]

Jeremy Havardi's recent study of British Second World War films does not dwell for long on the role of comedy, and just one Riley film is mentioned in a list of "light-hearted comedy capers."[201]

Other historians of British wartime cinema do briefly acknowledge the contribution of two Riley films in particular, *Old Mother Riley Joins Up* and *Old Mother Riley Detective*, but then move swiftly on to George Formby, whose ukulele-playing, gormless but lovable "little man" is now deemed to have won the war, in the cinema at least, almost single-handed. The exceptional popularity of Formby's films throughout the war is well-documented and needs no recapitulation here.[202] What is hard to understand however, is the fact that time and again, when Formby's phenomenal wartime film statistics are trotted out and marveled at, they are closely followed by almost equal statistics for Lucan and McShane, remarkable statistics which are then passed over almost without further comment. Jeffrey Richards, for instance, merely recorded the fact that "even Mother Riley was inveigled into joining up," and Brian McFarlane, in his discussion of director Lance Comfort, while going into a little more detail, nevertheless prefaces his comments apologetically with "*Old Mother Riley Detective* need not detain us for long. . . ."[203]

Unfashionable though it has been until very recently to confront the facts, it is abundantly clear that just before the war, and at its darkest hour, Lucan and McShane, without the benefit of Ealing Studios or Michael Balcon, were almost as popular as George Formby on screen, and just as popular on stage. And they certainly addressed a number of serious wartime issues, in their own idiosyncratic way, often with a sharper, less conformist or jingoistic tone than Formby. Even in the run-up to war, the Riley films were already addressing serious issues through comedy, and this aspect was merely intensified by the war. These issues were, class and justice in *Old Mother Riley*, 1937; women and politics in *Old Mother Riley MP*, spies and the war effort in *Old Mother Riley in Paris* (1938 but re-released in 1942 with the war-related new title *Old Mother Riley Catches a Quisling*); joining up and fifth-column spying in *Old Mother Riley Joins Up*; rationing and black market racketeers in *Old Mother Riley Detective*. Although not overtly concerned with war issues, *Old Mother Riley in Business* (September 1940), with its theme of the "small man" pitted against vast business conglomerates, could be seen as a kind of parable in praise of the communal efforts of ordinary local people against remote quasi-fascist dictatorships.

The following ten Riley films were released between late 1938 and early 1945;

Old Mother Riley in Paris (November 1938 and 1942)
Old Mother Riley MP (August 1939)
Old Mother Riley Joins Up (November 1939)
Old Mother Riley in Society (April 1940)
Old Mother Riley in Business (September 1940)
Old Mother Riley's Ghosts (April 1941)
Old Mother Riley's Circus (November 1941)
Old Mother Riley Detective (January 1943)
Old Mother Riley Overseas (December 1943)
Old Mother Riley at Home (May 1945)

Some of these films have already received a degree of attention from critics, and others still await analysis, unlike the nine films released during the same period by "national symbol" George Formby. Robert Murphy notes that "In the atmosphere of gloom and anxiety preceding the war a rash of spy films had emerged; *Q Planes, The Spy in Black, Spies in the Air, Among Human Wolves, The Four Just Men, An Englishman's Home* and *Traitor Spy*."[204] And Jeffrey Richards also points out that "spy films appeared to predominate throughout 1939."[205] But *Old Mother Riley in Paris* was released in November 1938, beating them all to it. Murphy also points out that "the excitement and upheaval of being conscripted into the armed services" inspired a group of "joining up" films, and he lists *All at Sea, Laugh It Off, Old Bill and Son, Somewhere in England* and *Old Mother Riley Joins Up*. Jeffrey Richards also notes that by 1940 comic films about the services were in vogue, and that "even Arthur Lucan was inveigled into joining the ATS to prove that *Old Mother Riley Joins Up*. Joining up films were almost obligatory for comedians of note and the trend lasted well into 1941."[206] But what has never been pointed out is that far from needing to be "inveigled," Mother Riley once again actually led the way. All the films listed above were released in 1940 or 1941, but *Old Mother Riley Joins Up* was in cinemas in November 1939, before all the others. As we have already noted, when war was declared all public places of entertainment were closed by order. Most appropriately, one of the first new films to appear after the re-opening of the cinemas was *Old Mother Riley Joins Up*.

The film is a joining up comedy, a services comedy, and a spy catcher drama, all rolled into one, and seasoned with Mother Riley's inimitable music-hall madness. It was not only great fun, when fun was desperately needed, but it also took some serious patriotic swipes at a number of targets. Above all, it is one of the earliest films, possibly the very first, to single out for *unequivocal* praise the contribution which women would make to the war effort, not in the home but in the armed forces. Today, this may not at first seem particularly novel or courageous, but one has only to read the opening pages of Jeffrey Richards' chapter on "Women at War" to realize that in 1939 Mother Riley, and even Kitty, were not just brave but also well ahead of their time.[207] Richards quotes Sue Harper, who maintained that "a certain stubbornness, narrowness and puritanism" concerning women's role meant that "personnel at the Ministry of Information were unable to develop a propaganda theory that permitted a coherent mode of address to female audiences." Even in wartime there was an insistence on women's traditional role in the home as helper and housewife, celebrated in many films, beginning with the Ministry's own *They Also Serve* (1940), most famously in Lean and Coward's *In Which We Serve* (1942) and then, at the end of the war, in *The Way to the Stars* (1946), in which "woman as an integral part of the engine of war has been replaced by a more traditional construction of woman as domestic and maternal."[208] Jeffrey Richards points out that "only a handful of films was devoted exclusively to women on war service, notably *The Gentle Sex* (1943) (the ATS) and *The Lamp Still Burns* (1943) (nursing)." But *Old Mother Riley Joins Up* was four years ahead of these films in its treatment of joining up, nursing, and the ATS. Critics may object that these are just comic travesties but that is an oversimplification; the mere mention of certain topics in wartime lent them a degree of seriousness, a kind of symbolic subtext of which both the MOI and the Censors were sometimes aware, as we shall see.

In *Old Mother Riley Joins Up* this serious message was firmly rammed home during the film's opening credits, which appear over a sequence showing platoons of smartly uniformed ATS women on parade, while a hearty baritone sings a stirring marching song, "Hats Off to the Women of England." The Rileys do not appear in this sequence, which seems entirely serious in both intention and execution. It fact it probably constitutes the longest piece of film up to that point showing uniformed British women drilling for service.

In a curious way this opening foreshadows a number of scenes in Leslie Howard's *The Gentle Sex* (1943). In the opinion of some critics, Howard "pokes a finger in the eye of outdated patriarchal condescension with a wonderful line in teasing irony that runs from the title itself, through the first line of Howard's narration."[209] I am not so certain. In the opening scene the narrator, in mackintosh and trilby, stands with his back to the camera on a footbridge in a railway station, looking down on a busy concourse. His voice is heard as that of an omniscient male observer, almost a puppet-master, or worse, a Svengali. "Women, women all over the place. This station's seething with women rushing about. What good can it do them? They think they're helping, I suppose." He then proceeds to choose, with a very deliberate literary allusion to Pirandello, and still with his back to the camera, his six, then "seven characters in search of. . . ." What is troubling is that he selects his "characters" in language uncomfortably reminiscent of something far more sinister, namely a stalker's victims. Here are three examples; "She's in the bag . . ." "This one, she looks worth following . . ." "Let's have her!" Howard then quotes poems by Walter Scott and Keats, both examples of the theme of the fickle inconstancy of woman. "O, Woman! in our hours of ease,/ Uncertain, coy, and hard to please . . ." (Scott). "Woman! When I behold thee flippant, vain,/ Inconstant, childish, proud, and full of fancies . . ." (Keats). The film does go on largely to dismantle this view of women, but some critics still maintain that "viewed today, this drama seems unbearably patronizing." This judgment often feels nearer the mark, and I doubt that even with audiences in 1943 many would have had the sophistication to grasp any intended "teasing irony." In Howard's narrator's closing words, again an omniscient voice-over, and again filmed literally looking down on the women, he completely undoes any anachronistically "modern" view of women. Howard's tone is not so much one of teasing irony as of old-fashioned chivalry bordering on the extremes of gender stereotyping. In fact, in the closing sequence his blend of omniscience and condescension becomes almost offensive. "There they are, our sweethearts, sisters, mothers, daughters . . ." They are not, after all, women in their own right but literally men's creatures, "You strange, wonderful, incalculable creatures. . . ."

No such patronizing chivalry or ambiguity of attitude colors the opening song-sequence of *Old Mother Riley Joins Up*. The song is a stirring paean of praise from men who acknowledge wholeheartedly the competence of women: "Hats off, to the women of England!" (The "Hats off, gentlemen!" at the end of *The Gentle Sex* is quite different in tone.) Given the distinct ambivalence with which the establishment viewed the *de facto* emancipation of women made inevitable by the demands of war, the lyrics of the opening number to a cheap Mother Riley comedy, are actually the most generous and unstinted tribute to the war work of the women, not "women's work," uttered by anyone at the time.

The nation has a job to do,
And who are helping to see it through?
Hooray! The women of England!'
From office, mansion, kitchen, stage,
And every rank and every age,
That's grand, they're lending a hand.
They've heard the nation's call,
Those [unclear] one and all.
Hats off, to the women of England,
Hats off to the brave and the fair!
In their khaki and their blue,
A splendid job they do,
They're helping us grin, they're helping us win,
They'll see our brothers through.
Hats off, to the women of England,
Hats off to all the women volunteers,
They're typists, maids and cooks,
Chorus girls and stars,
They're students from their books,
And barmaids from their bars,
Hats off to the Women of England,
They're the pride of the [unclear]

After the film's opening credits, we see Mother Riley handsomely attired as a District Nurse. A parade of volunteers, boy scouts and firemen is commanded by a bumbling general (H. F. Maltby) who ends up getting a good circus-style soaking by the incompetent fire brigade. They are all rather silly *men*, but moments later Kitty Riley qualifies as a doctor and joins a recruiting center, and Mother Riley joins the ATS. Although the audience was well aware that some kind of mayhem was about to ensue, they also knew that the indomitable Riley would somehow win through in a way which transcended comedy and slapstick and made an oblique but unmistakable comment on some aspect of society.

While sharing the indignities experienced by women attempting to join up at enrolment centers, Mother Riley declares rather sharply to the woman officer who is handling her roughly, "I can take it." Riley's curiously acid-toned "I can take it" seems to be a very early, and quite probably deliberately sarcastic, example of the slogan which later became the title of the short propaganda film *London Can Take It*, produced by the MOI in 1940 for the American market; a shorter version for domestic consumption was called *Britain Can Take it*. The upbeat tone of official propaganda, particularly in BBC radio programs, was not universally appreciated, and many workers found it "smug, artificial and condescending." In February 1941, a special investigation on listeners' attitudes to the progress of the war reported that although it was "the thing" to say "We can take it," this superficial cheerfulness masked deeper dissatisfactions.[210]

But how did the expression "we can take it" come to play such a powerful part in wartime propaganda? In 2008 the military historian and biographer Carlo D'Este retold the official version in his *Warlord: A Life of Winston Churchill at War, 1874-1945*. After the first large-scale bombardments of the London docks in September 1940, Churchill made a point of rushing to the scenes of devastation. At an air-raid shelter where some forty people had been killed by a direct hit, he found a large crowd of mostly poor people. "One might have expected them to be resentful against the authorities responsible," recalled his military secretary, Gen. Hastings Ismay, "but as Churchill got out of his car, they literally mobbed him. 'Good old Winnie,' they cried. 'We thought you'd come and see us. We can take it. Give it 'em back.' Tears flowed down Churchill's cheeks at the sight before him. Ismay heard an elderly woman exclaim: 'You see, he really cares; he's crying.'"

The veracity of this touching anecdote has often been challenged, most memorably by an elderly woman who remembered being present at this incident. When interviewed for the 1973 Thames Television series *The World at War*, she recalled that when Churchill gave his two-finger salute and said "We can take it," a cockney woman shouted back, "You ain't f***ing taking it mister, we are." Ever conscious of his place in history, Churchill wove the incident into his speech to the House of Commons on 8 October 1940, as if to confirm the official version and airbrush the other from the record." Neither by material damage nor by slaughter will the people of the British Empire be turned from their solemn and inexorable purpose. . . On every side, there is the cry, 'We can take it,' but with it, there is also the cry, 'Give it 'em back.'" But over a year before either Churchill or the cockney woman, Mother Riley's "I can take it!" in her joining up film, had given the expression nationwide currency in the specific context of preparations for the coming onslaught.

The extraordinary conditions of war at times actually highlighted class difference rather than class solidarity. In *Old Mother Riley Joins Up*, while waiting in the joining-up queue, an upper-class young woman is idly chattering to her posh friend who says she too would dearly love to join up—were it not for the Pekinese pet dog in her arms. These spoilt feather-brained gals are then contrasted unfavorably with some working-class girls in the queue, plain Janes with thick accents and "common" voices, but who are nevertheless determined to lend a hand, even after their day-shift in a factory. The idealized egalitarianism expressed in the film's opening song gives way here, and again later, to some rather sharper views of persistent class differences even among women at war. By a fascinating coincidence the playwright Howard Brenton has used a heavily ironic, even sarcastic version of this "we can give it back" anecdote in his *The Churchill Play*, and critic William Worthen has commented that

> The class war continues but has been concealed from public view by Churchill's rhetorical integration of class interests in a national mythology. Churchill's image of a unified 'Island Race' urges a common national interest, but in practice this myth reduces the working classes to minstrel-show puppets, acted on by historical forces they cannot presume to change.[211]

Riley, the "minstrel-show puppet" par excellence, seems at times to have been uncannily aware of the political implications of the charade in which she, and the common people, were forced to participate. As Worthen puts it "in a society where theatrical performance is at once an act of submission and of transgression . . . those who live to please must please to live."[212]

Like *Old Mother Riley in Paris*, *Old Mother Riley Joins Up* is also a spy catcher yarn with a deadly earnest theme; dastardly Nazi collaborators will stop at nothing to acquire the blueprints of a top-secret new weapon, and only Old Mother Riley, District Nurse turned raw recruit, can foil their plans. But only after a series of hilarious pantomime and music hall routines; electrocuting a patient, pitching a tent in the dark and ending up clown-like at the top of the pole; a parodic shadow striptease from inside a lighted tent; a four-arms-in-one-coat dance routine accompanied by an Irish jig to underline its music hall provenance; sleepwalking in a nightdress on a bicycle, an un-gendered nightmare Quixotic quest; and most surreal of all, serving the General coffee from her hot water bottle, and a cake topped with fake cherries from an old hat, with icing patterned by her late husband's false teeth. In extremis, and against all the odds, Mother Riley triumphs over spies and collaborators and is awarded a medal (a "gong"), which she makes literal in the closing shot by awarding an enormous dinner gong to Kitty's latest fiancé. This glorious farrago of the irreverently surreal and the absurd probably provided greater catharsis for the industrial classes than all the pious exhortations from on high to "grin and bear it."

In *Old Mother Riley in Society* the war is present, but mostly by implication. This odd but interesting film could be said to fall into three distinct parts, each reflecting the preoccupations of its producer, John Baxter. First there is a celebration of pantomime and backstage theater life. Kitty's new life in high society, the ball and the restaurant scene, are clearly meant as an implied indictment of inequality and conspicuous consumption, which we shall discuss later. The final scenes hark back to Baxter's *Doss House*, as Mother Riley loses job after job, ending up in a doss house among kind-hearted down-and-outs, until she is found by the very Tug Mulligan she had rescued in the opening scene. *Old Mother Riley's Circus* may be said to be a pure comedy, providing a brief moment of respite and much-needed escapism from the grim realities of 1941, although in passing Riley does mention the Home Guard, spitfires, coupons and rationing. The film also served as a nostalgic final outing among his beloved clowns and liberty horses for veteran director Thomas Bentley. But the Lucans' major contribution to morale in 1941 and 1942, apart from the road show, was the radio series from Bangor, which we have already discussed.

Mother Riley's most magnificent and hilarious piece of war work was undoubtedly the 1943 film *Old Mother Riley Detective*. The *Kinematograph Weekly* of 14 January 1943 noted perceptively that "Although the picture is mainly robust domestic pantomime, it is near enough to life to remind Black Marketeers and other public pests that the working classes are not easy game."The film also contained Kitty's one really successful song, for once convincingly integrated into the plot. Brian McFarlane noted that "Lance Comfort contrives a very evocative moment as [Kitty] is joined by a burst of community singing in the factory canteen to the tune of 'Let the Wheels Go round Together.'"[213] This song is undoubtedly a deliberate echo of the title of the film *They Keep the Wheels Turning*, released the previous year, in which women persuade a reluctant garage owner that (rather like the women in *The Gentle Sex*) they can service heavy vehicles just as well as men. McFarlane felt that "this moment of patriotic consensual activity . . . is at odds with the rest of the film's raucous good fun." On the contrary, it seems to me to catch perfectly the film's mood and tone from the outset, when audiences must have been impressed to learn that Mother Riley cleans the offices without pay as her contribution to the war effort, and when invited by Inspector Cole she instantly agrees, with a flourish of her shawl to the camera, to become "Old Mother Riley, Detective." In Lucan's war films the "raucous good fun" is often firmly based around "patriotic consensual activity" but never quite adopts the deferential, establishment-friendly stance to be found in the Formby films. Indeed, Riley's altruism in accepting no pay immediately makes her appear suspect in the eyes of one police officer, whose own baser motives are thereby subtly implied.

A full analysis of the reception of the Mother Riley films in Ireland, and among the Irish in Britain, would demand a separate study, but a couple of aspects of Mother Riley, Ireland and the war need to be mentioned at this point. The Irish wartime film censors rigorously excised anything which seemed to compromise Ireland's neutrality, and that meant cutting many words and scenes from British and American films. But by and large Mother Riley was deemed a harmless comic turn, sending up the British establishment, and when *Old Mother Riley MP* reached Dublin in January1940 the *Irish Independent* reported,

> Humor in new Film. Old Mother Riley in bonnet and shawl, standing in the British parliament, forcibly pleading for the 'Washerwomen of England,' is one of the many humorous scenes in *Old Mother Riley MP* which was shown to the trade at the Stephen's Green Cinema, Dublin . . . For his

performance in the title role Arthur Lucan may be ranked with the leading comedians.

A further article entitled "Irish Artistes in Film" declares the film to be "beyond all doubt the finest in that delightfully entertaining series featuring the old lady who has become one of screenland's hit characters." Ireland had known and admired Arthur Lucan for many years and he seems to have been adopted as one of the few acceptable versions of the stage-Irish stereotype. But even that could pose problems.

At the end of 1941 the BBC began a series of broadcasts from Bangor entitled *Irish Half Hour*, a title angrily contested by the prime minister of British Northern Ireland, Lord Craigavon, who wanted the title changed to *Éire Half Hour*. Claire Willis explains that the program was "ostensibly designed for Irish people serving in the British forces, but the real target was the Irish audience at home." Jimmy O'Dea, a Dublin comedian who was also popular in Britain, starred in his famous travesty role as Biddy Mulligan, the Pride of the Coombe, and as a shopkeeper in a series of skits on Irish small town life set in the fictitious Ballygobackwards, a forerunner perhaps of Llareggub in Dylan Thomas's *Under Milk Wood*, written thirteen years later. There were also more elevated contributions from singers of the caliber of Count John McCormack and Cavan O'Connor. The British press attaché in Dublin, John Betjeman, thought the program was of great propaganda value to Britain, at a time when Germany was making weekly broadcasts to Ireland in both English and Irish, a reminder that there was a darker and more serious side to Anglo-Irish relations at this time. Although Ireland, officially at least, remained neutral, senior members of the now banned IRA openly advocated Nazi help in removing Britain from the six northern counties, and they were in close and regular contact with members of Hitler's government. For his part, Lord Craigavon actively encouraged an invasion of the South. He wrote to Churchill in 1940 requesting that troops be used to install a new government in Dublin that would allow British ships to gain access to neutral Irish ports before they fell to the Nazis.[214]

Irish Half Hour might have been more effective as propaganda if there had been enough batteries in Ireland to power the radios.

But even then, as Claire Willis points out, with its "watered-down stereotypes of well-meaning, hopelessly disorganized Paddies with a fondness for drink," especially coming from the BBC, the show did not go down well with Irish listeners, and one Dublin critic claimed O'Dea "rivalled in vulgarity any stage Irishman performance of other years." By a curious coincidence, the two most famous stage-Irish "biddies" of all time, the Irishman O'Dea and the Englishman Lucan, were both in Bangor in 1942 (having great fun together, much to Kitty's annoyance) both recording for the BBC but for ostensibly different audiences. Whereas Mother Riley and Kitty were heard by millions and were unashamedly part of the British propaganda war effort, *Irish Half Hour* seems to have had a very limited audience in Ireland and any reference to, for instance, the reality of massive emigration was simply glossed over. In 1940-1941 alone, more than sixty thousand Irish people came to work in Britain. This was played down by the Irish media, and never mentioned in O'Dea's Ballygobackwards on the BBC, as it would certainly have been removed by the Irish censors. Pat Hillyard, Assistant Director of Variety at Bangor, was also worried by the forthcoming juxtaposition of the two brands of Irishness, and felt that *Irish Half Hour* and *Old Mother Riley* should not be broadcast on the same night. He gave several reasons for this: "*Old Mother Riley* which is phony Irish (Kitty McShane being Irish and always singing Irish numbers, and Arthur Lucan being Liverpool Irish) would run 8.15 to 9.00 p.m. on Saturday with *Irish Half Hour*, a program wholly Irish in conception following twenty minutes later at 9.20 to 9.50. Jimmy O'Dea and Arthur Lucan, the comedians of the two shows, each play 'dame.'" It was clearly felt that the clash of real and phony Irish might well ruffle sensibilities, so *Irish Half Hour* was moved to Tuesday nights.

Surprising though it may seem, the Irish censors did vet the Riley films, not all of which found their way instantly across the Irish Sea, because some clearly contained material which would have violated Irish neutrality. Although thousands of Southern Irish people were serving in the British forces, the Irish media were supposed to ignore the fact, and this undoubtedly explains why the film *Old Mother Riley Joins Up*, released in Britain in 1939, and celebrating the war effort of "The Women of England," was not released in Ireland until January 1942, three whole years late, by which time it was felt it could be seen as a harmless send-up. The film ran for just a week in Dublin and had a few showings around the country in 1942 and 1943. In Nenagh it was described as the Lucans' latest film, in which "they are in their glory as they turn the British Army upside down with their quaint antics . . . A feast of honest to goodness fun and a real cure for the Blackout Blues." The film then disappeared from Irish cinemas for ten years.

On a much darker note, there is in the Riley films just one example, but a glaring example, of a deeply insulting image of the Irish. I refer to the hideous portrait of Mother Riley's late husband, which is seen in the opening and final scenes of *Old Mother Riley's Ghosts*. At a time when thousands of Irishmen from all parts of the divided island were fighting in the British armed forces, it seems deeply regrettable that the scriptwriters and the censors were blissfully indifferent to a caricature of a racially degenerate, almost simian "Paddy" of the kind that had filled the pages of *Punch* in the nineteenth century; this does however reveal the degree to which the Irish could still be mocked and used as the butt of racial humor. I am neither hypersensitive on this matter, nor am I the first to point it out. Martin McLoone sees British cinematic representations of the Irish as innately violent and irrational, a "simian primitive" image from "a tradition of representation that continues to influence British perceptions of the Irish even today." McLoone refers to a simian caricature of Irish terrorists in the *Evening Standard* in 1982, and follows this with a reference to John Hill's view that "The effect of this cinematic tradition is to reinforce the ideological assumptions of nineteenth-century imagery, even if the cinema has rarely reproduced its crudity. He does refer to one film, *Old Mother Riley's Ghosts* from 1941, which comes close."[215] In the light of all this, there is no doubt in my mind that part of the success and appeal of Lucan's anarchic dame on the one hand, and her aspiring daughter on the other, lay in the psychological labyrinth of British cultural (formerly imperial) perceptions of the Irish, real or "stage," assimilating and "normalizing" Kitty, but in the case of her mother, often straying dangerously back toward what Lance Pettitt has called the "mayhem, mystery and madness that is 'Irishness.'"

Brian McFarlane praised director Lance Comfort's wartime "moment of patriotic consensual activity" when Kitty is joined in a burst of community singing in the factory canteen. But what critics have failed to point out about this, and many other scenes in the Riley films in general, is the rather delicately topical fact that Kitty McShane was not just genuinely Irish, but unmistakably southern Irish, hailing from the neutral Republic. As we have already noted, in 1940-1941 alone, more than 60, 000 Irish people came to work in Britain; even more noteworthy is the fact that a remarkably high proportion of these emigrants were single women. Between 1926 and 1936, and 1946 and 1951, more women than men left Ireland; work in America had become scarcer with the Depression, and Irish emigrants were required to provide £100 in capital or a guarantor. As a result, increasing numbers of young women, including many pregnant single women, came to England.[216] Louise Ryan, drawing upon Irish newspapers of the period, has suggested that the figure of the "emigrant girl" was central to Irish post-colonial discourses on emigration. She points out that "during the 1930s, the emigration of thousands of young Irish women to English cities such as London sparked widespread comment and criticism. The Irish press and the Catholic hierarchy in particular propagated an image of these vulner- able young women as lost and alone in the big, bad cities of England . . . Through her transgression of physical, cultural and religious spaces, she [the emigrant girl] encountered loneliness, danger and the risk of denationalization."[217]

When viewed in the light of these contemporary facts, Kitty's "Irish colleen" character acquires a new dimension and a deeper contemporary significance. For the thousands of young female Irish cinema-goers in Britain in the 1930s and 1940s, Kitty McShane became a reassuring role model. She constituted living proof that, in spite of the strictures of a stiflingly intolerant Catholic hierar- chy, and the resentment of diehard Republicans back home, there was in fact a safe place in British society for decent, hard-working Irish girls. They could find congenial employment and a degree of financial independence unheard of in Ireland. Like Kitty, they could "save up a few shillings to buy myself some nice new clothes" and perhaps, if they had the luck of Kitty Riley, they might even find a handsome English gentleman to lead them to the altar. For ordinary working-class young women, especially in the Irish diaspora, even Kitty's outrageously frilly frocks and onstage wedding gowns could be seen to have a symbolic significance, as the glittering and desirable alternatives to the drab hand-me-downs and clothing parcels from America on which so many ordinary people in Ireland depended at the time. For all the faults which Kitty's critics never tire of pointing out, her demonstrably immense popularity in the 1930s and 1940s was undoubtedly due in part to her following among aspiring Irish immigrant girls, many far prettier than she had ever been, who must have thought to themselves as they sat in the darkened cinemas, "If Kitty can make it, so can I!"

But above all else, Mother Riley's war work, her "target for tonight" as she once called Kitty's latest boyfriend, was to make the nation laugh and, perhaps even more effectively than Churchill's rhetoric, to raise the morale of the "industrial classes" in Britain's darkest hour. A telling illustration of this view has survived in a press photograph taken at the height of the blitz in September 1940. So powerful was the Riley effect that, even when she was not actually in the air raid shelters, her familiar and comforting presence was evoked to raise the spirits of bombed-out EastEnders. In the photograph, an enthusiastic crowd, mostly women and girls, watch as Marie Tully performs her impersonation of Old Mother Riley. The caption on the verso states (for the benefit of American readers) "Night Life in London. Marie Tully gave a brilliant impersonation of Old Mother Riley, a comedy character in British films, during 'Amateur Hour' in the Shoreditch Library air raid shelter. Meanwhile, Nazi bombs were falling on the outside city. 10/18/40."

In July 1940 the Lucans had contributed to the Ministry of Information's propaganda entertainment entitled "Rout the Rumor Rally" in Hendon Park. But by far the clearest evidence that the Lucans were consciously and actively involved in government war-time propaganda is to be found in several memoranda preserved in the BBC files at Caversham. Before the recording of the first episode of *Old Mother Riley Takes the Air* in 1941, Tom Ronald sent an internal memo to the Director of Variety sketching out the show's running order. The memo ends as follows: "Finale sketch called 'Old Mother Riley Goes to It.' The gist of it is that Kitty McShane has decided that she must do some form of war-work and naturally Mother Riley will not allow her daughter to start before she herself has sampled it. The first sketch in mind is that of a police-woman." This would seem to be the origin of the 1942 Columbia gramophone sketch *Old Mother Riley in the Police Force*, during which Mother says, "The men have gone from it and we must go to it!" Similarly, as we noted earlier, the gramophone sketch *Old Mother Riley on the Farm* is clearly an allusion to the trials and tribulations of "townie" girls in the Women's Land Army. Although Arthur's scripts for the radio sketches have not been published or studied, it seems reasonable to assume that they shared material with the gramophone sketches and the wartime films, and this suggests that, far from having propaganda material foisted on him, Arthur, supported by Kitty, was eager to contribute his own original comedy material with a strong patriotic twist. Firm evidence for this is to be found in another BBC Internal Memorandum, circulated by Tom Ronald in April 1942, just before the second radio series:

> "I went to see Lucan and McShane about the forthcoming series of Old Mother Riley and they told me that they are anxious to do some indirect propaganda in the show. This will in no way be blatant but just a sort of small pill with a lot of sugar coating. One idea they gave me was that Old Mother Riley was going to paper her kitchen. She stopped to think and realizes that she will be using a cupful of flour to make the paste, and if 12 million women in England decide to use this cupful of flour for papering their kitchen, the waste of flour in shipping space runs out to about 300 and something tons. The kitchen, instead of being re-papered, is washed down. This, of course, is just the bare outline and will be put over with the usual Mother Riley cracks.
>
> Lucan and McShane are perfectly prepared to get directions from time to time on any point of propaganda the Ministries may require, and they will do their best to write round these various things. I shall be grateful if you can let me know whether they may go ahead with this as they are now busy preparing scripts."

Approval was granted on 17 April, and this may have inspired Arthur to draw on the 1939 film *Old Mother Riley Joins Up* to create the "very amusing" ATS sketch to which Sybil Rowse referred in her letters. But if Arthur thought this particular sketch would be welcomed as a sugar-coated propaganda pill he was gravely mistaken. Instead, it drew a severe rebuke from the Director of Program Planning himself. On 23 July, G. D. Adams wrote to the Director of Variety, "Major Maschwitz told me today that Old Mother Riley has joined the ATS. This is not a good idea vis-à-vis the War Office and all the things we are trying to do. Could you please have her drafted back to civilian life by next Saturday."The fact that Maschwitz should have concerned himself with the doings of Mother Riley is quite astonishing, but it reveals the degree to which government departments infiltrated every aspect of public life in wartime. The vigilant Major Eric Maschwitz, who had had a long career in music, film and theater, was, by 1939, a high-ranking member of the Intelligence services. From November 1939, he served with the Secret Intelligence Service (Section sabotage). In 1940, he was assigned to the Special Operations Executive (SOE) and the Intelligence Corps. In 1942, he supervised radio programs for the troops, before transferring to the Political Warfare Executive (PWE). He ended the war as chief broadcasting officer with the 21st Army Group, leaving the army as a Lieutenant-Colonel.[218] There is a handwritten note by Pat Hillyard on the memorandum, confirming that the orders from on high were promptly obeyed; "Old Mother Riley back in civvies as requested." The ATS had just become a sensitive issue because, after secret trials in 1941 to assess their suitability, women were being incorporated (not without controversy) into male regiments to operate heavy searchlight equipment. Training had begun at nearby Rhyl, and the War Office would not tolerate frivolous or ambiguous publicity. So for once, even the anarchic and fearless "*Brünnhilde* of the back streets" was obliged to toe the line; but, as she put it a year later in *Old Mother Riley Detective*, "It's me war work!"

Without a doubt, throughout the war, whether on radio, gramophone, cinema screens, or live on stage and dodging the bombs as in South Shields, Old Mother Riley and her daughter Kitty helped not just Londoners but the whole nation to "take it," and in doing so they won the people's abiding gratitude and affection—and £30,000 a year! In 1940 Gracie Fields had had to leave Britain to save her Italian husband from possible internment. This was seen by many, quite unfairly, as a form of desertion. In an odd way, Mother Riley for a time took Gracie's place as the nation's favorite feisty working-class gal! After World War I, comedians George Robey and Harry Lauder had been honored, but only for their wartime charity work. After World War II, George Formby was awarded the OBE in 1946 for his contribution to the war effort, and "Our Gracie," reinstated as a national treasure, was finally made a Dame in 1979.[219] But, as a perfect example of what John Major has called "an institutionalized animus against music hall performers,"[220] Arthur Lucan's sterling efforts were studiously ignored by an establishment that was always unsure whether it mostly despised Old Mother Riley ... or feared her.

Chapter Fifteen: "A Bit of Scrag End." Images of Food in the Riley Films

The role of food imagery in cinema is not without considerable sociological interest, and images of food are of major symbolic significance in the Riley films. As James Keller has shown in his discussion of "the multiplicity of roles that culinary imagery can play in contemporary cinema," in many films food functions as a symbolic actor, and its images may be used as powerful markers of, among many other things, differences of gender, class and culture. Many of the food images in the world of Riley are far from the joyful, hyperbolic scenes of culinary abundance to be found, for instance, in the film *Babette's Feast*, or in Mikhail Bakhtin's celebration of the Rabelaisian literary banquet. In fact they are frequently the very opposite; images of a dearth or absence of food. As Keller has pointed out, "the reductive assumption that food in film always signifies desire reveals a very limited scrutiny of the body of works in this sub-genre."[221] Whereas Keller discusses food images in the context of erotic or other plea-surable desires, in most of the Riley films, especially those made during the war, images of hunger, shortage and rationing figure most prominently.

Food rationing in Britain came into force in 1940 and continued long after the end of the war. On 8 January 1940, bacon, butter and sugar were rationed. They was soon followed by meat, tea, jam, bis-cuits, breakfast cereals, cheese, eggs, lard, milk and canned and dried fruit. Strict rationing inevitably created a black market, and many things could still be had plentifully, but only for the right money. For this reason, any food images of upper-class or Rabelaisian abun-dance in the Riley war films are invested with ironic or judgmental intent, even in apparently comic contexts. Already, in the long, lean years before the war, unemployment and poverty had made shortages of food a fact of everyday working-class life. Riley's home address was "Ration Row, not far from the gas works," signaling to cinema audiences that she was not a film star in the usual sense but dwelt among ordinary people and shared their frugal lot. The presence of food images, and references to foods, real or figurative, may not be as profound or complex in the Riley films as those discussed by Gregory Stephens with reference to the films of Chaplin, but they are no less real or omnipresent, and they do have a clear symbolic function.[222]

Before the war, in *Old Mother Riley in Paris* (1938), there was steak and kidney pudding, but all mention (bar one) of steak then disappears until 1952. Even then, Mother Riley tells Baron van Housen, "I must be going now. You see, I left a bit of scrag end on to simmer." And Riley audiences were often reminded that merely boiling a kettle was dependent on being able to scrape together a shilling to put into the gas meter, something far beneath consideration in the charmed world of the Jack Hulberts and Cicely Courtneidges. When there *is* food to be had, Mother Riley, and decent British working-class people, like it plain. At breakfast on her first morning in the Briggs household, the butler informs Riley that they have "almost anything." "Have you got any bloaters?" she asks. "Any saveloys?" When told that they do not she says "I wonder what they live on in this house?" She finally settles for haddock, a "fat un" not a Finnan, and washes it down with cocoa.

The most basic items of working-class diet, a wedge of bread and butter and a cup of tea, are Mother Riley's attempted peace offering when, in *Old Mother Riley at Home*, Kitty threatens to leave home after a row. Mother leaves them outside Kitty's locked bedroom door, and Lucan's mimed gesture of bafflement and resignation at the refusal of the offering is one of the many genuinely touching examples of his silent performative skills. In *Old Mother Riley's Ghosts*, while sitting on a park bench, Mother Riley shares her sandwiches with a homeless stranger; this kind action of sharing simple food sets the plot rolling when the stranger turns out to be the brilliant inventor John Cartwright (silent film heart-throb John Stuart) who will eventually marry Kitty.

Another staple food item is the humble sausage, but now even further demeaned to become the cheap, adulterated sausage of wartime; when the lodger protests that sausages shouldn't be stored in the bread bin Riley retorts, "What d'you think these are made of?" As we note elsewhere, sausages also have a figurative, comic function; "he hates me like a sausage hates a frying pan;" "We made our money in sausages." And the hoary old, "How long will tea be, Ma?" "About four inches; it's a sausage!" (Compare Dan Leno's waiter sketch;

"How long would your steak be? Oh, about four inches I should say, about four inches.") Norman Robbins history of the evolution of pantomime is actually called *Slapstick and Sausages*. When in *Old Mother Riley in Society*, mother buys "A bit of middle and a few chips," as a treat for Kitty's supper, she is referring to the middle portion of a fish fillet, slightly better quality than the thin end, known as "a bit of tail." Fish and chips even manage to function here simultaneously for comedy and for pathos. Kitty is out late (again) so mother puts her fish and chips in the oven. They are devoured by drunken Tug Mulligan, who then passes out on the floor; in stark contrast to this homely squalor, Kitty, who has still not returned home, is being lavishly wined and dined elsewhere in far grander style than mother could ever hope to provide. Scenes such as these frequently highlight the contrast between Mother's adherence to simple working-class values, and Kitty's constant desire to rise above them.

Canned foods such as tinned salmon and sardines, peaches and pineapple, allowed the workers a cheap version of the dishes enjoyed in their fresh forms by the middle and upper classes; cans were often kept in the cupboard for a special occasion, and so became a form of savings, to be "spent" on high days and holidays. In *Old Mother Riley's Ghosts*, Mother plans to celebrate Jem the lodger's teaming up with the inventor, an unusual alliance of working and upper-middle class characters based on their equality of knowledge and ability. "I'm going to let myself go!" she announces, and produces a tin of salmon *and* a tin of peaches, saying "I've never had both together before!" When Kitty returns from work and reveals that she has been fired, Mother puts the peaches back in the cupboard and says "I hope you won't mind having the salmon without the peaches." When Jem enters and admits that he too has been fired, Mother slowly and sadly puts the salmon back into the cupboard and closes the door. The posh inventor gets the last (rationed) boiled egg in the house, and Jem has to make do with the water it was boiled in. As far back as "Bridget's Night Out" (1934), hard-up mother had offered to throw a party for Bridget by opening a tin of sardines and making a *strong* cup of tea, and as late as *Old Mother Riley Headmistress* (1950), when fire breaks out at the school mother saves her precious tins of still-rationed foods from under her pillow; her "invasion rations" as she quaintly calls them four years after the end of the war consist this time of a tin of pilchards and a tin of pineapple. Working-class reliance on a number of familiar tinned foods persisted long after Mother Riley hung up her tin opener, but she was surely unique in making them a symbolic marker of class distinction on stage and screen.

In many films, those who disdain simple food and drink are *ipso facto* suspect, and all elaborate or exotic foodstuffs which deviate from the homely British norm are usually a sign of some kind of snobbery or lack of authenticity, social, political or personal. In the war films this immediately signals the unpatriotic proclivities of spies, collaborators or empty-headed upper class twits. Restaurants in the Riley films function as privileged spaces in which the alimentary incompatibility of the classes is given comic demonstration. When, in a contravention of the solemn laws of the maternal melodrama, Mother and Kitty actually attempt to dine out together, glorious mayhem usually ensues. Mother Riley loves to lampoon the middle-class conventions of fine dining in elegant restaurants, and in several films she tries to bluff her way through her total ignorance of menus and manners, a recurrent theme of class-based comedy. Riley's table manners, or rather her lack of them, are rarely used to belittle her but are often used to exemplify her inability (or unwillingness) to conform to society's taboos and conventions. In the very first film, the wealthy Briggs family is horrified by the gross table manners of the old Match-seller they have been forced to take under their roof. At dinner she regales the Bishop with graphic descriptions of her indigestion. "Have you ever been under a railway bridge when a train went over? Well . . . ."

She noisily slurps her soup (a habit, says the hostess, picked up during her "rescue work") and she tips blancmange over the Bishop, a clear reference to a panto slop-scene. The diners are also shocked by Kitty's ignorance during dinner-table small-talk. When told that a Briggs ancestor died at Waterloo she enquires "Which platform?" Mother makes things worse by chiding her with "As if it mattered which platform!" (And she calls her Bridget instead of Kitty!) The stuffy formality of the dinner scene is highlighted when Riley's cockney ex-neighbors invade the house and, when invited to eat, spurn the dining room and instead go off singing and dancing to the more convivial kitchen. Another take on the artificiality, and cultural relativity, of table manners is to be found in *Old Mother Riley's New Venture*. When an Arab sheikh is Mother Riley's guest at a dinner party, the ignorance of etiquette all round, rather than becoming a racial or cultural slur, becomes a surreal and silly pantomime turn, as all the diners play stand-up-sit-down like O'Grady in the party game, and then slurp the contents of their finger bowls.

Like the finger bowls, the food consumed in high class establishments is depicted as elaborate, artificial, and therefore inauthentic. The very fact that a menu is in French is enough to make it not only pretentious but in 1938 politically suspicious, and in need of comic deflation. In *Old Mother Riley in Paris*, when dining in an elegant Parisian restaurant Riley decides to treat the incomprehensible menu as a racing card, and pick a winner with a pin. Pointing to the menu she says, "I'll have that an' that an' that an' that!" To which the waiter replies, "You can't have that Madam, that's the manager." When the manager takes her order, Mother tries to hide her ignorance by prissily repeating "Just a trifle" to whatever he proposes. This is taken literally by the waiters, who bring her a trolley loaded with dishes of trifle, thus providing her with the ammunition to end the scene with a circus or pantomime style custard pie attack on the other hapless diners.

A restaurant provides the setting for a more serious scene in *Old Mother Riley in Society*, the irony of which has escaped critics, too eager to condemn Baxter's supposed sentimentality. Mother Riley, homeless, destitute and estranged from Kitty, is washing up in the kitchen of a smart restaurant when she sees a whole chicken breast returned uneaten on a plate. She wraps it in a handkerchief and hides it under her shawl "in the family chest." Wartime working-class audiences would have sympathized with this, and disapproved not of Riley's petty pilfering but of the conspicuous waste of the restaurant diners among whom, by a perfect paradox, is Riley's own upwardly mobile daughter and her posh husband. At the beginning of the war, restaurants were not rationed and the rich could supplement their rations by dining out. Popular resentment against such glaring displays of inequality eventually led to food and price regulation in restaurants, so the glamorous restaurant scene in *Old Mother Riley in Society* served a propaganda purpose that is lost on today's audiences and critics. Another bitter-sweet touch in this restaurant scene is that the plaintive melody "No Matter Where You Are," which Kitty (dubbed by Celia Lipton) had earlier sung in the pantomime *Aladdin*, is now being played by the restaurant orchestra as a bright upbeat dance tune. This gives an ironic twist to Kitty's supposed anxiety about her lost mother, who is just yards away in the kitchens. This scene would have been more effective if Kitty as an actress could handle pauses in lines, and if she hadn't been gazing strangely off set and away from her husband while speaking to him, as if distracted by an invisible passer-by, a trick she repeats in a number of films.

But the wartime scriptwriters' deepest opprobrium was reserved for well-heeled, well-upholstered crooks, who profited from the hunger of others through the black market in food. This is the main theme of *Old Mother Riley Detective* (1943) and it is driven home by an upper-class but, for once, sympathetic detective, Inspector Cole, who explains to a momentarily deferential Riley in a rather pious propaganda speech that "The Food Controller is the mother of the whole nation, and his job is to see that everybody gets a fair share of food." Mother Riley is enlisted to help catch the suspected black market villain, the factory owner Mr. Popplethwaite. In a polished music-hall routine related to Lucan's Step washer sketch, Riley wheedles her way past Popplethwaite's housekeeper (played by Marjorie Rhodes) and into the kitchen where she sees well-stocked cupboards and shelves laden with ill-gotten food and drink beyond the wildest dreams of ordinary people. To help Inspector Coles, Kitty and Mother (once again in double travesty) manage to get themselves invited to dine out with the villain Popplethwaite, so that they can gather incriminating evidence of his unpatriotic racketeering. Mother Riley, masquerading as the beautifully dressed Mrs. Montgomery-Jones, is in one of her frequent lah-di-dah disguises, and this prompts a glorious moment at table when Mr. Popplethwaite addresses her by the posh pseudonym which she has by now completely forgotten. Lucan gives Popplethwaite a sudden look of utter stupefaction and says gruffly "Who?" Popplethwaite says, "I thought you said your name was Mrs. Montgomery-Jones?" Lucan, recovering his composure and his persona, lisps, "Oh yes, of course. Quite! But at the moment I'm travelling *in magneto*." (Riley elsewhere repeats her penchant for Latin malapropism when she tells her lawyer that something may be done *pro bono Pimlico*.)

When ordering dinner, Mrs. Montgomery-Jones first notes that the food is very expensive, "twice as dear as a milk bar," but then she deliberately conjures up a dream menu to tantalize hungry working-class audiences. "A nice juicy steak, four eggs on the top of one chip, some buttered toast and a cup of char." For rationed cinemagoers in 1943, this menu was utterly unobtainable, and restaurant scenes such as this and the one in *Old Mother Riley in Society*, even with comic interpolations, would have genuinely annoyed or angered the working classes who were surviving on ration-book coupons and "digging for victory." The mood of class-related luxury in this scene is further intensified when Mother is serenaded at her table by the violinist Alfredo Campoli, one of the finest classical musicians of the day. In using Riley to provoke the righteous indignation of the masses, director Lance Comfort seems to concur with his mentor John Baxter's belief that she was a far more efficacious communicator than official propaganda films. As we noted earlier, Baxter firmly believed that Riley's audiences left the cinema "with propaganda seeds planted in their mind to gain fruition later." In the final Riley film, *Mother Riley meets the Vampire* (1952), there was one last reference to food, when Baron von Housen (Bela Lugosi) offers to feed Riley a big juicy steak. Apart from its place in the plot, this first Riley film serving of beef since 1938 clearly celebrates the audience's knowledge that the worst of rationing was at last coming to an end. "Ooh, lead me to it!" says the lean and hungry Dame who for years had survived on bread-filled sausages, scrag-end, and "a bit of middle and a few chips."

Many of the preceding observations apply as much to drinking as to eating. Decent working people drink tea, beer or stout, and perhaps an occasional drop of gin. Coffee, wines, liqueurs and spirits are the dangerously exotic, quasi-immoral preserve of the middle and upper classes. Drink is inevitably used on occasion to signal Mother Riley's stereotypical Irishness; "Tipsy? There isn't enough of that stuff to make me dizzy let alone tipsy!" And asked by Kitty if whiskey improves with age, Mother replies, "The older I get the better I like it!" But images of drinking have some wider uses, especially to suggest the egalitarian conviviality of the old fashioned, English pub; *Old Mother Riley Overseas* (1943) begins with Mother Riley as the jovial landlady of the "Slip Inn," and ends back in the crowded pub where Kitty leads the singing of "There's no folk like the old folks ..."

The end of all food rationing in Britain did not come until July 1954, by which time Old Mother Riley, who should have been on her way to the planet Mars, had been dead for two months. But back in 1947-1948, Arthur Lucan as the Nurse in *Babes in the Wood* at the Bristol Hippodrome had brought politics into pantomime by singing the comedy chorus song "O Where Is My Sunday Potato?" While apparently light-hearted, the song was in fact a complaint about the potato rationing brought in in 1947 by the Labor government. The BBC briefly refused to pass the song for broadcasting, as its contrasting images of dearth and plenty might be construed as politically biased. By a curious coincidence, in the very same year, in David Lean's classic film of *Oliver Twist* there is a stunning example of the juxtaposition of images of hunger and plenty, in a scene not found in Dickens' novel but created by Lean and his fellow-scenarist Stanley Haynes, "writing in pictures," as Lean once put it. After the scene of the orphans eating their gruel in the canteen, the camera cuts to the workhouse overseers who are caught greedily feasting around a table laden with roast meats and pies. This seventy-four second scene is entirely silent apart from the repulsive noises of crunching, chomping and chewing made by the self-absorbed diners who are oblivious to the fact that Oliver and the orphans, "voracious and wild with hunger," are gazing longingly down on them from a gallery, like prisoners behind an iron grille. For avid cinemagoers at the time, this moment of high cinematic expressionism may well have brought to mind the image of Kitty McShane in a posh restaurant while her mother stole scraps from the scullery.

At a much lighter level, and in a way reminiscent of Chaplin, Mother Riley sometimes used objects in a deliberately absurd or inappropriate manner, as props to create the comedy of incongruity. Sausages in the bread bin; chicken in the "family chest;" cocoa for breakfast; fake cherries from an old hat on a cake patterned with her late husband's false teeth; coffee served from a hot water bottle; tinned food stored under her pillow. A large codfish on Mother Riley's fishmonger's slab looks up and speaks, so Mother says to her customer, "Oh! I haven't the heart! Have a kipper instead!" One of my favorite scenes of incongruity is in *Old Mother Riley in Society*. Mother, masquerading as Kitty's maid, arrives at the Morgan household and refuses to go round to the back door. "Straightforward Riley, that's me," she says, as she hands her bag to the horrified butler. "Here, take that, and show me to my room. I'm absolutely dying to loosen my corsets." Tea is served to Lady Morgan, but Mother Riley, the new maid, assumes it is for her. When Lady Morgan curtly explains, "Tea for one," Riley, unfazed, replies, "When are you having yours?" Then, realizing her mistake but undeterred, Riley blows down the teapot spout and drains Lady Morgan's teacup before declaring, "I was right, no sugar." We instantly understand that the egalitarian and non-conformist Riley will not last long "in Society," and she soon discovers that she is viewed as "a square peg in a round hole."

Whether in all-star movie classics or ramshackle Riley quota quickies, images of food and drink have often been used to condense and suggest lengthy and more complex arguments, their visual immediacy speaking louder—and faster—than words.

Chapter Sixteen: Unruly Women, Dangerous Dowagers and Old Mother Riley

In *Picturing the Past: The Rise and Fall of the British Costume Film*, Sue Harper notes that after the war, at the British Board of Film Classification, led by the prudish Colonel John Hanna, "Particular scorn was reserved for figures like Old Mother Riley and Frank Randle who appealed to a working-class audience," and Philip Gillett makes this crucial observation:

> Frank Randle and Old Mother Riley offer the escapism of preposterous plots involving larger-than-life characters. They rehearsed attitudes to employers which many workers must have yearned to emulate. If audiences never tried, they could at least leave the cinema with a healthy cynicism towards middle-class pomposity.[223]

To paraphrase Philip Gillett, Mother Riley also rehearsed attitudes and behavior towards men which many working-class women must have yearned to emulate, but outrageous and uninhibited self-expression was not the kind of behavior which the establishment now wished to foster among the post-war masses, especially the women. And it was not simply because Randle and Lucan were "as common as muck" that they were so severely judged but, far more ominously, precisely because they stirred up in their audiences, both male and female, the very fantasies of insubordination which were no longer to be encouraged. Andrew Spicer notes that the dark days of war provided a "liminal licensed space" for the lovable male fools and rogues of the Music Hall, and that Lucan, Formby, Hay and the Crazy Gang were followed by Arthur Askey, Tommy Handley, Frank Randle and Tommy Trinder, all of whose films "battled the pompous, the pretentious, the bullies and the kill-joys ... They had the license to mock constituted authority ... in the name of cheery 'common sense.'" But, as Spicer goes on to show, by the end of the war the individualistic insubordination of these various cheeky chappies was no longer deemed appropriate, and director Michael Balcon for one, was reluctant "to endorse an image of a self-assured and devil-may-care working class masculinity."[224] In such a climate, what chance did Mother Riley stand?

In *Women in British Cinema: Mad, Bad and Dangerous to Know*, Sue Harper may have caught exactly what it was that Colonel Hanna and his post-war censorship cronies found both so distasteful in general, and so disturbing about Old Mother Riley in particular. Harper points out that what she calls "Difficult Dowager" roles played by women in 1930s films did address "the big issues: desire, decay, death and revenge," but within the boundaries of certain social norms. She also acknowledges that these female stereotypes in 1930s cinema did "question stable gender definitions," concluding that "their playful assumption of masculine behavior is transgressive, but its edge is blunted by the comedy, and it serves to return the audience to a sense of comfort in the status quo."[225] Discussing a similar theme, Geoff King notes that "we laugh at figures that do not conform, thus reinforcing the solidity of our own often precarious identities."[226] Sue Harper goes on to show that film images of women after the war stressed the need for a return to traditionally gendered stereotypes, with the "desirable" female roles of good mothers and supportive wives re-assigned to their subordinate position within the patriarchal framework of the resurgent pre-war status quo. Sue Harper does, however, specifically acknowledge the exceptional case of Mother Riley: "We cannot discuss older, unruly females without dealing with the films of Old Mother Riley. In all the Old Mother Riley films, the heroine outrages the canons of good taste and is uninhibited in her pursuit of self-expression ... the fact that 'she' *is* a man deliberately muddies the issue." It does more than muddy the issue; the fact that Mother Riley is a man means that his/her transgressive "Difficult Dowager" comedy cannot be "blunted" by a return to a status quo ante which did not exist. In fact, as Lawrence Napper has noted, she simply "refuses to modify behavior ... reveling in the chaos she creates," and unlike, say, George Formby or, later, Norman Wisdom, "she displays no anxiety about the fact."[227]

For Sue Harper, the "ladies of misrule" do at least "usher in a short saturnalia, in which anarchy and bad behavior are the just rewards for a long life of conformity." Harper's perceptive observation was instinctively understood in Arthur Lucan's own day by Mother Riley's hugely loyal following, long after the war, among ordinary working-class women; theater managers called them "Arthur's Ladies," and many of them, as we noted earlier, accompanied their hero to his grave in Hull's Eastern Cemetery. I believe that the word "ladies" has to be heard with the inverted commas of irony. The father of a friend of mine remembered going to see Mother Riley at the Sunderland Empire in the late 1940s and when he came home he told his family that not only was the theater packed, but it was packed with what he called "fishwives." For these often downtrodden working women, Riley's belligerence and insubordination must have offered—albeit temporarily in the darkness of the cinema or theater—a form of catharsis, a kind of vicarious revenge on the menfolk who back in the family home could give them a "smack in the gob" without the slight-est fear of police intervention in what was euphemistically referred to as "domestic violence." There was more than a touch of grim reality in Mother Riley's wartime quip, "A married woman's Home Guard—the rolling pin."

Not content to confine herself to the permitted space of the pan-tomime dame, Riley's stage and screen excursions into the realms of social and political comment were becoming uncomfortable, con-fusing, and superfluous in a well-ordered post-war society in which hierarchies and conventions were largely restored. During the war, partly with the help of the likes of John Baxter, the people had been promised a brave new world of greater social and personal equality. The reality fell somewhat short of Baxter's naïve but well-intentioned utopian visions. What the people actually got, after the ground-breaking social innovations of the post-war Labor government, was a return to Churchill and the Conservatives in 1951.

Then, as rationing ended in the mid-1950s and employment and prosperity slowly returned, people began dimly to suspect that they could all be middle class now, and Mother Riley's staunchly proletarian back-street ways were something of an embarrassment, appreciated mainly by old women with long and bitter memories, and naughty children who had not yet been drilled into conformity. So with perfect comic timing, having upstaged a bemused American vampire and dismantled a scary robot (Riley cocking a snook at modern technol-ogy like Jacques Tati's Monsieur Hulot), after one last twirl round the

British stage without her darlin' daughter, Old Ma Riley obligingly kicked the bucket before they could fire her off to create extra-terrestrial mayhem on the planet Mars, an intended satire on the dawn of a "space age" which she did not live to see!

Though speculation may be idle, I firmly believe that, had Arthur Lucan lived for another ten years, he would have been "rediscovered" like his younger colleague Max Wall, who played in Alfred Jarry, Samuel Beckett and John Osborne. According to *The Guardian*, Max Wall in *The Entertainer* made Laurence Olivier look like an amateur. Arthur Lucan would have been a perfect Estragon to Max's Vladimir in *Waiting for Godot*, and a wondrous Mère Ubu to Wall's King Ubu in *Ubu Roi*.

Perhaps not entirely by chance, Lucan's last film had ended with an image strikingly reminiscent of the end of another film, a film which almost certainly influenced the very early development of Lucan's belligerent dame. Charlie Chaplin's *A Busy Day* (1914) ends with Chaplin, who plays the pugnacious and unfeminine wife, being pushed unceremoniously into the harbor. Paul Matthew St. Pierre describes the final scene as follows:

> At the climax, when the husband pushes his wife off the pier into the water, the movie's final shot depicts her fighting to stay afloat: her hat removed, her hairdo wet and undone, her women's clothing invisible under the water. The wife apparently sheds her gender and becomes Charlie Chaplin, crying out desperately for help, before finally sinking underwater as the movie comes to an end.[228]

The very same image closes *Mother Riley meets the Vampire*. Riley's wild motor-car and motor-bike chase in pursuit of the wicked Baron von Housen ends on the deck of a ship from which she is catapulted overboard into the water. Then, filmed like Chaplin with the same camera angle from above, her head bobs up inside a lifebuoy, and with chilling accuracy Riley—or is it Lucan?— shouts up at the camera, "This is the end!" Director George Minter was clearly paying homage to both Lucan and Chaplin, a point critics have hitherto overlooked or simply ignored.

In the final analysis, Arthur Lucan created in Old Mother Riley an anarchical comic "character and archetype" like the Harlequin of the *commedia dell'arte*, as he evolved in the popular eighteenth-century theater of the Paris fairs and the Théâtre Italien; Harlequin-Riley is verbose, loquacious, absurd, unpredictable, insubordinate, alternately violent and tender, protean, always different, yet somehow always the same. This utterly original and inimitable aspect of the Lucan-Riley phenomenon was well-understood by Paul Matthew St. Pierre:

> As a stage and film performer Arthur Lucan may have been identifiable primarily as Old Mother Riley, a pantomime dame and female impersonator, but as a character and archetype Old Mother Riley might be anybody she likes.[229]

By turns funny and sad, sublime and grotesque, real and fantastic, he/she incarnated and inhabited as no other actor has ever quite managed, the upside-down world of cathartic carnival and grotesque realism proposed by Mikhail Bakhtin in his theories of the novel and his study of *François Rabelais and His World*, a world which in recent years many critics, both British and American, have invoked in a variety of ways in their discussions of film comedy. David Sutton, for instance, speaks of the Blackpool of Gracie Fields in *Sing As We Go* as "an image of Bakhtin's carnival—a kind of liminal holiday zone in which the regulations of the workaday order are temporarily cast aside, a site for the very kinds of licensed transgression which the 'popular aesthetic' of British comedy represents."[230]

Given Mother Riley's hybrid nature and identity, she *herself* becomes "a site for the very kinds of licensed transgression" of which modern critics of British film comedy speak. But in Riley's case, as we have already noted when discussing Sue Harper's "Difficult Dowagers," Riley's transgressions are neither licensed nor temporary; her transgendered status maroons her forever in the gloriously surreal and anarchic world of pantomime, straddling the line between the sublime and the grotesque, between social realism and escapist fantasy. In a curious way, Mother Riley exerts a fascination similar to that of Peter Pan (a boy traditionally played by a woman), precisely because she belongs in an "other" world, like Peter Pan's Neverland, and, like Peter, she cannot "come back." Further consideration of the fascinating Freudian theme of the uncanny and its relation to theatrical illusion is sadly beyond the scope of the present volume.

In his discussion of film comedy, David Sutton notes the importance of George Orwell's essay on "the king of the saucy postcard," Donald McGill, with its "almost Bakhtinian" dualism of "noble folly" and "base wisdom," the contrasting but complimentary world-views of Don Quixote and Sancho Panza. In the "site" of Mother Riley's performing body or "body performative," these worlds frequently collide and Riley takes part in both the noble quest to right wrongs *and* the Orwellian "chorus of raspberries" from which Sutton's book takes its title. Indeed, when Mother Riley plays a cinema usherette in *Old Mother Riley's Circus*, a snoring, tipsy cinemagoer gives her the opportunity to provide a literal concretization of the Orwell-Sutton raspberry image. To silence the snorer Riley puts a gas mask on him; but instead of imposing silence, the gas mask acts as an instrument of comic transformation, and the passionate declarations of the onscreen lovers are now punctuated and trivialized by an absurdly childish counterpoint of raucous raspberries from the "gasbag" in the auditorium. This scene manages to be at once a vulgar joke and a sublimely absurd enactment of a piece of critical theory.

The more Mother Riley cries "I'm a Lady, I am, a Lady! And I defy you to prove it!" the more we are aware that she is not, never can be, never will be, and what is more, does not truly aspire to be any such thing! In her shamelessly ramshackle films, now rescued from oblivion and beginning to receive the serious attention they deserve, she remains to this day a joyfully (or sometimes troublingly) anarchic presence because she could not fully then, and still cannot today, be comfortably co-opted as an icon for any one group's social, ethnic, political, sexual or comedic agenda. She uncannily prefigured bits of them all, and cleverly, and knowingly, flirted with them all. But perhaps, given her uniqueness, like Groucho Marx, she did not care in the end to belong to any club that would accept her as a member.

Had impresario Lew Lake managed in the mid-1920s to transform Arthur Lucan and Bert Arnold into a double act without Kitty McShane, he would then almost certainly have tried to send "Lucan and Arnold" to Hollywood in the footsteps of fellow "Brits" Fred Karno, Charlie Chaplin, and Stan Laurel. Sadly, for some, there would then have been no Old Mother Riley, no darling daughter, and no series of blockbuster but ramshackle British comedy movies. Worse still, if Hollywood had failed to recognize and exploit his exceptional talents, we might today never have heard of Arthur Lucan at all.

On the other hand, I firmly believe that if the tide of film fortune *had* been taken at the flood, and had led on to victory, we might today pronounce the name Arthur Lucan with something approaching the admiration and respect with which we say Charlie Chaplin or Stan Laurel. Fortunately, the fifteen Riley films do remain, in spite of their many faults and imperfections, as a partial testament to the remarkable gifts of Arthur Towle, the Lincolnshire lad who became Arthur Lucan—the man who was Old Mother Riley—and a comedian of genius.

Appendix

The Pantomimes of Towle, Lucan and McShane 1895-1954

1895-1896 *Robinson Crusoe*. Shodfriars Hall, Boston. Arthur Towle, "a native."

1912-1913 *Cinderella*. Paisley. AL not KM.

1913-1914 *Cinderella*. Dudley. AL not KM.

1914-1915 *Little Jack Horner*. AL and KM's first together. Derby, Peterborough, Stafford.

1915-1916 *Little Jack Horner*. Hitchin, Coalville, Cinderford, Crewe.

1916-1917 No pantomime

1917-1918 *Little Jack Horner*. Dublin, Queen's.

1918-1919 *Little Red Riding Hood* Dublin, Queen's. (last Dublin Panto)

1919-1920 *Aladdin*. Pavilion Liverpool.

1920-1921 No pantomime

1921-1922 *Aladdin*. Glasgow.

1922-1923 *Babes in the Wood*. Glasgow.

1923-1930 No pantomimes.

1931-1932 *Dick Whittington*. Shakespeare Liverpool, Leeds, Wigan. Featuring George Formby in his first pantomime.

1932-1933 *Old Mother Hubbard*. Glasgow Empire.

1933-1934 *Jack and the Beanstalk*. Oldham Palace, Metropolitan and Empress Brixton.

1934-1935 *Old Mother Hubbard*. Liverpool Pavilion.

1935-1936 *Old Mother Hubbard*. Hull, Liverpool, Wolverhampton, Hulme.

1936-1937 *Old Mother Hubbard*. Lewisham.

1937-1938 *Old Mother Hubbard*. Leeds Empire, Sunderland, Liverpool.

1938-1939 *Aladdin*. South Africa.

1939-1940 *The Old Woman Who Lived in a Shoe*. Pavilion Liverpool.

1940-1941 "They will not play panto this year." Michael Lyon.

1941-1947 No pantomimes

1947-1948 *Babes in the Wood*. Hippodrome Bristol. AL, no KM. Fire, 16 February 1948.

1948-1949 *The Old Woman Who Lived in a Shoe*. Chatham, New Cross.

1949-1950 *The Old Woman Who Lived in a Shoe*. Wolverhampton, Norwich.

1950-1951 *The Old Woman Who Lived in a Shoe*. Boscombe.

1951-1952 *The Old Woman Who Lived in a Shoe*. Southampton. AL and KM's last performance together.

1952-1953 *Jack and the Beanstalk*. New Empire, Bristol. Arthur alone.

1953-1954 *Old Mother Hubbard*. Folkestone, Swindon. Arthur Lucan's last pantomime.

Notes

1 Steve King, assisted and edited by Terry Cavender, *"As Long As I Know, It'll be Quite Alright!" The Life Stories of Lucan and McShane*, Lancastrian Transport Publications, 1999. Terry Cavender passed away before the work was completed.

2 Leslie Halliwell, *Double Take and Fade Away*, Grafton Books, 1987, p. 28.

3 David Robinson, *The Great Funnies: a History of Film Comedy*, Studio Vista, 1969, p. 120.

4 Roger Wilmut, *Kindly Leave the Stage!: The Story of Variety, 1919-1960*, Methuen, 1985, p. 143.

5 John Fisher, *Funny Way to Be a Hero*, London, Muller, 1973, pp. 80-81. A new and augmented edition of Fisher's classic study appeared in November 2013.

6 Rachael Low, *The History of British Film*, Vol. VII, Allen and Unwin, 1985, p. 186.

7 Jeffrey Richards, *The Age of the Dream Palace: Cinema and Society in 1930s Britain*, Routledge, 1984; Anthony Slide, *The Great Pretenders*, Wallace-Homestead, Lombard, 1985; *Eccentrics of Comedy*, Scarecrow Press, 1998.

8 Elkan Allan, *Guide to World Cinema*, NFT, 1985.

9 Stephen Shafer, *British Popular Films 1929-1939: The Cinema of Reassurance*, Routledge 1997, p. 5.

10 Roger Wilmut, loc. cit.

11 *Magill's Survey of Cinema*, Vol. 4, Salem Press, 1981.

12 Geoff Brown with Tony Aldgate, *The Common Touch: The Films of John Baxter*, BFI, 1989, p. 73.

13 David Quinlan, *Quinlan's Illustrated Directory of Film Comedy Stars*, Batsford, 1992, p. 114.

14 *Drama*, British Theater Association, 1982, p. 29.

15 Betty Driver, *Betty, The Autobiography*, Granada Media, 2000, p. 104.

16 Ray Carradine, *Evergreen*, Summer, 1998, p. 98. Paradoxically, thanks to Alan Plater's over-generous assessment of Kitty's intellectual complexity, the best performance of her career was probably the one he wrote for Maureen Lipman in 1981; a *tour de force*, interpreted with chilling accuracy.

17 *Movie Maker*, Vol. 16, 1982, p. 175.

18 Jean-Louis Ginibre, *Ladies or Gentlemen: A Pictorial History of Male Cross-Dressing in the Movies*, 2005, Filipachi, New York, p. 46.

19 John Fisher, *Funny Way to Be a Hero*, (1973) p. 76.

20 Quoted by Patrick Newley in "Only One Old Mother Riley," *The Stage*, 9 February 2006.

21 Charlie Chester, *The Grand Order of Water Rats: A Legend of Laughter*, W. H. Allen, 1984, p. 33.

22 Sue Harper, *Picturing the Past: The Rise and Fall of the British Costume Film*, BFI, 1994, p. 97.

23 Jean-Louis Ginibre, *Ladies or Gentlemen*, p. 46.

24 http://cinecollage.net/screwball-comedy.htmlhttp://xroads.virginia. edu/~UG03/comedy/sbhome.html

25 http://www.bmonster.com/cult34.html

26 Dorothy Anger, *Other Worlds: Society Seen Through Soap Opera*, Broadview, 1999, p. 36.

27 Peter Stead, *Film and the Working Class: The Feature Film in British and American Society*, Routledge, 1989, p. 138.

28 Philip Gillett, *The British Working Class in Postwar Film*, Manchester University Press, 2003, p. 160.

29 Lance Pettitt, *Screening Ireland, Film and Television Representation*, Manchester University Press, 2000, p. 56.

30 "Ireland, the Empire and film" in *An Irish Empire? Aspects of Ireland and the British Empire*, ed. Keith Jeffery, Manchester University Press, 1996, p. 51.

31 By analogy with "American English" or "Australian English," the term "Irish English" is now preferred to the older "Hiberno-English."

32 Sue Harper, *Women in British Cinema: Mad, Bad and Dangerous to Know*, Continuum, 2000, p. 28.

33 Cf. Ben Elton: "Irishmen are not stupid and it's not funny to say they are—you can pretend for ten minutes and then your cover's blown. Women's tits are not funny and it's not funny to say they are. So where did we look, we looked around us, inside ourselves and in what we were doing— that's where the comedy was." In Roger Wilmut and Peter Rosengard, *Didn't You Kill My Mother In-Law: The Story of Alternative Comedy in Britain*, Methuen, 1989, p. 93.

34 *The Encyclopedia of British Film*, eds. Brian McFarlane, Anthony Slide, Methuen, 2005, p. 430.

35 Roger Lewis, "Freaks." http://www.anthonyburgess.org/mediablog/ freaks-by-roger-lewis

36 See Iona and Peter Opie, *Children's Games with Things: Marbles, Fivestones, Throwing and Catching, Gambling, Hopscotch, Chucking and Pitching, Ball-bouncing, Skipping, Tops and Tipcat*, Oxford University Press, 1997, p. 259.

37 *Magill's Survey of Cinema, English Language Films, Second Series*, Salem Press, 1981, p. 1778.

38 David Wilt, "Cynically Sentimental," in his blog on website http:// mexcine.tumblr.com

39 Peter Ackroyd, *Dressing Up, Transvestism and Drag: The History of an Obsession*, Simon and Shuster, 1979, p. 102.

40 Anthony Slide, *Eccentrics of Comedy*, p. 84. The first sentence is taken from an email from AS to me. In an interview in 2009, Ray Davies of The Kinks spoke about his song "The Village Green Preservation Society." "Old Mother Riley was a music-hall character. I thought it was a real old lady until I saw a documentary about her and discovered it was a man. Not a drag queen but a female impersonator. Definitely not camp or queenie. Just a bloke in a frock. There is a difference to the art form of the drag queen. Old Mother Riley was an extremely ugly man who looked even uglier as a woman."

41 A detailed study of theatrical cross-dressing is beyond the scope of the present volume. Discussions applicable to Arthur Lucan can be found in the following studies; Jean-Louis Ginibre, *Ladies or Gentlemen: A Pictorial History of Male Cross-Dressing in the Movies*, Filipachi, New York, 2005; Peter Ackroyd, *Dressing Up, Transvestism and Drag: The History of an Obsession*, Simon and Shuster, 1979; Geoff King, *Film Comedy*, Wallflower Press, 2002, especially Chapter four.

42 Roger Lewis, "Freaks."

43 Peter Ackroyd, op. cit., p. 64.

44 John Fisher, 1973, p. 72.

45 Danny La Rue with his "Wotcher, mate!" along with Dick Emery's Mandy, Kenny Everett's Cupid Stunt, and Lucas and Walliams' "Ladies" surely learned from Arthur the tricks of how to shatter the glamorous illusion in favour of comedy.

46 Arthur appears in Donald's graduation photograph at Trinity; Kitty stayed away.

47 Quotations from *Old Mother Riley in Society* and *Old Mother Riley's Circus*.

48 Roger Lewis, "Freaks,"

49 Sue Harper, *Picturing the Past: The Rise and Fall of the British Costume Film*, BFI, 1994, p. 150.

50 Brian McFarlane, *Lance Comfort* , Manchester University Press, 1999, p. 48.

51 *Re-Viewing British Cinema, 1900-1992: Essays and Interviews*, Wheeler W. Dixon ed., State University of New York Press, 1994, p. 2.

52 Norman Longmate, *How We Lived Then–A History of Everyday Life During the Second World War*, Pimlico, 1971, p. 407. In spite of its blimpish attitude to film comedy, the book does offer many fascinating insights into everyday life during the war.

53 Stephen Shafer, *British Popular Films 1929-1939: The Cinema of Reassurance*, Routledge 1997, p. 235

54 David Sutton, *A Chorus of Raspberries: British Film Comedy 1929-1939*, University of Exeter Press, 2000, reviewed by Tony Williams in *Film Quarterly*, Vol. 55, No. 1, (Autumn 2001) pp. 53-54.

55 Andy Medhurst, *National Joke: Popular Comedy and English Cultural Identities*, Routledge, 2007, see Introduction and pp. 63-64.

56 *British Comedy Cinema*, I.Q. Hunter, Laraine Porter eds., Routledge, 2012, p.6.

57 Paul Matthew St. Pierre, *Music Hall Mimesis in British Film, 1895-1960, On the Halls and on the Screen*, Fairleigh Dickinson University Press, 2009; Steven Fielding, "A Mirror for England? Cinematic Representations of Politicians and Party Politics, circa 1944–1964," *Journal of British Studies*, 47; I, 2008.

58 Sam Friedman, "Legitimating a Discredited Art Form: the Changing Field of British Comedy," *Edinburgh Working Papers in Sociology*, no. 39, July 2009, p. 11.

59 *The Comics: Old Mother Riley*, BBC North, screened BBC 2, 11 April 1980. *Bygones Special: The Life of Riley*, Anglia TV, 19 September 1980.

60 *The Independent*, 26 August, 1997. Patrick Newley's obituary for Rolland in *The Stage* similarly claimed that, "Lucan, a difficult man and an alcoholic, often missed performances either on stage or film-and was replaced by Rolland."

61 John Fisher, *Funny Way to be a Hero*, (New Edition), Preface Publishing, 2013, p. 100.

62 Josephine Tozier, *Among English Inns: The Story of a Pilgrimage to Characteristic Spots of Rural England*, L. C. Page, Boston, 1904, pp. 196-199.

63 From The Project Gutenberg EBook of *Jeremy*, by Hugh Walpole http://www.gutenberg.org/files/3474/3474-h/3474-h.htm

64 Martin-Harvey's companies toured the provinces with *The Only Way* in the autumn of 1899 and again in 1901. From September to November 1899 they played to packed houses with standing-room only in Birmingham, Hull, Sheffield, Manchester, Edinburgh and Dublin.

65 Leopold Lewis, *Henry Irving and the Bells: Irving's Personal Script of the Play*, Manchester University Press, 1980, p. 22.

66 Sigmund Freud to Yvette Guilbert, quoted in Kenneth S. Lynn, *Charlie Chaplin and His Times*, Simon and Schuster, New York, 1997, p. 349.

67 *The Cambridge History of British Theater*, Vol. 3, pp. 101-102.

68 Geoff J. Mellor, *They Made Us Laugh*, Kelsall, 1982, p. 69.

69 Trade poster for *Old Mother Riley Headmistress*.

70 The Percy Clifton who owned the Tower Ballroom in Skerries near Dublin from 1922 to 1947 had a wife, Mrs. E. Clifton (Lizzie?), and a son, Walter Clifton, who was a violinist.

71 Another Percy Clifton (real name George Dryden Knox) was successful around this time in musical comedy in London, including five years in *The Chinese Honeymoon* at the Strand Theater, and extensive touring in the provinces. He seems to be totally unrelated to the Musical Cliftons, and died in the 1920s while on tour in Australia and New Zealand. The Percy Clifton who made several spoken recordings for Zonophone around 1907 is almost certainly this George Knox. Two of Knox's two-hander comic sketches, "Buying the Christmas Dinner" with Yolande Noble, and "The Plumber" with Winifred Hare, are interesting as rare contemporary recordings of the kind of comic sketches which Arthur was learning to write and perform at this time. There was also an acrobatic circus act, The Three Clifton Brothers, Eccentric Railway Porters, doing the rounds at this time with "a screamingly funny absurdity entitled 'Ructions on the Railway,'" but there seems to be no link with the Musical Cliftons.

72 The names Danny, Vera and Alan Clifton are given by Steve King, but I have been unable to find a single reference to these names in any contemporary source, including the English and Irish press.

73 National Archives of Ireland website. http://www.census.nationalarchives. ie/exhibition/dublin/poverty_health.html See also Joseph V. O'Brien *"Dear, Dirty Dublin": A City in Distress, 1899-1916*, University of California Press, 1982.

74 I am most grateful to Maree Baker of The Skerries Historical Society for the information concerning the Cliftons at Skerries.

75 Seamus de Burca, "The Queen's Royal Theater 1829-1966," Dublin Historical Record, Vol. 27, No. 1 (December, 1973), p. 25. The Queen's closed in 1969 and was demolished in 1975.

76 For a brief account of the career of Gilbert Payne see Geoff J. Mellor, *They Made us Laugh*, Kelsall, 1982, pp. 80-81. In his piece on Arthur Lucan (pp.68-69) Mellor wrongly claims that Arthur was with Payne in 1910 and had not yet changed his name to Lucan. Mellor also wrongly states that the name change took place in 1913 when he met Kitty, and that Kitty was "only fifteen" when she married. *The Stage* for June 1911 shows that Arthur was already performing at Carnoustie as Arthur Lucan.

77 I possess several original Yo San postcards, including one sent and postmarked in July 1916. Because the verses speak of war and farewell they may have found renewed popularity after 1914.

78 Harry Flockton-Foster's granddaughter, Gillian Swift, also sent me photographs of her grandparents' concert party from the relevant years, with the names of all the members, and it is quite clear that Arthur Lucan was not among them. I believe Slim was thinking of the photograph of Payne's White Coons at Carnoustie in 1912.

79 Both of these pieces would appear to be brief adaptations of popular melodramas. *The Lights o' London*, a melodramatic play by George R. Sims, first produced in London on 10 September 1881. *The Race for Wealth* was possibly based on Mrs. Charlotte Riddell's 1886 novel of that name, on the perils of the big city.

80 See the poster at http://www.leodis.net/playbills/item. asp?ri=200341_48485965

81 Arthur told the same chorus girl, who was saddened by Kitty's treatment of Arthur, that he had been head over heels in love with Kitty, and that in spite of everything, in some odd way he still was.

82 Slim Ingram told me that right up to his last years Arthur still used his ruler. "Whenever anyone asked for an autograph the first thing he did was take the little ruler out of his front top pocket."

83 For an account of the many troubles which beset Dublin during these years see Padraig Yeates, *A City in Wartime, Dublin 1914-18*, Gill and MacMillan, 2011.

84 Philip Ryan, *The Lost Theaters of Dublin*, Westbury, 1998.

85 Quoted by Clair Wills, "Neutrality and Popular Culture," UCD scholarcast, Series 1, Spring 2008, p. 8.

86 In the late 1990s the archives and booking records of the Argyle Theater and other theaters managed by the Clarke family were acquired by the Harvard Theater Collection, Harvard University Library. They contain several references to Lucan and McShane.

87 All quotations from the Australian press are taken from the National Library of Australia's searchable database trove.nla.gov.au/newspaper

88 In 1898, in a "Grand Whitsuntide Programme" at the Tivoli music hall, Frank Latona appeared alongside a veritable pantheon of the greatest names in the history of the music hall; "Dan Leno, Vesta Tilley, Eugene Stratton, George Robey, Two McNaughtons, Harriet Vernon, Bessie Wentworth, Marie Loftus, Florrie Forde, Rawson and June, Lily Langtry, and a host of others."

89 "Sensational engagement of the world-famous comedienne from the London Coliseum, Jen Latona. Direct from Phenomenal Success on the Musgrove Tivoli Circuit. The most versatile artist in vaudeville. She accompanies herself most wonderfully but doesn't appear to be playing the piano, for she turns right round to her audience and tells them in song the quaintest stories imaginable. A Pianist, a Singer, and a Raconteur–all in one." *The West Australian*, 12 July 1924.

90 Jen Latona donated her scrapbooks to the Mayor of Fulham shortly
    before her death, but the Royal Performance programme was auctioned
    with her houses and their contents after her death in 1955. With
    characteristic generosity, Jen bequeathed the proceeds of the auction to
    the Variety Artists' Benevolent Fund. In 2009 a copy of the programme
    was offered for sale on the internet at $450.

91 All of Verne Morgan's reminiscences appeared in Steve King's biography. I
    have re-edited them to give them greater coherence and clarity.

92 John Fisher, (2013), p. 93.

93 Gordon Williams, *British Theater in the Great War: A Revaluation*,
    Continuum, 2005, p. 100.

94 Tom Towle, aged 39, was buried in Boston cemetery on 7 March 1895,
    section Q, plot number 242. Arthur must have known this and seems to
    have made no attempt to commemorate his father. The grave was never
    purchased, therefore no memorial was ever erected.

95 *The Western Morning News*, 25 April 1930.

96 Abridged from http://www.georgeformby.org/
    biography/a-jockey-treads-the-boards/

97 In 1932-1933 Formby toured Lancashire in Bert Loman's *Babes in the
    Wood*. Loman announced proudly that in its six-week tour the panto
    grossed £4,500 and was seen by 128,000 people. After a summer season
    at Blackpool, Formby toured his sell-out roadshow in Lancashire and
    Yorkshire. At Christmas 1933, Bert Loman's third contracted pantomime,
    Babes in the Wood at the Liverpool Pavilion, grossed £6,314 in six weeks
    and was seen by almost 150,000 people. Formby was now in the Lucan-
    McShane panto league, and only the Lucans could break his record, at
    the Pavilion the following Christmas. Bert Loman had kept his word, and
    Arthur and Kitty had played a small but crucial part in the irresistible rise
    of George Formby.

98 Paul Matthew St. Pierre, *Music Hall Mimesis in British Film, 1895-1960*,
    p. 80.

99 When I asked the BBC's Written Archives at Caversham to check the
    location of this broadcast, researcher Samantha Blake kindly informed
    me that "Lucan's contract would probably contain the information you
    want, but unfortunately his file for the period 1931-1938 was destroyed
    during World War II. I think at that time, that type of programme would
    probably have been transmitted live from a studio."

100 I am grateful to Roy Rust of Sibsey, Lincolnshire, for giving me copies of
    six sides of theater managers' reports on Lucan and McShane, spanning
    (with gaps) the years 1927-1938.

101 http://scotlandonscreen.org.uk/database/record.
     php?usi=007-000-002-111-C
102 Roy Busby, *British Music Hall: An Illustrated Who's Who from 1850 to the Present Day*, Paul Elek Incorporated, 1976, p. 116. Busby supports the claim of the Holborn Empire.
103 I am grateful to Vivyan Ellacott for this fascinating detail. He also added the serious reason for it. "But the glazed stuff is lethal; sharp-edged bits fly all over the place, even into the audience! The good old unglazed stuff just disintegrates as soon as it hits the floor."
104 The Souvenir Programme, "Argyle Theater 50th Broadcast" is preserved in the Wirral Archives, Argyle Theater collection, ZAR/2/2.
105 Not at the Metropole Theater Manchester in late June, as Steve King claimed. King places this accident some five months too late and in the wrong theater. Unfortunately, and rather surprisingly, I have been unable to find a single mention of the accident in the regional press.
106 Robert Murphy, Geoff Brown, Alan Burton, *Directors in British and Irish Cinema: A Reference Companion*, BFI, 2006, p. 434.
107 *The Times*, Tuesday 16 March 1937.
108 James Chapman, *Cinemas of the World: Film and Society from 1895 to the Present*, Reaktion, 2003, p. 405.
109 Thanks to Roy Rust who owns the original of this letter.
110 I am grateful to Alex Gleason, who is preparing *The British Film Music Encyclopedia*, for this information.
111 *The Cinema*, 26 March 1941, p. 9.
112 Paul Matthew St. Pierre, *Music Hall Mimesis in British Film, 1895-1960*, p. 122.
113 The BBC Written Archives at Caversham contain personal files for the Lucans covering the years 1939-1962, and lots of scripts on microfilm, including 14 episodes of *Old Mother Riley Takes the Air* from 1941 and 10 episodes of *Old Mother Riley and Her Daughter Kitty* from 1942. They also have the Christmas special, *Old Mother Riley's Christmas Party*, 25 December 1941.
114 I am deeply grateful to Mrs. Joan Towle for allowing me to reproduce her copy of Sybil Rowse's notes.
115 Columbia FB2663, 4 July 1941.
116 Columbia FB2663, 4 July 1941.
117 Columbia FB2685, 6 August 1941.
118 Columbia FB 2702, 6 August 1941.
119 All of the gramophone sketches can be heard on YouTube.

120 There is a photograph, dated 1944, of Sherwin in his "Riley" costume at http://britishvarietyartists.webs.com/jacksherwin.htm. Lucan's early stage make-up in "The Match-seller" was similar to Sherwin's, and was radically modified for filming.

121 Adapted from the *Monthly Film Bulletin*, May 1945, p. 59.

122 Anthony Slide, *Eccentrics of Comedy*, p. 91.

123 With thanks to Vivyan Ellacott for this excerpt from his boyhood reminiscences, written at my request.

124 Leslie Thomas, *In My Wildest Dreams*, Arlington, 1984, revised Arrow 2006, pp. 104-105.

125 Leslie Thomas, pp. 145-146.

126 Brian Blessed in Sharon Mail, *We Could Possibly Comment—Ian Richardson Remembered*, n.p.

127 Ricky Tomlinson, *Ricky*, Hachette Digital, 2008, n.p.

128 Terry Hallett, *Bristol's Forgotten Empire*, The Badger Press, Westbury, 2000, pp. 179-180.

129 Quoted in David Bret, *George Formby: A Troubled Genius*, Robson, 1999, p. 39.

130 http://www.supollard.co.uk/interview33.html

131 The review also reveals that Kitty was taken ill and that "Eileen Page, a promising young understudy, is playing the part of the daughter." Kitty was again missing in June 1948 at the Chelsea Palace, and Arthur played opposite another understudy, Edna Monks, supported by Willer Neal and George Beck.

132 http://thecynicaltendency.blogspot.co.uk/search?q=Arthur+Lucan He first blogged the sketch in May 2009.

133 Adapted from *Monthly Film Bulletin* 1949, p. 137.

134 http://www.theartsdesk.com/film/theartsdesk-qa-script-supervisor-angela-allen

135 Jack Le White and Peter Ford, *Rings and Curtains*, Quartet Books, 1992, pp. 211-218.

136 http://www.imdb.com/title/tt0043876/reviews

137 Brian Glanville, *Football Memories: 50 Years of the Beautiful Game*, Robson, 2004, p. 155.

138 http://www.bmonster.com/cult34.html

139 Roger Lewis, "Freaks."

140 These and the following facts were told to me by Arthur's granddaughter Marylyn, and Donald's widow Joan, when we met at Joan's house in St. Austell in August 2012. My thanks also go to Joan who allowed me to see and copy the letter from Arthur to Donald.

141 Roy Rolland interviewed in John Graham's 1980 BBC documentary.

142 Terry Hallett, *Bristol's Forgotten Empire*, p. 180.

143 Edward Thomas, *The Reluctant Star, A Biography of Malcolm Vaughan*, Ryefield Press, 2005, p. 49.

144 Philip Martin Williams and David L. Williams, *Wired to the Moon: Frank Randle-A Life*, History On Your Doorstep, 2006, p. 111.

145 Arthur's last two shows were just as popular down South as they were up North. For instance, in the month of August 1953 the show visited Folkestone, Eastbourne, Cheltenham, Exeter, and Weston-super-Mare.

146 In 1951 Arthur has also encouraged the young singer Donald Adams to audition for the D'Oyly Carte Opera Company, where he eventually became the leading bass-baritone.

147 John Fisher, 2014, p. 101.

148 Reminiscences gathered from Frank Seton and Roland Watson in the 1980s by the actors Nigel and Vivyan Ellacott. They kindly sent me copies in 2012.

149 "An Evening with Brian Murphy and Slim Ingram," DVD filmed at the Theater Museum Covent Garden, 15 September 2002.

150 Gilbert and Sullivan, *The Yeomen of the Guard*.

151 *The Manchester Guardian*, 19 May, 1954.

152 Reproduced by kind permission of Mrs. Joan Towle.

153 http://whirligigtv.yuku.com/topic/1393/Old-Mother-Riley?page=3#. Uh3Xuz9LPDg The film in question was probably *Old Mother Riley in Society*.

154 The imposing 1907 brick church, a grade II listed building, still stands in Spring Street but was closed for worship in 2009.

155 In 1956 the house was opened as the St. Nicholas Hostel for the Deaf by Prince Philip.

156 Quoted in Anthony Slide, *Eccentrics of Comedy*, p. 94.

157 By kind permission of Mrs. Joan Towle.

158 As we saw earlier, Arthur's version must be inaccurate as he was still in Boston long after his twelfth birthday.

159 Richard Anthony Baker, *Old Time Variety*, Pen and Sword, 2011, p. 174.

160 Ellis Ashton interviewed for *The Comics: Old Mother Riley*, BBC 2, 11 April 1980.

161 http://fleapit-movieexpress.blogspot.ie/2010/01/mother-riley-meets-vampiremy-son.html

162 Murray Charles Goldstein, *Naked Jungle: Soho Stripped Bare*, Silverback Press, 2005, p. 70.

163 Peter Jewell, "Collector's Tales," *Film History*, Vol. 20, Issue 2, 2008, p. 154.

164 The only Catholic Church located in Notting Hill is St. Francis of Assisi, Pottery Lane. Unfortunately no funeral records were kept there before 1987, but if Slim's clear recollection is correct (although he did not attend), St. Francis would seem to be the probable location for Kitty's Requiem Mass.

165 This information, together with photographs of her father and his two oddly different birth certificates, was given to me by Eileen Oldfield's granddaughter, Debbie Wilson. However, Eileen Oldfield made the same claim for the paternity of her second child, a claim which was categorically disproved within the Oldfield family, thus throwing into doubt the veracity of her earlier claim.

166 See the original painting, and Chaplin striking the pose at http://www.septembermorn.org/items/show/28

167 Ruth Barton, *Irish National Cinema*, Routledge, 2004, p. 56.

168 Barton, p. 60.

169 Pettitt, *Screening Ireland: Film and Television Representation*, p. 7.

170 For the first full-length study of this topic see Margaret Lynch-Brennan, *The Irish Bridget: Irish Immigrant Women in Domestic Service in America 1840-1930*, Syracuse University Press, 2009.

171 William H. A. Williams, *'Twas Only an Irishman's Dream: The Image of Ireland and the Irish in American Popular Song Lyrics, 1800–1920*, University of Illinois, 1996, pp. 135-136.

172 See also Kathleen Heininge's perceptive study, *Buffoonery in Irish Drama: Staging Twentieth-Century Post-Colonial Stereotypes*, Peter Lang, 2009.

173 Christopher Dowd, *The Construction of Irish Identity in American Literature*, Routledge, 2010, p. 18.

174 Maureen Waters, *The Comic Irishman*, State University of New York Press, 1984, pp. 41-56.

175 From Michael Quinion's World Wide Words, http://www.worldwidewords.org/qa/qa-ril1.htm The *Life of Riley* films and radio shows are totally unrelated and are all post-1937.

176 Quoted in William H. A. Williams, *'Twas Only an Irishman's Dream*, p. 217.

177 Scottish Music Hall Society, *Stagedoor, 75*, December 2006.

178 This article by the late Professor Jane Moody was originally on www.york.ac.uk It can still be found at http://istianjinelearning.org/christineakov/files/2013/08/PANT-O-MONIUM-RESEARCH-MATERIAL-1xy4kw3.pdf

179 Anne Varty, *Children and Theater in Victorian Britain*, Palgrave Macmillan, 2008, pp. 147-148.

180 Brian McFarlane, *Lance Comfort*, p. 49.

181 Paul Matthew St. Pierre, *Music Hall Mimesis in British Film*, 1895-1960.

182 Paul Matthew St. Pierre, p. 110.

183 Roger Lewis, "Freaks."

184 Peter Miles and Malcolm Smith, *Cinema, Literature & Society: Elite and Mass Culture in Interwar Britain*, Croom Helm, 1987, p. 28.

185 Jeffrey Richards, *The Age of the Dream Palace: Cinema and Society in 1930s Britain*, Routledge, 1984, p. 298.

186 David Sutton, *A Chorus of Raspberries*, p. 150.

187 See Philip Gillett on John Baxter, Frank Capra, and the view that "humor was the best way of making a serious point." Gillett, op.cit., pp. 169-173.

188 Robert Knopf, *The Theater and Cinema of Buster Keaton*, Princeton University Press, 1999, p.109. Replace Keaton with Lucan, and read the passage again.

189 Mary Ann Doane, 'The Moving Image: Pathos and the Maternal,' in Imitations of Life: A Reader on Film & Television Melodrama, ed. Marcia Landy, Wayne State University Press, 1991, p. 286. David Sutton, *A Chorus of Raspberries*, p. 150.

190 *Film*, British Federation of Film Societies, April 1975, p. 38.

191 http://www.imdb.com/title/tt0033975/reviews

192 George Melly, *Owning Up: The Trilogy*, Penguin, 2000.

193 John Fisher, (1973), p. 77.

194 *The Observer*, 18 April 1982.

195 "For the wedding the comedian dressed in a naval officer's suit." *Eccentrics of Comedy*, p.85. In fact, as we have already noted, the Lucan's wedding in 1913 must have been a much humbler affair.

196 *Magill's Survey of Cinema, English Language Films, Second Series,* Salem Press, 1981, p. 1779.

197 *New Society*, Vol. 32, 1975, p. 700.

198 http://www.britishpictures.com/arch_o1.html#Old_Mother_Riley_MP

199 Professor Richards made amends for this when he gave a paper on "Old Mother Riley and the War" at the London Cinema Museum on 12 October 2013.

200 Neil Rattigan, *This is England: British Film and the People's War, 1939-1945*, Associated University Presses, 200, p. 312.

201 Jeremy Havardi, *Projecting Britain at War: The National Character in British World War II*, McFarland, 2014, p. 90.

202 See Anthony Aldgate's chapter "Raise a Laugh; Let George Do It" in Aldgate and Richards, *Britain Can Take It: British Cinema in the Second World War,* Tauris, 2007, pp. 46-49.

203 Brian McFarlane, p. 48.

204 Robert Murphy, *British Cinema and the Second World War*, Bloomsbury, 2000, p. 44. See also his *Realism and Tinsel: Cinema and Society in Britain, 1939-1948*, Routledge, 1989, p. 191.

205 Anthony Aldgate, Jeffrey Richards, *Britain Can Take It: British Cinema in the Second World War*, p. 79.

206 Ibid.

207 Aldgate and Richards, op. cit., pp. 299-300.

208 Gill Plain, "Getting Things Straight for the Post War: Realigning Gender and Nation in *The Way to the Stars*," in *War-torn Tales: Literature, Film and Gender in the Aftermath of World War II*, Eds., Danielle E. Hipkins, Gill Plain, Peter Lang, 2007, p. 25.

209 Billy Mowbray, Notes for *The Gentle Sex* on Film4.com. See also Jeffrey Richards' chapter on Howard in *Britain Can Take It*, op. cit., pp. 44–75.

210 Siân Nicholas, *BBC Audience Research Reports Part 1: BBC Listener Research Department, 1937-c.1950*, Microform Academic Publishers, 2006, p. 11.

211 William B. Worthen, *Modern Drama and the Rhetoric of Theater*, University of California Press, Berkeley, 1992, p. 167.

212 Ibid., pp. 165-166.

213 Brian McFarlane, *Lance Comfort*, pp. 49-50.

214 The fraught relationship is explored by Ian S. Wood in *Britain, Ireland and the Second World War*, Edinburgh University Press, 2010.

215 Martin McLoone, "Traditions of Representation: Political Violence and the Myth of Atavism," in *Terrorism, Media, Liberation*, Ed. John David Slocum, Rutgers University Press, 2005, pp. 209-211. McLoone is discussing John Hill's essay "Images of Violence" in *Cinema and Ireland*, eds. Rockett, Gibbon, Hill, Routledge, 1988, pp. 147-193.

216 Taken from Benjamin J. Patterson, *Ethnic Groups USA*, Exlibris, 2008, pp.132-133.

217 Louise Ryan, Abstract, "Irish Female Emigration in the 1930s: Transgressing Space and Culture," *Gender Place and Culture*, 2001, published online: 14 Jul 2010. http://eprints.mdx.ac.uk/3618/

218 Adapted from http://en.wikipedia.org/wiki/Eric_Maschwitz

219 Other near-contemporaries who were honored after the war included Arthur Askey, OBE; Tommy Trinder, CBE; Elsie and Doris Waters, OBE. Will Hay would surely have been honored but died 1949. Other notable absentees from the honors list were Robb Wilton and, of course, Frank Randle.

220 John Major, *My Old Man: A Personal History of Music Hall*, Harper, 2012, p. 149.

221 James Keller, *Food, Film, and Culture: A Genre Study*, McFarland, 2006, p. 8.

222 Gregory Stephens, "Biting Back at the Machine: Charlie Chaplin's *Modern Times*," in online Sensesofcinema.com, 60, October 2011.

223 Philip Gillett, p. 192.

224 Andrew Spicer, *Typical Men: The Representation of Masculinity in Popular British Cinema*, Tauris, 2003, pp. 19-23.

225 Sue Harper, *Women in British Cinema,* pp. 27-28.

226 Geoff King, *Film Comedy*, Wallflower Press, 2002, p. 132.

227 *British Comedy Cinema*, I.Q. Hunter, Laraine Porter, eds., Routledge, p. 45. Geoff King notes that "Another, more extreme and further-reaching, example of male appropriation of the unruly woman is the deeply transgressive transsexual figure of Divine in the films of John Waters." Geoff King, *Film Comedy*, Wallflower Press, 2002, p. 138.

228 Paul Matthew St. Pierre, *Music Hall Mimesis*, p. 110.

229 Ibid., p. 129.

230 Sutton, *A Chorus of Raspberries*, p. 188.

Index
Numbers in **bold** indicate photographs

Lightning Source UK Ltd.
Milton Keynes UK
UKOW06f0639231017

311485UK00009B/740/P